W9-ABZ-908

DISCARD

RIGHT R
RIGHT

359 Perfect
for Beds
Containers, Fer

P

Storey Publishing

*The mission of Storey Publishing is to serve our customers by
publishing practical information that encourages
personal independence in harmony with the environment.*

Edited by Gwen Steege and Fern Marshall Bradley
Art direction and design production by Cynthia N. McFarland
Cover and interior design by Think Design, NYC

Cover photography credits:
Jacket front (clockwise from top right): © Ian Adams; © Ian Adams; © Paul E. Jerabek,
    9/7/1909–6/30/2008; © Ian Adams; © David Austin Roses Ltd.; © Rosemary Kautzky
Jacket back: © Ian Adams, top; © Ian Adams, middle; © Saxon Holt, bottom right;
    © Rosemary Kautzky, bottom left
Jacket flaps: © Ian Adams, front; author's photo (back) © Ian Adams
Jacket spine: © Ian Adams, top; © Paul E. Jerabek, 9/7/1909–6/30/2008, bottom
Interior photography credits appear on page 260

Indexed by Christine R. Lindemer, Boston Road Communications

© 2009 by Peter Schneider

All rights reserved. No part of this book may be reproduced without written permission from
the publisher, except by a reviewer who may quote brief passages or reproduce illustrations
in a review with appropriate credits; nor may any part of this book be reproduced, stored in
a retrieval system, or transmitted in any form or by any means — electronic, mechanical,
photocopying, recording, or other — without written permission from the publisher.

The information in this book is true and complete to the best of our knowledge. All recommendations are made without guarantee on the part of the author or Storey Publishing.
The author and publisher disclaim any liability in connection with the use of this information. For additional information, please contact Storey Publishing, 210 MASS MoCA Way,
North Adams, MA 01247.

Storey books are available for special premium and promotional uses and for customized
editions. For further information, please call 1-800-793-9396.

Printed in China by SNP Leefung Printers Limited
10 9 8 7 6 5 4 3 2 1

Library of Congress Cataloging-in-Publication Data

Schneider, Peter, 1959 Sept. 21–
    Right rose, right place / by Peter Schneider.
        p. cm.
    Includes index.
    ISBN 978-1-60342-438-7 (hardcover w/ jacket : alk. paper)
    1. Roses. I. Title.
SB411.S364 2009
635.9'33734—dc22
                                         2009013729

CONTENTS

INTRODUCTION   1

PART 1: THE VERSATILITY AND APPEAL OF ROSES   7

1 EVERYONE CAN GROW ROSES   9

• Choosing the Right Rose Matters a Lot
• A Few Words about My Garden

2 A ROSE FOR EVERY PURPOSE   17

• Species Roses
• Modern Roses
• Old Garden Roses
• A Final Word on Rose Classes
• Choosing Roses for Your Garden

PART 2: ROSES IN THE GARDEN AND LANDSCAPE   39

3 ROSES THAT CAN STAND ALONE   41

• Choosing a Site

4 GROWING ROSES IN HARMONY WITH OTHER PLANTS   63

• Roses in Beds and Borders
• Solving Problems with Roses
• Choosing the Right Spot

5 BEDDING AND CUTTING ROSES   125

• Choosing a Site for a Bedding Garden
• Bed Layout
• Enjoying Roses as Cut Flowers
• Choosing Bedding Roses

6 MINIATURE ROSES   161

• Using Miniatures in the Home Landscape

7 CLIMBING ROSES   171

• Convincing Climbers to Bloom Their Best
• Support Structures
• Climbers as Ground Covers
• Choosing Climbing Roses

8 TREE ROSES   193

• Types of Tree Roses
• Choosing the Right Varieties

9 ROSES IN CONTAINERS   199

• Container Roses as Garden Elements
• Planting and Caring for Container Roses

PART 3: GROWING ROSES   205

10 GETTING STARTED: Buying and Planting Roses   206

  • Twenty-First-Century Rose Shopping
  • Planting Roses

11 THE BASICS OF CARE: Food, Water, Mulch   220

  • Watering Roses
  • Feeding Roses
  • Mulch

12 DEALING WITH PROBLEMS: Insect and Animal Pests,
    Blind Shoots, and Diseases   227

  • Insects
  • Blind Shoots
  • Diseases
  • Animal Problems

13 UNDERSTANDING PRUNING: When, How, and Why   240

  • General Pruning Guidelines
  • Rose Pruning Specifics
  • Root Pruning

14 PREPARATION FOR WINTER: Timing and Techniques   247

  • Protective Mounds
  • Other Methods
  • Protecting Tender Roses

APPENDIX   251

  • Glossary
  • Resources
  • USDA Zone Map
  • Roses by Classification
  • Photography Credits

INDEX   256

INTRODUCTION

The single most important key to growing good roses is choosing the right rose in the first place. In this book I describe more than 350 reliable roses that possess special characteristics, have proven to be outstanding performers in my Ohio garden, and that are particularly useful for growing together with other plants. I have not written about any rose that I haven't actually grown.

Many books about roses are written from a Californian or English perspective, and thus offer little practical help to gardeners who live where winters are tough and roses must be too. Hardy shrub and heritage roses form the backbone of my garden. I enjoy hybrid teas and floribundas too but plant them carefully so that I can enjoy them as more than annuals.

Rose growing is not a theoretical exercise. It is soil and fertilizer, sunlight and rain, and living plants. Sometimes the realities of rose growing get lost in arguments for or against organic gardening. Applying pesticides and other chemicals routinely is expensive as well as harmful to the environment, but relying on organic remedies for every serious rose problem is not realistic, especially if you grow many roses in close proximity, or if you want to grow exhibition-quality roses. Of course, I'm startled to think about how many hundreds of gallons of toxic chemicals I dispersed into the environment in my first 20 years of rose growing. I feel a lot better now that I no longer use chemicals indiscriminately, and I like to think that my roses do too. Over the years my thinking about pest and disease control for roses has evolved to organic when practical; chemicals only when absolutely necessary.

I have spent the past 30 years intimately involved with the genus *Rosa,* growing over 2,000 different cultivars, and moving from a sheltered suburban garden where space was at a premium to a country garden with unlimited space but many more cultural challenges. In welcoming hundreds of visitors to our garden each year, I have become familiar with the questions and misconceptions gardeners most often have about roses. Along with my recommendations of roses and how to use them effectively in the landscape, this book also offers my answers to these common questions and problems that everyone faces in growing roses. You will find other great ideas in the gardens of your rose-growing neighbors and in nearby arboreta, horticultural parks, and botanical gardens. Roses that thrive in these places should also do well for you. And any roses you spy there that appear unhappy despite regular care are ones that you can cross off your list.

THE VERSATILITY AND APPEAL OF ROSES

Roses and people go way back. Our brains are hardwired with knowledge of roses: when we see a rose, we instinctively proceed to take in its fragrance (even after generations of not-so-fragrant roses, this primitive response remains strong). A bouquet of roses says something that no bunch of mums, tulips, or any other kind of flower can. The rose is emblematic of love, several nations, and numerous political parties, and it plays a symbolic role in some religions. A rose garden in bloom is one of the most beautiful and peaceful things many people can imagine, some kind of paradise.

CHAPTER 1

EVERYONE CAN
GROW ROSES

The roses that you often have seen grown in beds by themselves were very likely hybrid tea roses. They look good grown this way, and it makes them easier to care for. Fortunately, there is no need to segregate the rest of the rose kingdom. Climbers, miniatures, old garden roses, and the many different kinds of shrub roses are made for growing among perennials, evergreens, and other plants. What other genus offers examples that can grow tidily in a pot on your deck, provide months of nonstop color in the perennial border, form an impenetrable hedge, or send a cascade of bloom down from the tree it has been trained to climb? For one gardening challenge after another, roses provide colorful, fragrant solutions.

OPPOSITE The bold colors of the David Austin shrub rose 'Benjamin Britten' can create a powerful contrast in the garden.

DESPITE ALL THE POTENTIAL PLEASURES that they offer, roses have a reputation for being hard to grow. The people who do grow them successfully must be cranks, or obsessive, or maybe just very lucky.

Are roses really that difficult? No. If you can grow a marigold, you can grow a rose. Are roses trouble-free? No. But it's not specialized or expert care they require, it's simply regular attention. And just as mowing a lawn really isn't hard work, caring for roses isn't either. They require your attention for only a few hours each week during the growing season. The more time you spend with roses, the more enjoyable this time is likely to become. Roses repay a regimen of basic cultivation — water, food, mulch — with beautiful, plentiful blooms. But when you neglect a rose garden, watch how quickly it disintegrates into weeds, disease, and disorder. It doesn't take a lot of work to keep a rose garden going, but it takes only one long vacation to bring it all to a stop.

Roses really do give a lot back, in the enjoyment from being connected with nature, in the satisfaction from having your work rewarded with a garden full of blooms, and in the pleasure from sharing these roses with others. As you add more roses to your garden, you may join the many gardeners who have become interested in using roses in floral arrangements, in exhibiting specimen blooms, in the historical connections offered by heritage roses, or in propagating roses.

CHOOSING THE RIGHT ROSE MATTERS A LOT

Every week, I meet someone who tells me, "I can't grow roses." From listening to their stories, I have learned that almost everyone really *can* grow roses. The problem is that they've chosen to try and grow the wrong roses for their garden. No gardener can make a rose perform beyond its genetic potential. If you garden in Vermont, a rose that thrives in California might not be worth all the extra effort required to coddle it through your winter. If you live in Louisiana, the heritage rose you admired on a trip to New York might sulk much more than bloom in your garden. There are almost 15,000 different roses in commerce today. Many of them will thrive in your garden; others will not. You can't change your weather. What you can do is choose an appropriate rose in the first place.

Choosing the right rose at the start will save you a lot of effort and the potential for disappointment later. My best advice is: First, decide what is most important

OPPOSITE The modern gallica 'James Mason' grows like a weed and is smothered in bloom for a month each summer.

OPPOSITE The compact growth of 'Fair Bianca' makes it a shrub rose suitable even for the smallest gardens.

ABOVE The hybrid tea 'Double Delight' was the first rose I ever planted. Its changing colors and powerful fragrance hooked me on roses.

Monza, Italy, planting a rose that received a gold medal in Monza, Italy, is a good idea. If you live in Des Moines, it might not be. An All-America Rose Selection should be a reliable performer just about anywhere, but it may not be the very best rose for your neighborhood.

Decades ago, "patented" was a big selling point for new roses. Many nurseries still emphasize the fact that their roses are patented. The patent means only that someone has filled out a lot of paperwork and paid some fees to lawyers and the government, and of course that you and I cannot legally propagate the patented rose for sale. Some patented roses turn out to be disasters beyond the nursery greenhouses in which they were first admired; many unpatented roses have enjoyed outstanding garden careers.

Avoiding Slow-Death Syndrome

There are two kinds of rose failures — plants that die and plants that won't. Roses that die are easy to deal with. You dig them up and start over — with another rose or some other kind of plant. Roses that are unhappy but alive can be more difficult. They require the same care as any other rose (indeed, more) as you try to coax them into better health, and yet they provide little satisfaction. Some roses, particularly climbers, may take several years to become well established in your garden. But they should improve each season, building in size and vigor and not sliding backwards, getting smaller, starting to disappear. If your space is limited, cut your losses and eliminate the poor performers.

Roses don't change. There are many hundreds of roses that will perform brilliantly in your garden, but no amount of tender loving care can transform a rose that isn't right for you. Unless you have unlimited space, funds, and time, it isn't going to be worth the effort. Of course some roses may have more sentimental than garden value (your grandmother's favorite rose, the variety you carried in your wedding bouquet, a rose that shares a name with someone special to you). Roses like these deserve a place in our gardens as well as in our hearts, and providing whatever extra care they need will be a labor of love.

Because a rose will live for 25 years or longer, researching your rose choices has a big upside. A rose that gets off to a quick start, resists disease, and winters well is a rose that will become a highlight in your landscape. Planting an unsuitable rose only leads to disappointment and ultimately wastes time.

to you in a rose (color, height of plant, size and shape of bloom, suitability as a cut flower, masses of bloom in the garden, speed of repeat bloom, fragrance, disease resistance). Next, accept the fact that, unfortunately, you can't have it all. While each of us may have a different idea of what the perfect rose would be, that rose does not yet exist.

Once you've settled on your priorities, patronize mail-order rose nurseries and locally owned garden centers whose proprietors will understand what you want and can provide advice based on your conditions and their experience. Beware of roses sold at a big box or discount store. The varieties there may simply reflect what a supplier grew far too many of this year, or printed up far too many posters for last year.

If you admire an award-winning rose, find out why the award was given. The award might mean that the rose did spectacularly well in one specific place, or that it has proven reliable almost everywhere. If you live in

A FEW WORDS ABOUT MY GARDEN

The first rose I ever planted was the raspberry-and-cream hybrid tea 'Double Delight', when it was introduced as an All-America Rose Selection in 1978. It joined a few other roses already growing in my small backyard in suburban Cleveland: the famous 'Peace', a red hybrid tea that I could never definitely identify, and a maroon once-blooming climbing rose that I later learned was 'Dr Huey' (an escaped rootstock). 'Double Delight' did fantastically well, offering much more fragrance than 'Peace' and growing with lots more vigor than the old red hybrid tea. Encouraged by this success, the next year I planted more roses. They did well too. The year after that I made a new rose bed, then I pulled out a barberry hedge and made a rose hedge, and before long I had about 500 roses and not very much lawn. Although I grew all types of roses, I did not mix any other kinds of plants in with them. Rose gardening seemed easy. I could walk around the whole garden in five minutes, the garden hose reached wherever I wanted it to go, and — in a garden sheltered by houses, garages, and the neighbor's gigantic oak tree, as well as benefiting from the smudge pot effect of Lake Erie — I never had to worry too much about winter.

In those years I won a lot of trophies at rose shows and puzzled some established exhibitors by showing old garden roses and shrubs along with hybrid teas and floribundas. I imported roses from nurseries in Britain, Ireland, Germany, Belgium, France, and Switzerland. I was tempted to make more room for roses by creating a rooftop garden of potted roses on top of my garage, but I never actually went that far. If a rose didn't perform well, I dug it up and gave it away. I changed about 15 percent of the rose garden each year. After about a dozen years I had done all I could do on a 40' × 150' lot.

The Search for More Space

My wife, Susan, and I decided to make a new garden together, and we chose northern Portage County as a place convenient for both work and family. Susan then drove the rural back roads, stopping wherever a house was being built to see what kind of soil had come out of the basement. We later learned that the government published detailed maps of soil types throughout our region, but the basement tests proved to be accurate too, as well as giving us insight into various neighborhoods and home-builders. Eventually we bought a

section of an old farmstead that had been in hay for several years, and so started with a 5-acre blank slate. No trees, no buildings, no improvements, nothing but hay, groundhogs, and curious Holsteins staring at us from across the road. But we didn't have to put in a lawn. We had hay, and I mowed it.

Our soil is Canfield B, a sandy loam. Sometimes we miss the clay we had in our previous gardens, because watering is now a challenge in times of drought. On the other hand, we never have to wait for the soil to dry out and never lose a rose to the rotted roots that can result from poor drainage. Our garden is in USDA Zone 5b and has seen temperature extremes since 1993 ranging from 101°F to −26°F. We typically enjoy a springtime with plenty of rain, although it is rare for the roses to go unchecked by a late freeze. There are usually a lot of lightning storms in April and May, which inject nitrogen into the soil. After the roses bloom in June, summers become hot and often dry. Autumn can last a pleasantly long time, with frosts slowing the rose display in late September but often not ending it until well into October. Two years we even enjoyed roses from our garden on the Thanksgiving table. The ground usually freezes in mid-December, and if we're lucky the roses rest under a blanket of snow straight through until March.

Acres of Roses

Today we grow about 1,200 different roses spread over 8 acres. We've planted the roses that need the most care (the hybrid teas) closest to the house. We use soaker hoses to provide the hybrid teas with steady watering, and they receive regular meals of both organic and inorganic fertilizers. When necessary, we administer treatment for insects and disease. Our special care for hybrid teas continues into November, when we hill them up against winter. Some old garden roses grow a quarter mile away, and we don't run hoses that far. Many of our roses receive only rainfall along with a handful of fertilizer once or twice each spring. Although well mulched, the heritage and shrub roses are not sprayed with any chemicals and host healthy populations of lady beetles, praying mantises, and toads. They receive no winter protection. With room to grow as many roses as I want, I do not cull roses that perform poorly. Visitors to our Open Garden days each June get to see the laggards, looking even worse when struggling next to a star performer but proving the importance of choosing one's rose varieties with care.

'WINDRUSH', shrub/David Austin

'QUEEN ELIZABETH', grandiflora

'THÉRÈSE BUGNET', rugosa

'BELLA DONNA', old garden rose/damask

'ALEXANDER', hybrid tea

'PLEINE DE GRÂCE', shrub

'MAMAN TURBAT', polyantha

CHAPTER 2

A ROSE
FOR EVERY PURPOSE

The sheer number of roses available sometimes appears bewildering, and the categories into which they are classed seem to be little help in sorting them out. In addition to logical criteria such as appearance and how the rose actually grows, classification can depend on parentage, commercial considerations, or even the whim of a nurseryman. The often-byzantine requirements of rose show exhibitors play a disproportionate role in the assignment of rose classifications. Nevertheless, the following groups can be genuinely useful reference points when one is seeking a rose with a particular appearance or for a particular garden purpose.

SPECIES ROSES

In the species one sees roses as they grew before humans intervened. At home in the meadow or at the edge of a woodland, most species roses bloomed only once each year. Because their blooms were usually single-petaled, they were able to open easily even when growing in part shade. The hips they produced nourished birds, who planted rose seeds wherever they flew. Over time, insects spread pollen from one species to another, and thus natural hybrids appeared. Gardeners recognized, preserved, and propagated these hybrids long before they came to understand the process that created them, or embarked on anything like deliberate plant hybridization.

In nature, species roses are found only in the Northern Hemisphere. Breeders are often eager to incorporate species roses into their genetic pool to acquire more disease resistance or winter hardiness. *Rosa rugosa* provides the special toughness of a rose that grows on the windswept seacoasts of Manchuria, Korea, and Japan. The glossy leaves of *R. wichurana* have helped to bring more disease resistance into modern roses. Other distinctive characteristics of species roses — the water tolerance of *R. palustris,* which grows happily in swamps, or the eye-catching silvery gray foliage of *R. glauca* — have yet to be incorporated into the mainstream of modern roses.

BELOW *Rosa glauca* is notable for its silvery grey foliage. Like many species roses, its blooms are followed by attractive hips.

DESCRIBING ROSE BLOOMS

Single-petaled refers to blooms that have just one row of petals. In most cases this means five fully formed petals; the species *Rosa sericea* has only four. These are sometimes accompanied by small petaloids clustered at the base of the bloom. Single-petaled roses enjoy one day of perfect beauty. They typically close at sunset, and when they reopen the next morning will not appear as fresh.

'SCHARLACHGLUT', single-petaled

'LA BELLE SULTANE', semi-double

'BARONNE PRÉVOST', very double

'PASCALI', double

Semi-double refers to a rose that doesn't have enough petals to form a bloom that appears three-dimensional when viewed from the side. Any rose with more than one row of petals but less than 20 petals in total is considered semi-double. Buds of semi-double roses open quickly to flat, usually very pretty blooms, often made more attractive by wavy petals or an impressive display of stamens. Stripes show up particularly effectively on semi-double roses.

Double is used to refer to all rose blooms having 20 or more petals. Double roses can take one of various flower shapes, from the high-centered spiral of the hybrid tea to the cupped and quartered appearance of many heritage roses. Some old garden roses and David Austin introductions have as many as 200 petals.

Very double is a term often used to describe roses with 60 or more petals. These usually take more than a day to open even in the heat of summer. They can be enjoyed in their bud stage for longer than other roses, even though their buds are often not as elegant as those with fewer petals. They may have difficulty opening properly during rainy or foggy weather, or when autumn nights grow cool.

MODERN ROSES

The 1867 introduction of 'La France', the putative first hybrid tea, is such a watershed in rose history that every rose in every classification that has arisen since then is considered a modern rose. And so modern roses include hybrid teas, grandifloras, floribundas, polyanthas, large-flowered climbers, minatures, mini-floras, and shrubs — all classes that did not exist before 1867. Nearly all modern roses repeat bloom, but some early polyanthas, large-flowered climbers, and shrubs do not. Modern roses do not have to look "modern." Most of David Austin's English Roses are bred with the many-petaled form usually associated with old garden roses but are nevertheless shrubs — modern roses.

The hybrid tea is the genesis of the modern roses, but also its curse. Rose breeders spent generations trying to make roses in every other class look more like hybrid teas. This made roses *less* rather than *more* interesting, and only recently have many of the other classes become fully liberated from a slavish adherence to the spiraled, high-centered form of a hybrid tea bloom. Miniatures and mini-floras remain captives to the idea that hybrid tea form is the one best form for rose blooms.

'La France' is very fragrant, as were many of the early hybrid teas. By the middle of the twentieth century, most new hybrid tea introductions were not particularly fragrant, and many of the floribundas of that era had no fragrance at all. It would be unfair to condemn modern roses as a group for lacking fragrance, but the effort over the past 40 years to breed fragrance back into modern roses — by hybridizers such as Austin

'DOUBLE DELIGHT', hybrid tea

and Harkness in England and Dorieux in France — is something welcomed by all rose lovers.

Hybrid Teas

Hybrid teas are the roses that everyone knows best and some gardeners like least. These are the roses found in the front windows of flower shops, on the covers of greeting cards, and in the 1960s. If you want to cut roses for long-stemmed bouquets, no other class will be as useful. In the garden, though, you may often see too much of the long stem and too little of the rose. Too many hybrid teas have a stiff growth habit, poor disease resistance, and inharmonious colors. A vast bed of hybrid teas is unlikely to improve your garden as a whole, but no one will ever be unhappy to receive a bouquet of them.

With careful selection of more recent varieties, it is possible to grow hybrid teas of compact growth and good health, while still harvesting armloads of cut flowers.

Many gardeners still refer to "tea" roses. Hybrid teas originated in the nineteenth century with crosses between the hybrid perpetual and the tea. True teas are winter-tender plants suitable only for conservatories, greenhouses, and regions of California and the South (see discussion of tea roses under Old Garden Roses, page 31).

ROSE BREEDERS

Many rose nurseries are family firms, with breeders of the same surname working over a period of a century or more. Cocker, Dickson, Guillot, Harkness, Kordes, McGredy, Meilland, Poulsen, and Tantau are all families whose rose breeding work has extended over two or more generations. Most rose breeding families stay in one place, but Sam McGredy IV, moved in mid-career from Northern Ireland to the North Island of New Zealand, and Robert Harkness has now relocated the family's breeding operation from England to the south of France.

Principal breeders for the giant American firm of Jackson & Perkins, in chronological order, have been Nicolas, Boerner, Morey, Warriner and Zary. Weeks roses have been bred by O.L. (Ollie) Weeks and now Tom Carruth.

Floribundas

The ideal of the floribunda is a ready-made bouquet all on one stem. Plants are tidy, making perfect garden accents or impressive beds of the same or similar varieties. Some of the most charming varieties are single-petaled, or nearly so. While 20 to 30 informally arranged petals may be more common, other floribundas have clusters of blooms similar in form to smaller-scale hybrid teas. Anyone who has traveled in Europe and observed the vast rose beds along public highways might think that floribundas are primarily red; however, they do appear in every rose color. Floribundas disappoint when they have no fragrance — and too many lack scent — when they take too long between bloom cycles, and when old sprays hang on long enough to become a sodden mess after a big rain.

'BETTY PRIOR', floribunda

Grandifloras

When the stalwart cyclamen pink 'Queen Elizabeth' won the All-America Rose Selection award in 1954, it was viewed as too tall to be a floribunda, but with blooms not quite substantial enough to be called a hybrid tea. And so the grandiflora classification was concocted. While American nurseries and the All-American Rose Selection organization have provided us with a regular supply of "grandifloras" since then, there is no need to learn anything about them. 'Queen Elizabeth' turned out to be a one-of-a-kind rose, and all of the other so-called grandifloras are deficient in one respect or another when set against the 'Queen Elizabeth' template.

'QUEEN ELIZABETH', grandiflora

Polyanthas

Polyanthas are the ancestors of the floribundas, and some of them are more suited to museums than to contemporary gardens. 'The Fairy', the most widely grown rose in the world today, is a polyantha. Unfortunately, it comes in only one color, soft pink. (Various other polyanthas with "Fairy" in their name will not duplicate the stellar performance of 'The Fairy'). Many of the other most widely-grown polyanthas have serious defects including ugly, ranunculus-like blooms that never properly open as well as weak, spindly growth.

'THE FAIRY', polyantha

The ideal polyantha will produce humongous clusters of dainty blooms. 'The Fairy' does this on a nearly continuous basis throughout the summer. Others of its era may take a long time before displaying a second crop of blooms. Ignore the Dutch-raised polyanthas such as the Koster series, which were bred for forcing in pots under greenhouse conditions. For garden value, it is worth searching out some of the more-neglected polyanthas introduced in England and France in the early years of the twentieth century. The best of these are just like small-scale old garden roses (see pages 28–34), and can make charming edgers for beds of old garden roses. A few recent polyantha introductions, bred by Harkness in England and Jerabek in the United States, are superb garden roses.

'CROWN PRINCESS MARGARETA', David Austin shrub

Shrub Roses

As recently as a generation ago, "shrub" was a catch-all class for roses that didn't fit neatly into any other category. Oddballs, misfits, and one-of-a-kind roses all found a home under the shrub banner. Hybrid rugosas and hybrid musks were distinctive enough to become recognized subclasses within the shrub group. Today "shrub" incorporates most of the name-branded roses. Of course there are also noteworthy recent shrub roses that are not part of a corporate brand. When I hear "shrub rose," I think healthy and tough, and if the rose does not have both of those qualities I am disappointed. Here is a summary of some of the most popular name-branded and other shrub roses.

DAVID AUSTIN'S ENGLISH ROSES

These roses promise the fragrance and voluptuous full-petaled charm of antique roses combined with the repeat bloom of the modern ones. More recent introductions also have improved disease resistance and include colors that would have been unknown a century ago. This group is so large and diverse that David Austin has divided it into four subgroups: Old Rose hybrids, English Musk hybrids, English Alba hybrids, and the Leander group.

FLOWER CARPET ROSES

Bred by Noack of Germany, the Flower Carpet roses boast superior disease resistance and winter hardiness. Most are ground-hugging, although a few have a

'RED FLOWER CARPET'

more upright floribunda habit. 'Appleblossom Flower Carpet' is a paler pink mutation of the original 'Flower Carpet', but none of the others are directly related to one another, and the gardener who expects different colors of the same plant will be disappointed.

GÉNÉROSA ROSES

Introduced by the Guillot nursery, these are a French version of the English Roses. All have superior fragrance, some have excellent health. A few are not as vigorous or winter hardy as they should be.

KNOCK OUT ROSES

Bred by William Radler in Wisconsin, the Knock Out roses promise easy, floriferous growth on disease-resistant, winter-hardy plants. While the individual blooms are not elegant, the impact of such healthy roses in the landscape can be invaluable. The Knock Out roses are a triumph of marketing as well as rose breeding, and it is unlikely that they would have claimed so much territory in garden centers under their original name of "Razzleberry" roses.

'SONIA RYKIEL', générosa

'RAINBOW KNOCK OUT'

A ROSE BY ANY OTHER NAME WOULD PROBABLY SELL BETTER

Stupid names are another failing of polyanthas — although they're not the plants' fault. Naming a series of polyanthas after the Seven Dwarfs may have been clever marketing, but having one polyantha named 'Dopey' isn't. A British nursery recently repeated this mistake with a series of 12 roses named for signs of the zodiac. Consumers did not flock to a rose called 'Cancer', and even when its name was changed to 'The Crab', sales did not improve.

'CORAL MEIDILAND', shrub

'SIMPLICITY'

MEIDILAND ROSES

From Meilland of France, these roses are plants of various habits bearing great panicles of blooms, usually single-petaled or semi-double. All are designed for landscaping and look best when groups of the same variety are planted together. Most Meidilands provide bloom over a long period. Colors range from soothing to harsh.

OSO EASY ROSES

These are landscaping roses promoted for their disease resistance, all produced on their own roots. Most have attractive single or semi-double blooms and grow into low mounding shrubs. Because they represent the work of several different breeders, the Oso Easy roses may not share a kinship beyond the Oso Easy banner.

SIMPLICITY

From Jackson & Perkins of the United States, this is one of the oldest name-brand groups but also one of the least populated. All of the Simplicity roses display single- or few-petaled roses on a plant that is advertised as a hedge rose but will also incorporate easily into a perennial bed or other combination gardening scheme.

'CIBLES', hybrid rugosa

'BELINDA', hybrid musk

RUGOSAS

The healthy, wrinkled leaves that give this class its name are little changed from the species roses native to Hokkaido, Manchuria, and Korea. Hybridization has admitted many new colors into the rugosa family, which originally included only the white, pink, and purplish reds of the species rugosas. This group is beginning to see some real diversity in habit as well, with rugosas that work well as bedding plants or as groundcovers. Among the toughest of all roses, rugosas are not for fussy gardeners — rugosas dislike being pruned and are allergic to some chemical fungicides. Spray a rugosa and it may drop its leaves.

HYBRID MUSKS

No direct relation to the Musk Rose of Shakespeare, hybrid musks are shrubby plants characterized by gentle colors and healthy but nonaggressive growth. With large clusters of often-small blooms, they can look more at home with other garden plants than in a grouping of larger-flowered roses. They are among the best roses for incorporating into a mixed border. The majority of hybrid musks were bred by the Rev. Joseph Pemberton, an Englishman, at the beginning of the twentieth century and Louis Lens, a Belgian, at the century's end. Not all of the Pemberton creations are winter-hardy; his yellow and pastel orange shades are particularly tender.

EARTH-KIND ROSES

Roses receive the Earth-Kind designation if Texas A&M University determines that they will thrive with minimum, basic care. Not all Earth-Kind roses are shrubs, and because the initial evaluation did not consider winter hardiness, many are not appropriate choices for northern gardeners. Texas A&M has recently announced plans to more thoroughly investigate the winter hardiness of future designees.

'POLKA', large-flowered climber

KORDESIIS

Originally bred in Germany and later improved in Canada, the kordesiis are the most reliable repeat-blooming climbers for cold-winter gardeners. Most appear in vivid colors — there are few pastels or blends — on sturdy, sometimes stiff-growing plants. Foliage is typically glossy and disease-resistant. The one consistent fault of the kordesiis is their lack of fragrance.

Miniatures

There are two kinds of miniature roses. The first is a resilient little plant sold in garden centers and by reputable mail-order nurseries. Its blooms may resemble tiny hybrid teas, or it may produce a big mass of little blooms similar to a small-scale floribunda. Thanks to California rose breeder Ralph Moore, there are miniatures with striped blooms and mossed buds. While I have observed miniature roses put to interesting use in Tiny Town gardens featuring gnome dwellings and Lionel trains, many are reliable enough to fulfill important roles in the full-size landscape of normal gardens.

The second kind of miniature rose is sold in supermarkets and discount stores and often treated by consumers as a houseplant. It is bred to produce one spectacular burst of bloom before dying of exhaustion. While there have been exceptions, these miniatures rarely thrive outdoors. No rose is happy as a houseplant, but since these "throwaway" (as they are called in the trade) miniatures aren't happy in the garden either, the best way to enjoy them might be in passing at the supermarket.

CLIMBING MINIATURES

The best climbing miniatures are not the often-sprawly climbing mutations of well-known miniature varieties, but purpose-bred plants featuring petite blooms on tall plants. Many have a perfect pillar habit, others are more bushy. All should provide nearly continuous bloom and excellent health. Exemplified by the creations of British breeder Chris Warner, today's climbing miniatures make excellent garden plants wherever height is desired but a full-size climbing rose would be too large.

Climbers

Climbing roses come in all degrees of vigor, and the severity of your winters will have a huge effect on the success of climbing roses in your garden. A rose that topples pergolas in California might struggle to give an impersonation of a floribunda in Minnesota. Today's climbing roses are technically called "Large-flowered Climbers." The characteristic that differentiates them from the older climbers known as ramblers (see page 32) is not so much the size of their bloom (which varies greatly) but the fact that they are expected to offer this bloom repeatedly throughout the summer.

Roses lack tendrils or other natural means of attachment. Because they are not true climbers, they rely on the gardener for support.

'JEANNE LAJOIE', climbing miniature

MINI-FLORAS

The mini-flora classification was invented to assuage the complaints of rose show exhibitors and judges who felt that miniature roses were becoming too large. At some rose shows, the miniature "Queen of Show" was approaching the size of a floribunda. And thus many of the oversized miniatures were reclassified as mini-floras, and many new roses in this niche size are being bred and introduced. While few mini-floras are readily available outside of specialized channels, the best among them can be counted on for a dependable supply of cuttable blooms of the size a Victorian gentleman might put in his buttonhole, but often in startling modern colors. The enthusiastic exhibitors who fuss over mini-floras are happy to coddle them; if you aren't you may discover too many of them to be winter-tender, prone to disease, or reluctant to offer too many blooms at once.

'DR JOHN DICKMAN', mini-flora

'MME PLANTIER', old garden/alba

OLD GARDEN ROSES

Old garden roses include all roses in any of the classes that existed before the introduction of the first hybrid tea ('La France') in 1867. Some gardeners decide that they don't want anything to do with old garden roses because 1) they make gigantic plants that take up too much garden space and 2) they do not repeat bloom. Beyond this, many have long French names that are difficult to pronounce.

The names of these roses provide a living connection with history, and it can be fun to rent a French costume drama from Netflix and see how many albas and gallicas are walking around in human form (this helps with pronunciation too). Visit France and you will see that the same historical figures who were commemorated with roses also have streets and Metro stops named in their honor.

As for the principal charges against old garden roses, a few thoughts. Yes, many are gigantic plants. But just as many aren't. As with any other kind of rose, choosing carefully from the thousands of possibilities will result in the rose that is right for your garden. Members of the four original European classes of roses (alba, centifolia, damask, gallica) do indeed bloom only once each summer. This bloom is typically long and will usually include more flowers than almost any repeat-blooming rose will produce over a longer period of time in the same summer. Gardeners in my zone who insist on growing only repeat-blooming plants may limit themselves to floribundas, potentillas, and water lilies. I don't want to be so limited, and I find a once-blooming old garden rose every bit as important in my garden as a dogwood, a lilac, a rhododendron, or any other plant that blooms once each year.

Most old garden roses available today are fragrant. This does not prove that most roses of yesteryear were fragrant, compared to the many bred today that are not. It does mean that fragrant roses are more likely to be cherished and passed down from one generation to the next.

Albas

With distinctive blue-green foliage and flower colors that extend only from white through medium pink, albas are the class of old garden roses that are most easy to identify at a glance. Most albas mature into graceful tall shrubs that benefit from having twiggy interior growth removed. Their blooms are elegant but rarely large. Like apples and several other fruits, albas require chilling hours to perform well and won't be happy in climates without a real winter.

'FANTIN-LATOUR', old garden rose/centifolia

Centifolias

These are the hundred-petaled roses, more or less, forming a small but diverse class. Some centifolia bushes are large and sprawly, others are petite to the point of being proto-miniatures. Blooms can be shades of white through purplish pink to the bright cerise color that in the eighteenth-century rose world would have passed for red. Centifolias are also known as cabbage roses because of the way their petals fold over rather than for their size.

Damasks

The catalyst for the growth of the perfume industry in medieval Persia, the damask rose remains an important cash crop in modern-day Iran, Bulgaria, and Turkey. Most damasks appear in various shades of pink, and it would take a rose breeder at least two generations to breed the fragrance out of them. Damasks offer the largest flowers of the original European old garden roses. They are also among the toughest of all roses and don't mind being pruned after their one long annual display of bloom.

'LA VILLE DE BRUXELLES', old garden/damask

Gallicas

Purple roses. Striped roses. Almost-gray and kind-of-brown roses. They're all here, and usually on a plant that wants to spread into a thicket. Gallicas are notorious for sending up suckers from their roots, often feet or yards away from the original plant. In some situations this is useful (let's say you want a hedge), in others it can be a nuisance. You can control the tendency to sucker for a while by buying gallicas as budded rather than own-root plants. Eventually though, these too will sucker. Gallica blooms are rarely large, and the plants can be kept young by removing worn out canes every three or four years.

'BELLE DE CRÉCY', gallica

'SCARLET MOSS'

'CRESTED MOSS'

Moss Roses

Today moss roses are seen as emblematic of the Victorian age. In their day, however, moss roses were a fad, as gardeners and nurserymen sought mutations that displayed ever-greater degrees of moss (tiny pine-scented bristles) on rose stems and buds. Most moss roses were mutations of centifolias. The repeat-blooming ones were mutations of Portlands (see page 32). When a rose is selected for a bizarre characteristic it's not surprising that other virtues, such as good health or pleasing habit, may be absent. Moss roses are not the healthiest or easiest roses to grow, but they remain popular for the unique characteristic that gives them their name.

REMARKABLE MOSS ROSES

Rose moss offers attraction to three senses. First, the tiny red-green bristles on the sepals and peduncles of roses are a surprising treat for the eye. (In once-blooming mosses, the moss will usually be entirely green and often more abundant.) This glandular growth is particularly evident and attractive as a rose bud begins to unfurl; a fully open bloom obscures it all. Second, it feels good to the touch — soft and supple as fingers ripple over it. Third, it releases the fragrance of pine resin as you touch it. This surprising fragrance is completely separate from the fragrance of the rose bloom. The most dramatic example of moss appears on the sepals of 'Crested Moss', which despite its name and its moss, is technically a centifolia rose.

Chinas

Much is still mystery about the early China roses. Were they the creations of some ancient hybridizers, or spontaneous mutations that were recognized and preserved by observant Chinese gardeners? Whatever their origin, the repeat-blooming China roses revolutionized the rose world and live on in the genes of all of the repeat-blooming roses we grow today. You can grow these China roses with no trouble at all if you live in USDA Zone 7 or higher. A few, which I will describe later in this book, are winter-hardy farther north. Most Chinas put more effort into speedy bloom than elegant petal formation. They appear in all shades of pink, red, and purple, and also bequeathed us the color-changing characteristics found in such modern roses as 'Double Delight'.

Teas

In the elegant, nodding buds of the tea rose we find the genesis of the spiraled rose bud form that is still so prized today in the hybrid teas and in miniatures. Tea roses are really happy only where it is really warm. Northerners can grow them in conservatories, greenhouses, or in pots, but this is an effort repaid only to those with a deep appreciation of the tea's historical importance. Because of their spindly stems, weak necks, and papery blooms, authentic tea roses might disappoint the millions who still call the long-stemmed roses that come from the florist "tea" roses.

Noisettes

The first truly American class of roses, Noisettes were first developed in South Carolina in the early nineteenth century. These were the first repeat-blooming climbing roses, but most of them were never hardy enough to thrive in northern climates. Rose breeders used them a lot, but the result was improvement in other classes rather than hardiness in the Noisettes. By the end of their run many Noisettes were easy to confuse with teas. 'Manettii', a putative Noisette, is still used as a rose rootstock by nurseries in Mediterranean climates.

'MME ALFRED CARRIÈRE', Noisette

Ramblers

"My climber doesn't climb" is a frequent lament of the modern rosarian, especially those in climates with severe winters. It is certainly true that while climbers have been created with larger flowers, appearing more often and in every possible color, much vigor has been left behind. All of that vigor can be found in ramblers, many of which are strong enough to topple a garden arch or disappear up an apple tree. Ramblers typically produce huge sprays of relatively small blooms. They are the last roses to bloom each year, and often they are at their most glorious when hybrid teas and other modern roses are at rest following their first flush of bloom. Some ramblers are plagued by mildew, and almost all can be painful to prune. A few, such as the purple 'Veilchenblau', are mercifully free of thorns.

Heralded as a revolutionary way to use roses when first introduced in the 1980s, groundcover roses are nothing new at all. Peg the canes of a nineteenth-century rambler to the ground and voila! You've got yourself a groundcover rose.

'COMTE DE CHAMBORD', Portland

'AMERICAN PILLAR', rambler

Portland

Also called autumn damasks, the agreeable Portlands are compact, flower-filled bushes. Sometimes there is so much foliage that the blooms almost disappear into it, even when there are a lot of flowers. The bushy plants almost always make the most of any situation and are a reliable choice for herb gardens, borders, and even beds of one variety. Whenever you want an old garden rose that won't grow out of control, a Portland is a reliable choice. The Portlands represented a big step toward modernity in roses and were among the first to benefit from nineteenth-century nurserymen's understanding of how hybridization works. But breeders soon turned their attention to hybrid perpetuals and teas, and the maximum potential of the Portland was left unrealized. Had Portlands been extensively hybridized we might have enjoyed plants very much like David Austin's English Roses generations earlier.

Bourbons

Among the most fragrant of all roses, Bourbons produce voluptuous blooms on plants that can grow tall and lanky. The original Bourbon appeared as a natural hybrid on the Isle de Bourbon (now called Réunion) in the Indian Ocean, a spot on the globe where the repeat-blooming roses of China intersected with the old European roses that had been imported by French settlers. Bourbons can be enjoyed in northern gardens but require extra winter protection. For their impressively large blooms and mind-blowing fragrance, they are worth the extra care they demand.

'MME ISAAC PÉREIRE', Bourbon

Hybrid Perpetuals

Perpetual is an optimistic translation of the French word "remontant," which is used for plants that bloom again. It does not mean that they bloom all of the time, and many hybrid perpetuals don't. Some of the early hybrid perpetuals don't offer repeat bloom at all in my northern climate, and their informal, even scraggly, blooms may not be as immediately appealing to the eye as they are to the nose. In the later hybrid perpetuals one finds all of the strengths and shortcomings of the modern roses: huge blooms, long stems, and perfectly symmetrical flower form on plants that are subject to disease and look ugly when they're not in bloom. Hybrid perpetuals were bred for their blooms, and the plants on which they arrive may be gangly sprawlers or pathetic weaklings. Nineteenth-century gardeners often grew their hybrid perpetuals in cutting gardens hidden away from view. All hybrid perpetuals benefit from generous feeding. Whether you hide them away from general view is up to you. At their best, their flowers can be some of the most stunning roses you can grow.

'GÉNÉRAL JACQUEMINOT', hybrid perpetual

A FINAL WORD
ON ROSE CLASSES

Rose classification is subjective. Many roses could be easily slotted into a different class, and the classes often serve history and rose exhibitors more than logic or genetics. Nevertheless, learning about the various classes can provide an excellent, shorthand introduction to any rose you encounter. Floribunda? Big sprays of bloom. Polyantha? Bigger sprays of smaller blooms. Bourbon? Wonderful fragrance. Noisette? Not winter hardy for me.

CHOOSING ROSES
FOR YOUR GARDEN

Now that you've had an overview of the different classes of roses, you're ready to dive into the next section of the book: the individual rose profiles. I've organized these profiles not by class, but by garden use, such as, roses for bedding and roses for growing in harmony with other plants. Following the name of the rose, you'll find a quick listing of important facts about the rose: its class, its breeder (where known) with its country and date of introduction, bloom color, bloom size, degree of repeat bloom, height, and winter hardiness. For a few roses whose origins are obscure, I've indicated the country from which they came (France, China, and so on). I've chosen to recommend each of these roses because they've done so well for me. In the descriptions that follow, I highlight the specific advantages offered by each rose — the characteristics that make it different and better than other roses. I hope that within these portraits you will find the roses that are right for you.

A NOTE ABOUT ROSE HEIGHT
AND BLOOM SIZE

Throughout the rose descriptions, I report the dimensions that roses typically reach in my Ohio garden. Roses grown in locations with longer growing seasons should get taller; those in areas with tougher winters may well be shorter. Use heights only as relative guide. A rose that grows 8 feet for me might not for you, but in your garden it should still be taller than a rose that grows 5 feet for me.

Bloom size can also vary, but this is more dependent on season than on climate. In summer's heat, repeat–blooming roses usually produce flowers that are slightly smaller. Autumn blooms can be the largest of the year.

'TOUCH OF CLASS'

'SCABROSA'

'MARIA LIESA'

Attractive Hips

Don't remove spent blooms from these plants, and you will be rewarded with an increasingly colorful display of hips throughout the summer, persisting well into fall.

'Alba Semi-plena'
'Bourgogne'
'Cardinal Hume'
'Centenaire de Lourdes'
'Cibles'
'Corylus'
'Hansa'
'Henry Hudson'
'Louis' Rambler'
'Peter John'
'Pleine de Gràce'
Rosa arkansana
R. glauca
R. pomifera
R. pendulina
R. roxburghii normalis
R. virginiana
'Rosalita'
'Scabrosa' (photo at left)
'Scharlachglut'
'Thérèse Bugnet'
'Veilchenblau'
'Windrush'

Ground Covers

No rose is a true ground cover, but these varieties provide solutions for banks, terraces, and hard-to-reach areas.

'Blushing Lucy'
'Chevy Chase'
'Flower Carpet'
'Lady Elsie May'
'Maria Liesa' (photo at left)
'Palmengarten Frankfurt'
'Red Ribbons'
'Sommermorgen'
'Sweet Chariot'
'Veilchenblau'

Few or No Thorns

A joy to work with, these roses are perfect for flower arrangers, children's gardens, or anyone who hasn't had a tetanus shot.

'Fantin-Latour'
'Heritage'
'Lemon Blush'
'Mme Alfred Carrière'
'Maman Turbat'
'Maria Liesa' (photo at left)
'Marie-Jeanne'
Rosa pendulina
'Rosalita'
'Schoener's Nutkana'
'Smooth Velvet'
'Sommermorgen'
'Veilchenblau'
'Zéphirine Drouhin'

Flower in More than Half Shade

Almost any rose will grow in the shade, but few will flower successfully. Here are a few happy exceptions, all content with just three or four hours of sunlight a day.

'Belinda'
'Black Jade'
'Flower Carpet'
'Moonlight'
'Phyllis Bide'
'Queen Mother'
'Rainbow Knock Out'
R. arkansana
R. glauca
R. pendulina
R. virginiana
'Souvenir du Docteur Jamain'
'Veilchenblau'

Extraordinary Fragrance

Whether encountered in the garden or as cut flowers indoors, these roses provide a fragrance that will persist in your memory.

'Aloha'
'Auguste Renoir'
'Compassion'
'Dr. John Dickman'
'Double Delight'
'Electron'
'English Miss'
'Evelyn'
'Heritage'
'Ispahan'
'L'Aimant'
'Mme Isaac Péreire'
'Margaret Merril'
'Mister Lincoln'
'Oklahoma'
'Old Port'
'Paul Shirville'
'Perle von Weissenstein'
'Rose de Rescht'
'Sheila's Perfume'
'Sonia Rykiel'
'Souvenir de la Malmaison'
'Souvenir du Docteur Jamain'
'Spirit of Freedom'
'Sutter's Gold'
'Sweet Chariot'
'The McCartney Rose'
'Urdh' (photo at right)
'Variegata di Bologna'
'Vick's Caprice'
'Violette Parfumée'
'Yolande d'Aragon'

'DISTANT DRUMS'

Roses to Amaze Your Friends and Neighbors

Many roses are perfect for blending into a landscaping scheme, providing color and fragrance without overshadowing their companions. Not these — these are the roses that shout "Look at me."

'Aschermittwoch' (ghostly gray blooms)

'Crested Moss' (exaggerated moss)

'Distant Drums' (curious color combination; photo above)

'Goldelse' (perfectly spherical habit)

'Oranges 'n' Lemons' (amazing stripes)

'Pink Surprise' (exuberant bloom)

'Priscilla Burton' (bizarre "hand-painted" markings etched on its petals)

Rosa roxburghii (hips that look like chestnuts)

Rosa sericea pteracantha (extraordinary thorns)

'Rose Gaujard' (huge blooms; photo at right)

'Si' (tiny blooms)

'Silver Moon' (a rose that can cover a barn)

'Smooth Velvet' (completely thornless)

'The Mayflower' (remains completely healthy even when neighboring roses are diseased)

'Urdh' (whoever thought something named 'Urdh' could smell so good? photo at right)

'ROSE GAUJARD'

'URDH'

PART 2

ROSES IN THE GARDEN AND LANDSCAPE

Here in Ohio the rose parade begins in the middle of May, when the first species roses appear. The hybrid rugosas soon follow, and by early June every day brings more roses into bloom. Many ramblers do not flower until July, and by the time they finish, hybrid teas and miniatures are coming into their second cycle of bloom. Roses are the hardest-working plants in my garden, providing five months of color and fragrance, blooms to cut for bouquets, and ground-covering, lamppost-circling, tree-climbing structure.

CHAPTER 3

ROSES THAT CAN STAND ALONE

Some roses are substantial enough to stand on their own as a highlight in a mixed border, a stunning backdrop for a garden bench, or even in the middle of a stretch of lawn, in the same way you would use a small ornamental tree. Designers call these specimen plants, and while that sounds a bit clinical, it describes a plant whose appeal is not dependent on anything other than its own qualities. A specimen rose will bloom heavily, enjoy good health, and have a predictable habit.

PAGES 38–39
Disease-resistant and winter hardy, 'Flower Carpet' is a completely trouble-free edging rose.

OPPOSITE One of the toughest roses ever bred, 'Thérèse Bugnet' can spread over a large area.

ABOVE The compact climber 'Rosarium Uetersen' can also be grown as a free-standing shrub.

ABOVE RIGHT The exuberant 'Colette' is the best of Meilland's Romantica roses.

OPPOSITE The stalwart 'Captain Samuel Holland' benefits from vigorous pruning.

ROSES INTENDED as accents rather than specimens serve a different role and don't need to be outstanding in all regards. They accentuate other plants or a garden feature, and many roses can be desirable accent plants. But with specimen plants, more than anywhere else in the home garden, it is crucial to choose the right rose, because an inappropriate rose will be an unmistakable failure when displayed in such a prominent position.

Most of the roses I describe in this chapter are repeat-blooming shrubs. Species hybrids can also make great specimens, and they usually offer the added value of ornamental hips that form throughout the summer and ripen in the fall. In northern gardens, hybrid teas and floribundas will not grow large enough to serve well as specimen plants.

CHOOSING A SITE

Specimen roses are often sited where they can be enjoyed from a favorite window. When doing this, consider the rose's appearance throughout the seasons. In cold climates, few roses will keep their leaves over winter, even when planted close to a house. Some roses add structure to the garden even when they are leafless; others resemble dead sticks. Also consider rose hips and rose height when siting a specimen rose. A rose producing hips that prove attractive to birds can be a particular asset in the winter landscape. A large rose that produces all of its blooms at the top of the plant should not be planted too close to a window, unless the window is on the second floor.

BELOW The chestnut-like hips of *R. roxburghii normalis* provide garden interest long after the blooms are gone.

Lawn Roses

A few truly remarkable roses can be liberated from the rose bed, the mixed border, or foundation plantings and set by themselves in the middle of a lawn. When choosing a rose to feature in a lawn, it is important to gauge its ultimate size. Unlike trees, which usually grow straight up, many shrub roses will grow as wide as they are tall. Very thorny varieties may not be a good idea for lawns where children will be playing.

Roses are particularly vulnerable to herbicide damage. If you plant a specimen rose in a lawn, you should never spray liquid weedkillers in that vicinity. Even granular weedkillers should be used with great care. Make sure that your spreader device does not over-distribute the product. Check that runoff from rainfall or lawn watering will not carry the poison toward the rose. Chemical pre-emergent weed-preventing products are generally safe for use around roses, when used as directed. Corn gluten meal is an even safer alternative.

Roses in Wild Settings

Beyond the mowed lawn and the manicured border, larger properties may offer wild areas where specimen roses can truly shine. Here well-chosen roses can add mounds of solid color in a patchwork wildflower meadow, or provide continuing color in an orchard months after apple blossoms have fallen.

Roses as Hedges

Roses that grow large make great hedges. Using one variety will create a more formal effect, while mixing varieties can create a kaleidoscope of color. These won't exactly serve as living fences, because rabbits and smaller animals will always be able to find their way through. But a rose hedge that grows to 8 feet will keep out deer, so long as they can be prevented from eating it long enough for it to reach that height.

'PINK SURPRISE'

'PLEINE DE GRÂCE'

ROSES FOR HEDGING

Whether used along a property line or to divide areas of the garden into separate rooms, these roses will make a dense and colorful barrier.

LOW–MEDIUM
'Linda Campbell' (page 54)
'Petite de Hollande' (page 104)
'Rosa Mundi' (page 109)
'St. John's Rose' (page 111)
'Scabrosa' (page 113)
'Simon Robinson' (page 168)
'The Countryman' (page 119)
'Turbo' (page 121)
'White Roadrunner' (page 122)
'Wildeve' (page 122)
'Yesterday' (page 123)

TALL
'Antike 89' (page 177)
'Cibles' (page 47)
'Hansa' (page 91)
'Laura Ford' (page 183)
'Lemon Blush' (page 54)
'Perle von Weissenstein' (page 104)
'Pink Surprise' (page 56)
'Pleine de Grâce' (page 106)
'Thérèse Bugnet' (page 121)

A SHROPSHIRE LAD

CLASS: Shrub
BLOOM COLOR: Peach
BLOOM SIZE: 5"
INTRODUCED: Austin, England, 1996
REPEAT BLOOM: Monthly
HEIGHT: 7'
HARDINESS: Zones 5–9

Peachy-pink blooms, containing more than 90 petals arranged into a beautiful rosette that reveals itself as the plump buds open into wide, flat blooms. The color fades slightly even as the blooms hold their shape. The blooms are more weatherproof than most roses with this many petals. Rainfall will not ruin the display.

This strong-growing shrub can make an impressively large plant. Fortunately, it is more winter hardy than earlier David Austin roses of this color. Its height and upright growth make it an excellent choice as a hedge, or to wall off summer garden rooms. Plant as close as 18" apart for quick results as a hedge or wall.

By summer-pruning some canes (reducing them by one-third or more when removing spent blooms) you can ensure new blooms up and down the height of the plant. Left on its own, 'A Shropshire Lad' may eventually appear top-heavy with bloom.

RIGHT PLACE *Boundary hedge; garden room wall*

ALBA SEMI-PLENA

CLASS: Alba
BLOOM COLOR: White
BLOOM SIZE: 3½"
INTRODUCED: Europe, ancient
REPEAT BLOOM: None
HEIGHT: 7'
HARDINESS: Zones 4–7

A big, woody 7' plant whose cheerful semi-double blooms appear before most other roses are showing any color, a welcome hint of what is to come in the rose garden. The buds of 'Alba Semi-plena' are especially pretty against its large blue-green leaves. They open into loose, white blooms, which attractively frame the bright golden stamens. This is the only alba to make an impressive show of rose hips. The plant has strong bones and is an asset in every season. The canes of 'Alba Semi-plena' will grow gnarly and less productive after just a few years. These should be removed (a pruning saw may be necessary) to encourage new and more vigorous growth.

Although sold as a more compact version of 'Alba Semi-plena', the alba 'Sappho' grows almost as tall for me, without blooming as much.

RIGHT PLACE *Impressive hips; year-round interest*

'BOURGOGNE'

BOURGOGNE

CLASS: Hybrid Pendulina
BLOOM COLOR: Pink with white
BLOOM SIZE: 2"
INTRODUCED: Ilsink, The Netherlands, 1983
REPEAT BLOOM: None
HEIGHT: 8'
HARDINESS: Zones 4–9

"Rose is a rose is a rose." Except, perhaps, when it's grown for its hips. A hybrid from *Rosa pendulina,* 'Bourgogne' is covered in pretty little single-petaled flowers early in the season, medium pink with an indistinct creamy center. The real show comes later in the year, as 'Bourgogne' develops impressive bottle-shaped hips. These go through a stoplight progression of pigments, beginning a shiny green and gradually changing to yellow and orange before displaying a brilliant lacquered red color that persists into the winter. An 8' shrub covered in these amazing hips is a highlight of the autumn landscape. Branches with ripe hips will last well indoors when cut.

'Bourgogne' grows strongly. When it sprawls, a pair of lopping pruners can bring it back into bounds. It is quite winter hardy; the shrub will remain younger looking if you selectively remove canes as they reach several inches in diameter. Be sure to wait until late autumn to do this, otherwise you'll lose some of the show. You may notice seedlings popping up all around 'Bourgogne'. Few if any of these will be as praiseworthy as their parent, in either bloom or hip. To avoid confusion it may be best to destroy them.

When planting this rose, think of where you would like red hips in autumn rather than pink blooms in early summer. While 'Bourgogne' looks completely at home in a wild setting and will thrive without any care at all, you may want to plant it where you can easily observe the birds it will attract.

RIGHT PLACE *Hips create autumn interest and attract birds.*

'CIBLES'

CIBLES

CLASS: Hybrid rugosa	REPEAT BLOOM: Reliable
BLOOM COLOR: Magenta	HEIGHT: 9'
BLOOM SIZE: 2½"	HARDINESS: Zones 4b–9
INTRODUCED: Kauffman, Germany, 1893	

Having the most elegant growth habit of the hybrid rugosas, 'Cibles' makes a graceful vase-shaped shrub reaching 9'. It is draped in huge sprays of single-petaled, magenta-red blooms in June, enhanced on opening day by brilliant gold stamens. 'Cibles' offers scattered repeat bloom throughout the rest of the rose season and bears small, round, bright red hips in the autumn. This shrub's perfect habit and its interesting locustlike foliage makes it ideal as a stand-alone lawn specimen. 'Cibles' is an outstanding rose for northern gardens that deserves to be better known.

RIGHT PLACE *Landscape specimen; hedge*

'CAPTAIN SAMUEL HOLLAND'

CAPTAIN SAMUEL HOLLAND

CLASS: Shrub	REPEAT BLOOM: Reliable
BLOOM COLOR: Red	HEIGHT: 5' × 6' wide
BLOOM SIZE: 3½"	HARDINESS: Zones 4–9
INTRODUCED: Ogilvie, Canada, 1992	

Cheerful cherry red blooms emerge from pretty spiraled buds. This big shrub grows wider than tall, and its lime green foliage can make an interesting contrast to the usual deeper shades of green rose foliage. 'Captain Samuel Holland' is valuable as a specimen plant or as a constantly blooming member of a long rose border or hedge. 'Captain Samuel Holland' makes a better cut flower than most of the Canadian Explorer roses. It performs best when pruned severely in the spring.

RIGHT PLACE *Specimen; border or hedge; good cut flower*

A ROSE SANCTUARY

'Cibles' came to me from the Sangerhausen Rosarium in eastern Germany. Sangerhausen was established in 1903 to assemble all of the roses known at that time in one garden, and most contemporary breeders were eager to contribute their creations. The collection at Sangerhausen soon grew to several thousand roses. Through World War I, Germany's subsequent economic chaos, and the Nazi and Communist eras, the roses at Sangerhausen grew on. Finally, with the fall of the Berlin Wall and the reunification of Germany, the world was presented with a time-capsule garden full of wonderful roses that had been discarded or lost by a Western world often preoccupied with what's new. 'Cibles' is just one example of a superb heritage rose now available to the world again thanks to its preservation at Sangerhausen.

'COLETTE'

COLETTE

CLASS: Shrub   REPEAT BLOOM: Heavy
BLOOM COLOR: Apricot-pink   WIDTH: 6'
BLOOM SIZE: 4"   HARDINESS: Zones 4–9
INTRODUCED: Meilland, France, 1994

As David Austin's English Roses marched through the horticultural world in the 1980s staking out spots in garden centers, the pages of gardening magazines, and the minds of consumers who might not have otherwise followed rose developments, the world's major rose breeders raced to catch up with this phenomenon of old-fashioned-looking roses on modern repeat-blooming plants. The House of Meilland, responsible for the 'Peace' rose and a sizable minority of the roses you buy from a florist, came up surprisingly short with its line of Romantica roses. Most Romanticas looked exactly like hybrid teas, short and stout with glossy leaves and fat, sometimes confused-looking blooms. Some weren't even fragrant.

'Colette' is a glorious exception. It's a real shrub, graceful and wide, and not a rebranded hybrid tea. Its blooms are apricot-pink, appearing early in the year and repeating as quickly as any rose. It has outstanding winter hardiness and is untroubled by disease. 'Colette' reaches 5' tall × 6' wide in my garden.

A sport, first unimaginatively called 'Yellow Romantica' and recently renamed 'Lunar Mist,' offers all of the same plant qualities and lemon yellow blooms. It is especially valuable for the winter hardiness it brings to this color range.

RIGHT PLACE   *Groups of two or three plants; shrub borders*

CONSTANCE SPRY

CLASS: Shrub   REPEAT BLOOM: None
BLOOM COLOR: Pink   HEIGHT: 10' × 6' wide
BLOOM SIZE: 6"   HARDINESS: Zones 5–8
INTRODUCED: Austin, England, 1961

This was David Austin's first rose introduction, and it is very different from most of his subsequent creations. First, the plant is huge, reaching 10' × 6' in my garden. Second, it does not offer repeat bloom although its fluffy cup-shaped flowers, luminous pink with a softer reverse, do appear over a long time early in the season. When June temperatures stay out of the upper 80s we can enjoy three weeks of 'Constance Spry' each year.

Exceptionally winter hardy, 'Constance Spry' is full of vigor and clothed with healthy foliage all the way to the bottom of its canes. This makes it an ideal choice as a free-standing specimen rose. As a once-blooming rose it can be faulted only for failing to produce ornamental hips for autumn display. Over the years I've seen hips on 'Constance Spry' only a few times, and these have not contained viable seeds.

RIGHT PLACE   *Landscape specimen; can be trained to climb*

'CONSTANCE SPRY'

FRAGRANCE FANTASY

Nurserymen often have optimistic ideas about the fragrance of their rose introductions. Consumers are helped along with familiar points of reference: this rose smells like vanilla! or cloves! or raspberries! Many of these claims are becoming increasingly tenuous and even bizarre. For example, David Austin describes **'Constance Spry'** as having a fragrance like that of myrrh.

While almost everyone can agree on a rose's color, fragrance is perceived much more individually. I'm not sure if these figurative trips to the spice rack or fruit stand are always helpful — your nose will know if a rose is fragrant and if that fragrance is pleasing. As for 'Constance Spry', while I have no idea what myrrh smells like, I can vouch that 'Constance Spry' has a fragrance that is rich and pleasing, lasting even longer in the head than it does in the nose.

DORNRÖSCHENSCHLOSS SABABURG

CLASS: Shrub
REPEAT BLOOM: Steady
BLOOM COLOR: Pink
HEIGHT: 6'
BLOOM SIZE: 4"
HARDINESS: Zones 5–9
INTRODUCED: Kordes, Germany, 1993

Pure pink blooms on a towering shrub that blooms all summer long. The blooms have a lovely spiraled form, very much like that of a full-petaled hybrid tea, and a light but spicy fragrance. While its bloom could be mistaken for that of a hybrid tea, it is much more winter hardy. This is a rose that attracts attention, and visitors to our Open Garden Days always want to know more about it.

Although Susan and I maintain a record book and map for our own information, as well as having almost all of our roses in our heads, we try to keep all of our roses clearly labeled in the garden as well. (One visitor said, "I guess I could grow as many roses as you do, but I could *never* think of names for all of them.") 'Dornröschenschloss Sababurg' is the only rose where I'm tempted to continue the name onto a second label. Everyone always wants to know what this rose is called, but then aren't necessarily happy when they find out. Its name is not an asset outside of Germany, and in the rest of the world it is sometimes sold as 'Fairy Castle'.

RIGHT PLACE *Dooryard planting; mixed hedge*

'FANTIN-LATOUR'

FANTIN-LATOUR

CLASS: Centifolia
REPEAT BLOOM: None
BLOOM COLOR: Pink
HEIGHT: 6'
BLOOM SIZE: 4½"
HARDINESS: Zones 5–9
INTRODUCED: Origin unknown

No one knows where this rose came from, only that it isn't one of the roses that appears in the paintings of Henri Fantin-Latour (1836–1904). The American Rose

LONG-LASTING LABELS

Susan and I use cut-up mini blinds as plant labels. (Taste in window treatments has changed, and mini blinds often turn up for free on the side of the road on trash days; otherwise they are available for pennies at the Goodwill Store). It took us a long time to find a marker that was both legible and lasting. Most garden or laundry markers fade after just a year or two, and pencil is too light to be read from 5' or 6' away. Paint pens offered promise but were messy. Finally we found Allflex markers, used by dairy farmers to write numbers on the plastic ear tags worn by their cows. One must get these at a supply house where real dairy farmers shop; the "tractor" stores for city folk who have moved out into the country do not have them. Allflex markers are perfect for making rose labels. The ink persists out in the sun and rain and cold for four or more years.

Society says it was introduced before 1900, in which case M. Fantin-Latour could have enjoyed this excellent tribute in his twilight years. But no one has been able to point to a catalog listing this rose until the 1940s, when it apparently appeared out of nowhere, complete with the idea that it was introduced 40 years previously.

Wherever it came from, 'Fantin-Latour' is a beautiful and easy-to-grow rose, covered for as long as a month each spring with soft pink blooms. These have as many as 200 petals, growing more narrow as they reach the center of the flower, which often has a button eye. The plant grows 6' tall and wide in my garden, making an outstanding specimen shrub. Because it has very few thorns, it is easy to work and mow around. 'Fantin-Latour' will also be a winning member of a long border of heritage roses. It is officially classified as a centifolia, and it may be a natural hybrid between a centifolia and a Bourbon. Its one fault is a slight tendency to get black spot. To combat this, prune twiggy and weak growth hard after each annual bloom. (The black spot fungus finds it much more difficult to latch on to foliage connected to strong, vigorous canes.) Pruning after its annual bloom will not diminish its garden value, because there are no ornamental hips.

RIGHT PLACE *Heritage rose border; specimen plant*

GESCHWIND'S NORDLANDROSE

CLASS: Shrub	REPEAT BLOOM: Rare
BLOOM COLOR: Pink	HEIGHT: 7'
BLOOM SIZE: 3"	HARDINESS: Zones 4–9
INTRODUCED: Geschwind, Austria, 1884	

This rose is unstoppable. No matter how cold it gets in winter, no matter how hot or dry summer turns, in the face of wind or rain or hail . . . Whatever Mother Nature offers, 'Geschwind's Nordlandrose' stands up to it all, producing an abundance of many-petaled pink blooms. The blooms are not individually elegant, but their overall effect on the landscape is profound. My 7' shrub is covered top to bottom in bloom throughout June; the occasional flower appears later in the summer. This rose shines as a specimen shrub; don't bury it in a border where the blooms on the lower part of the plant could be hidden.

RIGHT PLACE *Specimen shrub; hedge*

'GESCHWIND'S NORDLANDROSE'

RUDOLPH GESCHWIND

Rudolph Geschwind was the greatest rose hybridizer of the Austro-Hungarian empire. His color palette did not extend much beyond pink, none of his roses has a catchy name, and most of his creations are hard to find today. But his roses are the perfect choice for the low-maintenance northern gardener. If you see a **Geschwind rose**, buy it. You will not be disappointed.

HOME RUN

CLASS: Shrub	REPEAT BLOOM: Heavy
BLOOM COLOR: Red	HEIGHT: 2'
BLOOM SIZE: 2"	HARDINESS: Zones 5–9
INTRODUCED: Carruth, USA, 2006	

One of the most exciting new roses of recent years, 'Home Run' provides nonstop dazzling color on a short, compact, extremely healthy plant. The single-petaled blooms are a red that is rich but bright at the same time, and they repeat with such rapidity that the concept of bloom cycles is almost meaningless. This rose is always in bloom.

Growing into a mound of just under 2', 'Home Run' is best thought of as a mini-shrub, much like 'Baby Love' (with which it pairs beautifully). This rose can be tucked anywhere you desire some bright red color, or planted on 1' centers for an ideal edge to a large bed.

RIGHT PLACE *Edging for large bed; container plant*

ISPAHAN

CLASS: Damask
REPEAT BLOOM: None
BLOOM COLOR: Pink
HEIGHT: 7'
BLOOM SIZE: 3"
HARDINESS: Zones 4–9
INTRODUCED: ancient, first recorded by Europeans in 1832

There are hundreds of pink heritage roses that bloom just once. Why is this one better than the rest? It makes a healthy, free-standing shrub. Its clear pink blooms show up from a long way off. It is completely winter hardy and has excellent resistance to disease. Its flowers usually appear in clusters, which can be cut as ready-made bouquets. And to my nose, it has the most persistent perfume found in any rose.

'Ispahan' grows easily to 7' or more and will occasionally sucker. It is named for the Iranian city where it is still used in the commercial production of attar of roses.

RIGHT PLACE *Free-standing shrub; fragrant hedge*

'JAMES MASON'

JAMES MASON

CLASS: Gallica
REPEAT BLOOM: None
BLOOM COLOR: Crimson
HEIGHT: 8'
BLOOM SIZE: 4"
HARDINESS: Zones 4–8
INTRODUCED: Beales, England, 1982

A modern hybrid of a gallica rose, 'James Mason' makes a billowing bush eager to sucker in every direction. It grows to 8' tall in Ohio and will spread indefinitely unless stopped by a pavement barrier — or a gardener with a spade. If you've ever wished for bamboo with large red blooms, plant 'James Mason'. Over the past few years I have been harvesting all of the suckers that 'James Mason' produces and transplanting them to the back of the property. Soon my back 3 acres will be completely fenced with a 'James Mason' hedge. Mowing controls suckers on my side, and my neighbor may enjoy a field of 'James Mason' until he brush-hogs.

Although there is no repeat of its bright crimson, 12-petaled flowers, it is hard to imagine anything more shocking than this rose in its full June bloom.

This rose was a late-in-life present for the actor James Mason from his wife Clarissa. For many years Clarissa Mason sponsored the James Mason Award, a different kind of rose prize. Most awards congratulate roses that haven't yet grown in anyone's garden. The James Mason Award recognizes varieties that had demonstrated stellar performance 10 years after their original introduction. Based on its productivity in my garden, the 'James Mason' rose would certainly qualify for its namesake award. It's one of the most dependable roses I grow.

RIGHT PLACE *Impenetrable hedge*

PETER BEALES

Nurseryman and author Peter Beales gets a lot of the credit for reintroducing heritage roses to gardeners in Britain and around the world. His 1985 book, *Classic Roses,* helped to bring heritage roses back into the mainstream. Beales achieved synergy before it became a buzzword, growing these classic roses at his nursery in Norfolk, England, and shipping them to his readers all over the world. He and his daughter Amanda have also hybridized many roses, of which **'James Mason'** is clearly the best.

JENS MUNK

CLASS: Hybrid rugosa
REPEAT BLOOM: Steady
BLOOM COLOR: Pink
HEIGHT: 6'
BLOOM SIZE: 3"
HARDINESS: Zones 3–9
INTRODUCED: Svejda, Canada, 1974

Its cotton-candy pink blooms are the brightest found on any of the Canadian Explorer roses, and the sturdy plant will be a bulwark wherever you place it. Well-armed with prickles, 'Jens Munk' can make an impenetrable hedge. Its bright color and summer-long bloom can also make it a focal point in a dull part of a home

'JENS MUNK'

landscape: It's perfect for brightening a background of conifers or a dark-colored building.

'Jens Munk' is a stalwart shrub, reaching 6' tall and almost as wide in my garden. More typically rugosa than most of the Explorers, 'Jens Munk' dislikes drought and will react poorly if sprayed with chemical fungicides.

RIGHT PLACE *Free-standing shrub; interplanting with conifers; hedge*

ONLY AS HARDY AS THEIR GENES

Although nurseries often advertise "northern grown for winter hardiness," a rose bred or grown in Canada is not inherently more winter hardy than one from California. A breeder working in Canada (or any cold-winter region) has the advantage of seeing first-hand how rose seedlings will react to cold. However, a California breeder can send prospects to cold-winter gardens for testing, and the large breeding operations do just that. Like everything else in roses, cold hardiness is all in the genes. Roses grown in a northern nursery have no special immunity to cold winters, especially considering that most of today's own-root roses will have spent their entire life inside a greenhouse, and field-grown budded roses will have spent their only winter at that nursery as dormant eyes, taking advantage of the hardiness of their rootstock.

That said, it is relevant to note that the Canadian government has sponsored two separate rose breeding programs aimed at creating winter-hardy roses. The Explorers, bred in Quebec from rugosas and *Rosa kordesii*, are usually large, impressive plants. Many of them waver between shrub and climber.

The Mordens, bred in Manitoba, have a more diverse pedigree. They are meant to be winter-hardy bedding plants (the pale pink 'Morden Blush' is the best of these).

JOHN CABOT

CLASS: Shrub	REPEAT BLOOM: Reliable
BLOOM COLOR: Pink	HEIGHT: 8'
BLOOM SIZE: 3½"	HARDINESS: Zones 4–9
INTRODUCED: Svejda, Canada, 1978	

Informal, shiny cerise pink blooms appear all summer long on this huge, tough plant. 'John Cabot' is quite disease resistant. Its extreme winter hardiness should complete the package of a trouble-free plant, but this winter hardiness can lull gardeners into complacency. Northern gardeners are often grateful for all of the live wood they find in the spring, and they want to keep every bit. This is an understandable reaction, but with 'John Cabot' it would be a mistake. This huge shrub will become top-heavy and unproductive if you don't make the effort to remove older canes.

'John Cabot' makes an impressive tall hedge, and as a stand-alone specimen plant it can duplicate the garden value of a massive rhododendron all summer long.

RIGHT PLACE *Tall hedge; can be trained to climb*

JUBILEE

CLASS: Hybrid perpetual	REPEAT BLOOM: Not in Zone 5
BLOOM COLOR: Purple	HEIGHT: 8'
BLOOM SIZE: 3"	HARDINESS: Zones 5–9
INTRODUCED: Walsh, USA, 1897	

'Jubilee' produces perfect sprays of rich purple blooms in astounding profusion for almost a month each summer. It's attractive on its own, harmonizes beautifully in a shrub border, and makes a perfect hedge. When cut young, its blooms last surprisingly well as cut flowers.

Although officially registered as a hybrid perpetual, 'Jubilee' is not a typical one. It provides impressive growth with no special cultural demands. It offers no repeat bloom for me, and its individual blooms are

'JUBILEE'

neither large nor remarkably fragrant. Assuming that I am growing the same rose that was introduced in 1897 (and contemporary descriptions seem to support this), I suspect that it was classified as a hybrid perpetual only because hybrid perpetuals were so popular at its time of introduction. Of all the purple-toned roses you can grow, this one offers the most agreeable combination of profuse blooms and hassle-free plant. I grow several specimens of this very useful rose around my garden; one even does reasonably well at climbing an 8' arch. In a warmer climate, it might even succeed completely at that.

RIGHT PLACE *Landscape and garden accent; shrub border; hedge; cut flowers*

'LA BELLE SULTANE'

LA BELLE SULTANE

CLASS: Gallica
BLOOM COLOR: Violet
BLOOM SIZE: 4"
INTRODUCED: origin uncertain, France, c. 1795

REPEAT BLOOM: None
HEIGHT: 6'
HARDINESS: Zones 4–8

The gallica 'La Belle Sultane' has been around for more than 200 years, and its sturdy petals display the darkest color in roses without crisped or browned petals. Its overall hue is a velvety deep violet, heading straight toward purple. As its violet buds unfurl, a band shaded as close to black as any rose can get surrounds the outer limits of each petal. The large semi-double blooms are illuminated by a boss of brilliantly gold stamens. The plant grows vase-shaped to about 6' when old, unproductive canes are regularly cleaned out. Neglected, it will mass into a shorter, less attractive plant.

Named for Aimée Dubucq de Rivery, a cousin of Empress Josephine, who was kidnapped by Barbary pirates while sailing the Mediterranean and ended up a celebrity member of the harem of Turkish sultan Abdulhamid I. Later she became a power behind the throne of her son, Sultan Mahmud II.

RIGHT PLACE *Heritage rose hedge; back of shrub border*

BLACK AND BLUE ROSES

We always want what we can't have, and rose breeders try to help us. Genetic engineers have been recruited to develop blue roses. They have made various predictions and promises, the first of which indicated that we would all be growing delphinium blue hybrid teas by 1999. Chromosomes from flowers that are naturally blue have been duly inserted into the ectoplasm of the rose. But the rose has balked; results so far have been disappointing, yielding nothing bluer than what traditional hybridization has already developed. Creating a black rose, on the other hand, should not require an advanced degree because all of the necessary ingredients already exist in roses. The problem, as has been pointed out by the renowned French rose breeder Alain Meilland, is that even if a rose were entirely black in the bud, its petals would absorb so much solar energy that they would crisp and burn as soon as they unfurled to meet the sunlight.

LA VILLE DE BRUXELLES

CLASS: Damask
BLOOM COLOR: Pink
BLOOM SIZE: 3½"
INTRODUCED: Vibert, France, 1836

REPEAT BLOOM: None
HEIGHT: 4'
HARDINESS: Zones 5–9

Perfectly quartered deep pink blooms appear for almost a month each spring on this healthy damask. The blooms will last indoors if cut when tight; mature blooms dry very well and are sought after by floral artists.

'LA VILLE DE BRUXELLES'

Every plant of 'La Ville de Bruxelles' makes the same perfectly shaped shrub, 4' tall × 5' wide in my garden. Its ideal leafy habit makes 'La Ville de Bruxelles' a perfect choice for repeating in the larger landscape, whether up a driveway or along a path, or at regular intervals in a long border. Each plant will look the same as the next, and all will be in bloom at the same time.

RIGHT PLACE *Along a driveway or path; at intervals in a long border*

'LEMON BLUSH'

LEMON BLUSH

CLASS: Alba

BLOOM COLOR: Yellow

BLOOM SIZE: 4"

INTRODUCED: Sievers, Germany, 1988

REPEAT BLOOM: None

HEIGHT: 10'

HARDINESS: Zones 4–8

For roses, yellow is the weakest link. Many yellow roses will not survive an Ohio winter without extraordinary protection efforts — heaps of sawdust or compost, mounds of soil imported from another part of the garden, Styrofoam igloos, or a landscaping blanket. Those that do survive may grow weakly, or prove prone to disease. 'Lemon Blush' has none of these problems. Its canes are tip-hardy to at least –10°F, it grows quickly to 10', and it's never troubled by disease. Even though its yellow buds fade to paler lemon blooms, it's the largest yellow rose bush I can hope to grow. This is one of the few roses that could be named for either color or scent.

Despite its massive size, this shrub is easy to garden with. It doesn't sucker or spread: 'Lemon Blush' stays right where you plant it. And because it is thornless, it's never a pain to prune or to work around.

RIGHT PLACE *Mixed rose hedge; can be trained over an arch*

THE BLUSH SERIES

'Lemon Blush' is one of a series of hybrid albas bred by a German amateur rose enthusiast. All have "Blush" in their name and grow to massive but amazingly uniform proportions. Blooms are much larger than the antique albas and fragrance is impressive, but after a stupendous early summer display there is no repeat bloom. 'Lemon Blush' is the most valuable of these, because its color is so rare and it makes such a pleasing contrast with pink old garden roses.

LINDA CAMPBELL

CLASS: Hybrid rugosa

BLOOM COLOR: Red

BLOOM SIZE: 3"

INTRODUCED: Moore, USA, 1990

REPEAT BLOOM: Good

HEIGHT: 6'

HARDINESS: Zones 4–9

Huge sprays of currant-red blooms erupt throughout the summer on this easy-to-grow rugosa hybrid. This is an archetypical cropper — a rose producing a huge crop of blooms, then resting before producing another. 'Linda Campbell' is a highlight of the landscape when it is blooming and an attractive bushy plant when it isn't. But this is not one of those roses that always has a couple of flowers on display. It's all or nothing, and when this rose is blooming the sprays it produces may simply be too large to cut for the house, unless you have an oversize house with Herman Munster furniture and gigantic flower vases.

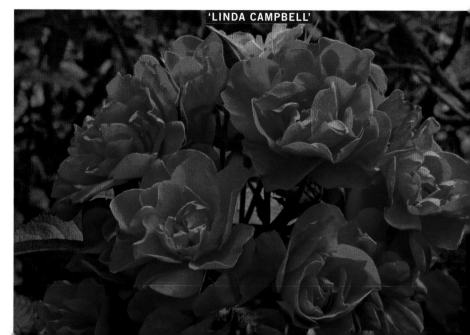

'LINDA CAMPBELL'

'Linda Campbell' is one of three excellent real (i.e., not purplish) red hybrid rugosas that grow over 6' tall. 'Hansaland' (Kordes, Germany, 1993) has a neater plant habit and more attractive foliage, but less substantial blooms. The brilliant, thorny 'Robusta' (Kordes, Germany, 1979) has unfortunately developed a tendency to get black spot over time.

RIGHT PLACE *Mixed shrub bed; low hedge*

'MME PLANTIER'

MME PLANTIER

CLASS: Hybrid alba	REPEAT BLOOM: None
BLOOM COLOR: White	HEIGHT: 6' or taller
BLOOM SIZE: 2"	HARDINESS: Zones 4–8
INTRODUCED: Plantier, France, 1835	

Like a giant snowball or a good viburnum, 'Mme Plantier' provides a vision of white from any direction. Because its growth is so uniform, and its three-week display of bloom so profuse, 'Mme Plantier' is ideally placed as a lawn specimen rose. In a border, its pure white blooms provide an effective contrast to any deeply colored flower and help to draw out paler tones in neighboring plants.

An alba hybrid, 'Mme Plantier' lacks the typical blue-green leaves of its family. Its lettuce green foliage would be a perfect backdrop for its 2", button-eyed blooms, if only it wasn't completely obscured by them. Like many white, once-blooming roses, it has a fresh scent similar to that of cold cream.

Some references describe 'Mme Plantier' as a shrub of medium height. It doesn't stop at medium for me and can be seen covering the sides of houses in southern Ohio.

RIGHT PLACE *Lawn specimen rose; endcap; climber in mild climates*

'MARCHESA BOCCELLA'

MARCHESA BOCCELLA

CLASS: Hybrid perpetual	REPEAT BLOOM: Heavy
BLOOM COLOR: Pink	HEIGHT: 6'
BLOOM SIZE: 3½"	HARDINESS: Zones 4–9
INTRODUCED: Desprez, France, 1842	

This is the best choice for anyone who wants an old garden rose that blooms throughout the summer. 'Marchesa Boccella' is a hybrid perpetual that really is perpetual, with a constant display of fragrant, powder-puff pink blooms on a plant that grows like a pillar to more than 6'.

Because 'Marchesa Boccella' is so winter-hardy it will tower over most other hybrid perpetuals for the first part of the rose year in the northern garden. Some of the others will have caught up or even grown past it by September. It makes a tidy hedge and is a superb ever-blooming specimen plant. 'Marchesa Boccella' benefits from the regular removal of old canes; left on its own it will grow into a much less productive thicket.

RIGHT PLACE *Hedge; fragrant garden*

A SHOW STORY

'Marchesa Boccella' is inextricably confused with the Portland rose 'Jacques Cartier'. Indeed, the flowers of 'Marchesa Boccella' are often hidden beneath its foliage, a characteristic of the Portlands. But if it is a Portland, 'Marchesa Boccella' is one that grows almost twice as tall as any of the others in my garden.

When I began exhibiting roses in the early 1980s, the Cleveland Rose Society included old garden roses in its show schedule as a kind of grudging afterthought to the myriad classes available for hybrid teas and every conceivable combination of hybrid teas (three red hybrid teas; one red, one white, and one pink hybrid tea; five hybrid teas that have won the AARS award, newly introduced hybrid tea . . .). While other types of roses were divided by color classes, old garden roses were divided only by the middle of the alphabet, A–L and M–Z. One canny exhibitor (growing perhaps one old garden rose) regularly won both awards with two specimens of the same rose, one shown as 'Jacques Cartier' and the other as 'Marquise Boccella' (as 'Marchesa Boccella' was spelled in those days). Today little has changed. Old garden roses are divided by date of introduction, with one trophy for those introduced before 1867 and one for everything that came later. Since 'Jacques Cartier' was introduced in 1868, you can imagine what happens.

PETER JOHN (photo, page 3)

CLASS: Hybrid musk	REPEAT BLOOM: Reliable
BLOOM COLOR: Apricot-pink	HEIGHT: 5'
BLOOM SIZE: 4"	HARDINESS: Zones 4–9
INTRODUCED: Jerabek, USA, 2003	

A beautifully shaped shrub with apricot-pink flowers, 'Peter John' is tremendously winter hardy for a rose of this color. Fully double blooms appear in sprays all summer long, and those that aren't deadheaded are likely to form attractive hips. There is only a slight scent. It is registered as a hybrid musk because of its affinity to the German hybrid musk 'Nymphenburg', on which it is an improvement in both hardiness and floriferousness. Its foliage and blooms will show to

perfect advantage in front of a gray stone wall. 'Peter John' is also substantial enough to grow as a lawn specimen. A grouping of three or five plants will create a sea of color all summer long. In addition to its value as a specimen plant, 'Peter John' makes a stunning hedge when planted on 4' centers.

RIGHT PLACE *Group planting; hedge; autumn hips*

PINK SURPRISE

CLASS: Hybrid bracteata/rugosa	BLOOM SIZE: 4½"
	REPEAT BLOOM: Reliable
BLOOM COLOR: Pink fading to white	HEIGHT: 5' × 8' wide
	HARDINESS: Zones 4–9
INTRODUCED: Lens, Belgium, 1987	

And the surprise, several garden visitors have noted, is that it isn't pink. Long pink buds open to platter-sized, single-petaled blooms of pearlescent pink that will fade

'PINK SURPRISE'

to white in the summer sun. Autumn blooms are often more genuinely pink. This is a beautiful shrub, covered in lustrous light green foliage and blooming nonstop throughout the rose year. Its clusters of blooms cover the plant from top to bottom.

Descended from rugosas, but with a more relaxed habit than many in that group, 'Pink Surprise' grows 5' tall × 8' wide in my garden. It would grow even wider if I let it. This rose needs no special care beyond the occasional removal of old canes.

RIGHT PLACE *Hedge; season-long interest*

LOUIS LENS

Louis Lens began his career breeding worthy but conventional roses such as the hybrid tea 'Pascali'. Later on he devoted himself to bringing healthy species blood into modern roses. Although he is most noted for his line of hybrid musks, he also did pioneering work with *Rosa bracteata, Rosa filipes,* and *R. helenae.* A few of these experiments have not proven hardy for those who enjoy something more severe than a Belgian winter, but **'Pink Surprise'** is spectactularly cold resistant.

RALPH'S SOUTH AFRICAN ROSE

CLASS: Mystery
BLOOM COLOR: Pink
BLOOM SIZE: 3"
INTRODUCED: ex-South Africa
REPEAT BLOOM: None
HEIGHT: 7'
HARDINESS: Zones 5–9

'Ralph's South African Rose' is one of the most interesting and rewarding found roses that I grow (see Lost and Found Roses, page 58.) Brought back as cuttings by Ralph Moore from South Africa, and then propagated at his California nursery, this rose blooms with almost unbelievable profusion in June, with blooms and sprays of blooms emerging from every node along its long, branching canes. The plush, 100-petaled flowers are mid-pink with just a hint of lavender, with a fragrance that travels through the garden.

This rose does not appear in Gwen Fagan's comprehensively illustrated landmark book, *Roses at the Cape of Good Hope,* which documents the heritage roses lost and found in South Africa. Some rosarians have dubbed this 'Ralph's South African Bourbon.' Indeed, the flowers have all of the fullness and fragrance of a

Bourbon. But no other Bourbon is hardy to its tips over an Ohio winter, and it shows no willingness to offer repeat bloom in this climate. The true ancestry of this rose remains a mystery.

RIGHT PLACE *Mixed rose hedge; can be trained as a climber*

ROSA EGLANTERIA

ROSA EGLANTERIA

CLASS: Species
BLOOM COLOR: White with pink
BLOOM SIZE: 1½"
ORIGIN: Europe
REPEAT BLOOM: Occasional
HEIGHT: 5'
HARDINESS: Zones 5–9

The Sweet Briar Rose is famous for releasing a scent of green apples from its foliage after a rain, or when its leaves are rubbed between one's fingers. Its blooms are delicate, single-petaled white with pink. Although the plant's small foliage contributes to an overall dainty impression, it is healthy and tough. And its multitude of thorns are something to be reckoned with.

Its prickliness makes *Rosa eglanteria* (also known as *R. rubiginosa*) an excellent barrier hedge. I had the idea of planting this behind a garden bench, so that I could sit and absorb its fragrance after a summer rain. Although sitting on a wet bench ultimately proved unappealing, *R. eglanteria* has no problem dispersing its foliar scent throughout the garden, easily enjoyed by ambulatory gardeners.

There is a gall wasp that seeks out *R. eglanteria*. It does no real harm, and the round, mossy galls it leaves on the stems can either be left as curiosities or cut away.

RIGHT PLACE *Barrier hedge; wherever fragrant foliage can be enjoyed*

HYBRID EGLANTERIAS

In the 1890s Lord Penzance of Surrey, England (a cousin of Oscar Wilde), introduced a whole series of eglanteria hybrids, including ones named after himself and Lady Penzance. Each of these offers some enhancement: larger bloom, brighter color, more compact habit. As a whole, however, they are much more prone to disease than their species parent and may be of most interest to collectors.

ROSA POMIFERA

CLASS: Species	REPEAT BLOOM: None
BLOOM COLOR: Pink	HEIGHT: 6'
BLOOM SIZE: 1½"	HARDINESS: Zones 5–9
ORIGIN: central Europe	

The Apple Rose produces the largest hips in the rose kingdom. The fact that the bristly seedpods don't really look like apples, even when they are fully red, shouldn't dissuade anyone from growing this fascinating rose as a specimen, or as part of a spectacular hedge. The hips are good to eat too, so long as you haven't sprayed them with chemicals. Its pink, crinkly, single-petaled blooms appear over a long period in June, emerging from buds that at first hint that they might produce red blooms. The flowers appear by themselves and in small clusters. The foliage of *Rosa pomifera* is interesting in its own right, covered in a down that gives its green leaves a silvery sheen. This species rose grows 6' in my garden; judicious pruning can encourage it to grow wide as well as tall. It will sucker freely if you let it.

LOST AND FOUND ROSES

Roses are a living link with history not just through their names (which often conjure historical associations) but in themselves, as all roses are one piece of an original whole. Hybrid roses are in the first instance grown from a seed. After that, the resulting seedling, unique in the world, is propagated by cuttings or by bud-grafting. All subsequent plants form a link in one continuous chain stretching back through the years to that one original plant. So the alba you enjoy in your garden today is not just the same variety that Empress Josephine enjoyed at Malmaison, it is part of the same plant.

Sometimes rose identities become muddled. Labels are lost, a nursery makes a mistake, authoritative rosarians are insistent but confused. There are undoubtedly a number of old garden roses known by names today that are completely different from the names they enjoyed in their heyday. Other heritage roses are discovered at abandoned homesteads, in roadside ditches, or in old cemeteries without being attached to any name at all. Keen rosarians known as rose rustlers search out these forgotten roses and provide a great service by preserving and propagating them.

A small percentage of these found roses are almost certainly varieties with no past whatsoever. They could be the result of a spontaneous mutation or of a seedling planted by a bird, and no amount of searching through old rose books and nursery catalogues will ever reveal an identity that never existed.

When a rose with no known identity is discovered, it is often given a study name, enclosed in double quotation marks to indicate its provisional nature. This often credits the finder or the place where the rose was found. Eventually, everyone hopes, the rose can be reunited with its true identity. Sometimes the truth hurts. For example, the rose discovered by heritage rose rustlers in Texas and christened "Katy Road Pink" was not some forgotten treasure from Texas' pioneer past, but 'Carefree Beauty', a shrub rose developed by Dr. Griffith Buck at Iowa State University and introduced in 1977.

An excellent semi-double form is called 'Duplex' or Wolley-Dod's Rose, after the English clergyman who thought he had discovered it in 1900. In fact, rose literature shows that he was just the latest in a line of rediscoverers of a rose that has been in existence since at least the eighteenth century. But could there possibly be a more perfect name for a late Victorian clergyman rosarian than Charles Wolley-Dod?

RIGHT PLACE *Specimen plant; hedge; edible hips*

ROSA ROXBURGHII NORMALIS

CLASS: Species	REPEAT BLOOM: None
BLOOM COLOR: Pink	HEIGHT: 15'
BLOOM SIZE: 3"	HARDINESS: Zones 4–9
ORIGIN: China	

This is one of the largest rose plants I grow. Reaching 15' in height, it would grow as wide if I let it. Its single-petaled, clear pink blooms are the largest of any species rose, popping up all over the plant early each season. A deeper pink version is also available from specialist nurseries. While these blooms do not last long, they are soon followed by large burred hips that look very much like chestnuts (hence its popular name, the Chestnut Rose; see photo of hips, page 44).

An added attraction, rare in roses, is a flaky ornamental bark. I would not seek out *Rosa roxburghii normalis* solely for its bark as I would many birches or a paperbark maple, for example. However, the flaky bark does let this large rose work as an ornamental tree. Because it will dwarf almost all other roses, as well as many other plants, this is how *R. roxburghii normalis* is best used. Birds love it, and it's a trouble-free plant for any gardener who owns a pruning saw. Unlike some trees with ornamental bark, this rose will not suffer from sunscald if you prune away a lot of branches to showcase the bark. If you have room in your garden for a dogwood or an ornamental pear, you have room for this remarkable rose.

Although I prefer the simple beauty of *R. roxburghii normalis,* a double-petaled version of this rose is readily available, usually sold as *R. roxburghii.*

RIGHT PLACE *Ornamental tree*

ROSA ROXBURGHII NORMALIS, BARK

ROSA ROXBURGHII NORMALIS, BLOOM

ROSA VIRGINIANA

CLASS: Species   REPEAT BLOOM: None

BLOOM COLOR: Pink   HEIGHT: 4'

BLOOM SIZE: 2"   HARDINESS: Zones 5–9

ORIGIN: Northeastern USA and Canada

The first rose to grow in my garden. I found this nice plant growing at the back of our property, in the shade of the maple trees that the early settlers allowed to grow up in the no-man's-land between their farms. *Rosa virginiana* has everything you'd want in a wild rose: luminous deep pink blooms with glowing golden stamens, large round hips that color up very well, and a plant whose foliage turns autumn colors in tune with the maples — golden yellow, bright orange, scarlet red. The plant makes a tidy 4' thicket, suckering slowly. It is one of the last roses to bloom each spring, usually not starting until all modern roses have finished. Planted in the understory of deciduous trees it will provide a perfect echo to their autumnal color display.

R. virginiana alba (also known as *R. carolina alba*) is essentially the same rose with white blooms. There is a double-petaled version called *R. virginiana plena* ('Rose d'Amour'). It is probably a natural hybrid of *R. virginiana* mixed up with something else, rather than a mutation. The blooms of *R. virginiana plena* are very pretty, but the plant is not as tough or persistent.

RIGHT PLACE *Understory plant; tolerates shade*

ROSARIUM UETERSEN

CLASS: Large-flowered climber   REPEAT BLOOM: Good

BLOOM COLOR: Pink   HEIGHT: 7'

BLOOM SIZE: 4½"   HARDINESS: Zones 5–9

INTRODUCED: Kordes, Germany, 1977

Deep pink roses with subtle salmon tones. Most often sold as a climber, 'Rosarium Uetersen' makes a perfectly rounded 7' shrub for me, covered with large blooms in the full-petaled style typical of old garden roses. The foliage is glossy and abundant.

When I first saw this rose pictured in the Kordes catalog in the early 1980s I thought the company must have had some employee in their advertising department cutting out pictures of the rose and pasting them all over the plant. (This was years before Photoshop.) I couldn't believe so many large blooms could appear at one time on one rose plant. But it's true — the bloom is incredibly profuse, and the plant healthy and trouble-free.

RIGHT PLACE *Free-standing shrub or short climber*

'ROSARIUM UETERSEN'

SCHARLACHGLUT

CLASS: Gallica

BLOOM COLOR: Red

BLOOM SIZE: 4"

INTRODUCED: Kordes, Germany, 1952

REPEAT BLOOM: None

HEIGHT: 7'

HARDINESS: Zones 4–8

Large single-petaled blooms of blood red, followed in the fall by equally impressive red hips. This is a majestic gallica, worthy of a prime location. Its bloom color is vibrant and pure, making it ideal for growing against a light-colored building or as a lawn specimen. It would overpower most companions in a mixed border. Sometimes sold as 'Scarlet Fire' or 'Scarlet Glow'.

When a sucker of the *Rosa canina* rootstock emerged in the middle of my 'Scharlachglut' plant, I decided to leave it be. The two bloom at the same time, the pretty white and pink blooms of *R. canina* contrasting beautifully with the bold red 'Scharlachglut'. In the fall they display an abundance of quite different but very attractive rose hips. Fortunately, 'Scharlachglut' is strong enough to stand up to its understock, and both plants reach about 7' in height. I do limit the *R. canina* to three canes but otherwise sit back and enjoy the show.

I won't say "Don't try this at home" but I will say that in most cases it's a bad idea to let an understock grow. To make an Upstairs/Downstairs combination such as 'Scharlachglut'/*R. canina* work, you must have two roses of relatively equal vigor. This is usually impossible because most roses used as rootstock are tremendously vigorous. *R. multiflora*, especially, will choke anything else out. 'Scharlachglut'/*R. canina* is a rare winning combination. I would be intrigued to see 'Dr Huey', a dull maroon climbing rose often used as a rootstock in California, in combination with a vigorous light yellow or pale apricot climbing rose. That could be an appealing and interesting combination as well.

RIGHT PLACE *Against a light-colored building; landscape specimen; mixed border*

SCHARLACHGLUT

CHAPTER 4

GROWING ROSES IN HARMONY WITH OTHER PLANTS

A rose garden is often thought of synonymously with a bed of roses — a collection of roses grown by themselves, apart from other plants. Many roses are perfectly happy when planted this way, and some gardeners continue to resist the idea of planting roses with other plants. Yet so many roses are remarkably harmonious. They welcome the company of other plants, and they can improve a perennial border or collection of small shrubs even as these companion plants make the rose appear more vibrant and effective than it might be on its own. Repeat-blooming roses demonstrate their unequaled flower power in a perennial border or in a collection of larger shrubs. Plant roses and you won't lack for color, from the time that the spring-blooming shrubs and bulbs finish all the way until frost.

OPPOSITE David Austin's 'Gertrude Jekyll' associates perfectly with *Nepeta* 'Six Hills Giant' and foxglove.

The American hybrid tea 'Summer Dream' (not to be confused with the English floribunda 'Summer Dream' described on page 155) grows happily with *Clematis paniculata*.

ROSES IN BEDS AND BORDERS

It's a basic garden design principle that a mixed border — a collection of deciduous shrubs such as roses, along with perennials and bulbs — works properly when at least one-third of its components are blooming at any one time. Thus, any plant that does not bloom for at least one-third of the growing season is not pulling its weight. All repeat-blooming roses pass this test with flying colors. Once-blooming roses do not, although those that produce ornamental hips should receive bonus points. But there are few other flowering shrubs hardy in Zone 5 that would meet this artificial criteria, and many remain happy and useful members of mixed borders.

In general, no classification of rose is as well-suited for the mixed border as is the hybrid musk. The growth habit of many hybrid musks is graceful, and their flowers usually appear in big, airy sprays. The classification most ill-suited for mixed plantings is the hybrid tea. Many hybrid teas are indeed "blooms on a stick" (as are, for example, dahlias), and the stick part looks particularly ugly when it carries no bloom. A few recent hybrid teas are well suited for mixed plantings, and they are noted in this section. Few roses look attractive when out of bloom or during the long winter months. But let's be fair: the list of garden plants that are unreservedly great for 12 months a year in the northern garden is quite short.

Some floribundas and many of the shorter shrub roses are ideally suited for growing in a perennial bed (what used to be called an herbaceous border). Usually floribundas with smaller flowers are best suited for this work, as a single plant of a large-flowered floribunda can look heavy and out of place in a perennial bed. Whatever rose you choose to include in a perennial bed, expect it to be the highlight, the exclamation point, the largest, and possibly the longest-lived component.

SOLVING PROBLEMS WITH ROSES

In the descriptions that follow I recommend several roses as ideal for problem areas or neglected parts of the garden. Numerous roses can thrive with minimal care in areas neglected only because we don't visit them often. Ground-cover shrub roses are ideal solutions for slopes or sunny embankments where plants with an upright habit either look out of place or require too much care. And if the problem is an eyesore you want to conceal, just choose a rose of appropriate height.

ROSES IN THE SHADE

Almost any rose will grow in a shady spot, but it won't bloom there or will grow unattractively leggy trying to do so. When I was obsessively importing new roses from Europe in the 1980s, I had to keep them in quarantine beds away from other roses. I finally ended up using a shady patch between my house and the neighbor's that had formerly been devoted to impatiens. The area received about an hour of sun each day. When they bloomed at all there, large-flowered roses such as hybrid teas were abnormally small. Floribundas usually failed to make the clusters of bloom I expected, producing lonely-looking solitary blooms. I could keep these roses alive for their two-year quarantine period, but I never witnessed their true potential until I moved them to a sunnier part of the garden.

Although too much shade is hard on roses, almost all roses are very happy with a little shade. (This is especially true of the roses pictured here.) In my experience, a mixture of 70 percent sun and 30 percent shade is the best combination for most roses. A location with some afternoon shade is often ideal. The morning sun can dry the dew or any nighttime rain off of the rose foliage, and the roses will be protected from burn during the heat of the day. Roses in full sun are not as happy as roses in part shade: their blooms are smaller, their coloration less intense, and the plants less vigorous. There's a reason places like England and Portland, Oregon, are considered ideal climates for growing roses, and it isn't sun. I never realized how important my suburban neighbor's giant oak tree was to my roses until I moved out to the country, planted roses in a hay field, and left them out in the sun all day. Sixteen years later I finally have some shade from trees I've planted myself, and the roses are very happy in it.

The deep shade of evergreens is never satisfactory for roses, but early blooming, single-petaled roses usually do well near deciduous trees, since these roses will form their buds before the trees leaf out each spring. This is why species roses are often so happy at the edge of, or even just inside, woodlands.

'VEILCHENBLAU'

'BELINDA'

'BLACK JADE'

'PHYLLIS BIDE'

Roses that we can fully integrate into our gardens are almost always healthier than they would be if grown only with other roses. Growing roses all by themselves (monocropping) is an open invitation to all of the pests and diseases that prefer roses. You might as well display a target that encourages bugs to "stop here!" A rose bed with a serious pest problem often prompts a chemical response from the concerned rosarian, and this usually makes the problem even worse as beneficial insects are destroyed along with the troublemakers. Nature has a cycle in which plants face predation but inevitably recover and prosper. The introduction of pesticides makes this impossible, as various pieces are removed from the natural puzzle. In nature we do not find roses growing by themselves separated from the rest of the plant world. They are at the wood's edge, next to the columbine, in the meadow, near the Joe Pye weed, or trying their best to scale a small tree.

CHOOSING THE RIGHT SPOT

Because of their growth habits, colors, and bloom period, the following roses are especially recommended for growing in harmony with other plants. When adding roses to an existing border or creating a new one, there are just a few cautions to observe. Roses develop many small feeder roots near the surface of the soil, and because of these they will rarely be happy if surrounded with perennials that must be frequently divided, or bulbs that must be dug each year. Roses won't thrive if they have to compete with shallow-rooted trees such as birches and large maples. Well-fed, well-watered roses are remarkably tolerant of roots from deep-rooted trees and larger shrubs.

Roses can do most of the work in a mixed border from one month after the first spring frost right through to the end of the growing season. Spring bulbs such as daffodils can add a lot of color during the time when roses aren't blooming, and forsythia, daphnes, azaleas, and peonies can help bridge the flowering gap between the bulb season and rose time. With just a few exceptions, roses don't offer much in the foliage color department beyond green. Here heucheras and other perennials can provide contrast, as can small trees that offer autumn color. Rose blooms can be shocking or soothing, depending on their companions and your taste. If you enjoy blue and purple perennials, you may not want to mix in bright orange roses. Then again, you might, and that's okay too.

It's easy to incorporate well-chosen roses into an existing perennial bed or mixed border without anyone realizing that they are new additions. Roses are perfect for this purpose, because people have always expected them to be there.

ABRAHAM DARBY

CLASS: Shrub	REPEAT BLOOM: Steady
BLOOM COLOR: Apricot	HEIGHT: 6'
BLOOM SIZE: 6"	HARDINESS: Zones 5–9
INTRODUCED: Austin, England, 1985	

'Abraham Darby' is a beautiful plus-size rose that can be overpowering when not used thoughtfully in the garden. I wouldn't want to be without its massive cup-shaped, fragrant blooms in changing shades of apricot and buff, but I also don't like to see them looming over everything else, often in an overeager sort of way.

To keep this 6' shrub in balance with our garden, my wife devised a triangular bed, 6' × 6' × 6', surrounded by three 'Skyrocket' junipers and an edging of winter-hardy 'Green Velvet' boxwood. 'Abraham Darby' is dwarfed by the junipers and cascades gracefully over the boxwood. We have repeated these triangular beds at each corner of our most formal area of the rose garden, each with a different set of roses. Nothing else works so well as the tall Austins.

I also grow Austin's apricot orange 'Evelyn' (described later in this chapter) in one of these beds. This is one of my favorite roses, for both its intricate petal-packed form and its extravagant fragrance. Unfortunately, it is not reliably winter hardy in Zone 5. The boxwood helps to shelter it from the worst of the winter, and 'Evelyn' is usually waiting there to welcome another spring, sending out its first growth when 'Abraham Darby' has already accelerated past 3'.

RIGHT PLACE *In beds and borders with other large-scale plants*

'ABRAHAM DARBY'

ADELAIDE HOODLESS

CLASS: Shrub	REPEAT BLOOM: Steady
BLOOM COLOR: Red	HEIGHT: 4'
BLOOM SIZE: 2½"	HARDINESS: Zones 4–9
INTRODUCED: Marshall, Canada, 1972	

A tough red rose from the Canadian prairies, 'Adelaide Hoodless' makes big sprays of bright crimson blooms — sometimes so many of them that its relatively thin branches will tip under their weight. The individual blooms are small, and their form is best described as informal. Repeat bloom is steady, and this rose is often blooming while its neighbors are at rest.

This is the most successful example of *Rosa arkansana* appearing in hybridization. Just one generation separates this rose from the species, from which it inherits tremendous winter hardiness but maybe not quite enough black spot resistance. Like its grandparent, 'Adelaide Hoodless' thrives with little care and can tolerate drought. Indeed, fussing can't improve it, and I would not waste this rose on a highly improved patch of garden. 'Adelaide Hoodless' is the perfect rose to plant anywhere your hose or sprinkler cannot reach.

While her name evokes images of a reverse Little Red Riding Hood, Adelaide Hoodless (1858–1910) was a real person, a Canadian dedicated to improving the education of rural women and founder of the Women's Institutes.

RIGHT PLACE *Low-maintenance areas*

AGNES

CLASS: Hybrid rugosa
BLOOM COLOR: Yellow
BLOOM SIZE: 3"
INTRODUCED: Saunders, Canada, 1900
REPEAT BLOOM: Rare
HEIGHT: 4½'
HARDINESS: Zones 5–9

One of the first roses to bloom each spring, its arching canes are covered with amber yellow flowers for two or three weeks (or until it rains). The medium-sized blooms are full petaled, but the petals are thin and won't last when cut.

A cross between *Rosa rugosa* and *R. foetida persiana*, 'Agnes' has unfortunately inherited all of the latter's propensity for black spot. I recommend it anyway, for the excitement of the first roses of the year. Growing amid the conifers around our front porch, its blooms are a star attraction while its subsequent black spot is never noticed.

This remains the best winter-hardy yellow hybrid rugosa. 'Topaz Jewel' is a great repeat bloomer and more strongly yellow, but unfortunately it is not winter hardy in Zone 5.

RIGHT PLACE *With conifers; mixed shrub border*

ANGEL FACE

CLASS: Floribunda
BLOOM COLOR: Lavender
BLOOM SIZE: 3"
INTRODUCED: Swim & Weeks, USA, 1969
REPEAT BLOOM: Good
HEIGHT: 2'
HARDINESS: Zones 5–9

While gardens have been at least potentially sated with purple roses recently, there is still a lot of room for improvement in the lilac-lavender shades. 'Angel Face' endures because of a lack of winter-hardy competition and its superb fragrance. This is a squat floribunda, reaching just over 2' in my garden. Its ruffly blooms appear on sprays that often jut out at odd angles from the bush, which is unattractive when not in bloom. For all of these reasons, 'Angel Face' will be much more satisfactory when grown among perennials such as pale-colored phlox. These will do much to disguise the growth deficiencies of 'Angel Face', while enhancing the beauty of its flowers.

RIGHT PLACE *Perennial border*

ANNA ZINKEISEN

CLASS: Hybrid spinosissima
BLOOM COLOR: White
BLOOM SIZE: 3"
INTRODUCED: Harkness, England, 1982
REPEAT BLOOM: Steady
HEIGHT: 5'
HARDINESS: Zones 5–9

A seriously underappreciated rose, interesting for its complicated ancestry of *Rosa spinosissima* and *R. californica*, and genuinely valuable for its masses of fully double, white-gold blooms. These appear in clusters on a stalwart, prickly bush. Bloom is massive in June and steady throughout the rest of the summer. Growing to 5' tall and wide, 'Anna Zinkeisen' is large enough to be a specimen shrub, but it appears more useful in the border where its elegant structure qualifies it as a centerpiece plant and its soft color accentuates whatever may be blooming nearby.

RIGHT PLACE *Landscape and garden accent; mixed border*

'ANGEL FACE'

'ARMADA'

ARMADA

CLASS: Shrub

BLOOM COLOR: Pink

BLOOM SIZE: 4"

INTRODUCED: Harkness, England, 1988

REPEAT BLOOM: Good

HEIGHT: 5'

HARDINESS: Zones 5–9

'Armada' produces sprays of big, rich pink blooms on a glossy-leaved, disease-resistant shrub, growing 5' tall and just as wide in my garden. It asks for no special care beyond deadheading, which will prompt repeat bloom. One of the strengths of 'Armada' is its ability to produce blooms all up and down its height, and not just at the top of the plant. To take advantage of this display, it should not be hidden in the middle of a mixed border. I use 'Armada' to line my driveway. It is also effective as a short screen.

RIGHT PLACE *Along driveway; short screening plant*

ASPIRIN-ROSE

CLASS: Floribunda

BLOOM COLOR: White

BLOOM SIZE: 2"

INTRODUCED: Tantau, Germany, 1997

REPEAT BLOOM: Good

HEIGHT: 2' × 3' wide

HARDINESS: Zones 5–9

A very useful rose, growing just 2' tall and 3' wide and clothed in glossy foliage. It is covered in masses of glistening white blooms, blushed pink as they first open. 'Aspirin-Rose' is the epitome of the healthy, modern rose when massed, but individual plants are also useful

THE INTRICATE TASK OF BREEDING ROSES

To be successful, a rose breeder must be able to identify roses that make good parents. These are not always the same roses that have desirable characteristics, because some superb roses are also infertile or unable to pass along a particular trait. With experience, the breeder learns that due to recessive genes some roses are able to distribute characteristics that they do not have themselves. This is often the case with fragrance.

Then the breeder must be able to sort through thousands of seedlings from each cross and quickly decide which might merit further evaluation. Rose seedlings first bloom when they are just a few months old, and the breeder has only a solitary bloom above a few pairs of leaves on a tiny plant inside a greenhouse to inform his first decision.

Sometimes an extraordinary rose will appear — a color break, a rose with incredible vigor, a seedling that doesn't want to stop blooming. These should be easy enough to spot.

I wonder if it is harder for a breeder to pick out the rose that is exactly what he was seeking at the time when a group of seedlings bloom for the first time. **'Armada'** is exactly that rose, a cross between the climber 'New Dawn' and the hybrid tea 'Silver Jubilee'. It looks and grows exactly like what one would most want from that particular cross, if you could adjust the dials on a rose-hybridizing machine and order up exactly what you wanted.

as specimen plants, at the front of the border, and trailing over landscape timbers.

Named in Germany for the 100th anniversary of Bayer aspirin, this rose is sometimes sold as 'Special Child' in the United States.

RIGHT PLACE *Mass planting; landscape and garden accent; front of mixed border; trailing over landscape timbers*

BABY FAURAX

CLASS: Polyantha

BLOOM COLOR: Amethyst

BLOOM SIZE: 1"

INTRODUCED: Lille, France, 1924

REPEAT BLOOM: Good

HEIGHT: 2'

HARDINESS: Zones 5–9

Charming amethyst flowers on a dependable little polyantha. Rarely reaching 2' for me, it's the perfect rose for the front of the border and also quite happy in a pot. 'Baby Faurax' wants to bloom all of the time, and it benefits from deadheading. Pronunciation hint: this rose is pronounced "Fair-ax."

RIGHT PLACE *Front of mixed border; container plant*

'BABY LOVE'

BABY LOVE

CLASS: Miniature
BLOOM COLOR: Yellow
BLOOM SIZE: 1½"
INTRODUCED: Scrivens, England, 1992

REPEAT BLOOM: Continuous
HEIGHT: 18"
HARDINESS: Zones 5–9

Bright yellow, single-petaled blooms smothering a compact 18" plant make this the perfect tuckable rose, fitting seamlessly into a bed of perennials. Its uncomplicated blooms also make it at home with most annuals. Plant 'Baby Love' anywhere you'd like a continuous display of yellow blooms, and just snip old ones off to hurry along a new batch.

A descendant of *Rosa davidii*, 'Baby Love' is one of four modern roses that appear completely immune to black spot in my garden. (The others are David Austin's dusky pink 'The Mayflower', the original pink 'Flower Carpet', and its paler sport 'Appleblossom Flower Carpet'). Because it is so healthy without spraying and maintains such an attractive compact habit, 'Baby Love' also makes a terrific accent plant in berry patches and near vegetable gardens.

RIGHT PLACE *Mixed border of perennials or annuals; accent plant near edible gardens; container planting*

BARONNE PRÉVOST

CLASS: Hybrid perpetual
BLOOM COLOR: Pink
BLOOM SIZE: 4"
INTRODUCED: Desprez, France, 1842

REPEAT BLOOM: Reliable
HEIGHT: 5'
HARDINESS: Zones 5–8

One of the most dependable old garden roses, this hybrid perpetual belongs in every garden because: 1) it has the beautiful, full-petaled form of the classic old garden roses; 2) it offers repeat bloom as swiftly as any modern roses; 3) it takes up no more room than a hybrid tea; 4) it has a wonderful fragrance; and 5) it requires no special care.

Generally, the hybrid perpetuals became less winter hardy as they were more extensively hybridized. As an early hybrid perpetual, 'Baronne Prévost' winters just fine. Its one fault is a susceptibility to black spot, where that disease is a problem, but this is no worse than with most contemporary hybrid teas. Planting it away from disease-prone roses will go a long way toward minimizing this potential problem. 'Baronne Prévost' will add a lot of fragrance to a grouping of Canadian Explorer roses or other healthy shrubs.

There is a paler pink mutation called 'Oderic Vital', which is only slightly less vigorous.

RIGHT PLACE *Mixed border*

'BARONNE PRÉVOST'

BASYE'S PURPLE ROSE

CLASS: Shrub
BLOOM COLOR: Purple
BLOOM SIZE: 2½"
INTRODUCED: Basye, USA, 1968

REPEAT BLOOM: Good
HEIGHT: 5'
HARDINESS: Zones 5–9

A remarkable rose that is purple in every respect. Most visitors to your garden will be drawn to its intensely purple, single-petaled blooms that appear in profusion in spring and regularly thereafter. Serious gardeners will appreciate its purplish foliage, which makes a great contrast in a mixed planting. Even the stems and thorns are plum colored. And no one will even know that if you cut into a stem of 'Basye's Purple Rose' it will actually bleed purple. Unless, of course, you bring secateurs along on your garden tours and show them.

This is a lanky plant reaching 5' in my garden, with frequent suckers. Its leggy appearance will be improved by an underplanting of lower-growing roses or some other complementary plant, such as forget-me-nots.

RIGHT PLACE *Mixed border; foliage gardens*

BELINDA

CLASS: Hybrid musk
BLOOM COLOR: Pink
BLOOM SIZE: 1½"
INTRODUCED: Bentall, England, 1936

REPEAT BLOOM: Steady
HEIGHT: 5'
HARDINESS: Zones 5–9

The most winter hardy of all of the Pemberton-Bentall hybrid musks, 'Belinda' is a tougher version of its sister 'Ballerina'. (That's a beautiful rose, loved around the world, but not really up to northern Ohio winters.) 'Belinda' produces humongous sprays of simple blooms, bright pink with a white center. Bright yellow stamens quickly fade to a dead brown color and can be a distraction when viewing the sprays close-up. From a distance, the color impact of 'Belinda' is impressive, and it continues nonstop throughout the summer. The plant grows 5' tall and wide for me; it will be larger in milder climates. It requires nothing in the way of special care, is happy in full sun or half-shade, and will be at home either in a busy mixed border or by itself in a problem corner of your property.

RIGHT PLACE *Mixed border; landscape and garden accent; tolerates half shade*

BELINDA'S DREAM

CLASS: Shrub
BLOOM COLOR: Pink
BLOOM SIZE: 3"
INTRODUCED: Basye, USA, 1992

REPEAT BLOOM: Steady
HEIGHT: 3½'
HARDINESS: Zones 5–9

Advertised for its excellent disease resistance, this shrub rose may be more valuable on two other counts. One, it has a narrow, upright growth habit that makes it an unselfish member of any mixed planting. It won't overshadow anything else, it will simply grow straight up (to 3½' in my garden). Two, it performs spectacularly well in heat, and even tolerates drought better than most other roses.

Buds are medium pink, opening into fully double blooms with an old-fashioned look. They may not open properly in cool, damp weather. There is unfortunately little fragrance.

RIGHT PLACE *Mixed border*

'BELINDA'

'BELLA DONNA'

BELLA DONNA

CLASS: Damask
BLOOM COLOR: Pink
BLOOM SIZE: 3"
INTRODUCED: ex-France, 1844
REPEAT BLOOM: One long annual bloom
HEIGHT: 5'
HARDINESS: Zones 5–9

We first called this mystery rose "Zeke's Pink" after the Akron rosarian who gave it to us. Then we met up with Rick Strebler, who recognized it as the rose he had dubbed "Portage County Rose," a variety that could be found growing at old homesteads, in fields, and in ditches all over the county. Finally the southern Ohio heritage rose authority Clyde Everett visited our garden and identified it as 'Bella Donna', an identification that has been reinforced by all of the literature we've subsequently read.

'Bella Donna' is a damask that blooms for over a month each spring, after polar winters and mild ones, cool weather or hot, rain or shine. Its silver-dollar-sized blooms are medium pink, with petals organized into symmetrical quarters. A three-week period of intense, bush-covering bloom is followed by two or more weeks of scattered bloom, with the last blooms of the season often hidden deep inside the plant. 'Bella Donna' grows to 5' and sends out frequent suckers. You'll always have starts to give to your rose-growing friends, which is

exactly how 'Bella Donna' got passed all around Portage County. If you don't harvest young suckers, they will eventually encroach on neighboring plants.

I'll never know if some intrepid early rosarian-settler actually imported this from France or merely brought it to Ohio from faraway New York. But once it was grown here, 'Bella Donna' certainly made itself at home. Its origin might be obscure, but its future is guaranteed. 'Bella Donna' is here to stay.

RIGHT PLACE *Mixed border; hedge*

BELLA ROSA

CLASS: Floribunda
BLOOM COLOR: Pink
BLOOM SIZE: 2"
INTRODUCED: Kordes, Germany, 1981
REPEAT BLOOM: Good
HEIGHT: 2'
HARDINESS: Zones 5–9

The beauty of this rose is in its exuberant mass of bloom, covering the short plant at monthly intervals throughout the summer. The pink flowers are not that attractive individually — they can suffer from weather spotting and stamens that age to an ugly brown — but there are just so many of them that the rose more than earns its keep.

'Bella Rosa' is sold as a floribunda, but it is shorter than others in that class and may be best thought of as a mini-shrub, useful wherever a pocket of pink color is needed in the garden.

RIGHT PLACE *Almost anywhere*

BELLE DE CRÉCY (photo, page 29)

CLASS: Gallica
BLOOM COLOR: Mauve shades
BLOOM SIZE: 2½"
INTRODUCED: Hardy, France, 1829
REPEAT BLOOM: None
HEIGHT: 4'
HARDINESS: Zones 5–8

Grow this rose and you will know why they were once called the Mad Gallicas. Its buds are red, but they quickly reveal petals of deep pink, lilac, magenta, and purple, before finally fading into a curious but pleasing shade of slate gray. Sometimes there is a green pip at the middle of the bloom that just adds to the general color confusion. This is a great rose to grow for potpourri. Not only are its petals very fragrant, but they keep their colors when dried. 'Belle de Crécy' grows to 4' and is healthier than many gallicas. (Photo, page 29.)

I was inspired to grow 'Belle de Crécy' and most of my gallicas in circular beds about 12' across after visiting the Royal Botanical Gardens in Burlington, Ontario, Canada. I plant my roses closer together than the Botanical Garden does, no more than 3' apart, and before long they are sending out suckers into each other's territory. Most gallicas will bloom at the same time, and this close planting creates a patchwork of color that would be hard to engineer any other way.

RIGHT PLACE *For potpourri; mixed border*

BELLE ISIS

CLASS: Gallica	REPEAT BLOOM: None
BLOOM COLOR: Pink	HEIGHT: 6'
BLOOM SIZE: 3"	HARDINESS: Zones 5–8
INTRODUCED: Parmentier, France, 1845	

A lovely soft pink gallica that makes a great counterpoint to the strong colors of many in this class. Small powder-puff blooms appear in great profusion each June; a rain will make the bush tumble over under their weight.

'Belle Isis' grows strongly to 6' and suffers almost no dieback over winter. It is a grandparent of David Austin's 'Constance Spry' and so an ancestor of many of his English roses.

RIGHT PLACE *For color relief in a mixed rose planting*

'BELLE STORY'

BELLE STORY

CLASS: Shrub	REPEAT BLOOM: Reliable
BLOOM COLOR: Pink	HEIGHT: 4'
BLOOM SIZE: 4"	HARDINESS: Zones 5–9
INTRODUCED: Austin, England, 1984	

A different kind of English rose from breeder David Austin, 'Belle Story' has 35 petals but gives the effect of a semi-double rose. Soft pink petals open wide to reveal a captivating bunch of golden stamens. There is a persistent musky fragrance. Repeat bloom is excellent and the plant healthy.

'Belle Story' makes a bushy shrub, 4' × 4'. It is useful both in the mixed border and as a reliable endcap to a roses-only bed. Some roses have exceptionally good years and some off years. 'Belle Story' has the virtue of consistency, and it can be counted upon for dependable performance year after year.

RIGHT PLACE *Mixed border; as an accent in a roses-only bed*

'BELLE ISIS'

'BETTY PRIOR'

BETTY PRIOR

CLASS: Floribunda

REPEAT BLOOM: Good

BLOOM COLOR: Pink

HEIGHT: 2½'

BLOOM SIZE: 2½"

HARDINESS: Zones 5–9

INTRODUCED: Prior, England, 1935

With this rose we see the polyantha transforming into the floribunda (a class which was at first called "hybrid polyantha"). 'Betty Prior' carries forward the big sprays of bloom found on the polyantha along with the compact, bushy habit of the plant. Like the polyanthas, it starts to bloom late, after most other roses. But then nothing can stop it until frost. Like later floribundas, 'Betty Prior' has larger flowers, and they are not crammed together in the sprays.

Its single-petaled blooms are deep pink with an almost red reverse, fading to an overall medium pink.

'Betty Prior' is a great choice for a group planting in a large border. Five or seven plants will provide constant color throughout the summer and for many years to come.

RIGHT PLACE *Several plants in large mixed border*

A LUCKY FIND IN THE BACK

Last spring I was poking around the forlorn-looking roses set out on the sidewalk in front of a discount close-out store. The roses offered at places like these are problematic. In the first place, they have usually been coated in wax to keep them fresh. In many cases, the wax does such a thorough job that the rose bush never actually grows. Their roots have been butchered so that they can be squeezed into a plastic bag, where along with some sawdust they will stay for weeks or even months. These roses often come from factory farms, where keeping names straight is not a priority. (Indeed, these businesses sometimes name their roses incorrectly, in order to cheat patent or trademark regulations.) So why was I shopping there? Apart from curiosity, I was looking for 'Just Joey', an exquisitely beautiful but very winter-tender apricot hybrid tea from England that has occasionally turned up in such outlets. I won't spend $20 to buy 'Just Joey' from a reputable nursery, because I know it will not survive my winter, no matter how well I protect it. But I will spend $3 at a closeout store to enjoy 'Just Joey' as an annual.

Anyway, a sales person noticed my interest in the roses and asked if I wanted to see the rest of them. "The rest of them?" "Yes, we have tons more in the back." "The back" turned out to be an unrefrigerated storeroom, where great big cardboard boxes of Texas-grown roses were stacked up. Inside each box were 100 bareroot roses in their colorful plastic bags, and they'd been there for at least two months. I was welcomed to search through these boxes for anything I might like to buy, and it was certainly discouraging to see so many dead and dying roses. But I did find 20 or so plants of **'Betty Prior'**, all looking good. It's one tough rose.

BIRDIE BLYE

CLASS: Shrub

BLOOM COLOR: Pink

BLOOM SIZE: 3"

INTRODUCED: Van Fleet, USA, 1904

REPEAT BLOOM: Good

HEIGHT: 5'

HARDINESS: Zones 5–9

In Britain, cattle breeders took the lead in early efforts at rose hybridizing. In America, it was medical doctors, as the United States Department of Agriculture employed Dr. Walter Van Fleet to breed better roses scientifically. Van Fleet is best remembered for his ramblers such as 'American Pillar', 'Silver Moon', and 'Dr W Van Fleet', but 'Birdie Blye' remains an underappreciated, indestructible gem.

This shrub rose comes from a cross between a tea rose and a rambler, and it grows into a 5' shrub. It's very much like a winter-hardy China rose, with loosely formed light pink flowers appearing all summer long. The healthy foliage is pale green, and the canes have few thorns. The flowers make a constant impact in the garden but shatter quickly when cut. It's the perfect rose for the mixed border, but it can also be valuable in wilder parts of the garden because it thrives with no care whatsoever. 'Birdie Blye' is going to grow, and it's going to bloom. It's indestructible.

RIGHT PLACE *Mixed border; naturalistic settings*

BLUSH HIP

CLASS: Alba

BLOOM COLOR: Pink

BLOOM SIZE: 3"

INTRODUCED: origin uncertain, c. 1840

REPEAT BLOOM: None

HEIGHT: 5'

HARDINESS: Zones 4–8

A beautiful rose with a mysterious background, 'Blush Hip' is classified as an alba but lacks the blue-gray foliage typical of that class. Bright pink buds open to blooms that soon fade to rose pink (but are always deeper than what would normally be called "blush"). And it doesn't set any hips.

Never mind, this is a quality rose that maintains an ideal rounded habit, 5' in my garden. I use it very effectively as part of a circular bed featuring gallica roses (see page 29). 'Blush Hip' provides a color that is a soothing contrast to the wild purples and stripes of the gallicas on an exceptionally healthy, foliage-filled plant.

RIGHT PLACE *Good contrast to gallica roses*

BONICA

CLASS: Shrub

BLOOM COLOR: Pink

BLOOM SIZE: 3"

INTRODUCED: Meilland, France, 1983

REPEAT BLOOM: Reliable

HEIGHT: 3'

HARDINESS: Zones 5–9

When 'Bonica' became the first-ever shrub rose to receive the All-America Rose Selection award, the public relations people had a lot of work to do. Its ruffled pink blooms lacked the classic, spiraled hybrid tea form that had become emblematic of AARS selections, even the floribundas and climbers. Rose show exhibitors were still important as trend-setters in the world of rose commerce, but rose shows offered few trophies for shrub roses. And people with small gardens would be scared of planting a rose called a shrub.

The publicity campaign for 'Bonica' touted it as a carefree choice for the modern garden, a rose that didn't need to be pampered, a rose that would provide strong repeat bloom throughout the summer and wouldn't die over winter, and even as a plant that would provide habitat for nesting birds. All true (although I have never seen any birds nesting in mine), and all in a tidy 3' × 3' package, compact enough for any garden.

Many of the promises made about 'Bonica' have been more completely fulfilled by later introductions. It did not herald a new range of similarly sized shrub roses, but many healthy twenty-first-century floribunda roses grow to 'Bonica' proportions. 'Bonica' isn't perfect: during periods of persistent rain, it will get black spot. Its ability to produce ornamental hips was overstated. And it doesn't have any fragrance. But 'Bonica'

'BONICA'

remains a safe landscaping choice, and it opened the door (and American rosarians' minds) to the possibilities presented by subsequent introductions. The shrub rose was here to stay.

'Royal Bonica' is a mutation with more petals and larger blooms. Its flowers are one shade deeper. 'Denise Grey' is a shrubbier, close relative of 'Bonica' introduced in Europe in 1988. Even though it is particularly well-suited to northern gardens, 'Denise Grey' has never enjoyed wide distribution in the United States. It is worth seeking out from specialist mail-order rose nurseries, such as those included in the *Combined Rose List* (see page 254).

RIGHT PLACE *Mixed border*

BRIGHT SMILE

CLASS: Floribunda	REPEAT BLOOM: Good
BLOOM COLOR: Yellow	HEIGHT: 2½'
BLOOM SIZE: 3"	HARDINESS: Zones 5–9
INTRODUCED: Dickson, Northern Ireland, 1981	

A cheerful rose, short for a floribunda, with well-proportioned sprays of clear yellow blooms. It is one of the first floribundas to bloom each spring, and it fades less than other yellow floribundas. This rose does not respond well to simple deadheading (the removal of spent blooms). It must be cut back severely after each bloom, or the subsequent bloom will suffer small size and weak stems. Because the compact plants can look ravaged after a strong summer pruning, 'Bright Smile' is a better candidate for the front part of a mixed border rather than for a bed consisting only of roses.

RIGHT PLACE *Front of a mixed border*

BRITANNIA

CLASS: Polyantha	REPEAT BLOOM: Good
BLOOM COLOR: Red	HEIGHT: 18"
BLOOM SIZE: 1½"	HARDINESS: Zones 5–9
INTRODUCED: Burbage, England, 1929	

With simple single-petaled flowers instead of the convoluted, complicated flower forms found in some of its contemporaries, 'Britannia' appears a very modern polyantha. Blooms are bright red with a white center, appearing yellow because of all of the fresh stamens. These show up in well-spaced sprays all summer long.

'Britannia' grows just 18" tall and makes a superb low edge at the front of a large border. It also excels when grown in a pot.

RIGHT PLACE *Low edging at front of large mixed border; container plant*

'CARDINAL DE RICHELIEU'

CARDINAL DE RICHELIEU

CLASS: Gallica	REPEAT BLOOM: None
BLOOM COLOR: Purple	HEIGHT: 4½'
BLOOM SIZE: 3"	HARDINESS: Zones 5–7
INTRODUCED: Parmentier, France, 1840	

Impossibly purple, this once-blooming gallica is a curiosity that is also full of vigor and health. Its blooms are small and packed with petals. Indeed the unfurling process lasts for several days, not stopping until the blooms have fallen apart. In certain light its purple may appear to be blended with charcoal, slate, and other shades of gray. No one notices the departed blooms as there are so many fresh ones opening each day over a two- to three-week period. Almost certainly having some China in its ancestry, 'Cardinal de Richelieu' has shinier foliage than the typical gallica, and its smooth stems make it easy to garden around. This 4½' rose rarely suckers and is unhappy only in extreme heat. If your climate usually welcomes your roses' first bloom with 90°F temperatures, 'Cardinal de Richelieu' may not be for you.

Shade, however, is not the answer. This rose won't show to its best advantage in a dark corner of the garden or next to conifers. It makes a glorious sight surrounded by white and pale pink foxgloves, which bloom at the same time.

RIGHT PLACE *Combined with white or light-colored perennials in a mixed border*

CARDINAL HUME

CLASS: Shrub
BLOOM COLOR: Purple
BLOOM SIZE: 2½"
HARDINESS: Zones 5–9
INTRODUCED: Harkness, England, 1984

REPEAT BLOOM: Continuous and heavy
HEIGHT: 4' × 6' wide

A fascinating and useful shrub, growing wider than tall and covered in great panicles of purple blooms. The individual blossoms unfold claret red with perfect buttonhole form before opening wide and becoming completely purple. 'Cardinal Hume' is eager to set hips if not disbudded, and these can make an excellent orange display in the autumn. It has good winter hardiness but will catch black spot in a rainy year. Its ultimate size has been 4' tall × 6' wide in my garden, and it fits in very well with the softer colors of the Pemberton and Lens hybrid musks. Its flowing habit and strong repeat bloom also makes it a great choice for the mixed border.

For many years David Austin treated this as an honorary English Rose in his catalog. Harkness raised a pink shrub rose from the same cross that produced 'Cardinal Hume'. Called 'Rochester Cathedral', it is tough and healthy but lacks both the neat form and fascinating color of 'Cardinal Hume'.

RIGHT PLACE *Mixed border*

CAREFREE DELIGHT

CLASS: Shrub
BLOOM COLOR: Pink
BLOOM SIZE: 2"
INTRODUCED: Meilland, France, 1994

REPEAT BLOOM: Heavy
HEIGHT: 5' or taller
HARDINESS: Zones 5–9

One of the best of all landscaping roses, 'Carefree Delight' is effective cascading over a short fence, forming a dense hedge, or covering a hard-to-reach area such as a sunny embankment. In milder climates, it can even be trained as a climber. At the Park of Roses in Columbus, Ohio, 'Carefree Delight' is a star attraction. Planted en masse it forms a fluid mound that serves to delineate a garden room in a completely effective yet informal way.

'CAREFREE DELIGHT'

'Carefree Delight' also associates beautifully with other plants. Its foliage is small and its individual blooms about the size of a quarter, so there is no risk of it appearing out of scale with its neighbors the way some large-flowered roses can. Blooms are soft pink with a cream eye and appear nonstop in billowing sprays all summer long. They fit in perfectly with veronica and other lavender and blue perennials.

RIGHT PLACE *Cascading over a fence; dense hedge; ground cover; climber (in mild climates); mixed border*

CELSIANA

CLASS: Damask
BLOOM COLOR: Pink
BLOOM SIZE: 3"
INTRODUCED: unknown, The Netherlands, before 1700

REPEAT BLOOM: None
HEIGHT: 5'
HARDINESS: Zones 5–9

A charming damask, whose blooms nod on thin stems. Opening from red buds, its petals unfurl to reveal a

'CELSIANA'

'CHAMPLAIN'

silvery pink, semi-double bloom highlighted by pretty golden stamens. As the blooms fade to white you can almost watch the color changing before your eyes. 'Celsiana' is especially beautiful when the sun shines on, and almost through, its petals.

'Celsiana' grows upright to 5'. Its pale green foliage makes a nice contrast when planted with other heritage roses or in a border of mixed shrubs. Like other damasks, it does not produce hips of any great beauty.

RIGHT PLACE *With other heritage roses; in mixed shrub border*

CENTENAIRE DE LOURDES

CLASS: Floribunda

BLOOM COLOR: Pink

BLOOM SIZE: 3½"

REPEAT BLOOM: Reliable if deadheaded

HEIGHT: 3½'

HARDINESS: Zones 5–9

INTRODUCED: Delbard-Chabert, France, 1958

Big silvery pink blooms on a stalwart plant that some nurseries sell as a floribunda, and others offer as a shrub. It is truly an in-betweener, with more vigor than the typical floribunda, more compact flower clusters than the typical shrub. 'Centenaire de Lourdes' reaches 3½' in my garden, where it provides heft in a mixed rose-and-perennial border featuring many more airy, single-petaled flowers. Its repeat bloom is excellent so long as flowers are snipped off as they age. Otherwise you will get a good crop of hips, which are attractive in their own right.

This is the kind of rose one wishes would come in every color, and indeed there is a 'Centenaire de Lourdes Rouge'. Introduced in 1992, it is an entirely new rose, not a mutation, and appears unlikely to achieve the impact of the 1958 introduction.

The original 'Centenaire de Lourdes' rose is usually sold under its proper name in the United States and Canada. In the early 1960s, British nurseries may have thought that a rose name with religious overtones wouldn't sell and renamed this rose 'Mrs Jones'. (History does not tell us who this Mrs Jones might have been, but this was a decade before the Billy Paul song.)

RIGHT PLACE *Mixed border*

CHAMPLAIN

CLASS: Shrub

BLOOM COLOR: Red

BLOOM SIZE: 3½"

REPEAT BLOOM: Good

HEIGHT: 3' × 4' wide

HARDINESS: Zones 4–9

INTRODUCED: Svejda, Canada, 1982

The best choice for pure red rose blooms in a mixed border, 'Champlain' combines an ability to bloom constantly with a pleasing wider-than-tall habit. It reaches 3' tall by 4' wide in my garden and rarely suffers any winter dieback. Its blooms appear all summer long in well-proportioned clusters on sturdy stems.

RIGHT PLACE *Mixed border*

THE NEWEST SPECIES ROSE

Most people who have gotten species roses named after themselves did so by tramping around China in the nineteenth century and discovering things that were completely novel to Westerners. In the 1940s, Wilhelm Kordes did what only nature should be able to do and created his own species rose. *Rosa kordesii* has large, bright pink blooms and the shiniest, most mirrorlike foliage imaginable. Even though it was raised from the seed of a hybrid rugosa, it comes true from seed itself, which is the simplest definition of a species rose. Anyway, its sprawly growth and lack of repeat bloom has disqualified *R. kordesii* from most gardens, even as hybridizers around the world seek to incorporate its unique qualities into modern roses. From *R. kordesii* comes much of the winter hardiness and health of **'Champlain'** and the other Canadian Explorer roses.

CHARLES DE MILLS

CLASS: Gallica
BLOOM COLOR: Purple/crimson
BLOOM SIZE: 4"
INTRODUCED: France, before 1746

REPEAT BLOOM: None
HEIGHT: 5'
HARDINESS: Zones 5–8

Incredible blooms of purple-crimson, swirling around with other spokes from that part of the color wheel, in a large, long-lasting bloom. This is one of the best and largest-flowered of the gallicas, blooming for a good three weeks each year. The origin of this rose is uncertain, and its true name may be 'Bizarre Triomphant'. Like all once-blooming roses, it will reward a good dose of fertilizer applied early in the year. 'Charles de Mills' is a heavier feeder than most once-blooming roses, and it will also benefit from organic topdressings applied throughout the year.

The 5' arching plant is tougher than it looks and will eventually sucker to fill in a large area. It will stand up straighter if staked, tomato-cage style. I grow 'Charles de Mills' with other gallicas, but it could form a stunning part of a mixed border for any gardener willing to pay attention to its suckers.

RIGHT PLACE *Mixed border*

'CHARLOTTE'

'CHARLES DE MILLS'

CHARLOTTE

CLASS: Shrub
BLOOM COLOR: Yellow
BLOOM SIZE: 3½"
INTRODUCED: Austin, England, 1993

REPEAT BLOOM: Good
HEIGHT: 3'
HARDINESS: Zones 5–9

Some of David Austin's yellow English Roses are not tough enough for an Ohio winter. 'Charlotte' is. This is a perfect example of rose hybridization accomplishing exactly what one would want it to. 'Charlotte' has a dose of rugosa blood, which no doubt accounts for its winter hardiness, and yet in appearance it is every bit as refined as the more tender yellow English roses. Its scent is even that of the very tender nineteenth-century tea roses.

'Charlotte' grows to a robust 3' in my garden, often producing its blooms in massive clusters. The yellow color is most intense at the center of the bloom. Outer petal edges are often framed in white, which will gradually spread as the flower fades. 'Charlotte' works well with delphiniums and other blue and lavender perennials that can match its height.

RIGHT PLACE *Mixed border with tall blue and lavender perennials; tree rose*

COMPLICATA

CLASS: Gallica/hybrid

BLOOM COLOR: Pink

BLOOM SIZE: 5"

INTRODUCED: origin uncertain

REPEAT BLOOM: None

HEIGHT: 7'

HARDINESS: Zones 5b–8

While its gallica/macrantha ancestry may be a source of debate, and its name apparently a reference to a distinctive crease found in its petals, there is nothing complicated about the simple beauty of this rose's large single-petaled pink blooms. This rose is one of the most cheerful sights of June, and something I look forward to seeing each year.

Although it does not require support, 'Complicata' has an awkward habit and is sometimes recommended for growing into small trees. This strategy can disguise much of its wayward growth, but the blooms (which usually appear individually rather than in the great clusters of the classic tree scramblers) can disappear as well. 'Complicata' would be a marginal tree-climber here in Zone 5, knocked back to nothing after a tough winter. I use it most effectively near the end of a long border of heritage roses, none of which mind its intrusions, and a few of which match its 7' height. This relatively out-of-the-way location makes 'Complicata' a destination rose in June. The fact that it is a relatively unattractive plant the rest of the year is something that no one else will ever notice. 'Complicata' is not the best choice for a small garden, but it will reward gardeners who have sufficient space.

RIGHT PLACE *Large gardens; end of the rose border*

'COMTE DE CHAMBORD'

perfect habit for a rose bed and will also contribute reliably to a mixed border.

This rose is confused in commerce with one called 'Mme Boll'. In the United States, you are likely to get the same rose no matter which of these names you specify.

RIGHT PLACE *Rose bed; mixed border*

COMTE DE CHAMBORD

CLASS: Portland

BLOOM COLOR: Pink

BLOOM SIZE: 3½"

INTRODUCED: Moreau-Robert, France, 1860

REPEAT BLOOM: Reliable

HEIGHT: 3½'

HARDINESS: Zones 5–9

One of the most rewarding old garden roses, offering a fantastic return for the small amount of space it consumes. The richly colored blooms of 'Comte de Chambord' are classic rose pink, shading to a pearlescent color at their edge. They often appear in well-spaced sprays, repeat quickly, and can be faulted only for not standing up to rain. This Portland grows upright (to 3½' in my garden) but not leggy: it is covered in foliage from top to bottom. 'Comte de Chambord' has the

CONRAD FERDINAND MEYER

CLASS: Hybrid rugosa

BLOOM COLOR: Silver-pink

BLOOM SIZE: 4"

INTRODUCED: Müller, Germany, 1929

REPEAT BLOOM: Repeats if deadheaded

HEIGHT: 7–8'

HARDINESS: Zones 5–9

A century ago, adventurous hybridizers spent a lot of their time crossing very hardy rugosa roses with very tender teas and Noisettes. They were hoping, I'd imagine, for some happy medium of tea flower form and delicate color, reinforced by rugosa toughness. That rarely happened, but 'Conrad Ferdinand Meyer' is an excellent example of what often did. It's a huge plant, sprawling in all directions, covered early in the season with large blooms of a delectable silver pink. It has a wonderful fragrance and can be encouraged to repeat bloom by rigorously removing every last spent flower.

'Conrad Ferdinand Meyer' is too sprawly to make a good lawn specimen plant, but it is quite useful for introducing color into a wilder corner of the garden, where it will thrive with no special fuss. This rose is also perfect for masking air-conditioning units or other unsightly objects. Although this rose has always been quite healthy for me, it is reported to be a martyr to rust where that disease is a problem. Like other rugosas, it resents being sprayed with fungicides.

'Conrad Ferdinand Meyer' has been an important parent of David Austin's English Roses. It has a white sport called 'Nova Zembla'.

RIGHT PLACE *Naturalistic gardens; screening*

CORAL MEIDILAND

CLASS: Shrub

REPEAT BLOOM: Reliable

BLOOM COLOR: Pink

HEIGHT: 4'

BLOOM SIZE: 2"

HARDINESS: Zones 5–9

INTRODUCED: Meilland, France, 1993

This is the best of the many Meidilands I have grown. A very clean-looking rose, 'Coral Meidiland' has bright

'CORAL MEIDILAND'

single-petaled blooms of pure coral pink set amid shiny foliage. It blooms a little later than most other roses in the spring, but once started it does not stop blooming until there is an autumn freeze. 'Coral Meidiland' does not require deadheading; spent blooms will drop away on their own as new growth emerges. Single-petaled roses such as this are the easiest of all roses to incorporate into a mixed border, since they provide a lot of color without ever overpowering their neighbors. Originally introduced and sold in France as 'Douceur Normande'.

RIGHT PLACE *Mixed border*

MEIDILANDS

All of the Meidiland roses have big clusters of relatively small blooms. But their growth habits are far from uniform. 'Red Meidiland' is essentially a ground cover; 'Pink Meidiland' grows bolt upright. 'Ice Meidiland' forms a mound. 'Cherry Meidiland' is healthy and free-blooming, but it has a harsh color that makes it difficult to blend into a garden. **'Coral Meidiland'** has a relaxed, slightly spreading habit with thin, flexible stems that makes it perfectly at home in the middle of any mixed border. Its blooms look particularly alive when placed next to larkspur or other purple perennials.

CORYLUS

CLASS: Rugosa/nitida hybrid

REPEAT BLOOM: None

BLOOM COLOR: Pink

HEIGHT: 3'

BLOOM SIZE: 2½"

HARDINESS: Zones 4–9

INTRODUCED: LeRougetel, England, 1988

A rose for all seasons, 'Corylus' has abundant, bright green, crinkly foliage in spring and summer; in fall, it colors in the manner of a maple tree to yellow and orange. Its five-petaled, bright pink blooms appear for almost a month, and they are followed in due course by attractive round hips. Even as its foliage drops in the winter, its fruit will continue to attract birds.

'Corylus' grows to a uniform 3' × 3' shrub. It would be an asset in any mixed border, and I find it most useful in association with other kinds of shrubs. It blooms just after the lilacs and before the deutzia, and it will be

'CORYLUS'

full of attractive hips when the heptacodium is coming into its full bloom.

RIGHT PLACE *Mixed border; shrub border*

THE LUCK OF THE CROSS

Even though any species rose should breed true from seed, they are complex enough that a cross between any two species roses should produce thousands of possible outcomes. English plants-woman and author Hazel LeRougetel had the good luck to find **'Corylus'** from a cross between the species roses *Rosa nitida* and *R. rugosa*. You or I could cross *R. nitida* and *R. rugosa* for many years without ending up with a rose as good as **'Corylus'**, let alone one that is better. *Corylus* is the Latin name for hazel, so LeRougetel, with a wink, named this rose for herself. The less-elegant but just-as-hardy Canadian rose 'Métis' is a close relative.

COUNTRY DANCER

CLASS: Shrub   REPEAT BLOOM: Reliable
BLOOM COLOR: Pink   HEIGHT: 3'
BLOOM SIZE: 3"   HARDINESS: Zones 5–9
INTRODUCED: Buck, USA, 1973

Some roses have their day: one morning each summer when they are full of bloom and their leaves are full of health, they light up the garden. Other roses have their year: because there is more rain than usual, or less, or it's hotter or cooler, they become much happier in your garden than they ever have been before. Other roses are almost boring in their predictability: they grow and bloom well, day after day, year in and year out. 'Country Dancer' is one such rose. Plant enough roses like 'Country Dancer' and your rose garden will look good all of the time.

'Country Dancer' grows 3' tall × 3' wide, bushy and full of good health. Its double blooms are bright pink and wavy, with a pleasing fragrance.

RIGHT PLACE *Mixed border; rose beds*

'COUNTRY DANCER'

COUNTRY LIVING

CLASS: Shrub
REPEAT BLOOM: Good

BLOOM COLOR: Pink
HEIGHT: 3'

BLOOM SIZE: 3"
HARDINESS: Zones 5–9

INTRODUCED: Austin, England, 1991

An intriguing and beautiful English rose, soft pink, with small, petal-packed blooms appearing in modest sprays. The thorny plant grows narrow and not very tall (3' in my garden). It fits in very well with perennials of about the same height; it's an especially beautiful companion for some of the taller hybrid lavenders.

'Country Living' is winter hardy and healthy, except for a susceptibility to downy mildew when weather conditions favor that disease.

RIGHT PLACE *Mixed border with perennials of about the same height*

CROWN PRINCESS MARGARETA

(photo, page 22)

CLASS: Shrub
REPEAT BLOOM: Good

BLOOM COLOR: Apricot/yellow
HEIGHT: 4½'

BLOOM SIZE: 6"
HARDINESS: Zones 5–9

INTRODUCED: Austin, England, 1999

Whopping big blooms of apricot to almost orange, depending on the weather. These fade to nearly yellow while holding onto an exquisitely perfect rosette form and filling the surrounding area with their fragrance. It makes a sturdy shrub, 4½' tall in my garden.

David Austin's catalog depicts 'Crown Princess Margareta' climbing over an arch. It absolutely isn't going to do that in Zone 5, but it does winter well enough, and its large apricot blooms make a strking statement in the mixed border in midsummer.

RIGHT PLACE *Mixed border*

DAINTY BESS

CLASS: Hybrid tea
REPEAT BLOOM: Good

BLOOM COLOR: Pink
HEIGHT: 3'

BLOOM SIZE: 4"
HARDINESS: Zones 5–9

INTRODUCED: Archer, England, 1925

The famous single-petaled hybrid tea, introduced at a time when being a hybrid tea would boost the sales of any rose, however unlikely. Today, because shrub roses are so popular, we undoubtedly have shrub roses that would not have been called that in another era.

'DAINTY BESS'

'Dainty Bess' displays five wide petals of ordinary pink, brought to life by the dramatic purple filaments of its stamens. While blooming all the time, the plant is not very well clothed in foliage. And so it is a perfect recruit for the mixed border, where its stunning blooms will appear at about the 3' level, and phlox or some other vigorous perennial can be used to disguise its foliar shortcomings.

RIGHT PLACE *Mixed border*

DAYDREAM

CLASS: Shrub
REPEAT BLOOM: Good

BLOOM COLOR: Mauve
HEIGHT: 2' × 3' wide

BLOOM SIZE: 2"
HARDINESS: Zones 5–9

INTRODUCED: Lim, USA, 2005

A healthy, spreading shrub covered with dime-sized, single-petaled blooms of amethyst-mauve.

'DAYDREAM'

Extraordinarily healthy and winter–hardy, this shrub grows to 2' tall × 3' wide in my garden. Its one drawback is a lack of contrast between the dark green foliage and the blooms. 'DayDream' will be a much more effective garden performer if situated next to white, yellow, or light pink roses or perennials.

RIGHT PLACE *Mixed border near white, yellow, or light pink roses or perennials*

'DISTANT DRUMS'

DISTANT DRUMS

CLASS: Shrub	REPEAT BLOOM: Good
BLOOM COLOR: Mauve/tan	HEIGHT: 3'
BLOOM SIZE: 3½"	HARDINESS: Zones 5–9
INTRODUCED: Buck, USA, 1984	

Brunette buds open to informal blooms in a confection of tan and mauve, all swirled together. It will be a little more tan in hot weather, and a little more mauve in cool. Unlike most novelty roses, whose path into commerce is greased by an odd color even though the plant may be disease prone or doesn't want to actually bloom, this one is genuinely healthy and floriferous. Although classified as a shrub, its habit is very much like a floribunda. And because its unusual color is neither strident nor harsh, 'Distant Drums' blends effortlessly into a border of perennials.

Like most Buck roses, 'Distant Drums' makes a 3' shrub in my garden. It's a long-lived rose, looking just as fresh and healthy today as when I first planted it shortly after its introduction.

In 1999 a rose called 'Kaleidoscope' became an unlikely All-America Rose Selection winner. Its color

is similar to 'Distant Drums', but it lacks vigor. 'Distant Drums' is in every respect a better rose.

RIGHT PLACE *Mixed border; rose beds*

GRIFFITH BUCK

Dr. Griffith Buck spent several decades at Iowa State University breeding better roses. Although his hybrids are known for winter hardiness, they lack the hardy-to-the-tips constitution of the Canadian Explorers. What they do have is the ability to come roaring back after severe winters. Prune out the dead wood, and then stand back.

EGLANTYNE

CLASS: Shrub	REPEAT BLOOM: Reliable
BLOOM COLOR: Pink	HEIGHT: 4'
BLOOM SIZE: 4"	HARDINESS: Zones 5–9
INTRODUCED: Austin, England, 1994	

One of the best of David Austin's English Roses, 'Eglantyne' blooms steadily all summer long on a tough, healthy plant growing to a nicely rounded 4'. The blooms are clear medium pink, opening wide to a saucer shape that displays dozens of small petals in a particularly beautiful way. If used for cut flowers, the blooms should be cut when they are no more than one-half open. The rose blends perfectly with Austin's

'EGLANTYNE'

other introductions — both those that grow shorter and those that get quite tall — and also makes an impressive standard, or tree, rose.

This rose has no connection to the eglantine roses, hybrids of *Rosa eglanteria*. It is named for Eglantyne Jebb, the founder of Save the Children, an organization that works to improve the lives of children in need in the United States and around the world. 'Eglantyne' has already enjoyed a longer rose career than 'Save the Children', a short-lived red floribunda that appeared in 1986.

RIGHT PLACE *Mixed border; rose border; as tree rose*

'ESCAPADE'

ESCAPADE

CLASS: Floribunda	REPEAT BLOOM: Reliable
BLOOM COLOR: Pink	HEIGHT: 4'
BLOOM SIZE: 3"	HARDINESS: Zones 5–9
INTRODUCED: Harkness, England, 1967	

One of the most carefree roses ever bred, 'Escapade' produces big sprays of cheerful semi-double blooms all summer long. These are mauve-pink mixed with white. They are backed by healthy lettuce-green foliage that makes a healthy counterpoint to the usual darker shades of rose leaves. There is no better floribunda for the mixed border, but I also enjoy the contrast it provides in a long bed of floribundas. Taller than the average floribunda, 'Escapade' reaches 4' in my garden.

This is a rose that everyone likes. One of my mentors in roses prided himself in growing only hybrid teas and miniatures that could compete for Queen of the Show in rose competitions. One year he ordered 'Esmeralda', a hot new exhibition hybrid tea, from a nursery in Canada that apparently organized its rose field in alphabetical order. A field marker was misplaced, and everyone who ordered 'Esmeralda' received 'Escapade' instead. After his initial disappointment, my friend reconciled himself to 'Escapade', couldn't bring himself to dig it up, and for many years touted it as the only floribunda — and the hardest-working rose — in his garden.

RIGHT PLACE *Mixed border; floribunda bed*

EUGÈNE DE BEAUHARNAIS

CLASS: China	REPEAT BLOOM: Good
BLOOM COLOR: Purple	HEIGHT: 18"
BLOOM SIZE: 2½"	HARDINESS: Zones 5b–9
INTRODUCED: Hardy, France, 1838	

One of the few China roses that has proven reliably hardy in northern Ohio, 'Eugène du Beauharnais' provides an endless supply of ruffly purple blooms on a short, thorny plant. It may reach only 18" in height, and it will be happy anywhere the soil has been fortified with manure or other organic amendments. Growing on its own roots, it has not needed any special winter protection in my garden. In practical terms, it fulfills the garden role of a miniature rose that can be tucked in anywhere a spot of color is desired, with the added historical interest of having been named for Napoleon's stepson.

RIGHT PLACE *Rock garden; miniature garden; container*

EVELYN

CLASS: Shrub	REPEAT BLOOM: Good
BLOOM COLOR: Apricot	HEIGHT: 3'
BLOOM SIZE: 5"	HARDINESS: Zones 6–9
INTRODUCED: Austin, England, 1991	

The most fragrant rose I grow, 'Evelyn' is also a prolific bloomer. Its large, intricately formed blooms are bright apricot, eventually fading gracefully to pink. As cut flowers they will perfume a room. 'Evelyn' makes a bushy shrub just over 3' tall and almost as wide. For a description of how I use 'Evelyn' in my garden, see the 'Abraham Darby' entry on page 67.

'EVELYN'

Each November I provide 'Evelyn' with a heaping mound of compost or a bushel basket full of sawdust as winter protection. Without this, it would not survive a Zone 5 winter. As an alternative, it can be grown in a half-barrel or other large container and moved to a garage or other sheltered place for the winter. I don't take these special measures for any other shrub rose; for its beauty and its fragrance 'Evelyn' is worth it.

RIGHT PLACE   *Container planting*

FELICITAS

CLASS: Shrub	REPEAT BLOOM: Heavy
BLOOM COLOR: Pink	HEIGHT: 2' × 5' wide
BLOOM SIZE: 2"	HARDINESS: Zones 5–9
INTRODUCED: Kordes, Germany, 1998	

Simple bright pink flowers on a shiny-leaved shrub that likes to spread, without ever getting very tall. An eight-year-old plant is barely 2' tall in my garden, and at least 5' wide. The cheerful blooms appear over every

'FELICITAS'

part of the plant. 'Felicitas' makes a real impact in the border, flowers floating above foliage like anemones in the air. One plant of 'Felicitas' can improve a large area without suckering or disrespecting its neighbors. Although its wiry stems appear long enough to cut, the blooms do not last well indoors. In every other respect this plant is a winner: super health, total Zone 5 winter hardiness, constant repeat bloom. Named in honor of Felicitas Svejda, pioneering breeder of the Canadian Explorer roses.

RIGHT PLACE   *Mixed border; mass planting*

'FÉLICITÉ PARMENTIER'

FÉLICITÉ PARMENTIER

CLASS: Alba	REPEAT BLOOM: None
BLOOM COLOR: Pale pink	HEIGHT: 4½'
BLOOM SIZE: 2½"	HARDINESS: Zones 5–8
INTRODUCED: Parmentier, France, 1834	

A delicately beautiful alba, whose pom-pom blooms of pink (fading to white) appear in large clusters. Its fragrance is as delicate as its flowers, memorable without being overpowering. The plant is covered in healthy bluish-green leaves, making narrow growth to 4½'.

'Félicité Parmentier' provides a great many flowers in a relatively small space. It is not always pleased with competition, however, and I have found it to be much happier as a part of a well-spaced border of once-blooming roses (where it will still be blooming after most of the others are finished) than as part of a mixed border or surrounded by perennials.

RIGHT PLACE   *Rose border*

FESTIVAL FANFARE

CLASS: Shrub

BLOOM COLOR: Orange striped
with white

BLOOM SIZE: 3½"

INTRODUCED: Ogilvie, England, 1986

REPEAT BLOOM: Good

HEIGHT: 5'

HARDINESS: Zones 5–9

One of the most profuse of all of the striped roses, 'Festival Fanfare' makes gigantic trusses of simple blooms, a pastel coral orange wildly striped in chalk white. The 5' plant can appear lanky and sparse when not in bloom, but it fits perfectly into a mixed border where its bloom explosions will always attract interest. This is a mutation of 'Fred Loads' (Holmes, England, 1968) whose unstriped blooms are a brighter coral orange.

RIGHT PLACE *Mixed border*

FISHERMAN'S FRIEND

CLASS: Shrub

BLOOM COLOR: Red

BLOOM SIZE: 4½"

INTRODUCED: Austin, England, 1988

REPEAT BLOOM: Reliable

HEIGHT: 4'

HARDINESS: Zones 5–9

Not the largest of David Austin's red roses, or the most powerfully fragrant, or the most intricately formed. But 'Fisherman's Friend' is a completely reliable rose, healthy and winter hardy and eager to repeat bloom. It is without doubt the best rose ever named after a cough drop. Its thorny bush grows to 4'. The bold color and consistent bloom offered by 'Fisherman's Friend' calls out for a strong contrast, and I provide that by surrounding it with white phlox.

RIGHT PLACE *Mixed border, near white or light-colored plants*

FLOWER CARPET

CLASS: Shrub (used as
groundcover)

BLOOM COLOR: Pink

BLOOM SIZE: 1½"

INTRODUCED: Noack, Germany, 1991

REPEAT BLOOM: Good

HEIGHT: 18" × 4' wide

HARDINESS: Zones 5–9

Most roses make poor edging plants. Even those with a relatively short habit often grow leggy, or appear to do so because they have lost their lower leaves to black spot or spider mites. But the rose sold in the pink pot at garden centers everywhere is incredibly useful as an edger, for providing color in difficult places, and around ponds. 'Flower Carpet' is densely clothed in tiny, shiny dark green leaves that are attractive in their own right. For this reason I would be happy to plant a problem area with 'Flower Carpet' even if it bloomed much less often.

I've used the Flower Carpet roses in several different ways in my garden. The most effective planting is the original pink 'Flower Carpet' and its blush-colored sport, 'Appleblossom Flower Carpet', around the rocks that line one end of a lily pond. They thrive here, reaching almost 4' wide while growing only 18" tall, spreading over the rocks in a very natural-looking way and dangling their flower stems over the water. These Flower Carpets thrive even as nearby dwarf conifers have become less dwarf, leaving the Flower Carpets in more than half shade. I would never use pesticides around a pond, and because 'Flower Carpet' is completely disease resistant in my garden, it's not something I even need to think about.

'Flower Carpet' is insanely easy to root from cuttings. I sometimes think I could just drop the cuttings on the ground and come back a week or so later to find new plants. (Even though 'Flower Carpet' is protected by both plant patent and trademark, it is perfectly legal in the United States to grow new plants for your own use, so long as you do not sell them.)

RIGHT PLACE *Edging plant; ground cover; tolerates half shade*

'FLOWER CARPET'

MORE FLOWER CARPET ROSES

'Appleblossom Flower Carpet' is just as disease proof as the original, producing the same masses of small, double-petaled blooms. The rest of the **Flower Carpet** roses are not directly related. 'Red Flower Carpet' is an excellent rose, but much more like a floribunda in its growth than a groundcover (for photo, see page 22). Although healthy and colorful, 'Coral Flower Carpet' is not as winter-hardy as the others. 'Yellow Flower Carpet' turned out to be an utter disappointment, a straggly grower and quite susceptible to black spot. The "Next Generation" of Flower Carpets, which began with the launch of 'Scarlet Flower Carpet' in 2007, promises a return to the original principle of completely healthy, ground-hugging plants.

FLOWER GIRL

CLASS: Shrub
BLOOM COLOR: Pink
BLOOM SIZE: 2½"
INTRODUCED: Fryer, England, 2000
REPEAT BLOOM: Reliable
HEIGHT: 3½'
HARDINESS: Zones 5–9

This shrub is one of the roses I recommend most often for use in a mixed border. Its light pink, semi-double flowers appear in large sprays produced with amazing regularity throughout the summer. The flowers are as delicate and dainty as the plant is tough. This rose is eager to grow and doesn't mind competition from nearby perennials or from gardeners who take all of its sprays as cut flowers. Cut it, and it just gets busy growing more.

'Flower Girl' is much more popular in the United States than it turned out to be in its native England. The best way to think of it may be as a half-size hybrid musk, growing 3½' tall and 2½' wide, perfectly suited to today's smaller gardens.

RIGHT PLACE *Mixed border*

FOCUS

CLASS: Hybrid musk
BLOOM COLOR: Pink
BLOOM SIZE: 2½"
INTRODUCED: Lens, Belgium, 1984
REPEAT BLOOM: Dependable
HEIGHT: 4½'
HARDINESS: Zones 5–9

This is a hybrid musk quite different from most of the others. Its habit is sturdy and upright, reaching 4½' in my garden. Its blooms, a light pink that fades gracefully to cream, are packed with almost 100 petals and appear in large, well-shaped sprays. It blooms a little later than most roses in spring but then continues blooming throughout the summer. Its stems make great ready-made bouquets when cut, usually showing pink-shaded and white blooms at the same time, and its fragrance somehow seems more powerful indoors.

This rose has an appearance we instantly think of as "old-fashioned" even though the only old-fashioned roses anything like this are some of the early twentieth-century polyanthas, one-third of the size of 'Focus'. Sometimes sold as 'Sweet Bouquet' in the United States.

RIGHT PLACE *Cutting garden; mixed border*

FRÜHLINGSMORGEN

CLASS: Shrub
BLOOM COLOR: Pink/yellow
BLOOM SIZE: 4"
INTRODUCED: Kordes, Germany, 1942
REPEAT BLOOM: Sparse
HEIGHT: 6'
HARDINESS: Zones 5–9

One of the first roses of spring, wide single-petaled blooms of pink and pale yellow, with crimson stamens. These appear all up and down its arching canes for a

'FRÜHLINGSMORGEN'

good three weeks in a massive and unforgettable display. Once it is complete, you will see only scattered bloom for the rest of the year. The plant grows to 6' and is really unattractive when not in bloom: its foliage is dull, and there simply isn't enough of it to cover the gangly canes. As a specimen shrub, 'Frühlingsmorgen' will let you down 49 weeks of the year. Incorporated into a mixed border, though, it can be a star. False indigo *(Baptisia australis)* usually blooms at the same time as 'Frühlingsmorgen'. A violet indigo will make a lovely contrast, and the indigo will have no problem concealing the rose's foliar deficiencies for the rest of the summer.

There are five "Frühlings-" hybrid spinosissimas from Kordes, ranging across the color spectrum. Each is a distinctive rose and well worth seeking out for exuberant spring bloom.

RIGHT PLACE   *Well in the middle of a mixed border*

'GÉNÉRAL JACQUEMINOT'

GÉNÉRAL JACQUEMINOT

CLASS: Hybrid perpetual	REPEAT BLOOM: Above
BLOOM COLOR: Red	average
BLOOM SIZE: 4½"	HEIGHT: 5'
	HARDINESS: Zones 5–9
INTRODUCED: Roussel, France, 1846	

Important in rose history as an ancestor of nearly all of the deep red roses we grow today, "General Jack" is still worth growing in its own right. Like all hybrid perpetuals, it demands to be well fed and well watered. Unlike many of them, it has a manageable habit, maxing out at 5' of bright green growth. Given attention, it will reward you with lots of pretty crimson buds throughout the summer, each with the kind of fragrance we wish every rose would offer. For a startling contrast, consider planting 'Général Jacqueminot' amid a patch of anthemis or other daisylike flowers.

RIGHT PLACE   *Mixed border*

'FUCHSIA MEIDILAND'

FUCHSIA MEIDILAND

CLASS: Shrub	REPEAT BLOOM: Reliable
BLOOM COLOR: Fuchsia	HEIGHT: 4'
BLOOM SIZE: 2"	HARDINESS: Zones 5–9
INTRODUCED: Meilland, France, 1991	

Intensely fuchsia, this Meidiland pairs dramatically with any white flower that can keep up with it. Growing 4' × 4', 'Fuchsia Meidiland' has perfect vigor: all energy goes into producing new blooms, none is wasted on growing out of bounds. Rarely out of bloom, very healthy, and winter hardy.

RIGHT PLACE   *Mixed border near white flowers*

GEORGE VANCOUVER

CLASS: Shrub	REPEAT BLOOM: Reliable
BLOOM COLOR: Red	if deadheaded
BLOOM SIZE: 4"	HEIGHT: 4'
HARDINESS: Zones 4–9	
INTRODUCED: Ogilvie, Canada, 1994	

This has the most attractive habit of any of the Canadian Explorers, growing into a nicely rounded bush of about 4' tall. This makes it a good choice for repeating several times in a border, where each plant of 'George Vancouver' will look just like the next. Large cherry

'GEORGE VANCOUVER'

GO AND COME

While a cross between two species roses might produce one of thousands of different results, the ancestry of modern hybrid roses is so complex that a cross between any two of them has been estimated to produce a potential 17 million different outcomes. It's nothing as simple as crossing a red hybrid tea with a yellow hybrid tea and getting an orange hybrid tea. No matter what you cross you're most likely to get a pink rose, and a single-petaled one at that. Rose breeders contend with varieties that don't want to pass on their most desirable characteristics, or that have infertile pollen, or that won't set seeds. Many hybrid roses have what the German hybridizer Wilhelm Kordes called "go and come" characteristics, traits that disappear for a generation before reemerging, perhaps, in second-generation seedlings.

red blooms appear abundantly in spring, usually in clusters of four to seven flowers, and its hips will be swelling even before the flowers fade. These should be deadheaded to encourage better repeat bloom. 'George Vancouver' is indifferent to winter cold, but not as drought resistant as some of the other Explorers. Keep it well watered for best performance.

RIGHT PLACE *Repeated in mixed border*

GRACE ABOUNDING

CLASS: Floribunda	REPEAT BLOOM: Good
BLOOM COLOR: Cream	HEIGHT: 4'
BLOOM SIZE: 3"	HARDINESS: Zones 6–9
INTRODUCED: Harkness, England, 1968	

Envision a perfect cross between a floribunda and a hybrid musk. It would be a healthy, slightly spreading plant, taller than the average floribunda, displaying its sizable blooms in big sprays, and eager to provide repeat bloom. 'Grace Abounding' is exactly that rose, with wheat-colored buds opening into creamy gold blooms that quickly mature to white. This rose is just as valuable in the cutting garden as it is in the mixed border, where its soft color and habit of displaying its sprays above its foliar growth makes it a star. 'Grace Abounding' blooms a little later than most floribundas, and it has a bit of the winter tenderness of the pastel-colored hybrid musks. A simple shovelful of dirt or sawdust keeps it alive over an Ohio winter.

RIGHT PLACE *Mixed border; cutting garden*

GREAT WALL

CLASS: Shrub	REPEAT BLOOM: Reliable
BLOOM COLOR: Red	HEIGHT: 5'
BLOOM SIZE: 2½"	HARDINESS: Zones 4–9
INTRODUCED: Lim, USA, 2005	

Bristling with good health and large bright cerise semi-double blooms, 'Great Wall' is almost never out of bloom. New growth sprouts from all over the plant, so flowers rarely have stems of any cuttable length. Avoid summer pruning or tinkering with this rose. Just let it grow and bloom anywhere you'd like a bright swath of color but don't require rose blooms that are individually impressive. 'Great Wall' works especially well when planted in multiples of three or five plants. This rose

'GREAT WALL'

from Ping Lim, the innovative hybridizer for Bailey Nurseries, is hardy to its tips in zone 5. Named for the Great Wall of China, it seems satisfied at 5' in Ohio.

RIGHT PLACE *In company with three or five plants*

GREETINGS

CLASS: Shrub

BLOOM COLOR: Purple with white

BLOOM SIZE: 3"

INTRODUCED: Zary, USA, 1999

REPEAT BLOOM: Heavy

HEIGHT: 4'

HARDINESS: Zones 5–9

An easy-growing shrub, growing to a well-branched 4' and constantly covered in bright semi-double blooms, purple-red with a white eye. These often display a delicate striped effect. Blooming in large sprays, 'Greetings' makes an impact from a distance, where it may not at first be recognized as a rose. 'Greetings' is one of the most distinctive roses in the garden, at home in any perennial bed, but it does not last well as a cut flower. It is healthy and very winter hardy.

RIGHT PLACE *Mixed border*

'HAKUUN'

HAKUUN

CLASS: Floribunda

BLOOM COLOR: White

BLOOM SIZE: 2"

INTRODUCED: Poulsen, Denmark, 1962

REPEAT BLOOM: Monthly

HEIGHT: 2'

HARDINESS: Zones 5–9

Billowing clusters of milk-white blooms appear on this 2' floribunda at regular intervals throughout the summer. Winter hardy, disease resistant and eager to repeat bloom, this rose was decades ahead of its time and should be better known today. Its habit is upright, fireplug size, and valuable anyplace where you want a lot of white for three or four months of the year. When you cut a spray with any kind of a stem, there won't be too much plant left. While new growth will start quickly, 'Hakuun' does benefit from leafy perennial neighbors that can conceal this unappealing stage in its growth cycle. It is an ideal white highlight for a perennial bed. Hakuun is Danish for "white cloud."

RIGHT PLACE *Perennial bed; container planting*

'HANSA'

HANSA

CLASS: Hybrid rugosa

BLOOM COLOR: Purple-red

BLOOM SIZE: 4½"

INTRODUCED: Schaum & VanTol, The Netherlands, 1905

REPEAT BLOOM: Scattered

HEIGHT: 6'

HARDINESS: Zones 4–9

A hybrid rugosa supercharged with vigor, 'Hansa' grows to 6' and spreads via suckers as far as you will let it. Its healthy foliage is leathery and bright at the same time, covering the slightly arching plant from top to bottom. Blooms are purplish red, fully double, opening in a charming fanlike manner. They have a strong spicy scent that travels well throughout the garden. 'Hansa' will start forming large, round hips immediately after its spring bloom. It will have a strong bloom period again in the fall, even if these hips are left to ripen. Expect a scattering of bloom throughout the middle of the summer and you won't be disappointed.

'Hansa' will swamp weak neighbors, but it is useful in combination with other large, tough plants. It also makes a super hedge. This is a rose that requires no special care at all. Anyone can grow 'Hansa'.

Because they are native to the rough seacoasts of north Asia, rugosas are often recommended for their salt tolerance. I decided to test this out by digging up some 'Hansa' suckers and planting them along the road, with the permission of the farmer who grows corn and soybeans in the field across from my house. Here they thrived, despite a winter that saw the snowplow go by several times each week. And even after I learned that my township had saved money by switching from salt to cinders for road ice control, I remained impressed with 'Hansa'. Rugosas are definitely cinder-resistant plants! Then New York City had a blackout that was eventually blamed on tree branches falling on a power line a few miles from here. So the local electric company became obsessive about clearing any living growth beneath its lines. While it was extremely unlikely that 'Hansa' was ever going to reach 25' in height and interfere with the nation's electrical grid, the plants were in due course cut down. They keep trying to come back, but they rarely get beyond 2' or 3' before the electric company sends someone out to cut them down again. This constant pruning has prompted 'Hansa' to sucker even more aggressively, and it has now colonized a large area. Soon some of it will be beyond the electrical "no-grow" zone and free to grow and bloom to its full potential.

RIGHT PLACE *Mixed border with large plants; hedge; roadside planting*

HAPPY CHAPPY

CLASS: Shrub	REPEAT BLOOM: Nearly
BLOOM COLOR: Multicolored	constant
BLOOM SIZE: 2"	HEIGHT: 1' × 2' wide
HARDINESS: Zones 5–9	
INTRODUCED: Ilsink, The Netherlands, 1999	

Full of changing colors, the single-petaled blooms of 'Happy Chappy' begin as bright apricot-yellow and progress to orange and finally deep pink. The combination of all of the colors at once on a healthy low-growing plant is impressive. This rose reaches just over 1' tall in my garden, while spreading to more than 2'. It's perfect at the front of any border where its exuberant colors won't distract from a more subdued scheme.

'HAPPY CHAPPY'

Whenever it seems to me that roses are being given ever more stupid names, I open a daylily catalog and I'm reassured that things in the rose world really aren't that bad.

RIGHT PLACE *Front of border; tree rose*

HEAVEN ON EARTH

CLASS: Floribunda	REPEAT BLOOM: Steady
BLOOM COLOR: Apricot	HEIGHT: 2½"
BLOOM SIZE: 7"	HARDINESS: Zones 5–9
INTRODUCED: Kordes, Germany, 2004	

Peachy apricot, its 7" blooms are the largest found on any floribunda. Sprays typically consist of just two or three blooms; others arrive as solitary specimens. When fully open these may not be recognized as roses, which can make it a surprising feature in a mixed border. (Imagine a novel-colored peony that blooms

'HEAVEN ON EARTH'

throughout the summer.) Grouped with other floribundas, 'Heaven on Earth' may just look out of place, and it may overwhelm its neighbors in a perennial bed. This rose provides plentiful color in a small space, and in addition to its value in the mixed border, is one of the best accent roses for smaller gardens. A couple of blooms is enough to make a real impact; covered with a dozen, this plant offers an unforgettable display. This rose rarely has stems long enough to be in proportion with its giant blooms. However, cut blooms look great when floated in a glass bowl indoors. Habit is short and wide, and 'Heaven on Earth' has the same excellent health we have come to expect in recent Kordes floribundas.

RIGHT PLACE *Mixed border; accent in small garden*

'HENRY HUDSON'

HENRY HUDSON

CLASS: Hybrid rugosa
BLOOM COLOR: White
BLOOM SIZE: 3"
INTRODUCED: Svejda, Canada, 1976
REPEAT BLOOM: Good
HEIGHT: 3' × 4' wide
HARDINESS: Zones 4–9

Growing wider than tall, 'Henry Hudson' is a Canadian Explorer rose with strong rugosa characteristics. The fully double blooms begin as pink buds, opening to white, providing a two-tone effect. Bright orange hips provide more color still and are often ripe by July, just as the second crop of blooms is beginning.

A very tough rose that thrives with little care, 'Henry Hudson' proves that something other than 'Stella d'Oro' daylilies can grow happily in the parking lot of fast food restaurants. Its resistance to salt makes it an excellent rose to plant at the entrance to your driveway. Its white blooms will reflect moonlight and headlights, making your entrance appear even brighter at night. And if 'Henry Hudson' gets run over, it will grow back.

RIGHT PLACE *Driveway entrance*

HERITAGE

CLASS: Shrub
BLOOM COLOR: Pink
BLOOM SIZE: 4½"
INTRODUCED: Austin, England, 1984
REPEAT BLOOM: Reliable
HEIGHT: 5'
HARDINESS: Zones 5–9

Beautiful and tough, 'Heritage' produces scads of delicate, full-petaled blooms on a plant that is much hardier than its lax, almost thornless growth might suggest. The 70-petaled blooms are seashell pink with a commanding fragrance, almost always appearing in sprays. They open from deeper pink buds into a perfect cup shape. After this point they are prone to fall apart, so 'Heritage' is not recommended as a cut flower. This is not a problem in the garden, as more blooms are always on the way. Grows to 5' in my garden, and it doesn't mind being cut back hard when it starts to get leggy. 'Heritage' is the ideal rose for the mixed border. If you

'HERITAGE'

have room, grouping three plants of 'Heritage' will provide a spectacular display.

RIGHT PLACE *Mixed border*

HERMOSA

CLASS: China

BLOOM COLOR: Pink

BLOOM SIZE: 2½"

INTRODUCED: Marchesseau, France, before 1837

REPEAT BLOOM: Reliable

HEIGHT: 2½'

HARDINESS: Zones 5–9

Remarkably winter hardy for a China rose, 'Hermosa' gives northern gardeners a chance to see why Chinas were called "monthly roses." It blooms so dependably throughout the season that I sometimes don't recognize it when it's not in bloom. The double blooms are bright rose pink, at their prettiest when upright buds, like glowing pink candles. Later, they appear to shy away from view when the weight of an open bloom causes it to nod back into the plant. Growing about 2½' tall, it can be planted as part of a floribunda bed, but it will be happier in a more sheltered position, such as a foundation planting.

There is a climbing sport called 'Setina' which I have not grown.

RIGHT PLACE *Foundation planting*

HOT COCOA

CLASS: Floribunda

BLOOM COLOR: Brown

BLOOM SIZE: 3"

INTRODUCED: Carruth, USA, 2003

REPEAT BLOOM: Good

HEIGHT: 3½'

HARDINESS: Zones 5–9

Rusty buds open to blooms that are chocolate brown when you're lucky and dull orange when you aren't. Plants are healthier and more vigorous than most of the other brown roses (which are officially referred to with the apple or potato term of "russet" by the American Rose Society). 'Hot Cocoa' has an upright floribunda habit with moderate-sized sprays of large ruffly blooms. I have been impressed with its winter hardiness here in Zone 5.

The gardener does not have too many chocolate-colored roses to choose from, or brown-shaded flowers of any genus, and 'Hot Cocoa' will bring smiles wherever its unusual color is allowed to stand on its own. It will be most effective situated next to plants blooming in white, lemon, or blush, and pointless near electric pink or shocking orange.

'HOT COCOA'

One of the nation's leading home improvement stores inexplicably sells this rose complete with its own miniature wooden trellis. The trellis will not look any better at home, or serve any purpose, because 'Hot Cocoa' is not in any way a climbing rose.

RIGHT PLACE *Mixed border near white, lemon, or blush plants*

INDIGO

CLASS: Portland

BLOOM COLOR: Purple

BLOOM SIZE: 3"

INTRODUCED: Laffay, France, 1830

REPEAT BLOOM: Reliable

HEIGHT: 3½'

HARDINESS: Zones 5–9

Its compact size makes 'Indigo' ideal for even small gardens. Purple blooms appear continuously throughout the summer on the tidy, stiff growth typical of a Portland rose. 'Indigo' is fragrant, but not as fragrant as it looks. This is not a moss rose, but you can see the beginning of moss on its bristly stems. It is quite winter hardy, and while black spot and powdery mildew may each appear late in the season, they do no real harm.

This suckers very freely for a repeat-blooming rose. Unlike the aggressive suckers produced by some

'INDIGO'

gallicas, the suckers form neat little small versions of 'Indigo' 3 or 4 feet from the mother plant. During the growing season, once a sucker appears and is growing well, separate it from the mother plant with a few sharp thrusts of a spade. Come fall it will be easy to dig up and plant somewhere else or give to a gardening friend.

RIGHT PLACE *Mixed border; rose bed*

INTERNATIONAL HERALD TRIBUNE

CLASS: Floribunda
BLOOM COLOR: Purple
BLOOM SIZE: 2"
INTRODUCED: Harkness, England, 1984

REPEAT BLOOM: Continuous
HEIGHT: 18"
HARDINESS: Zones 5–9

A long name for a short rose, 'International Herald Tribune' is a small, tough floribunda with loads of semi-double purple blooms. In my garden it is often the first floribunda to bloom each year. The flowers begin primarily purple; a white eye emerges and enlarges as the flowers mature. These appear in cheerful clusters on top of the 18" plant. If there is any other purple perennial hardy to Zone 5 that blooms continuously for four or more months, I am not aware of it. This is a rose that you can tuck anywhere near the front of a border where a strong dash of color is desired throughout the summer. Growth is twiggy, and while simply snapping off spent blooms will encourage new growth, pruning a little lower will make that growth stronger and stems cuttable.

Because its dense foliage reaches all the way to the ground, 'International Herald Tribune' can be one of the first roses to show spider mite damage when that pest is present. Removing the lowest leaves can deny spider mites a foothold.

RIGHT PLACE *Front of border*

JACQUELINE DU PRÉ

CLASS: Shrub
BLOOM COLOR: White
BLOOM SIZE: 3½"
HARDINESS: Zones 4–9
INTRODUCED: Harkness, England 1988

REPEAT BLOOM: Reliable with
proper care
HEIGHT: 3'

Large, semi-double, creamy white blooms open to a cupped shape, revealing golden stamens supported by extraordinary raspberry pink filaments. This startling display, coupled with the pretty curves of the simple

'JACQUELINE DU PRÉ'

blooms, make this a particularly photogenic rose. Its perfect beauty can stop hearts as well as camera shutters. 'Jacqueline du Pré' is one of the first repeat-blooming roses to appear each spring, and it blooms especially strongly in the cool of the autumn. It dislikes heat waves and may be less productive during the summer if not well watered. This is a short, sturdy 3' shrub that is equally at home near the front of a large rose border or as a highlight plant in a perennial bed. It dislikes being pruned; fortunately, it is quite winter hardy. Like almost all roses introduced by Jack Harkness, 'Jacqueline du Pré' has a pleasing fragrance.

RIGHT PLACE *Front of a rose border; accent in a perennial bed*

KATHLEEN FERRIER

CLASS: Floribunda
BLOOM COLOR: Pink
BLOOM SIZE: 3"
HARDINESS: Zones 5–9
INTRODUCED: Buisman, Netherlands, 1952

REPEAT BLOOM: Big sprays
every 6 weeks
HEIGHT: 5'

This is a rose that throws all of its energy into making great sprays of semi-double, deep pink blooms, fading attractively to salmon. Unfortunately, it does not devote much effort toward foliage; the plant looks sparse beneath the blooms and ugly without them. This is a problem easily solved by using 'Kathleen Ferrier' in a mixed setting rather than for bedding. Sold sometimes as a floribunda, sometimes as a shrub, it reaches 5' for me. It's very winter hardy, and I suspect it gets some black spot only because I grow it next to 'City of London', the most notorious black-spotter in my garden.

RIGHT PLACE *Mixed border*

'LADY ELSIE MAY'

LADY ELSIE MAY

CLASS: Shrub

BLOOM COLOR: Pink

BLOOM SIZE: 2½"

INTRODUCED: Noack, Germany, 2002

REPEAT BLOOM: Reliable

HEIGHT: 2' × 4'

HARDINESS: Zones 5–9

Bright coral pink, shading to orange in cool weather, this is a rose that glistens with good health. From the breeder of the Flower Carpet roses, 'Lady Elsie May' grows into a splendid wide shrub, spreading 4' in my garden while reaching just past 2' in height. It makes a spectacular edging along a large-scale border, and its toughness recommends it for planting in difficult situations. Blooms are just barely double, and you may have to get up very early in the morning to observe the pretty camellia-like half-open stage. The fully open blooms persist attractively, and new growth and blooms appear even when spent blooms are not removed.

RIGHT PLACE *Edging for large border; ground cover*

LADY HILLINGDON

CLASS: Tea

BLOOM COLOR: Yellow

BLOOM SIZE: 4"

INTRODUCED: Lowe & Shawyer, England, 1910

REPEAT BLOOM: Monthly

HEIGHT: 4½'

HARDINESS: Zones 5b–9

The true teas are great garden and cut-flower plants in warm places: southern USA, southern France, Australia, conservatories, and greenhouses. Most will not survive in the north, but 'Lady Hillingdon' is a happy exception. I have grown several teas in pots, which can be stored as dormant plants in the garage over winter or nursed along indoors. 'Lady Hillingdon' is the only tea that survives outdoors for me.

And it doesn't just survive; it prospers. By the height of each summer it has grown into a 4½' tall bush covered in elegant amber buds. These fade to yellow as they open into blooms that are large enough to bend over their stems, in typical tea fashion. The new growth is purple, which makes a great contrast with the buds and blooms. 'Lady Hillingdon' is quite healthy. If one takes the nodding blooms as charming rather than a defect, then its biggest problem is petals that are not thick enough to withstand rainy weather.

Too gangly for bedding, 'Lady Hillingdon' will be a luminous member of any mixed border. Its hardiness comes from its timing. Most teas actually survive winters in Zone 5 but fail because they start growing too early each spring and are cut down by multiple freezes while more sensible roses are still dormant. 'Lady Hillingdon' waits, and it usually dodges the late freezes as effectively as do most of the yellow hybrid teas of yesteryear. Indeed, as one of the last teas to be introduced, it is likely that 'Lady Hillingdon' has a dose of hybrid tea somewhere in its background. Despite this, it has all of the outward charm of a true tea. For those in warmer climates, there is also a climbing version.

RIGHT PLACE *Mixed border*

LÉDA

CLASS: Damask

BLOOM COLOR: White

BLOOM SIZE: 3"

INTRODUCED: Origin uncertain, before 1827

REPEAT BLOOM: Very rare

HEIGHT: 5'

HARDINESS: Zones 5–8

Nicknamed the Painted Damask, 'Léda' brings a modern look to old garden roses. From red buds, its blooms open as creamy white, with just a touch of red at the tip of each quilled petal. These appear in small clusters all over the plant. Normally a once-bloomer, in some years 'Léda' produces a few blooms later in the summer.

Growing 5' tall and 6' to 7' wide, this beautiful rose is substantial enough to serve as a specimen plant. But its big wide leaves and sturdy growth make it a perfect companion for some of the other great shrubs of the northern garden: deutzia, lilac, and weigela, and in my garden these are its neighbors.

RIGHT PLACE *Landscape and garden accent; mixed shrub border*

LEVERKUSEN

CLASS: Kordesii

BLOOM COLOR: Yellow

BLOOM SIZE: 3"

INTRODUCED: Kordes, Germany, 1954

REPEAT BLOOM: Sparse

HEIGHT: 7'

HARDINESS: Zones 5–9

The first of the yellow kordesiis, this grows into an attractive, upright 7' shrub. While most kordesiis are climbers, 'Leverkusen' shows no desire to climb in my garden and requires no support. It's a cheerful addition to the mixed border, and it also works very well against red brick. Brilliant yellow buds quickly fade to lemon yellow blooms. Most blooms appear one to a stem, but it is not uncommon to see some sprays as well. Bloom is much more profuse at the start of the season than at the end. After most winters I find about a foot of good wood left on 'Leverkusen', and once pruned it begins regrowing vigorously from that.

RIGHT PLACE *Mixed border; effective against red brick*

YEARNING FOR YELLOW

More than 50 years after the introduction of **'Leverkusen'** the search for really winter-hardy yellow shrub roses continues. 'J P Connell' (1987) was a curiously lethargic addition to the family of Canadian Explorers. 'Morden Sunrise' (1999) in the Canadian Parkland series is a deeper yellow, edged pink, but it has a habit no more substantial than that of a floribunda. I am enthusiastic about 'Tahitian Moon' (introduced by Lim in 2004), which grows vigorously to 5' and is covered throughout the summer with pale yellow blooms, edged light pink later in the season. Someday gardeners will have a reliably winter hardy rose with the habit of 'Leverkusen', the floriferousness of 'Tahitian Moon', and a dazzling bright yellow color. But it's not here yet.

LITTLE RAMBLER

CLASS: Shrub

BLOOM COLOR: Pink

BLOOM SIZE: 1½"

INTRODUCED: Warner, England, 1994

REPEAT BLOOM: Reliable

HEIGHT: 5'

HARDINESS: Zones 5–9

A rose that defies classification, producing the charming clusters of bantam blooms enjoyed on magnificent old ramblers, but on a 5' plant that flowers all summer long. Blooms are pale pink fading to white, so that there are often blooms of two colors in one spray. They emerge from every nook and cranny of the arching shrub, and it may be difficult to find a stem long enough to cut. The plant is healthy and quite winter hardy. It can be employed in a difficult situation quite effectively: around here, it disguises my trash cans perfectly. It makes a spectacular tree rose in its native England; unfortunately, no American nurseryman has offered it this way. Sometimes sold as 'Baby Rambler'.

RIGHT PLACE *Screening*

MME HARDY

CLASS: Damask

BLOOM COLOR: White

BLOOM SIZE: 3"

INTRODUCED: Hardy, France, 1832

REPEAT BLOOM: None

HEIGHT: 5'

HARDINESS: Zones 5–9

The most famous white old garden rose has been justly praised for its pure white color and intricately swirled form, the trademark green pip at its center, and its cool, refreshing fragrance. It has also been claimed as a parent (of the American climber 'Colonial White') even though it is sterile, the green pip replacing the sex parts. This is a rose unlike other damasks, indeed unlike any other rose.

'MME HARDY'

Roses that bloom only once each year do so on old wood. Thus, pruning them in the spring will take away all of the bloom for that year. For this same reason, we can't expect once-blooming roses to flower the first year after planting. (See chapter 13 for details on pruning roses.) When I was new to roses, I was so keen to grow 'Mme Hardy' after seeing it at the Garden of Roses of Legend and Romance in Wooster, Ohio, that I immediately sent in an order to Pickering Nurseries in Ontario. That fall they sent me a giant-sized bare-root plant, so long of cane that I decided not to prune it back before planting, as a prudent gardener would have. Instead, I covered it with a big beige plastic bag and misted it daily to keep the long canes hydrated while the plant had time to grow roots. The plant went into dormancy with its long canes still green and plump, and sure enough, 'Mme Hardy' made buds and bloomed that first spring. And it has done so ever since.

Despite the beauty of its flowers, 'Mme Hardy' is not a perfect plant. It is vigorous but also lax in its growth, and it dislikes competition from aggressive neighbors. It may be most effectively used as a focal point in an herb garden or, with generous spacing, in a border of similar-sized damask or alba roses. 'Mme Hardy' grows to 5' for me and only occasionally suckers.

RIGHT PLACE *Focal point in herb garden; mixed rose border*

MME ISAAC PÉREIRE

CLASS: Bourbon	REPEAT BLOOM: Good
BLOOM COLOR: Pink	HEIGHT: 6'
BLOOM SIZE: 4½"	HARDINESS: Zones 6–9
INTRODUCED: Garçon, France, 1881	

One of the most beautiful of the old garden roses, with large deep pink blooms blessed with a powerful and pleasing fragrance. That's the good news. The bad news is that the plant is gangly, with lax canes sprawling to 6' in my garden, and prone to black spot. However, the black spot does not slow bloom production, and by situating the plant in a mixed border the disease will not be noticed, while the flowers will attract a lot of attention. To enjoy indoors, cut buds while they are still unfurling.

This rose responds very well to pegging down. If its long canes are trained to run along the ground, they will produce new growth and bloom from every internode. If you have enough room, this is a spectacular

'MME ISAAC PÉREIRE'

way to enjoy 'Mme Isaac Péreire'. There is a lighter pink mutation called 'Mme Ernst Calvat'. It produces a higher proportion of misshapen flowers than does 'Mme Isaac Péreire'.

RIGHT PLACE *Mixed border; fragrance garden*

MLLE CÉCILE BRUNNER

CLASS: Polyantha	REPEAT BLOOM: Good
BLOOM COLOR: Pink	HEIGHT: 4'
BLOOM SIZE: 1½"	HARDINESS: Zones 6–9
INTRODUCED: Ducher, France, 1881	

This is the Sweetheart Rose, famous as a boutonniere rose in earlier times. If your grandfather wore a bowler hat and used a walking stick, he may have cut a bloom of 'Mlle Cécile Brunner' to place in his lapel before walking to the train station each morning. Or, if he was like mine and played hooky from the steel mill to watch the Pirates at Forbes Field, he almost certainly did not. But his wife might have enjoyed it in her garden just the same.

A polyantha unlike any of its classmates, 'Mlle Cécile Brunner' produces light pink blooms exactly like perfectly formed miniature hybrid teas, and lots of them. It grows into a bushy plant, to 4' in a good summer, and was traditionally planted by the back door to make snipping boutonnieres convenient. This placement will also help it in colder climates. A cross between a polyantha and a tea, 'Mlle Cécile Brunner' is less winter hardy than most of the other roses I am recommending, and heat radiating from your house will help it survive the winter.

A climbing version can be a glorious sight in warmer climates. In Zone 5 it climbs and winter-kills without producing very many blooms at all.

RIGHT PLACE *Dooryard garden*

MAMAN TURBAT

CLASS: Polyantha

BLOOM COLOR: Pink

BLOOM SIZE: 1"

INTRODUCED: Turbat, France, 1911

REPEAT BLOOM: Reliable

HEIGHT: 2'

HARDINESS: Zones 5–9

One of the best of the old polyanthas, 'Maman Turbat' delivers the charm of an old garden rose on a compact, perpetually flowering plant. Its many-petaled blooms appear in shades of pink on a disease-resistant plant that grows about 2' tall and wide. These are typically presented in sprays of a dozen or more lightly fragrant blooms that last well when cut. 'Maman Turbat' is ideal for planting in front of a bed of heritage roses, or for growing in a pot. This is a charming, genuinely useful rose that should be much better known.

RIGHT PLACE *Cutting garden; front of rose bed; container plant*

'MAMAN TURBAT'

MARIE-JEANNE

CLASS: Polyantha

BLOOM COLOR: White

BLOOM SIZE: 1"

INTRODUCED: Turbat, France, 1913

REPEAT BLOOM: Unusual

HEIGHT: 4'

HARDINESS: Zones 5–9

A polyantha that is halfway to being a hybrid musk, and quite useful in mixed plantings. Blush pink buds open

'MARIE-JEANNE'

to petal-packed white blooms, larger and more intricately formed than those of most polyanthas. These appear in almost unbelievably lavish sprays in early summer. Because most blooms appear at the top of the relatively narrow 4' plant, it is ideal for the middle part of a mixed border. Its canes are nearly thornless and therefore painless to work around. Repeat bloom is poor, but 'Marie-Jeanne' produces more blooms in its one profuse month than other roses its size do over two, or more, years.

RIGHT PLACE *Mixed border*

MARJORIE FAIR

CLASS: Hybrid musk

BLOOM COLOR: Red

BLOOM SIZE: 1"

INTRODUCED: Harkness, England, 1977

REPEAT BLOOM: Reliable

HEIGHT: 4'

HARDINESS: Zones 5–9

Often sold as 'Red Ballerina', this rose differs from its parent (the famous 1937 hybrid musk 'Ballerina') in two fundamental ways. One, its blooms are white surrounded by crimson instead of pink. And two, it is a zone hardier than 'Ballerina'. I must provide winter protection to enjoy 'Ballerina' here in Zone 5, and even then it's not at its best. 'Marjorie Fair' gets along fine without any winter protection.

This busy plant grows 4' tall and usually a little wider, throwing out great sprays of its single-petaled

'MARJORIE FAIR'

SEARCHING FOR GOOD SPORTS

If you grow enough roses long enough and observe them carefully, you will eventually find a mutation, or "sport," of your own. From my own garden, I have a version of Austin's 'The Countryman' with only about 20 petals, instead of the 110 customarily found on blooms of the original plant. This is not in any way an improvement; it's just different. Very few mutations are in fact improvements, and some that would be breakthroughs turn out to be unstable. An unstable sport will switch back and forth between the original and the sported version; sometimes blooms will be half one way and half the other. Often one bloom in a spray may be in some way different, but color or petal mutations that do not consist of an entire cane producing the new type of flower will generally not prove to be stable when propagated.

If you discover a mutation you may simply enjoy it as part of the original plant until that cane eventually dies. But by propagating the sport you will 1) determine whether or not it is a stable mutation and 2) preserve it. Patent protection does not apply to mutations that are clearly distinct and different from the original. If your mutation can be successfully propagated there is no reason why you cannot name and introduce the new rose.

blooms all summer long. This is a very healthy rose that requires nothing in the way of special care, and it provides color month after month. To enhance the impact of its color, try planting it amid white or pale pink summer-blooming phlox.

RIGHT PLACE *Mixed border near white or pale pink phlox*

MARY ROSE

CLASS: Shrub	REPEAT BLOOM: Continuous
BLOOM COLOR: Pink	HEIGHT: 4'
BLOOM SIZE: 4"	HARDINESS: Zones 4–9
INTRODUCED: Austin, England, 1983	

The most dependable of all of David Austin's roses, 'Mary Rose' is a constant bloomer on a 4' shrub that ignores winter cold and summer heat and is remarkably tolerant of drought. Its color is a strong rose pink. We run no water to the rose bed in which 'Mary Rose' grows, and when rains fail us and other roses begin to show signs of stress, 'Mary Rose' grows happily forward. I believe that 'Mary Rose' is in bloom for more days each summer than any other large-flowered rose I grow. It starts early, finishes late, and is hardly ever without bloom in between.

'Mary Rose' has a degree of genetic instability, demonstrated by the numerous mutations (or sports) it has produced. There is an excellent pastel pink sport called 'Redoute'. This has all of the 'Mary Rose' qualities in a softer color. An equally tough white mutation is called 'Winchester Cathedral'. This sometimes displays blooms striped in 'Mary Rose' pink. While it has never been authorized or released by the Austin organization, a fairly stable selection of this secondary sport circulates among collectors as 'Striped Mary Rose'.

RIGHT PLACE *Mixed or rose border; tree rose*

'MARY ROSE'

MOONLIGHT

CLASS: Hybrid musk
BLOOM COLOR: White
BLOOM SIZE: 2"
INTRODUCED: Pemberton, England, 1913
REPEAT BLOOM: Good
HEIGHT: 5' or more
HARDINESS: Zones 5–9

Informal, milky white blooms appear in well-spaced clusters all over this healthy hybrid musk. Everything is in proportion; the sprays of bloom set perfectly against the shiny leaves. And it's a great choice for illuminating a shady corner of the garden. Like most of Pemberton's hybrid musks, or most any light-petaled rose that blooms in large sprays, 'Moonlight' does well in some shade. 'Moonlight' reaches 5' for me, and it can be kept shorter with frequent summer pruning. I have seen it used beautifully as a climber in warmer climates.

Not all of the Pemberton/Bentall hybrid musks are reliably hardy in cold-winter climates. Among the most commonly available varieties, 'Buff Beauty' and 'Penelope' are not winter hardy without lots of extra protection in Zone 5. 'Moonlight' thrives.

RIGHT PLACE *Mixed border; climber in warm climates; tolerates shade*

MORGENROT

CLASS: Shrub
BLOOM COLOR: Red
BLOOM SIZE: 3"
INTRODUCED: Kordes, Germany, 1985
REPEAT BLOOM: Reliable
HEIGHT: 3'
HARDINESS: Zones 5–9

There is no other winter-hardy, repeat-blooming rose that produces large, single-petaled red blooms on a compact plant. The plant develops into a perfect 3' mound and arrives at its good health without the benefit of glossy leaves. The clematis-like blooms are bright red, with a white eye at the center of the flower. They usually appear singly; sometimes there will be a cluster of three to five blooms. It is one of the first shrub roses to bloom each spring, and it repeats steadily throughout the summer.

This is a dramatic and incredibly useful plant. If you imagine the mixed border as a symphony, with each plant performing a specific part, 'Morgenrot' plays the cymbals.

RIGHT PLACE *Mixed border*

MOUNTBATTEN

CLASS: Floribunda
BLOOM COLOR: Yellow
BLOOM SIZE: 3½"
INTRODUCED: Harkness, England, 1982
REPEAT BLOOM: Reliable
HEIGHT: 5½'
HARDINESS: Zones 5–9

Sold as a floribunda, but it's too tall to be a useful bedding rose. The brilliant yellow blooms of 'Mountbatten' appear with regularity throughout the summer, both individually and in well-spaced clusters. It's a rose that's almost always in bloom, and while rarely so profuse to be a showstopper, its good health and ruffled blooms are very useful in a mixed border where foliage is too often relied upon to provide good yellow color. 'Mountbatten' makes a worthwhile cut flower, and cutting long stems will encourage it to bloom instead of just making new growth.

RIGHT PLACE *Mixed border; cut flower*

'MY HERO'

MY HERO

CLASS: Shrub
BLOOM COLOR: Red
BLOOM SIZE: 2½"
INTRODUCED: Lim, USA, 2003
REPEAT BLOOM: Good
HEIGHT: 3'
HARDINESS: Zones 4b–9

Sometimes it's easy to confuse vigor with winter hardiness. Many roses have the vigor to bounce back quickly from a tough winter, even when starting the growing season with almost no live wood. Northern gardeners depend on these roses. But roses that are truly winter hardy, hardy to the tips of their canes, are also important. These roses keep their shape from one year to the next, and they give the gardener an important measure of predictability. They offer year-round structure in the border because they don't disappear for several months as roses that must be pruned back to the ground do.

'My Hero' is one such hardy rose, growing just 3' tall but not dying back one bit. Its blooms are a bright red, appearing most usually in small clusters. They are completely double, which is unusual for a self-cleaning rose. 'My Hero' will drop all of its petals all by itself, and because it is sterile will keep producing new buds without the message of "Mission Accomplished" that signals other roses to slow down because seeds have been successfully set.

RIGHT PLACE *Mixed border; low-maintenance areas*

NASHVILLE

CLASS: Shrub	REPEAT BLOOM: Reliable
BLOOM COLOR: Pink striped	HEIGHT: 2'
with white	HARDINESS: Zones 5–9
BLOOM SIZE: 2½"	
INTRODUCED: Poulsen, Denmark, 1992	

This is the most impressive of the shorter striped roses. 'Nashville' has semi-double blooms of bright magenta, with chalk stripes that vary in their intensity. Some blooms will present a vivid contrast; in others the effect will be more subtle. It flowers in large clusters, so contrasts appear between the different blooms in one spray as well as between the colors on each bloom. The leafy, compact plant blooms early in the spring and keeps going all summer, maintaining a remarkably uniform growth habit. It never grows beyond 2' for me, and I've used it most effectively massed as an underplanting in an island bed featuring prestonia and josiflexa lilacs. Most years this early rose will bloom at the same time as these late-blooming lilacs, and the contrast with white lilacs such as 'Agnes Smith' is particularly striking.

Originally introduced as 'Christopher Columbus' in Europe, this rose sailed the ocean blue and became 'Nashville', one of a series of Danish roses named for American cities.

RIGHT PLACE *Underplanting in shrub bed*

'NEARLY WILD'

NEARLY WILD

CLASS: Floribunda	REPEAT BLOOM: Nearly
BLOOM COLOR: Pink	continuous
BLOOM SIZE: 2"	HEIGHT: 2½'
HARDINESS: Zones 5–9	
INTRODUCED: Brownell, United States, 1941	

Clusters of single-petaled rose pink blooms that might be more charming if they weren't so ubiquitous. This wasn't ever the most-planted rose in the United States, but it probably has the greatest rate of survival. It does not catch any of the rose diseases in the summer, and it won't die over the winter. Despite its health, it can look sparse as part of a bed of floribundas. It is more useful sharing space with perennials, where its simple flowers will blend in well but its color will unfortunately offer nothing novel. If I could choose one rose to come in every color, or at least any other color, this would be it.

RIGHT PLACE *Perennial border*

OLD PORT

CLASS: Floribunda	REPEAT BLOOM: Good
BLOOM COLOR: Purple	HEIGHT: 3'
BLOOM SIZE: 3½"	HARDINESS: Zones 5–9
INTRODUCED: McGredy, New Zealand, 1990	

If David Austin had introduced this rose, no one would argue that it isn't a shrub (and many would be grateful that Austin had finally produced a superior purple rose). In reality, 'Old Port' is marketed as a floribunda, even though it is hardly typical of that class. Its powerfully fragrant blooms are large, and sometimes out of proportion with the compact plant. They appear singly and in small clusters, and they can take more than a week to open all the way through their 100-plus petals. I grow this rose in the front row of a bed of Austin's English Roses, and it fits in very well.

RIGHT PLACE *Front of rose border*

OPEN ARMS

CLASS: Shrub	REPEAT BLOOM: Excellent
BLOOM COLOR: Pink	HEIGHT: 6' × 8' wide
BLOOM SIZE: 2"	HARDINESS: Zones 5b–9
INTRODUCED: Warner, England, 1995	

Like a man without a country, 'Open Arms' is a rose without a class. It is often cataloged with Chris Warner's climbing miniatures, even though it lacks their narrow, upright growth. In England, many rosarians refer to it as a rambler, even though it offers excellent repeat bloom. The American Rose Society calls it a climbing polyantha, even though it doesn't climb and isn't much like a polyantha. 'Open Arms' builds into a graceful mound of arching stems covered in blooms. Its semidouble flowers emerge as bright coral pink, fading to soft pink. After 10 years the ultimate height of the plant appears to be 6', spreading even wider.

So I will call it a shrub, although there is no other shrub rose exactly like it. 'Open Arms' is very healthy and hardy enough for all but the most extreme Zone 5 winters. Its habit is too awkward for a rose bed, but it can be a dramatic accent in a wilder part of the garden. I keep several random plants in my orchard, carrying the apple blossom idea forward long after the real ones have fallen.

RIGHT PLACE *Naturalistic planting*

ORANGES 'N' LEMONS

CLASS: Shrub	REPEAT BLOOM: Reliable if
BLOOM COLOR: Orange striped	deadheaded
with yellow	HEIGHT: 5'
BLOOM SIZE: 4"	HARDINESS: Zones 5b–9
INTRODUCED: McGredy, New Zealand, 1992	

People often ask the "If you could grow only one rose . . ." question. That's tough, but "If you could grow only one *striped* rose" is easy. 'Oranges 'n' Lemons' is unique among all modern roses: a vigorous, healthy shrub with large sprays of boldly striped orange-and-yellow blooms. Bright orange and pure yellow. The effect is as close as a rose can get to tropical, and because the blooms are fully double they last much longer than fewer-petaled striped roses. 'Oranges 'n' Lemons' makes an upright, bushy shrub to 5' in my garden. This rose attracts attention: use it to draw garden visitors down a path or to electrify a dull corner. Remove spent blooms as soon as they lose their attractiveness to hurry up the next cycle of bloom.

RIGHT PLACE *Mixed border; garden accent*

'PALMENGARTEN FRANKFURT'

PALMENGARTEN FRANKFURT

CLASS: Shrub	REPEAT BLOOM: Good
BLOOM COLOR: Pink	WIDTH: 3'
BLOOM SIZE: 2½"	HARDINESS: Zones 5–9
INTRODUCED: Kordes, Germany, 1988	

Many ground-cover roses appear as if they'd been manufactured in the Boring Rose Factory, but this one has real character. This is as close to a genuine ground cover as a rose can get. Its growth is entirely procumbent, with new shoots extending sideways instead of straight up. Its ruffly raspberry pink blooms appear in big clusters that lie down as easily as the plant does. 'Palmengarten Frankfurt' grows about 3' wide, and it looks charming spilling over a brick or stone walkway. It has outstanding disease resistance. If planted in an area where children or pets play, or food is grown, it can easily go without fungicide sprays.

RIGHT PLACE *Ground cover; organic gardens*

PEARL DRIFT

CLASS: Shrub
REPEAT BLOOM: Regular
BLOOM COLOR: White
HEIGHT: 2½' × 4' wide
BLOOM SIZE: 4"
HARDINESS: Zones 5–9
INTRODUCED: LeGrice, England, 1981

Pearlescent buds open to flat, silvery white blooms that cover the plant several times each summer. Its sprays are large but anchored by stocky stems that never grow out of bounds.

This is an ideal rose for foundation plantings. Its pearly blooms are particularly attractive against brick and among conifers, and its mirror-bright leaves are attractive in their own right between bloom cycles. Grows 2½' tall × 4' wide for me. Because it grows wider than tall, 'Pearl Drift' is often incorrectly described as a ground-cover rose. But there is nothing creepy-crawly about it, and it would look awkward on an embankment. 'Pearl Drift' is simply a shrub rose with an angular and low habit of growth.

RIGHT PLACE *Foundation planting, especially against a dark building or conifers*

PERLE VON WEISSENSTEIN

CLASS: Gallica
REPEAT BLOOM: None
BLOOM COLOR: Pink
HEIGHT: 7'+
BLOOM SIZE: 3½"
HARDINESS: Zones 4–8
INTRODUCED: Schwarzkopf, Germany, 1773

The first rose recorded to have been bred in Germany, 'Perle von Weissenstein' is a gallica with many characteristics of a centifolia. The plant grows tall, over 7', and is covered in fat pink buds each spring. Like peonies, these will not open properly in wet weather. When June is dry, 'Perle von Weissenstein' in its full bloom is a glorious sight, with a powerful fragrance that carries throughout the garden. The fully open blooms are packed with more petals than I can count, rich pink washed with mauve. Once opened properly, they last a long time. I grow this rose as part of a border of heritage roses. When weather prevents it from opening properly, the overall effect does not suffer.

Note that some nurseries have this rose confused with a purple imposter. A phone call or email should confirm that a nursery is selling the pink gallica you want. And if the nursery does not know what color its roses are, find a different nursery.

RIGHT PLACE *Rose border*

'PETITE DE HOLLANDE'

PETITE DE HOLLANDE

CLASS: Centifolia
REPEAT BLOOM: None
BLOOM COLOR: Pink
HEIGHT: 2'
BLOOM SIZE: 1½"
HARDINESS: Zones 5–9
INTRODUCED: Origin uncertain; before 1800

A charming, small heritage rose that will fit easily into any garden. 'Petite de Hollande' reaches just over 2' in my garden and grows almost as wide. Its small, very double blooms are a glowing medium pink, perfectly in proportion with the size of the plant. This is the one nonrecurrent rose that I recommend for growing in containers. It makes such a beautiful, unified display in June that it can be more fully appreciated close up in an 18" pot. This can then be retired to an out-of-the-way location for the remainder of the growing season.

Healthy, tough, and winter hardy, 'Petite de Hollande' also makes a very effective short hedge. It is officially classified as a centifolia, but like the gallicas propagates itself via suckers. This habit can disqualify it from use at the front of a mixed border.

RIGHT PLACE *Short hedge; container planting*

PINK PROSPERITY

CLASS: Hybrid musk   REPEAT BLOOM: Regular
BLOOM COLOR: Pink   HEIGHT: 4'
BLOOM SIZE: 2"   HARDINESS: Zones 5–9
INTRODUCED: Bentall, England, 1931

One of the most rewarding of the hybrid musks, 'Pink Prosperity' blooms in great big clusters of small petal-packed florets. Buds that can be almost red in cool weather open to beautiful rose pink blooms, which fade pleasingly to white. It takes a long time for all of the blooms in a spray to open. The result is a dramatic spray of blooms in white and shades of pink.

This is one of the later hybrid musks from the Pemberton/Bentall breeding line, and it anticipates the improvements that would be later bred into the class by Louis Lens. It forms an attractive bush, growing about 4' tall and wide, and never appears sparse or gangly. Even though they are huge, the sprays appear on stems that are strong enough for cutting. I interplant 'Pink Prosperity' with once-blooming heritage roses. It fits in well, doesn't mind if its neighbors start to crowd, and provides strong doses of color throughout the summer. This rose is healthy and much more winter hardy than its parent, the regular 'Prosperity'.

RIGHT PLACE *Rose border*

BELOW 'Pink Prosperity' with the white shrub rose 'Dentelle de Bruges' (Lens, Belgium, 1991)

'PLAISANTERIE'

'PINK PROSPERITY'

PLAISANTERIE

CLASS: Hybrid musks   REPEAT BLOOM: Good
BLOOM COLOR: Multiple   HEIGHT: 5'
BLOOM SIZE: 2"   HARDINESS: Zones 5–9
INTRODUCED: Lens, Belgium, 1996

A magnificent color-changing rose, often displaying purple and buff yellow blooms within the same sprays on a graceful 5' plant. Pink, apricot, and even brownish tones can also be found on the five petals of this rose, which is as close as northern gardeners can get to the famous color-changing China rose 'Mutabilis'. ('Mutabilis' is not one of those marginally hardy roses that can be coaxed through a northern Ohio winter with a shovelful of compost or an earthen mound. It is so tender that its winter survival can be guaranteed only by growing it in a tub and bringing it indoors for the winter, just as we do with fig trees.)

'Plaisanterie' is the most colorful of Lens' many excellent hybrid musks. It looks its best when surrounded by its white, pale yellow, and soft pink relatives in the hybrid musk class.

RIGHT PLACE *Rose border, especially with white, pale yellow, or soft pink roses*

'PLEINE DE GRÀCE'

PLEINE DE GRÀCE

CLASS: Shrub
BLOOM COLOR: White
BLOOM SIZE: 2½"
INTRODUCED: Lens, Belgium, 1983

REPEAT BLOOM: None
HEIGHT: 8'
HARDINESS: Zones 4b–9

Pure white single-petaled flowers in bold clusters on a shrub that can reach monstrous proportions if left unpruned. Canes are armed with particularly fierce, curved prickles. These make this rose effective as an impenetrable barrier but also something you're going to want to situate well away from pathways and areas that need mowing. 'Pleine de Gràce' is large and impressive enough to be a specimen rose, with a graceful arching habit, but because of its dangerous thorns it is safer to incorporate it into a border. This shrub is covered in thousands of blooms each June, and an equal number of beautiful round orange hips each September. The hips make such a strong display that I would not plant this rose any place where orange would make me uncomfortable. 'Pleine de Gràce' is a unique and rewarding rose for large gardens. Sometimes sold in America as 'The Songbird Rose' (because of the nesting possibilities it offers).

RIGHT PLACE *Impenetrable barrier hedge*

PRINCESS ALICE

CLASS: Floribunda
BLOOM COLOR: Yellow
BLOOM SIZE: 3"
INTRODUCED: Harkness, England, 1985

REPEAT BLOOM: Good
HEIGHT: 4'
HARDINESS: Zones 6–9

Bright yellow florets in huge sprays, rising up like beacons of good cheer in the garden. This is one of four Harkness floribundas that share very similar growth habits. 'Anne Harkness' is caramel-apricot, 'By Appointment' buff, and the disappearing-from-commerce 'Harkness Marigold' orange. All bloom later than most other floribundas, at the end of June in northern Ohio, when the polyanthas and ramblers are also blooming for the first time. These floribundas have a lanky growth habit and can appear a bit sparse in foliage. They are ideal for instant bouquets. They fit into a mixed border more effectively than a floribunda bed, where both their habit and bloom time will put them out of synch with most everything else. If you do use these floribundas as bedding plants, plant them closer together than usual for floribundas. Cut back hard to ensure continued production of quality sprays.

RIGHT PLACE *Mixed border*

'PRINCESS ALICE'

QUEEN MOTHER

CLASS: Shrub
BLOOM COLOR: Pink
BLOOM SIZE: 2½"
INTRODUCED: Kordes, Germany, 1991

REPEAT BLOOM: Good
HEIGHT: 2'
HARDINESS: Zones 5–9

Even though numerous other roses named for members of Britain's royal family have done well commercially in the United States, this one has never tallied up the sales it deserves. It might be the best of them all. 'Queen Mother' is a compact shrublet, growing 2' × 2' and covered in pale pink flowers that are just barely double — as its sepals drop, a brief salute to hybrid tea form occurs before the petals reflex into a relaxed, open form highlighting attractive yellow stamens. The plant is the picture of health, with glossy deep green foliage. This rose looks great grown in a pot, and because it never grows out of bounds it can be tucked anywhere in the home landscape. It tolerates partial shade and has no problems over winter.

RIGHT PLACE *Container planting; tolerates shade*

RAINBOW KNOCK OUT

CLASS: Shrub
REPEAT BLOOM: Excellent
BLOOM COLOR: Pink/yellow
HEIGHT: 3' × 4' wide
BLOOM SIZE: 2½"
HARDINESS: Zones 4–9
INTRODUCED: Radler, USA, 2007

The most charming of the Knock Out roses, 'Rainbow Knock Out' blooms with the same reckless abandon as its brand-mates, always making new buds before old blooms have a chance to fade. The five-petaled blooms here are soft pink, enlivened by a strong yellow center. When you can spot it beneath the bloom explosion, the foliage is rich green and healthy. Like the other Knock Outs, 'Rainbow Knock Out' is very winter hardy. Expect mature plants to reach 3' tall by as much as 4' wide; my cluster of three plants looks lovely planted in front of purple coneflowers. Planted 18" apart, 'Rainbow Knock Out' would make a dense ribbon of color at the edge of a curving border of larger plants.

RIGHT PLACE *Mixed border, especially as edging plant; tolerates shade*

'RAINBOW KNOCK OUT'

RED RIBBONS

CLASS: Shrub
REPEAT BLOOM: Reliable
BLOOM COLOR: Red
HEIGHT: 2' × 3'
BLOOM SIZE: 2½"
HARDINESS: Zones 5–9
INTRODUCED: Kordes, Germany, 1990

A luminous shade of red that catches and amplifies sunlight, 'Red Ribbons' makes a strong impact from hundreds of feet away. One plant is dazzling; a group can be overpowering. Grows 2' tall by 3' wide and is never out of bloom. The blooms are larger than those found on most ground-cover roses. Healthy and winter hardy, it asks only that you keep old canes cut out of its center. An almost blinding effect can be achieved by planting this rose with purple salvia. Originally introduced as 'Mainaufeuer' in Germany.

RIGHT PLACE *Ground cover*

REGENSBERG

CLASS: Floribunda
REPEAT BLOOM: Good
BLOOM COLOR: Mauve-pink
HEIGHT: 2'
BLOOM SIZE: 3"
HARDINESS: Zones 5–9
INTRODUCED: McGredy, New Zealand, 1979

A charming member of the hand-painted family, featuring mauve-pink designs etched on a creamy background. The blooms are just barely double, and they show off the hand-painted effect handsomely when fully open. The compact plant is quite healthy and winter hardy.

Too short to fit into a floribunda bedding scheme, it is ideally used as an accent plant in any sunny spot where a 2' mass of color is desired. It also makes a superior tree rose when budded on an 18" or 24" stem. (See chapter 8.)

RIGHT PLACE *Garden accent; tree rose; container planting*

RHAPSODY IN BLUE

CLASS: Shrub
HEIGHT: 5' (much taller in warm climates)
BLOOM COLOR: Purple
BLOOM SIZE: 3½"
HARDINESS: Zones 6–9
REPEAT BLOOM: Good
INTRODUCED: Cowlishaw, England, 2003

Not really blue, but a breakthrough in vigor for a purplish rose. The semi-double blooms appear in big sprays on a plant that may reach climber proportions

'RHAPSODY IN BLUE'

considered double; they open quickly and you will most often enjoy them as open blooms. Some will appear in vast sprays, others in more modest clusters, and some as individual blooms.

RIGHT PLACE *Bedding; mixed border; landscape or garden accent*

A WORTHY AWARD

I'm skeptical of most European rose awards because of their limited scope and often-curious judging practices. (Winners are sometimes chosen by politicians, or schoolchildren, or the nurseries themselves.) But I have come to trust the German ADR (Anerkannte Deutsche Rose) award as an excellent predictor of good health and winter hardiness. **'Romanze'** is a recipient of this award that has proved its worthiness with more than 20 years of healthy growth.

---

in mild climates. 'Rhapsody in Blue' settles in at a satisfied 5' for me, without growing very wide. New blooms are bright purple and may appear almost blue at dawn and dusk. They get darker as they age, and they may eventually reach an unattractive combination of smoky purple and wilted brown. This is your signal to cut off the spray, making sure to cut low enough to keep the plant within bounds.

I grow this dynamic rose in the gravelly soil over the septic leach field. The rose doesn't mind, and it associates beautifully with the Russell lupines that are also happy there.

RIGHT PLACE *Wherever a startling color is desired*

ROMANZE

CLASS: Shrub
BLOOM COLOR: Pink
BLOOM SIZE: 4"
INTRODUCED: Tantau, Germany, 1985
REPEAT BLOOM: Good
HEIGHT: 4½'
HARDINESS: Zones 5–9

A true multipurpose rose, 'Romanze' is effective as a taller bedding rose, in a mixed border, or even on its own as a specimen plant in a spot where a larger grower would be out of place. Growing 4½' tall and wide, 'Romanze' is a picture of good health. Its deep, slightly dusky pink blooms have just enough wide petals to be

ROSA ARKANSANA

CLASS: Species
BLOOM COLOR: Pink
BLOOM SIZE: 2"
HARDINESS: Zones 4–9
ORIGIN: Central North America
REPEAT BLOOM: One very long flush
HEIGHT: 2'

A short, tough plant that makes itself at home almost anywhere: sun or three-quarters shade, wet soil or dry, a difficult site or the loam of a well-made perennial bed. It will sucker freely if you let it, but it can be easily kept to a spread of 2' to 3' with twice-annual root pruning, as described on page 246. Simply use a perennial

R. ARKANSANA 'PEPPERMINT'

spade to renew a boundary for *Rosa arkansana*, or to slice off a new one. This is a cheerful, carefree rose, and once gardeners see it at its best, most will want to enjoy more of it.

The single-petaled, candy pink blooms appear over a long period, usually six weeks in my garden. So even though it does not repeat bloom, it is in bloom for half of the summer. I am particularly fond of the selection called 'Peppermint' (Craig, USA, c. 1984), which features gently striped flowers. In either case, the hips are small and round, ripening with a blush of red, just like a summer apple.

RIGHT PLACE *Mixed border; tolerates three-quarters shade*

ROSA GLAUCA (photo, page 18)

CLASS: Species	REPEAT BLOOM: None
BLOOM COLOR: Pink	HEIGHT: 2' or more
BLOOM SIZE: 1"	HARDINESS: Zones 5–9
ORIGIN: Central Europe	

Also called *Rosa rubrifolia,* and sometimes the Red-leaf Rose, this species rose does have red leaves when young, with stems that are almost purple. Mature foliage is the gray of autumn clouds. This rose produces crucial foliage for serious flower arrangers, and it can also be quite effective wherever gray foliage is desired in the garden. Plants such as *R. glauca* provide important relief to a summer garden that can sometimes appear as a sea of green.

R. glauca is generally unhappy during short, wet summers and carefree during long, dry ones. It can tolerate a fair amount of shade and, unlike many wild roses, does not sucker aggressively. After many years my plant is only 2' tall × 3' wide, and I wonder if it would be bigger if we didn't cut so many stems for use in arrangements.

The small, light pink blooms open in the morning and attract bees for a few hours before afternoon breezes carry the petals away. While the individual flowers are insubstantial, there are a lot of them and they continue to appear over a long period. Their clusters are more attractive (and persistent) when they grow into round, shiny mahogany-red hips.

Some adventurous hybridizers have employed *R. glauca* in their breeding programs, with mixed results. 'Carmenetta' (Preston, 1923) is not very different from the species. It is reported to be more winter hardy, but this must be a difference that becomes apparent in Zone 4, because I do not see it in my own garden. The most interesting hybrid I have grown is the Canadian 'Louis Riel' (Zubrowski, 1996), which carries *R. glauca*'s distinctive gray foliage into a more upright plant with single-petaled white blooms that recur throughout the summer.

R. glauca may grow less true to type than most species, since there can be a lot of variation in foliage and bloom color from plant to plant.

RIGHT PLACE *Tolerates shade*

'ROSA MUNDI'

ROSA MUNDI

CLASS: Gallica	REPEAT BLOOM: None
BLOOM COLOR: White striped with red	HEIGHT: 4'
	HARDINESS: Zones 5–8
BLOOM COLOR: 3"	
INTRODUCED: ex-Europe, <1581	

'Rosa Mundi' (*Rosa gallica versicolor*) has been in cultivation for over 400 years. It may not have been the first striped rose, but it was the first one to gain a name and fame. Although its origin is obscure, its distribution has been massive, giving 'Rosa Mundi' an uninterrupted place over centuries of rose garden history. Its bold cerise-red stripes and creamy white intervals appeared as a mutation of *R. gallica officinalis* (the Apothecary's Rose), and occasionally one or more canes will revert to the original form. This provides added interest and contrast, and it can be managed with judicious pruning.

Growing 4' tall and wide, 'Rosa Mundi' makes a spectacular low hedge. It is also at home in the herb garden, the mixed border, and any place where a strong color impact is desired. No, it does not offer repeat bloom.

But over its two weeks of annual bloom 'Rosa Mundi' will produce more flowers than any repeat-blooming rose does in a year.

Often incorrectly italicized, 'Rosa Mundi' is believed to have gotten its name from "The Fair Rosamund" (Jane Clifford), mistress of England's twelfth-century King Henry II, even though the rose itself is not that old.

RIGHT PLACE *Low hedge; herb garden; mixed border*

ROSA PENDULINA

CLASS: Species

BLOOM COLOR: Red

BLOOM SIZE: 2"

ORIGIN: Alpine Europe

REPEAT BLOOM: None

HEIGHT: 4'

HARDINESS: Zones 4–8

One of the great simple beauties of the rose kingdom, *Rosa pendulina* welcomes each spring with a striking display of single-petaled, light red blooms. Its thornless stems are red too when they are young, and so are its hips, which last well into winter. This species rose suffers no dieback at all in northern Ohio, and it maintains a tidy 4' × 4' habit. I grow this rose in the shade of maple trees, and after it blooms it becomes obscured by hostas. In the fall, the hostas die back to reveal the glorious hips of *R. pendulina*.

RIGHT PLACE *Tolerates shade*

ROSA SERICEA PTERACANTHA

CLASS: Species

BLOOM COLOR: White

BLOOM SIZE: 2"

ORIGIN: Himalayas

REPEAT BLOOM: None

HEIGHT: 5'

HARDINESS: Zones 5b–9

Here are the most astonishing prickles in rosedom, often 1½" long, bright red, and translucent. Plant this

rose where its thorns can catch the morning or afternoon sun, or cut its stems to enjoy them on a windowsill. Like the species *Rosa sericea,* the flowers of *R. sericea pteracantha* have but four petals. Apart from this novelty they are not very interesting: white, insubstantial, and fleeting.

The thorns become less red and impressive as they age, so for the most effective display the plant must be continually cut back to encourage new stems and new thorns. I no longer worry about seeing any blooms on *R. sericea pteracantha,* so I cut it back severely each spring. This also helps to keep the plant in bounds, and with such pruning it can be a respectable member of a perennial border. A rich soil or high nitrogen fertilizer will encourage abundant new growth and plenty of spectacularly thorny stems to harvest for flower arrangements.

RIGHT PLACE *Mixed border*

ROSALINA

CLASS: Hybrid rugosa

BLOOM COLOR: Pink

BLOOM SIZE: 2½"

INTRODUCED: Kordes, Germany, 1992

REPEAT BLOOM: Reliable

HEIGHT: 3'

HARDINESS: Zones 4–9

A refined hybrid rugosa, growing into a 3' drift of healthy growth topped with single-petaled, deep pink blooms, smaller than any of the species rugosas. Repeat bloom is excellent throughout the summer. This plant pairs beautifully in our garden with 'Goldmound' spirea, which reaches exactly the same size.

RIGHT PLACE *Mixed shrub border*

RUGOSA QUIRKS

Rugosas have a reputation for trouble-free growth, earned on the basis of their winter hardiness, disease resistance, and eagerness to grow vigorously without supplemental feedings. However, they do have their quirks. Most resent being sprayed with chemical fungicides and can develop discolored foliage as a result. Few rugosas experience disease severe enough to even raise the thought of fungicides, but if you've planted them among roses that are disease prone, it can be difficult to remember to skip over the rugosas when you're spraying the others.

A second anomaly is that entire canes of rugosa growth can suddenly turn brown and die. I believe that this is connected with inconsistent watering, as it most often happens during a drought or after a gully-washer.

ROSALITA

CLASS: Hybrid musk
BLOOM COLOR: White
BLOOM SIZE: 1½"
HARDINESS: Zones 5–9
INTRODUCED: Lens, Belgium, 1997

REPEAT BLOOM: Reliable if deadheaded
HEIGHT: 3' × 6'

Mighty sprays of lovely single-petaled white blooms, each with a stunning display of golden stamens, decorate this versatile rose. A hybrid musk that grows wider than tall, 'Rosalita' can spread 6' while growing only 3' tall. While tough enough to thrive in a wild area, it deserves a place where it can be enjoyed every day. Its low but wide habit is especially useful in a bed that curves or forms a semicircle. The canes have relatively few thorns and are no problem to work around, if you are growing 'Rosalita' in a mixed border. Its 1" blooms are very much like miniaturized versions of 'Sally Holmes' (see page 113). In climates where that rose grows tall, a fascinating display results when 'Rosalita' is planted at its base.

Deadheading speeds repeat bloom, but it is worth leaving at least a few sprays of spent blooms to enjoy the autumn hips, which ripen to an unusual coral orange color. This is one of the few roses bred from the species *Rosa helenae*.

RIGHT PLACE *Naturalistic plantings; curved or circular beds; mixed border*

ROSE DE RESCHT

CLASS: Portland
BLOOM COLOR: Purple-red
BLOOM SIZE: 3"
INTRODUCED: Origin uncertain, France, 1840s?

REPEAT BLOOM: Reliable
HEIGHT: 2½'
HARDINESS: Zones 5–9

This Portland rose offers the most reliable repeat bloom of any winter-hardy old garden rose. Its purple-red

'ROSE DE RESCHT'

blooms are not large and may not be noticed at all in the pandemonium of the spring rose bloom explosion. But in the quiet of autumn 'Rose de Rescht' becomes a star.

The plant is quite compact, reaching only 2½' in my garden. It can grow inward rather than up or out, so it benefits from regular thinning of unproductive growth, which can otherwise become a haven for spider mites. Taking cut flowers with as long of a stem as possible can also help the plant stay on the right track, as will severe spring pruning in gardens south of Zone 6.

The extremely fragrant 'Rose de Rescht' is a popular feature in herb gardens, and its petals are a useful ingredient in potpourri.

RIGHT PLACE *Herb gardens*

RUSH

CLASS: Hybrid musk
BLOOM COLOR: White/pink
BLOOM SIZE: 2"
INTRODUCED: Lens, Belgium, 1983

REPEAT BLOOM: Heavy
HEIGHT: 3½'
HARDINESS: Zones 5–9

One of Louis Lens' best hybrid musks, 'Rush' combines a compact 3½' habit with nearly constant bloom. The small, single-petaled flowers are white with a variable pink border, appearing in large but well-shaped clusters. This is the rare hybrid musk that fits in perfectly well in a floribunda bed, where it will make most floribundas look stingy with their bloom. It is extremely effective near the center of a mixed border, where it can be depended on for profuse bloom right up until frost. 'Rush' was bred from 'Ballerina' but is much more winter hardy.

'Rush' was voted the "Rose of the Century" in Lyon, France, in 1983. This award would be more impressive if Lyon did not choose a Rose of the Century every year.

RIGHT PLACE *Floribunda bed; center of mixed border*

ST JOHN'S ROSE

CLASS: Species hybrid
BLOOM COLOR: Pink
BLOOM SIZE: 2½"
INTRODUCED: Origin uncertain

REPEAT BLOOM: None
HEIGHT: 3'
HARDINESS: Zones 5–9

This is the famous Holy Rose of Abyssinia, also known as *Rosa richardii* and *R. sancta*. It has been cultivated by the Coptic Christians in Ethiopia for a long time; in the 1940s, C. C. Hurst postulated that it was a hybrid of *R. gallica* that had made its way to Africa from the Middle East in ancient times. A garland of roses discovered in an Egyptian tomb and believed to date from about 300 A.D. has been associated with this rose. Some recent scholars are skeptical about all of this. They distrust Hurst (a geneticist who married his cousin), and they ask why this rose does not appear in European records until about 1890. Of course, many people around the world have enjoyed roses without keeping records about them — or sharing their records with Europeans.

This is a simple rose, blooming once each year with fragile, crinkly five-petaled blooms of light pink that can appear to be washed with a pale mauve cast. These typically appear in sprays that look lovely on the bush, but sparse when cut. In the garden, 'St John's Rose' is most useful when thought of as a reined-in species rose. It provides all of the simple beauty of a wild rose, while maintaining an even, relatively low height (it makes a 3' mound in my garden). And it won't sucker. Its foliage is unremarkable and can easily disappear into a border after its one annual bloom is complete.

RIGHT PLACE *Mixed border*

'SALET'

SALET

CLASS: Moss	REPEAT BLOOM: Abundant
BLOOM COLOR: Pink	HEIGHT: 5'
BLOOM COLOR: 3"	HARDINESS: Zones 5–9
INTRODUCED: Lacharme, France, 1854	

The most reliable of all of the moss roses, 'Salet' offers as abundant a repeat bloom as any old garden rose.

The blooms are light pink, luminous from a distance and individually beautiful. The blooms often appear in small clusters that can be cut and enjoyed indoors. Its powerful fragrance is what perfumers might call "pure rose."

'Salet' makes a nice bushy plant, to 5' for me, avoiding the lanky growth of many mosses. It is also relatively healthy and not prone to the debilitating powdery mildew that besets this family. 'Salet' should be planted where its buds can be enjoyed within easy reach, such as along a walkway, and where hands can easily discover its moss.

If you want to sample other moss roses, consider the silvery pink 'Gloire des Mousseux', which has the largest blooms of any moss rose. For the most spectacular display of moss, grow the once-blooming, deep pink 'Crested Moss'. Another choice is the intriguing 'Goethe', which displays sprays of tiny, single-petaled, dark pink blooms on a 6' plant, bristly moss extending all up and down its stems.

RIGHT PLACE *Along a path or walkway*

MANLY MILDEW

The first moss rose I ever grew was 'Deuil de Paul Fontaine', which I found in the famous catalog of Roses of Yesterday & Today, Watsonville, California. They described it as "A man's Moss rose. Nothing comparable in rosedom!" Well, after growing it for just a short time I discovered that the only thing incomparable about it was the powdery mildew. In its first year, its canes and leaves were all completely coated with white fungal growth. This made a startling contrast with the deep crimson-purple blooms, which were themselves deformed because of the mildew. But I don't recommend growing 'Deuil de Paul Fontaine' for the variegated effects created by its disease problems.

The next year I bought an expensive fungicide, which did a reasonable job of bringing the mildew under control. But it really wasn't worth the expense or effort, and after two years I abandoned 'Deuil de Paul Fontaine' and tried some other moss roses. Most of these were pink and thus perhaps more suited to womenfolk, in the logic of catalog writers.

'SALLY HOLMES'

SALLY HOLMES

CLASS: Hybrid musk	REPEAT BLOOM: Steady
BLOOM COLOR: White	HEIGHT: 3–10' depending on
BLOOM SIZE: 3½"	climate
HARDINESS: Zones 5–9	
INTRODUCED: Holmes, England, 1978	

A spectacular rose, with billowing sprays of single-petaled white blooms, larger in their individual dimensions than other hybrid musks. A spray of 'Sally Holmes' blooms can easily be as large as a basketball. Its stems are pliant, with slightly elongated, dark green foliage. Under favorable conditions the overall effect can be like that of a hydrangea in the garden, if you can imagine a hydrangea that grows much taller than wide.

More than most roses, the growth of 'Sally Holmes' will be guided by your microclimate. I grow one plant in front of my porch, where the warmth from the house helps to bring it through the winter. In a good year, 'Sally Holmes' reaches 6' or 7' and sprawls charmingly onto the porch. I grow a second plant in a much more unprotected perennial bed, where it rarely achieves more than the 3' height typical of a floribunda, even though its bloom is profuse. In Australia and California 'Sally Holmes' is treated as a climber and can reach great heights. The more winter you have, the less of 'Sally Holmes' you will enjoy.

Once a collector's item, 'Sally Holmes' is now available almost anywhere roses are sold. Beware: many plants coming onto the market are infected with mosaic virus. Avoid this by purchasing 'Sally Holmes' from a reputable rose nursery that will guarantee their stock to be virus free.

RIGHT PLACE *Mixed border; climber in warm climates*

ROBERT HOLMES

Most rose hybridizers name and introduce too many of their creations. There are commercial pressures to do so and, like everyone else, rose breeders have egos. An amateur hybridizer who kept his ego under control, Robert Holmes named only a few roses. They are all individual, excellent contributions to the world of roses. Apart from the orange-flowered shrub 'Fred Loads', they are all white. **'Sally Holmes'** is the only one that is easy to find. If you ever come across 'Fairy Snow' or 'Surf Rider', bring them home too.

SCABROSA

CLASS: Hybrid rugosa	REPEAT BLOOM: Reliable
BLOOM COLOR: Magenta	HEIGHT: 4'
BLOOM SIZE: 3½"	HARDINESS: Zones 4–9
INTRODUCED: Harkness, England, 1950	

This is an ugly name for a beautiful rose, which is essentially a refined version of the species *Rosa rugosa*. It was introduced by the Harkness nursery at a time before they were breeding roses, and it's uncertain where it came from (something that sprang up at the nursery? something sent in by a customer?) or why it was called 'Scabrosa'. *Scabrosa* is Latin, more or less, for "rough rose," but it may have been only a misread label.

In any case, this is an easy-to-grow and rewarding rose, full of rugosa good health and featuring large single-petaled magenta blooms. The flowers have some of the same crinkliness found in rugosa foliage. These appear in profusion at the beginning of the rose season, and with dependable regularity throughout the summer. There is no reason to deadhead, because the

'SCABROSA'

113

development of large, tomato-shaped hips does not deter the production of new buds. The blooms do not last well when cut, but the hips do.

This rugged rose will thrive in a neglected area of a landscape, and it can also be a carefree ornament among larger perennials. It grows 4' tall and wide for me, with occasional suckers.

RIGHT PLACE *Naturalistic areas; mixed border*

'SCEPTER'D ISLE'

SCEPTER'D ISLE

CLASS: Shrub   REPEAT BLOOM: Reliable
BLOOM COLOR: Pink   HEIGHT: 6'
BLOOM SIZE: 3½"   HARDINESS: Zones 5–9
INTRODUCED: Austin, England, 1996

Less packed with petals than many David Austin introductions, 'Scepter'd Isle' has about 45 petals that expand quickly into a cup shape, which opens just far enough to reveal pretty golden stamens within. The blooms are a luminous clear pink, perfectly set against the dark green foliage and glowing from across the garden. There is a strong fragrance. 'Scepter'd Isle' grows

postlike to 6' in my garden and is very seldom out of bloom. If you have a path leading up to a climbing rose, 'Scepter'd Isle' is the perfect rose to plant right before you get there.

RIGHT PLACE *Rose border; dooryard*

SCHOENER'S NUTKANA

CLASS: Species hybrid   REPEAT BLOOM: None
BLOOM COLOR: Pink   HEIGHT: 3'
BLOOM SIZE: 3"   HARDINESS: Zones 4–8
INTRODUCED: Schoener, USA, 1930

A cross between *Rosa nutkana* and a hybrid perpetual, this is the most enduring creation of Georg Schoener, a German immigrant priest who aimed to incorporate native American species into the gene pool of modern roses. One could create an interesting garden using only roses bred by the clergy, and 'Schoener's Nutkana' is one of the most individual. Its intensely pink, single-petaled blooms open to reveal a disc of gigantic yellow stamens, and the petals continue opening until they are practically tucked in behind the disc. Although it is healthy, the foliage is not particularly attractive. The stems are nearly thornless, so this is an easy rose to work around, and it will be an asset in any area where its unusual blooms can be appreciated. It grows 3' tall × 4' wide in my garden. Because it offers neither repeat bloom nor impressive hips, it is best sited in an area where other plants, such as Japanese maples, will provide autumn interest.

RIGHT PLACE *Mixed border*

SEBASTIAN KNEIPP

CLASS: Hybrid tea   REPEAT BLOOM: Good
BLOOM COLOR: White   HEIGHT: 6'
BLOOM SIZE: 4"   HARDINESS: Zones 5–9
INTRODUCED: Kordes, Germany, 1997

A strong plant with sprays of large 100-petaled creamy white blooms, arranged with the classic symmetry of a quartered heritage rose and filled with a rich, fruity fragrance. Its long flower stems are perfect for cutting. This is a tough, disease-resistant plant that will perform well under difficult conditions. It does not require the tender loving care demanded by most hybrid teas. Its repeat bloom is unusually swift for a rose with so many petals, and it requires no winter protection in Zone 5.

RIGHT PLACE *Rose border; cutting garden*

NOT QUITE HYBRID TEAS

The primacy of the hybrid tea means that many roses that aren't really hybrid teas are called hybrid teas by their introducers, who are interested in selling as many roses as possible. Although sold as a hybrid tea, **'Sebastian Kneipp'** is not really one, just as 'Heirloom', a petal-packed purple rose introduced by Jackson & Perkins in 1972, is not a hybrid tea even though it has always been sold as one. The breeder Rev. Joseph Pemberton wanted to call all of his creations hybrid teas too. Fortunately, a rose society official talked him out of this, and that is why they are known as hybrid musks.

'SIMPLICITY'

SIMPLICITY

CLASS: Shrub
REPEAT BLOOM: Reliable
BLOOM COLOR: Pink
HEIGHT: 4'
BLOOM SIZE: 3"
HARDINESS: Zones 5–9
INTRODUCED: Warriner, USA, 1978

The first in the Jackson & Perkins line of landscaping roses. Since other colors have been released, 'Simplicity' is now sometimes known as 'Pink Simplicity'. This is a pretty rose that is often misused. Jackson & Perkins unfortunately advertised it as a "living hedge," and so thousands of Americans have planted 'Simplicity' along their driveways. This rarely works. In cold-winter areas, 'Simplicity' suffers too much dieback to make an effective hedge. It spends half of the summer getting back to where it was the autumn before. Elaborate methods of winter protection are usually eyesores, and so are not suited to the prime position in the landscape often given to 'Simplicity'. If you're a Zone 5 gardener enduring 'Simplicity' in this manner, don't hesitate to move your plants to the perennial garden. They will be much happier, and so will you.

Beyond this, 'Simplicity' is usually planted too far apart. If your lawn mower fits between the individual plants that compose your hedge, it's not really a hedge. In Zone 5, if I were to plant 'Simplicity' as a hedge, I would space the plants just 12" apart.

Just because it doesn't make a good hedge in northern gardens doesn't mean 'Simplicity' isn't a good rose. Its semi-double pink blooms are not without charm, and it is very quick at repeat bloom. It is healthier than most roses introduced in the 1970s. Growing to no more than 4' tall, it is most effectively used in a mixed border, or as an anchor in a bed of tall perennials. (For a living hedge, look to the hybrid rugosas.)

RIGHT PLACE *Mixed border; anchor plant in a bed of tall perennials*

'SNOWBELT'

SNOWBELT

CLASS: Polyantha
REPEAT BLOOM: Reliable
BLOOM COLOR: White
HEIGHT: 2½'
BLOOM SIZE: 1"
HARDINESS: Zones 4–9
INTRODUCED: Jerabek, USA, 1997

More blooms than you'd think possible on one little rose. So many blooms cover 'Snowbelt' that it is often difficult to find a stem long enough for cutting bouquets. 'Snowbelt' makes a tidy 2½' polyantha in our garden, smothered in semi-double white blooms for weeks each June. Repeat bloom is also strong, and while old blooms don't need to be removed to encourage new ones, the plant will look much tidier if you make this effort. This is a perfect rose for foundation plantings. Or if you can imagine a place in your yard where you'd like to have a white azalea blooming all summer long, that is where you should plant 'Snowbelt'.

In Ohio, the snowbelt is the northeast area of the state where winter snowfall is increased by weather systems traveling over the unfrozen waters of Lake Erie. Paul Jerabek bred and evaluated his roses in the heart of this snowbelt, and all of his creations can be counted on for winter hardiness.

RIGHT PLACE *Foundation plantings*

SOMMERMORGEN

CLASS: Shrub	REPEAT BLOOM: Good
BLOOM COLOR: Pink	HEIGHT: 2' × 4' wide
BLOOM SIZE: 2½"	HARDINESS: Zones 5–9
INTRODUCED: Kordes, Germany, 1991	

Although nurseries like to promote their "ground-cover" roses, no rose is a true ground-cover plant that will colonize a barren hillside or embankment, smothering any weed that tries to grow up beneath it. To enjoy groundcover roses in a neglected area of the landscape you may need to employ landscaping fabric, or be prepared to go weeding in between them. Weeding around 'Sommermorgen' is relatively easily, since it has few prickles. Its growth is healthy and vigorous, to about 4' wide while growing only 2' tall. Its blooms are semi-double, a delicate but effective shade of pink. Often sold as 'Baby Blanket' in the United States.

RIGHT PLACE *Ground cover*

SONIA RYKIEL

CLASS: Shrub	REPEAT BLOOM: Good
BLOOM COLOR: Pink	HEIGHT: 3'
BLOOM SIZE: 6"	HARDINESS: Zones 5b–9
INTRODUCED: Guillot-Massad, France, 1993	

'Sonia Rykiel' is one of the most fragrant roses I grow, and it is crammed with petals in the style of a Bourbon. Its color is coral pink, a modern shade that would have been revolutionary a century ago. Its foliage is modern-

'SONIA RYKIEL'

looking too and it will attract some black spot when that disease is a problem. It has proven reliably winter hardy in my garden, even though I am growing it on *Rosa soulieana,* a less-than-hardy climbing rose that is sometimes used as a rootstock in France.

The blooms of 'Sonia Rykiel' can be huge, and its stems are rarely strong enough to hold them upright. This lolling effect can be quite effective when displayed in a half-barrel or other elevated large container. It

GÉNÉROSA ROSES

The cover of the Guillot rose catalog proclaims, "Créateur de Roses Anciennes & Générosa." Not too many nurseries can make that kind of claim. Their "ancient" roses include the first hybrid tea and the first polyantha, developed in the nineteenth century.

"Générosa" is their own name for new-old roses: the Guillot breeders were not the first to revisit the heritage rose in order to give it up-to-date colors and repeat bloom, but there are several fascinating examples in this series including **'Sonia Rykiel'** and 'Martine Guillot' (see page 144).

Générosas are meant to compete with David Austin's English Roses, and are based on the same idea (healthy, repeat-blooming roses combining modern colors with the full-petaled form and memorable fragrance of heritage roses). So far, though, they are much more of a mixed bag. Too many are weaklings, and the yellow and apricot ones are not reliably winter hardy in Ohio. In most cases, the fragrance is superb, and there is no reason not to believe that the best of the Générosas are yet to come.

The Générosa roses have had a hard time finding a market in the United States. First, two nurseries squabbled over who had rights to introduce them. Then the nursery that won that argument went bankrupt. Today, several Générosas are available from a few discerning specialist nurseries.

can also be useful in the front row of a border. 'Sonia Rykiel' should not be sited in the middle of a perennial bed where its blooms can disappear into its neighbors' foliage.

RIGHT PLACE *Large container planting; front of mixed border*

'SOPHY'S ROSE'

SOPHY'S ROSE

CLASS: Shrub
BLOOM COLOR: Red
BLOOM SIZE: 2½"
INTRODUCED: Austin, England, 1997
REPEAT BLOOM: Reliable
HEIGHT: 2½'
HARDINESS: Zones 5–9

A delightful yet tough little rose, very much like a winter hardy version of a China rose. 'Sophy's Rose' has about 80 narrow petals of luminous light red. It's very healthy and winter hardy, and repeats its bloom as quickly as any modern rose. Growing to a rounded 2½' it disappoints only in its weak fragrance.

The beauty of this little rose would be lost in a mixed border. It is superb for growing in pots, looks at home in the herb garden, and would also make an interesting counterpoint in a bed of floribundas.

RIGHT PLACE *Container planting; herb garden; accent in bed of floribundas*

SOUVENIR DU DOCTEUR JAMAIN

CLASS: Hybrid perpetual
BLOOM COLOR: Red
BLOOM SIZE: 3½"
INTRODUCED: Lacharme, France, 1865
REPEAT BLOOM: Good
HEIGHT: 7'
HARDINESS: Zones 5–9

Most of the roses that are happy in partial shade closely resemble a species rose: blooms that are white or light pink, with few petals per blossom. They typically grow wider than tall and display their blooms in big sprays. This one is completely different: it's a tall hybrid perpetual, with full-petaled blooms of a crimson as close to black as a rose can get, brought to life by bright yellow stamens.

'Souvenir du Docteur Jamain' is a lanky grower even in full sun. In the partial shade of a house or other building it will get even lankier, but it's not a noticeable difference. However, its blooms are much happier when protected from total sun. They take longer to open, last longer, and present a more fully satisfying unburnt color. These blooms are as strongly fragrant as they look.

RIGHT PLACE *Tolerates partial shade*

SPIRIT OF FREEDOM

CLASS: Shrub
BLOOM COLOR: Pink
BLOOM SIZE: 5"
INTRODUCED: Austin, England, 2003
REPEAT BLOOM: Reliable
HEIGHT: 3½'
HARDINESS: Zones 5–9

Each blossom on 'Spirit of Freedom' has about 200 petals, which may approach the theoretical maximum

'SPIRIT OF FREEDOM'

possible for flowers that actually open. Yet it opens very well, in all but the wettest weather, and provides a strong display of a soft color — a pure, soft pink washed delicately in mauve. Its fragrance is rich, its repeat bloom excellent, and its large, cupped blooms will lend weight to a mixed planting. 'Spirit of Freedom' makes healthy, bushy growth to 3½' for me.

RIGHT PLACE *Mixed border*

'STANWELL PERPETUAL'

ENGLISH ROSES: GOOD, BETTER, BEST

There are over 150 of David Austin's English Roses from which to choose. Depending on what you are seeking, you can go wrong. Many of the early ones (those named after the characters in *The Canterbury Tales* for example) are weaklings that won't stand up for themselves in a mixed border. I still admire the ethereal beauty of the blooms of 'Canterbury' itself, but a vision of it just barely peeking over the top of its name tag isn't a real strong recommendation. When vigor arrived at the David Austin nursery in the 1980s, repeat bloom suffered. Roses such as 'Leander' grew like weeds but rarely bloomed after June. Today everything has come together for the new roses with the charm of the old, and you should expect any new Austin introduction to be vigorous, disease resistant, and in bloom each month of summer. Some still face winter hardiness challenges: the recent introductions 'Harlow Carr' and 'Spirit of Picardy' did not successfully overwinter for me. If you're a collector you may want them all; otherwise, choice is a matter of personal preference or even how much you like a name. Because I live and garden in Freedom Township, Ohio, I like the name **'Spirit of Freedom'** a lot. And the rose has not let me down.

This is one of the oldest repeat-blooming roses suitable for the northern garden, and one of the best roses ever bred by a bee and perhaps planted by a bird. It popped up in the London garden of a Mr. Lee, on the site of what is now Heathrow Airport, almost certainly a seedling from a spinosissima pollinated by an early Portland rose.

RIGHT PLACE *Naturalistic planting; cut flowers*

'TEASING GEORGIA'

STANWELL PERPETUAL

CLASS: Hybrid spinosissima   REPEAT BLOOM: Good
BLOOM COLOR: Blush   HEIGHT: 4'
BLOOM SIZE: 3"   HARDINESS: Zones 4b–8
INTRODUCED: Lee, England, 1838

A beautiful rose, buff pink fading to white and full of fragrant petals. These arrive on a rough 'n' ready plant that is much tougher than its dainty leaves might suggest. It has the appearance of a restless rose, always sending out strong growth away from its center. This is not a plant for a highly manicured part of the garden, but it excels where it faces a little competition, from bossy yarrow, for example. Grows 4' tall and wide in my garden, where I keep it close to the house because 'Stanwell Perpetual' makes a great cut flower.

TEASING GEORGIA

CLASS: Shrub   REPEAT BLOOM: Good
BLOOM COLOR: Yellow   HEIGHT: 4'
BLOOM SIZE: 4½"   HARDINESS: Zones 5b–9
INTRODUCED: Austin, England, 1998

The most refined of David Austin's golden roses, 'Teasing Georgia' displays its large blooms in sturdy sprays. Each bloom is large in itself; because they arrive in groups the overall effect is multiplied. Each cup-shaped, 100-petaled bloom is golden yellow in its center, contrasting beautifully with pale yellow outer petals. This rose can be an invaluable part of a mixed border, providing a strong color impact on a healthy, winter-hardy plant.

The curious name is thanks to the German television personality Ulrich Meyer. He arranged to have this rose named for his wife, the journalist Georgia Tornow.

RIGHT PLACE *Mixed border*

THE COUNTRYMAN

CLASS: Shrub	REPEAT BLOOM: Sporadic
BLOOM COLOR: Pink	HEIGHT: 4 ½'
BLOOM SIZE: 4"	HARDINESS: Zones 4–9
INTRODUCED: Austin, England, 1987	

A completely trouble-free rose from David Austin, 'The Countryman' makes an excellent 4½' hedge in my garden. It will also add structure to the border and is at home when grouped with other winter-hardy shrubs such as deutzia and weigela. Its deep pink, ruffly blooms appear profusely in June and in patches after that. They have a strong rose fragrance that carries well. This is the most winter-hardy Austin introduction that I have grown, sometimes suffering no winter dieback at all. It is also commendably healthy.

'The Countryman' is often compared to the Portland roses, and some of its blooms do disappear beneath its foliage in the Portland manner. But let's be completely honest: most Portlands bloom more. The value of this rose is in its ruggedness.

RIGHT PLACE *Hedge; mixed border; shrub border*

THE FAIRY

CLASS: Polyantha	REPEAT BLOOM: Continuous
BLOOM COLOR: Pink	HEIGHT: 3'
BLOOM SIZE: 1½"	HARDINESS: Zones 4b–9
INTRODUCED: Bentall, England, 1932	

Seventy-five years after its introduction, this is the world's most popular rose in terms of plants sold each year. 'The Fairy' is a durable polyantha with big sprays of soft pink flowers stretching all up and down its pliable but thorny canes. Its foliage is shiny and healthy, in scale with the small size of its flowers. 'The Fairy' is

'THE FAIRY'

unbothered by a Zone 5 winter. 'The Fairy' turned out to be the perfect rose for concealing our wellhead, as a part of a circular bed featuring ornamental grasses. It blooms later than most other roses, and it's not really relevant to speak about repeat bloom because there is no break to divide initial from repeat. Once 'The Fairy' starts, it does not stop until frost.

There are several clones of 'The Fairy' in commerce. The best makes a 3' hump of color, with canes arching gently in all directions. Inferior versions feature rampant growth and sprawl at the expense of bloom. Although you can always find discount plants, it is wise to purchase 'The Fairy' from a reputable specialist rose nursery. It is spectacular as a gently weeping tree rose.

RIGHT PLACE *Mixed border; landscape accent; tree rose*

ANN BENTALL

Even though she bred two of the five most widely grown roses in the world today ('The Fairy' and the pink-and-white hybrid musk 'Ballerina'), Ann Bentall has never been admitted into the pantheon of "Great Hybridizers." To some extent, this is sexism. It may also be classism: Bentall was an employee of Rev. Joseph Pemberton, and there is often an assumption that she was merely introducing the leftover seedlings after his death. She certainly continued Pemberton's work, just as many of the universally recognized Great Hybridizers continued the work of their father, their grandfather, or their corporation. For a full account of Ann Bentall's contribution to the rose world, read Hazel LeRougetel's *A Heritage of Roses*. For a full appreciation, grow **'The Fairy'**.

THE INGENIOUS MR FAIRCHILD

CLASS: Shrub
REPEAT BLOOM: Good

BLOOM COLOR: Pink
HEIGHT: 5' or taller

BLOOM SIZE: 4½"
HARDINESS: Zones 5–9

INTRODUCED: Austin, England, 2003

When you picture a rose in your mind, you probably see a high-centered hybrid tea, just like the roses from a florist's shop. Or perhaps you imagine a many-petaled heritage rose like the ones your grandmother grew. Some roses don't fit either of those templates, though. They actually look more like something other than a rose. The Grootendorst series of hybrid rugosas, for example, have flowers that look just like carnations. And the Koster series of polyanthas look very much like ranunculus. 'The Ingenious Mr Fairchild' looks just like a peony.

The blooms are rich pink with some lilac shades, heavily covering a strong plant that reaches 5' for me and might grow taller if I let it. It starts blooming just as the real peonies are finishing for the year, and it continues right on until frost. Don't hesitate to cut blooms with long stems; this will keep the plant bushier and more productive. The large blooms have a memorable fruity fragrance. It will pick up some black spot when that disease is rife, but this does not appear to diminish its vigor or productivity. In my garden, any black spot is easily and beautifully disguised by 'Snow Hill' salvia.

This rose's name is a nod to Thomas Fairchild. Working with sweet williams from 1717–1720, he is credited as the first European to hybridize a plant.

RIGHT PLACE *Mixed border; cutting garden*

THE MAYFLOWER

CLASS: Shrub
REPEAT BLOOM: Reliable

BLOOM COLOR: Pink
HEIGHT: 3'

BLOOM SIZE: 3½"
HARDINESS: Zones 5–9

INTRODUCED: Austin, England, 2001

A tough English Rose that has traded in some of its charm for complete black spot resistance. While under trial, 'The Mayflower' grew under a decrepit old climbing rose that rained down black-spot-infected leaves all around. 'The Mayflower' never succumbed, and neither has it ever shown black spot in my garden, where its companions are other David Austin roses (of which only 'Golden Celebration' is really a notorious black-spotter). Unfortunately, 'The Mayflower' looks like the ugly duckling among the sophisticated, refined blooms of other recent Austin introductions. Although its repeat bloom is good, its medium-sized blooms are not particularly intricately formed or elegant, its color is ordinary, and its fragrance is light. 'The Mayflower' would do better for me in a tougher part of the garden, someplace where it could show off its blooms without regular care and not be shown off by its more exquisite cousins. It would be a good choice for that patch between the driveway and the neighbor's yard, or as a replacement for that overgown old spirea. 'The Mayflower' is a rose I'd highly recommend to anyone who thinks they can't grow roses, or who has had problems with black spot.

Medium pink with over 140 petals, some of them very short. 'The Mayflower' makes a stocky 3' shrub in my garden, packed with healthy leaves.

RIGHT PLACE *Naturalistic planting*

THE McCARTNEY ROSE

CLASS: Hybrid tea
REPEAT BLOOM: Good

BLOOM COLOR: Pink
HEIGHT: 3'

BLOOM SIZE: 5"
HARDINESS: Zones 6–9

INTRODUCED: Meilland, France, 1995

One of the few hybrid teas that won't look out of place in a mixed border, 'The McCartney Rose' is also one of

'THE McCARTNEY ROSE'

the most fragrant hybrid teas ever bred. Blooms are a clear, rich pink, beginning as elegant buds that spiral open quickly to the high-centered form that is typical of hybrid teas before finishing as a gorgeous full-petaled open bloom. Like most hybrid teas, it requires extra winter protection when grown in the open in Zone 5; in a mixed setting it will usually receive sufficient shelter from its neighbors.

Named for Paul McCartney, the former Beatle, and not to be confused with 'The Macartney Rose' *(Rosa bracteata)*, a single-petaled white rose named for an eighteenth-century diplomat and plant collector. That Macartney is definitely not winter hardy in Zone 5.

RIGHT PLACE *Mixed border*

'THÉRÈSE BUGNET'

THÉRÈSE BUGNET

CLASS: Hybrid rugosa	REPEAT BLOOM: Reliable
BLOOM COLOR: Pink	HEIGHT: 5'
BLOOM SIZE: 3"	HARDINESS: Zones 4–9
INTRODUCED: Bugnet, Canada, 1950	

One of the first roses to bloom after a severe winter, this rugosa hybrid is absolutely indestructible. Its blooms are fluffy, medium pink, with a pleasant spicy scent. It keeps on blooming whether or not old blooms are deadheaded, and left on its own 'Thérèse Bugnet' will display blooms and ripening hips at the same time in autumn.

Suckering freely, this rose will quickly colonize a substantial area. This makes it valuable on banks and other hard-to-reach places. It can also serve as a perennial bed traffic officer. If you have something annoying like gooseneck loosestrife on the march, just put 'Thérèse Bugnet' in its path. That will stop it. 'Thérèse Bugnet' grows to 5' tall for me. Its width is almost indeterminate, due to its rapid suckering.

Any professional would have been happy to have bred this rose, but roses were only a hobby for the long-lived Georges Bugnet, French-born novelist of Western Canada.

RIGHT PLACE *On banks and other hard-to-reach areas*

TURBO

CLASS: Hybrid rugosa	REPEAT BLOOM: Reliable
BLOOM COLOR: Pink	HEIGHT: 5'
BLOOM SIZE: 3½"	HARDINESS: Zones 5–9
INTRODUCED: Meilland, France, 1993	

This fascinating hybrid has rugosa ancestry from both its seed and pollen parents, mixed with some modern floribunda. The result is a healthy plant that grows more stolidly upright than most rugosas, with glossy leaves. Its wide-petaled, deep pink blooms are just barely double, and they open quickly. They often appear in clusters that can be too heavy for their stems, creating a charming cascading effect. Bloom is massive in spring and nearly continuous thereafter. Unlike most rugosas, it does not readily set hips.

I value 'Turbo' as a dependable 5' hedge. Its fierce prickles will deter dogs, hikers, children, meter readers, and even that bane of the winter garden, the snowmobiler. It is equally at home in the mixed border, where both its foliage and blooms will lend a glossy sheen.

RIGHT PLACE *Hedge; mixed border*

VARIEGATA DI BOLOGNA

CLASS: Bourbon	REPEAT BLOOM: None in cold
BLOOM COLOR: White striped	climates
with red	HEIGHT: 11'
BLOOM SIZE: 5"	HARDINESS: Zones 6–9
INTRODUCED: Bonfiglioli, Italy, 1909	

The most stunning striped blooms in the rose world, and a rose I find worth growing despite its unsuitability to my climate. Here are massive, extraordinarily fragrant blooms of cream-striped purplish-red. If you are lucky, and care for this rose well, you may receive three blooms a year (not three cycles, three *blooms*) each borne individually on top of a gangly 11-foot cane. And if you are one of those gardeners who likes to stay on top of diseases, this one can help you out. 'Variegata di Bologna' will show powdery mildew before any other rose in the garden, and it has attracted rust to gardens that had never seen it before. It is a tribute to the beauty of this mutation of a Bourbon rose discovered in Italy (and too often mispronounced by American rose exhibitors as "Variety of Boloney") that 'Variegata di Bologna' has persisted in catalogs and gardens for a century, despite its multitude of faults. This rose is grateful for a little support, and when placed carefully (in the midst of David Austin's English roses, for example, or behind some ornamental grasses tall enough to screen its foliar deficiencies), 'Variegata di Bologna' retains the ability to shock us on the day it finally blooms.

RIGHT PLACE *Far back in the mixed border*

WHITE ROADRUNNER

CLASS: Hybrid rugosa	REPEAT BLOOM: Good
BLOOM COLOR: White	WIDTH: 4'
BLOOM SIZE: 3"	HARDINESS: Zones 4–9
INTRODUCED: Uhl, Germany, 2003	

A pure white hybrid rugosa with attractive, clean growth spreading to 4' wide. Foliage is light green when new, and in combination with the single-petaled blooms gives an impression of springtime even in mid-August. Hips color up well but are smaller than on other rugosas. This trouble-free rose is perfect near the front of a large border, in poor soils, and for beginning gardeners.

From the same breeder, 'Pink Roadrunner' is another very tough rose, although in a more ordinary color. And 'Romantic Roadrunner'? That's even deeper pink.

RIGHT PLACE *Front of a large border*

WILDEVE

CLASS: Shrub	REPEAT BLOOM: Good
BLOOM COLOR: Pink	HEIGHT: 4'
BLOOM SIZE: 3½"	HARDINESS: Zones 5–9
INTRODUCED: Austin, England, 2003	

Ruffly full-petaled dusky pink blooms, sometimes touched with apricot and fading to a delicate blush. They make the most impressive sprays of any David Austin creation. The plant grows quickly into a robust,

'WILDEVE'

slightly arching shrub that covers a 4' area with attractive foliage and lots of bloom. Healthy and completely winter hardy, 'Wildeve' is a rose that I didn't pay much attention to at first but have come to appreciate more each year. It returns a lot of garden value for very little effort, and I have now employed it as an endcap for mixed beds.

RIGHT PLACE *End of mixed beds; tree rose*

'WINDRUSH'

WINDRUSH

CLASS: Shrub	REPEAT BLOOM: Good
BLOOM COLOR: Yellow	HEIGHT: 4'
BLOOM SIZE: 4"	HARDINESS: Zones 5–9
INTRODUCED: Austin, England, 1984	

Not a typical David Austin introduction, 'Windrush' produces masses of lemon yellow blooms on a tough, hardy plant. Its blooms are semi-double, most beautiful when fully open. Its thin stems will often bend under the weight of a spray with many blooms. The soft color is a perfect antidote to anything harsh and shows up well against the dark background provided by conifers. It is also one of the few roses to be effective when grown with black-eyed Susans.

To enjoy attractive rose hips on 'Windrush' simply leave some blooms on the plant, without deadheading. 'Windrush' has enough vigor to keep on blooming even as it sets seed and its hips ripen. It spreads to about 4' while growing as tall in my garden.

RIGHT PLACE *Against a background of dark conifers*

'YESTERDAY'

YESTERDAY

CLASS: Polyantha	REPEAT BLOOM: Reliable
BLOOM COLOR: Pink	HEIGHT: 3'
BLOOM SIZE: 2"	HARDINESS: Zones 5–9
INTRODUCED: Harkness, England, 1974	

A charming and very useful rose, growing into a 3' mound of shiny leaves with dainty sprays of small blooms, pink maturing to lavender with a white eye. 'Yesterday' blooms all summer long. This is a perfect rose to plant in a perennial bed, so long as you don't mind it making some of your less floriferous perennials look unproductive. It fits in perfectly with white, mauve, blue, and soft yellow flowers. It also makes an effective low hedge.

'Yesterday' has a complicated parentage. It was introduced as a polyantha, despite being two generations removed from any true members of that class. It does look very much like an improved polyantha. It shares the habit and profuse bloom of 'Snowbelt' (page 115) and 'Zenaitta' (below), polyanthas bred a generation later by Paul Jerabek.

RIGHT PLACE *Mixed border; low hedge*

YOLANDE D'ARAGON

CLASS: Portland	REPEAT BLOOM: Reliable
BLOOM COLOR: Pink	HEIGHT: 4½'
BLOOM SIZE: 4"	HARDINESS: Zones 5–9
INTRODUCED: Vibert, France, 1843	

One of the handful of old garden roses that every rosarian should enjoy, the Portland 'Yolande d'Aragon' produces its 100-petaled blooms reliably throughout the summer and has a fantastic fragrance. It is tidy enough (with narrow growth to just 4½' tall) to fit well into any rose garden or mixed border. Its deep pink blooms enjoy softer highlights, and they open flat to reveal an intricate arrangement of quill-shaped petals, like a star within a star within a star.

Its blooms are huge, and they often appear in big, heavy clusters. Remarkably, the stems are usually able to support this weight. However, care should be taken that the plant is not rocked out of the soil by gusty winds. This is a sure death sentence for a budded plant over winter in a cold climate, and while an own-root plant may survive it will be weakened. The best solution to this potential problem is to the cut the large sprays to enjoy indoors.

RIGHT PLACE *Rose garden; mixed border*

ZENAITTA

CLASS: Polyantha	REPEAT BLOOM: Constant if
BLOOM COLOR: Orange-red	deadheaded
BLOOM SIZE: 2"	HEIGHT: 3' or more
HARDINESS: Zones 5–9	
INTRODUCED: Jerabek, USA, 1991	

Bright scarlet-orange, this is the most intensely colored of any polyantha. Its blooms appear in vast sprays on a glossy-leaved plant that rewards deadheading with a constant supply of new blooms.

'Zenaitta' is great for bringing a splash of vivid color to a more muted perennial bed. In a bed of hot colors it will also shine. It does best in full sun and won't be too happy tucked underneath a larger plant. Grows vigorously to 3' in Ohio; it can get much bigger in warmer climates.

RIGHT PLACE *Mixed border*

CHAPTER 5

BEDDING
AND CUTTING ROSES

The traditional way to grow roses — in a bed by themselves — is still the most effective way to display most hybrid teas and floribundas. Hybrid teas are now healthier than ever. As long as you choose them wisely, your rose bed will not look like an abstract mass of sticks when it is not in bloom. Floribundas have always been perfect for mass planting, and now they offer a more complex range of colors and bloom types as well as healthier growth. Some of today's floribundas even have noteworthy fragrance.

OPPOSITE Easy-to-grow 'Queen Elizabeth' provides lots of cuttable blooms all summer long.

THE IDEA of using roses as bedding plants, planted all by themselves, is deeply ingrained. When Susan and I open our garden each June, we have learned to keep an eye out for a long-time rose society member who uses his cane to rub out "weeds" (perennials) in beds where we grow roses with other plants. Beds where roses are grown all by themselves look right to him. They will be a source of dazzling summer color and nearly constant cut flowers.

CHOOSING A SITE FOR A BEDDING GARDEN

When Susan and I planned our rose garden, we pictured hybrid teas in a formal setting about 400' behind the house on what we called Rose Hill. This has puzzled garden visitors from California and West Virginia, who have looked across the garden and wondered, "Where's this hill?" Fair enough, it's a Rose Slope that only feels a lot like a hill when you are pushing a wheelbarrow full of soil amendments. On this incline we designed a garden of concentric circles modeled roughly after Elizabeth Park, a municipal rose garden we had admired in Hartford, Connecticut. We built the beds, planted the hybrid teas, and sat back — only to watch them die. This was partly due to a drought that began in the year we planted the hybrid teas and did not fully break until four years later. It was also due to our inexperience with the location, and ultimately to the unsuitability of hybrid teas to a garden where they may not receive pampering every day.

So we started over, and today our hybrid teas thrive in beds much closer to the house, where they are the first to receive our attention. We highly recommend that you choose a site close to your house for your bedding garden too. Now, our Rose Hill is filled with happy hybrid rugosas, Canadian Explorers, German shrub roses, and old garden roses, along with about a dozen hybrid teas that have survived for all of this time.

RIGHT The best of Guillot's Generosa roses, 'Martine Guillot' combines the elegant buds of 19th-century tea roses with Zone 5 hardiness. Here, growing in the author's garden in Freedom Township, Ohio.

BED LAYOUT

A single row of roses rarely makes a satisfactory bed. I have planted some hybrid perpetuals single file, but they grow so tall that the effect is really that of a narrow hedge separating portions of the garden. If you plant three rows of roses in a bed, you should achieve an impressively full-looking effect, but it will be difficult to give the roses in the middle row the care they deserve. Two rows, staggered, is usually the perfect approach and with properly chosen varieties will produce a lush display. Whatever length you decide on for your rose bed, planting taller varieties at its center and shorter ones near either end will prove most effective.

In addition to good drainage and fertile or improved soil, the ideal site for a rose bed will receive full sun in the morning and some shade in the afternoon. Generous sunlight is required to produce cutting roses on strong stems; shade during the heat of the day will help to make those blooms even more impressive. Spacing will depend on your climate and the varieties chosen, but it is much better to space a little too closely than too far apart; generous spacing produces undesirable gaps. Height is not a critical factor in planning a cutting garden because today's most productive cutting roses have been effectively homogenized — nearly all floribundas grow about 2½ feet tall in my garden, and most hybrid teas 3½ to 4 feet. This makes them excellent for bedding. The height will vary, of course, by climate but the uniformity will not. I space floribundas 12 to 18 inches apart and hybrid teas 20 inches here in my Zone 5 gardens. A bed of older hybrid teas, grown primarily for historical interest, are quite happy and not at all overcrowded at just over 12 inches apart.

Floribundas often look best when planted in multiples of the same varieties. Since few hybrid teas bloom as heavily as a floribunda, the investment in multiple plants of the same variety won't pay the same dividends. The principle value of the hybrid tea is in the armloads of cut flowers it will produce. If it looks good in the landscape, that's a bonus. A large rose bed containing all different varieties may end up resembling the horticultural version of a stamp collection rather than a well thought-out garden. But that's exactly what I enjoy in my front yard: 100 floribundas, all different, each offering something that its neighbor does not.

A beautiful rose bed can be created by combining floribundas and hybrid teas. Just keep in mind that most of the hybrid teas will grow taller, and that most of the floribundas will take longer to repeat bloom. For best results, stick to the recent healthier, bushier hybrid teas and not the old favorites sold at discount and big box stores. Mixing it up in the rose bed can help avoid the problem of "croppers" — roses that produce a massive flush of bloom, and then sit and rest for what might seem like too long. Planting an assortment of roses can almost guarantee that some of them will be in bloom at any one time throughout the summer.

Catch me when I'm behind on weeding and I'll joke that I have living mulch in some of my rose beds. But I don't, they're just weeds, and I've never found a groundcover that works well to underplant bedding roses in my climate. Rose beds are most productive, and most attractive, when they are well mulched. (For more on mulch, see page 224.)

BLOOM CYCLES

Much is written about discordant rose colors. For example, an orange rose like 'Domstadt Fulda' shouldn't be planted next to an electric pink rose, such as 'Electron'. It is true they will clash, but generally only once each year. After the big spring bloom, roses have different repeat cycles. In my garden these can vary from 28 to more than 60 days. In general, roses with fewer petals on shorter stems repeat more quickly than those with lots of petals on long stems, and one-bloom-per-stem roses will be back with their second bloom before cluster-flowered ones. (Actually, some one-bloom-per-stem roses may be approaching their third bloom cycle before a cluster-flowered rose displays its second crop.) Whether you seek out or avoid startling color contrasts is up to you. But after the initial burst of bloom each spring, it will be out of your hands. The roses will bloom when they want to.

OPPOSITE 'Electron' in the cutting garden at Fellows Riverside Gardens, Youngstown, Ohio.

ENJOYING ROSES AS CUT FLOWERS

If you buy a rose from a florist and take it apart, petal by petal, you will almost certainly count a total of 30 to 40 petals. That is the magic number of petals for a rose that will present a pleasing shape and be capable of holding that shape for an extended time. Of course, roses with fewer petals can be enjoyed as cut flowers too. The rule to remember is that the fewer petals a rose has, the sooner it should be cut.

- Single-petaled roses, such as 'Sally Holmes', should be cut just as their sepals are coming down.
- Hybrid teas are best cut when about one-third open.
- Many-petaled roses, such as most of David Austin's introductions, should be left to open more fully on the bush. Austin is now breeding roses specifically for the cut flower trade, and the popularity of many-petaled roses in wedding bouquets and floral arrangements is increasing each year.

A bed of roses is meant to supply cut flowers, but not too many, too soon. Robbing any rose of most of its foliage at once can be a potentially fatal blow. On several occasions in my early days of rose exhibiting, I butchered most of a young rose bush to bring it to the show, and so I know from personal experience that losing a rose bush to win a trophy (or have cut flowers indoors) does not feel good for more than one day. Wise gardeners never remove more than one-third of a rose bush at any one time.

For the largest possible blooms, disbud 'Electron' and other hybrid teas by removing all the side buds that develop around the terminal bud on each stem. This can be easily done with your thumb and forefinger when the buds are quite small. Using secateurs for this delicate operation will too often result in decapitation of the bloom whose size you are trying to increase.

Roses should be cut either first thing in the morning or late in the afternoon. Their sugar and water content is highest at these times, and the roses will last longer. Cut with sharp pruners, and then recut the stem underwater — this will prevent air bubbles from traveling up the stem and causing the flower to wilt. Take stems as long as you want, but don't remove more than half of the plant's total foliage at one time. Remember, the longer the section of stem you cut, the longer it will take the rose to produce a new bloom. Cutting just above an

outward facing bud eye will keep the plant shapely.

If you don't want to cut a stem, or your rose hasn't made one, roses can be enjoyed indoors floating in a bowl. A 6-inch clear glass (or crystal) bowl works perfectly for one bloom; larger bowls can display several different blooms at once.

A long-stemmed cut rose will last longer if conditioned by plunging it up to its neck in 100°F tap water and storing in a cool place (50°F is ideal) for several hours. If you are cutting roses in advance for a wedding, dinner party, or other special event, keep them in a cool, dark place. If refrigerating, cover each bloom with a plastic bag to keep it fresh, and make certain your refrigerator doesn't cycle in freezing territory. Most roses can be refrigerated for three days with little loss of substance. They must go into the refrigerator dry — roses wet from rain or dew will spot under refrigeration. Apples release a gas that causes roses to open faster, so they should not be refrigerated with roses.

Floral preservatives really work, but a little sugar and bleach works almost as well. Use a teaspoon of sugar and a few drops of bleach per quart of water. Simply changing the water each day, and recutting the stem under water, does a lot to extend the life of cut roses. Most roses should last a week indoors, and recutting the stem under water every other day will extend vase life even further.

If you grow baby's breath, you can make rose bouquets just like the ones sold in many supermarkets. Larkspur works perfectly with roses, and asters and snapdragons are dependable bouquet companions. Asparagus fern can add some green foliar interest. Both the foliage and flowers of snow-in-summer will fit well into a bouquet of miniature roses. Because most miniature roses lack fragrance, a little lavender can help a lot. As you grow more roses you may find that the most rewarding bouquets are those created with several different kinds of this most versatile flower.

CHOOSING BEDDING ROSES

The following collection of rose descriptions is by no means encyclopedic, or even a listing of all of the bedding and cutting roses that I admire. It does include all of the roses that really shine, year after year, in my own garden, despite tough winters and with less care than more fussy gardeners might provide.

Note: Because all hybrid tea and floribunda roses for bedding and cutting are repeat bloomers, that category is omitted at the start of their descriptions. Height is listed for some roses but not for hybrid teas or floribundas, since they tend to fall in a uniform height range — 3½ to 4 feet and 2½ feet, respectively, in my garden.

ABOVE Too tall for bedding, 'Queen Elizabeth' is at home in this dooryard garden.

'ALEXANDER'

ALEXANDER

CLASS: Hybrid tea
BLOOM SIZE: 4"
BLOOM COLOR: Orange
HARDINESS: Zones 6–9
INTRODUCED: Harkness, England, 1972

If you want an orange rose, 'Alexander' is the orangest. Its vermilion is unfading and demands attention from across the garden. If this attention is accompanied by supplementary food and extra water, 'Alexander' will be happy. It's a heavy feeder, but it rewards extra care with a solid garden performance. This is one of the tallest-growing hybrid teas, and so a place at the center of a rose bed will keep it from overshadowing its neighbors. Except when it blooms.

MY LOVE IS LIKE AN ORANGE, ORANGE ROSE?

Some people think that roses lost their way back in the 1950s, when they started getting so orange. I can see this point of view. Pink is peaceful, orange is jarring. But both, certainly, have their place, even if it might not be next to one another.

Pelargonin, the pigment responsible for geranium red, arrived in roses in 1943 via the rose we know as 'Independence' (its original German name, 'Sondermeldung' — "Special Announcement" — is a better name for a rose that heralded so much). 'Independence' itself was an ugly rose, but through its genes we now have all kinds of orange and coral shades that hadn't appeared in roses before.

AMBRIDGE ROSE

CLASS: Shrub
REPEAT BLOOM: Reliable
BLOOM COLOR: Pink
HEIGHT: 2½'
BLOOM SIZE: 3"
HARDINESS: Zones 5b–9
INTRODUCED: Austin, England, 1990

So many of David Austin's English Roses are outsize personalities, potential stars in a full-scale border. This compact one excels as a bedding plant. Its habit is short and rounded, covered throughout the summer with apricot-pink blooms that fade gracefully to pale pink. The flowers are very full, opening from a cup shape into a beautiful rosette. They carry that same myrrh fragrance found in 'Constance Spry' (see page 49).

This rose grows to 2½' and takes up the same amount of space as a floribunda. It is also valuable as a tree rose, and quite attractive when grown in a large pot or urn.

AOTEAROA NEW ZEALAND

CLASS: Hybrid tea
BLOOM SIZE: 4½"
BLOOM COLOR: Pink
HARDINESS: Zones 6–9
INTRODUCED: McGredy, New Zealand, 1989

Easy to grow, and rewarding both for the beautiful shape of its pale pink blooms and for their strong fragrance. Flowers can be disbudded to bloom one per stem, but they are more effective in the garden and as cut flowers when left to form a spray. This hybrid tea forms a healthy, attractive bush and never seems to miss the stems that are cut.

Aotearoa is the Maori name for New Zealand. This rose is sometimes sold as 'Aotearoa', sometimes as 'New Zealand', and sometimes as both. There is a white mutation that is marketed as 'Full Sail' in the United States. It is identical to the original in every respect except for color.

AUGUSTE RENOIR

CLASS: Hybrid tea
BLOOM COLOR: Pink
BLOOM SIZE: 6"
HARDINESS: Zones 5b–9
INTRODUCED: Meilland, France, 1992

One of the few winning members of the Romantica brand, 'Auguste Renoir' produces massive peony-shaped blooms, deep pink and richly fragrant. This rose is happiest in hot, dry locations, where repeat bloom will be swiftest. Its blooms may not open properly in cool, wet weather.

Its habit is just like that of any other hybrid tea, and 'Auguste Renoir' is useful for providing a fragrance stop in a hybrid tea bed that may otherwise leave visitors using a lot of imagination when they stop to smell your roses.

BELLE ÉPOQUE

CLASS: Hybrid tea
BLOOM SIZE: 3½"
BLOOM COLOR: Copper
HARDINESS: Zones 6–9
INTRODUCED: Fryer, England, 1994

A tall hybrid tea with captivating bronze blooms, most beautiful when they approximate a parchment brown color. The slender buds are in line with the narrow growth habit of the plant, which can be spaced closer together than other hybrid teas. Hybrid teas in this color are usually weaklings, or winter tender, but 'Belle Époque' grows with commendable vigor and has no problem with an Ohio winter, given the minimum shovelful of compost or sawdust protection.

While the ideal hybrid tea would produce one large bloom on a long, straight stem, most will in fact bloom in sprays if they are not disbudded (removing side buds and leaving one terminal bud to bloom). 'Belle Époque' always wants to spray, and to me it is more attractive and makes a bigger impact in the garden this way.

This is the most recent of several roses named 'Belle Époque'. It's the only one that isn't pink.

BERNSTEIN-ROSE

CLASS: Floribunda
BLOOM SIZE: 3"
BLOOM COLOR: Yellow
HARDINESS: Zones 5–9
INTRODUCED: Tantau, Germany, 1987

Deepest yellow to amber, this full-petaled floribunda can't be mistaken for any other rose. Roses of this color are often winter tender, or shy to bloom, or both. 'Bernstein-Rose' needs no special winter protection in Zone 5, and it blooms strongly throughout the summer. Its blooms appear in modest clusters, which last well when cut. This rose has a perfect habit. It is most effective when planted with orange and orange-red floribundas.

Not named for any particular Bernstein; *bernstein* is the German word for amber.

'BRIDE'S DREAM'

BRIDE'S DREAM

CLASS: Hybrid tea
BLOOM SIZE: 4½"
BLOOM COLOR: Pink
HARDINESS: Zones 5–9
INTRODUCED: Kordes, Germany, 1985

The light pink hybrid tea 'Bride's Dream' is so sturdy that one somewhat unscrupulous East European nursery has been using it as a rootstock, bud-grafting other roses onto cuttings of 'Bride's Dream'. This makes for confusing suckers, but whether it arrives on purpose or accidentally in your garden, 'Bride's Dream' is definitely worth keeping. It is hardy and productive, and its only real fault is that its streamlined, urn-shaped blooms will weatherspot in damp conditions.

WEATHERSPOTTING

It doesn't have to rain for rose petals to weatherspot: a succession of cool nights and/or foggy mornings will cause many roses, including **'Bride's Dream'**, to develop unsightly splotches on their petals. This is a natural phenomenon — just as rose blooms get smaller in extreme heat, they develop imperfections when it is damp. If you absolutely want to avoid this, you can protect developing buds by shielding them with bonnets made from wax paper. Manufactured sandwich bags will work for all but the largest blooms; for these you may need to make your own bonnets.

'BRIGADOON'

BRIGADOON

CLASS: Hybrid tea   BLOOM SIZE: 4"

BLOOM COLOR: Orange/pink   HARDINESS: Zones 5–9

INTRODUCED: Warriner, USA, 1992

A tall hybrid tea that is remarkably healthy and winter hardy. Unlike most hybrid teas, 'Brigadoon' requires no winter protection in Zone 5. Its blooms are a blend of coral orange and pink, changeable with the weather. The cutting stems are as long as you'd expect from a plant this tall, and taking cut flowers encourages the production of more long stems. Simply deadheading spent blooms will produce a profusion of smaller blooms on much shorter new growth.

CANDELLA

CLASS: Hybrid tea   BLOOM SIZE: 4"

BLOOM COLOR: Red/white   HARDINESS: Zones 5b–9

INTRODUCED: McGredy, New Zealand, 1990

A hybrid tea in a bold shade of red with a stark white reverse. The effect is especially dramatic as the buds are unfolding. Garden visitors often ask to see 'Snowfire', a well-remembered hybrid tea from 1970 in this same color scheme. I refer them to 'Candella', which is healthier and more vigorous.

CHANELLE

CLASS: Floribunda   BLOOM SIZE: 3"

BLOOM COLOR: Apricot   HARDINESS: Zones 6–9

INTRODUCED: McGredy, Northern Ireland, 1959

The healthiest floribunda of its era, 'Chanelle' produces pretty sprays of delicate creamy apricot blooms, on a vigorous plant that (rare for a floribunda) appears attractive when it is not in bloom. The blooms have a high-centered hybrid tea shape, and their one fault is an inability to stand up to rain. Even a brief shower will leave 'Chanelle' looking soggy, spotted, and unattractive.

When the British gardening guru Christopher Lloyd famously dug up all of his roses and replaced them with tropical-looking plants, 'Chanelle' is one of the few that Lloyd decided to keep. It is perfectly winter hardy in Zone 6 and south. I am happy to give it a shovelful of mulch each fall; this is all it needs to soldier through my Zone 5 winters.

'CHARLES AZNAVOUR'

CHARLES AZNAVOUR

CLASS: Floribunda   BLOOM SIZE: 4"

BLOOM COLOR: Pink/white   HARDINESS: Zones 5–9

INTRODUCED: Meilland, France, 1988

A wonderful bedding floribunda, with a perfect compact habit and informal, wavy, semi-double blooms of cream edged in pink. These typically appear in large sprays, and these sprays arrive on long stems that are good for cutting. Repeat bloom is extraordinary, and disease resistance is above average. This rose can be faulted only for lack of fragrance, and blooms that weatherspot after rain or a heavy dew. A great rose for hot, dry climates, this is one of the most popular roses in Australia, where it is known as 'Seduction'.

Sometimes sold as 'Matilda' in the United States, but be sure you are getting this pink-and-white floribunda and not the red grandiflora of that name. A version called 'Gala Charles Aznavour' has more pink suffusion into the creamy petals.

CHORUS

CLASS: Floribunda   BLOOM COLOR: Orange
BLOOM SIZE: 4"   HARDINESS: Zones 5b–9
INTRODUCED: Meilland, France, 1975

An easy-to-grow floribunda, straddling the line between orange and red. Blooms are large for a floribunda, and packed with petals. They usually appear in clusters of three to five blooms, but since they are so large the effect is equal to a rose that produces smaller blooms in larger sprays. The plant is compact, with an ideal habit for bedding.

CLIO

CLASS: Hybrid perpetual   REPEAT BLOOM: Good
BLOOM COLOR: Pink   HEIGHT: 4'
BLOOM SIZE: 6"   HARDINESS: Zones 5–9
INTRODUCED: Paul, England, 1894

One of the largest hybrid perpetual blooms, and also one of the most beautiful. Visitors to my garden often mistake this rose for one of David Austin's introductions. Huge blush pink blooms seem illuminated from within. Each one has more than 100 petals, which arrange themselves into an intricate, sunken cup shape. Enjoy them in the garden; 'Clio' does not last well when cut.

In my climate, this stout plant never sends out the long shoots that often catch powdery mildew on other hybrid perpetuals. Its compact 4' habit recommends it as a stunning bedding rose.

DAY BREAKER

CLASS: Floribunda   BLOOM SIZE: 3"
BLOOM COLOR: Peach/amber   HARDINESS: Zones 5–9
INTRODUCED: Fryer, England, 2004

Perfectly shaped pastel peach-and-amber blooms on a shrubby floribunda that is always producing healthy new growth. Flowers often appear as part of large sprays that can be cut as instant bouquets. This rose

'DAY BREAKER'

makes a good argument for patience: it took two years to establish in my garden but has been a star performer ever since.

DICKY

CLASS: Floribunda   BLOOM SIZE: 2½"
BLOOM COLOR: Coral-salmon   HARDINESS: Zones 5–9
INTRODUCED: Dickson, Northern Ireland, 1983

A template for the perfect floribunda, 'Dicky' produces ideally proportioned and often huge sprays of lovely florets of an even coral-salmon color. Each bloom is flawless in both its own progression through bud and bloom to open flower, as well as in its position in the overall spray. A rose with no known idiosyncracies: plant it, water it, feed it, and it won't let you down.

Sold as 'Dicky' in the United States, it is properly called 'Anisley Dickson', a tribute to the breeder's wife.

DOMSTADT FULDA

CLASS: Floribunda   BLOOM SIZE: 4"
BLOOM COLOR: Orange-red   HARDINESS: Zones 5–9
INTRODUCED: Kordes, Germany, 2004

Use with caution: this is the brightest orange of any floribunda. This stocky, healthy rose produces startling sprays of semi-double blooms that open wide to make a solid mass of intense orange-red color. They will last well as cut flowers if taken as tight buds. Once the blooms open, they are most effective if left on the bush.

'Domstadt Fulda' repeats more quickly than most floribundas, and it's unlikely that its bloom cycles will synchronize with whatever you plant next to it. However, white or yellow companion roses would be much more effective than pink or purple, even if the bloom overlap occurs only once a year.

DOUBLE DELIGHT

CLASS: Hybrid tea   BLOOM SIZE: 4½"
BLOOM COLOR: Red/white   HARDINESS: Zones 5b–9
INTRODUCED: Swim & Ellis, USA, 1977

This fragrant cream-raspberry blend proves how endearing a rose can be despite its faults. 'Double Delight' has ugly foliage that becomes diseased when you don't spray it and suffers phytotoxic reactions when you do. This was the first rose I ever planted, and a couple of thousand roses later I can think of lots of better roses that never would have gotten me hooked. There is much to be said for those intangible qualitites of a rose often summarized as "charm."

One in every 20 or so blooms of 'Double Delight' is stunningly perfect in its color and form. Every bloom is intoxicatingly fragrant. A very large bed of 'Double Delight' will be disappointing because of the unattractive foliage and growth that appears uneven — 'Double Delight' doesn't grow into a pleasantly rounded bush but produces canes of varying height. A few plants of 'Double Delight' will almost always be a highlight in a bed of mixed hybrid teas.

'DOUBLE DELIGHT'

ELECTRON (photo, page 129)

CLASS: Hybrid tea   BLOOM SIZE: 4½"
BLOOM COLOR: Pink   HARDINESS: Zones 5–9
INTRODUCED: McGredy, Northern Ireland, 1973

A workhorse of a hybrid tea that survives with minimal care and thrives with just a bit more than that. The hot pink blooms arrive in profusion in June and regularly thereafter. Unlike most other hybrid teas of its generation, 'Electron' matures into a bush that isn't embarrassing when not in bloom. It also boasts an extraordinarily powerful fragrance. Originally named 'Mullard Jubilee'.

ELINA (photo, page 195)

CLASS: Hybrid tea   BLOOM SIZE: 6"
BLOOM COLOR: Yellow   HARDINESS: Zones 5–9
INTRODUCED: Dickson, Northern Ireland, 1983

There is no more dependable yellow hybrid tea than 'Elina', a rose that represents a real step forward in hybrid tea breeding. Genetically it's half a floribunda, bringing the toughness and heavy bloom of the floribundas into the hybrid tea class while maintaining the large bloom size and long stems everyone wants in a hybrid tea. The primrose yellow is soft, but consistent and steady. It brings out the color of anything planted next to it. The plant is robust and bushy, full of health, and a star in any rose bed.

Dickson Nurseries grows a small number of roses for sale to the public, and it depends upon royalties and sales of naming rights to fund its hybridizing program. 'Elina' was originally named 'Peaudouce' after a popular European brand of disposable diapers. After the contract for that naming expired, everyone was free to call this wonderful rose 'Elina'.

ENGLISH MISS

CLASS: Floribundas   BLOOM SIZE: 3"
BLOOM COLOR: Pink   HARDINESS: Zones 5–9
INTRODUCED: Cant, England, 1977

Although shorter than most floribundas, 'English Miss' has a perfect habit for bedding. Its blooms appear in varying shades of soft pink and have petals sturdy enough to stand up to wet weather. They typically appear in large sprays; these are tempting to cut, but before doing so gauge how much plant will be

135

left behind. If 'English Miss' has produced three large sprays at once, it will be wisest to leave two of them on the bush. Extremely fragrant for a floribunda, this rose is perfectly hardy in Zone 5.

FABERGÉ

CLASS: Floribunda   BLOOM SIZE: 3"

BLOOM COLOR: Pink   HARDINESS: Zones 5–9

INTRODUCED: Boerner, USA, 1969

This floribunda, producing perfectly scaled-down hybrid tea blooms, is equally valuable as a bedding and cut-flower rose. Its blooms are soft coral pink, enlivened by a patch of yellow on the reverse of each petal. The leathery foliage is healthy, and the plant's spreading habit helps fill out a rose bed even when 'Fabergé' is not in bloom.

FAIR BIANCA

CLASS: Shrub   REPEAT BLOOM: Regular

BLOOM COLOR: White   HEIGHT: 3½'

BLOOM SIZE: 3"   HARDINESS: Zones 5b–9

INTRODUCED: Austin, England, 1982

Wide sprays of elegant, fully double, pure white blooms appear regularly on long, cuttable stems. The blooms often display a cute button eye; they always have a pleasing fragrance. A generation after its introduction, 'Fair Bianca' is still the best white rose bred by David

Austin. Austin's catalog now recommends this rose for "Mediterranean climates." There are many ways to describe Ohio's climate. Mediterranean isn't one of them, but this rose does very well here too.

Although cataloged and sold as a shrub rose, 'Fair Bianca' has the habit and all of the good qualities of a superior floribunda, and in my garden it is a stellar member in a bed of about 80 floribundas.

'FOLKLORE'

FOLKLORE

CLASS: Hybrid tea   BLOOM SIZE: 5"

BLOOM COLOR: Orange   HARDINESS: Zones 5b–9

INTRODUCED: Kordes, Germany 1977

A gentler color than the usual orange hybrid tea, and softened even further by a pastel buff reverse. These blooms arrive on a tall, tough plant that offers outstanding winter hardiness. Stems are often crooked, which could be a negative if you seek a perfectly uniform bouquet of long-stemmed blooms. But this makes 'Folklore' a bonus for ikebana enthusiasts, and it has no effect whatsoever on its impressive garden display.

'European Touch' is the best of several mutations of 'Folklore' — its flowers are the biscuit color that shows up on the reverse of 'Folklore' petals. 'European Touch' sometimes reverts to 'Folklore', or throws blooms that are a hodgepodge of orange and biscuit.

'FAIR BIANCA'

FOUNTAIN

CLASS: Hybrid tea (technically)   HEIGHT: 5'
BLOOM COLOR: Red   HARDINESS: Zones 5–9
BLOOM SIZE: 5"
INTRODUCED: Tantau, Germany, 1970

This rose has it all — huge ruffly crimson blooms with an intoxicating scent, a healthy and bushy habit, and winter hardiness. It has suffered from something of an identity crisis, sold as a hybrid tea in some parts of Europe and a shrub in others. It is actually most useful when used as a large (to 5') floribunda. 'Fountain' may have been a generation ahead of its time, because its habit is right in line with some of the best, most vigorous floribundas being introduced in Germany today. Although it has never benefited from the push of a large commercial nursery in the United States, it is available from specialist growers and certainly deserves to be more widely grown.

GARDEN PARTY

CLASS: Hybrid tea   BLOOM SIZE: 5"
BLOOM COLOR: White   HARDINESS: Zones 5b–9
INTRODUCED: Swim, USA, 1960

A creamy ivory burnished with a delicate mauve edge. 'Garden Party' is the healthy parent of 'Double Delight', and it remains a garden asset despite a slight tendency to mildew. This one fault can be minimized by planting 'Garden Party' in an open situation where the breeze can help blow the mildew away. Avoid planting it in a corner or a crowded area.

'GEBRÜDER GRIMM'

GEBRÜDER GRIMM

CLASS: Floribunda   BLOOM SIZE: 3½"
BLOOM COLOR: Orange   HARDINESS: Zones 5–9
INTRODUCED: Kordes, Germany, 2002

Bright coral orange with a pale yellow reverse, these pretty buds open to wide, ruffly blooms that last a long time. The plant is healthy and productive, as happy in the cool of autumn as it is in summer's heat.

This floribunda has a slight tendency to sprawl, which can be prevented by cutting sprays with long stems, or by simply cutting back a third of the growth after each bloom cycle. Choosing an inside-facing eye when cutting back will provide an additional brake on any unwieldy growth. As with many German roses, this rose has picked up additional names as it has traveled around the world. In the United States and Canada it is often sold as 'Grimm Brother's Fairy Tale'.

GELBER ENGEL

CLASS: Floribunda   BLOOM SIZE: 3"
BLOOM COLOR: Yellow   HARDINESS: Zones 5–9
INTRODUCED: Kordes, Germany, 2003

A revolutionary yellow floribunda with superb health and winter hardiness. Bright yellow blooms appear all over a plant whose foliage glistens with good health. These 22-petaled blooms usually array themselves in big sprays but occasionally appear on their own. They have a pleasant but not overpowering fragrance. 'Gelber Engel' is usually sending out new growth even before its current set of buds have time to open. The plant reaches 4½' in my floribunda bed, taller than most of its compatriots but right at home next to 'Escapade' or 'Stadt den Helder'.

A ROSE BY ANY OTHER NAME

A professional rose breeder can make money in three ways: 1) by propagating and selling plants; 2) by receiving royalties from others who propagate and sell plants that the breeder has patented, or whose names the breeder has protected via trademark; and 3) by selling naming rights for a rose to an individual, corporation, or organization.

An offshoot of method 3 is by donating naming rights to charities, thus earning tax advantages as well as goodwill. That is how we get 'Crocus Rose', named not for the pretty little springtime bulb but for the charity whose acronym stands for Colo-Rectal Cancer Understanding and Screening.

'GELBER ENGEL'

Good as this rose is — and if you are only going to plant one yellow floribunda, make it this one — there is still room for improvement. The flowers eventually fade to off-white, and the sprays would ideally be more symmetrical in their arrangement. But these are nit-picks at a rose that is miles ahead of the yellow floribundas that came before it.

GEMINI

CLASS: Hybrid tea   BLOOM SIZE: 5"
BLOOM COLOR: Pink/white   HARDINESS: Zones 6–9
INTRODUCED: Zary, USA, 2000

A vigorous and reliable hybrid tea, producing abundant bloom throughout the summer. 'Gemini' is a blend of cream and coral pink, its urn-shaped blooms lasting a long time. Its perfectly shaped flowers appear both singly and in well-spaced sprays of three to five.

'GEMINI'

When Jackson & Perkins decided to start producing some hybrid teas on their own roots, 'Gemini' was one of the first roses chosen. It certainly does not need a kick-start from a rootstock to get off to a good start.

GENE BOERNER

CLASS: Floribunda   BLOOM SIZE: 3"
BLOOM COLOR: Pink   HARDINESS: Zones 5–9
INTRODUCED: Boerner, USA, 1969

The efforts of hybridizer Gene Boerner took the flori-bunda from its polyantha roots of a huge number of relatively formless blooms on short, twiggy plants to an ideal of seven to nine relatively large blooms, each mimicking the shape of a hybrid tea, on a long stem well-suited for cutting or exhibiting. The rose 'Gene Boerner' is the apogee of this ideal: a very clean and even pink blossom color; slender, elegant buds; and a plant that grows with vigor to nearly 4'. It remains an excellent, if unfragrant, rose for bedding and cutting.

GENE BOERNER

Known as "Papa Floribunda," Gene Boerner was a tireless promoter of the rose. Active in an era when men still wore hats, he was famous for keeping a rose bloom under his. Whenever anyone complained that roses just weren't fragrant anymore, he would doff his hat, remove the rose, and invite all around to sample its scent. It was a neat trick, but in the real world people want roses to be fragrant in gardens, and as cut flowers, and not particularly after having been kept under a hat all day. Most of Boerner's rose creations for Jackson and Perkins were not fragrant, and the seedling chosen posthumously to bear his name is not either.

GLAD TIDINGS

CLASS: Floribunda   BLOOM SIZE: 3"
BLOOM COLOR: Red   HARDINESS: Zones 5–9
INTRODUCED: Tantau, Germany, 1988

A superior red floribunda, notable for its ideal bedding habit (2½' in my garden), intensely red blooms, and symmetrical sprays of urn-shaped blooms. It is called 'Lübecker Rotspon' in its native Germany; we can thank the British for bestowing the 'Glad Tidings' name when it was chosen as Rose of the Year there. Remarkably free of powdery mildew for a red floribunda, it also boasts excellent winter hardiness.

GOLDELSE

CLASS: Floribunda BLOOM SIZE: 3"
BLOOM COLOR: Amber HARDINESS: Zones 5–9
INTRODUCED: Tantau, Germany, 2000

Intense amber gold blooms cover this remarkable floribunda, which makes a perfectly round 18" diameter bush. Every plant has the same spherical habit, making an incredibly impressive display when planted en masse, or when used as a tree rose. Outside of Germany, this rose is sometimes sold as 'Bowled Over'. One nursery advertises it as "The Bowling Ball Rose."

Very healthy and winter hardy. The fully double flowers usually appear in small clusters, and repeat bloom is rapid.

GOLDMARIE

CLASS: Floribunda BLOOM SIZE: 3"
BLOOM COLOR: Yellow HARDINESS: Zones 5–9
INTRODUCED: Kordes, Germany, 1982

The closest thing to a gold color in a healthy floribunda, 'Goldmarie' blooms profusely on an upright plant with slightly stiff foliage. Its flowers are deep yellow to almost gold, unfading, with just a thin edge of pink-red in cool weather. Established growth typically carries modest clusters of three to seven blooms, while basal breaks may erupt into humongous sprays of bloom. Flowers are just barely double but last a long time on the bush.

European nurseries maintain trademark rights by reusing names. Kordes introduced a previous 'Goldmarie' in 1958 and a subsequent one in 1998. To avoid confusion, this one is sometimes sold as 'Goldmarie 82'.

H C ANDERSEN

CLASS: Floribunda BLOOM SIZE: 3"
BLOOM COLOR: Red HARDINESS: Zones 5–9
INTRODUCED: Poulsen, Denmark, 1986

Brightest red blooms on a healthy plant that grows more upright than many floribundas. Repeat bloom and disease resistance are both exemplary; one almost wouldn't expect a rose named for the creator of fairy tales to be so practical. Like almost all red floribundas, this one has no fragrance. Sometimes sold in this country as 'America's Choice.'

HANNAH GORDON

CLASS: Floribunda BLOOM SIZE: 4"
BLOOM COLOR: White/red HARDINESS: Zones 5–9
INTRODUCED: Kordes, Germany, 1983

An easy-to-grow floribunda whose vigor almost qualifies it as a shrub. The 5' plant is covered all summer in cheerful blooms, ivory edged in raspberry red. These are most attractive when fully open, displaying a wavy picotee effect. Blooms appear both singly and in modest clusters.

'Hannah Gordon' is hopelessly confused in commerce with 'Nicole', a floribunda of the same color from the same breeder. The real 'Nicole' has blooms with fewer but more substantial petals, and a much more compact habit of growth.

The impressive but little grown 'Schloss Balthazar' has blooms that are super-sized versions of 'Hannah Gordon' on a plant that is a foot or so shorter.

'HANNAH GORDON'

HOME & GARDEN

CLASS: Floribunda BLOOM SIZE: 3½"
BLOOM COLOR: Pink HARDINESS: Zones 5–9
INTRODUCED: Kordes, Germany, 2002

A floribunda with full-petaled light pink flowers in large, perfectly arranged sprays. The plant is extraordinarily healthy. This is a great example of the good things that can happen when other classes of roses are liberated from a slavish adherence to the high-centered, spiraled hybrid tea form. The 80-petaled blooms of 'Home & Garden' take much longer to open

'HOME & GARDEN'

JEMA

CLASS: Hybrid tea   BLOOM SIZE: 6"
BLOOM COLOR: Apricot   HARDINESS: Zones 5b–9
INTRODUCED: Perry, USA, 1981

A hybrid tea with huge blooms of a captivating apricot color, often tinged with pink in cool weather. The egg-shaped buds move very quickly to wavy, fully open blooms and hold their beauty at this stage for a long time. The plant can grow in an awkward, angular manner; to avoid this, prune it to inward-facing eyes. Roses of this color are often winter tender, but 'Jema' is not. Thus, it makes a fine substitute for the hybrid tea 'Just Joey', which is one of the most popular garden plants in many parts of the world but is unsuitable in cold-winter areas such as Ohio.

HOW TO NAME A ROSE

Rose breeders receive inspiration for rose names from many different sources. Family members usually receive priority. Some have named roses for military commanders under whom they served; others for their dogs. Television personalities are always popular, as are people willing to pay to have a rose named after themselves. Breeder Astor Perry named most of his roses after peanut towns — important centers of peanut cultivation in the southern United States. **'Jema'** was a happy exception.

JOHN F KENNEDY

CLASS: Hybrid tea   BLOOM SIZE: 5"
BLOOM COLOR: White   HARDINESS: Zones 6–9
INTRODUCED: Boerner, USA, 1965

I missed out on this rose for many years because I had decided (without actually growing it) that its popularity was due to the sentiment people attached to its name. That was a big mistake on my part — this is a very dependable and fragrant garden rose. The big white hybrid tea blooms appear with clockwork regularity throughout the summer, on a healthy, bushy plant.

'John F Kennedy' is a perfect example of a rose that is dismissed by the exhibitors who make up the majority of Rose Society membership (in this case, because its form does not feature a perfectly spiraled center) but remains a valuable rose in everyone else's gardens.

than a flower with 35 hybrid tea-like petals would, and they last longer once they are open. Because of this they provide more color in the garden at both the beginning and end of a bloom cycle. And color in the garden is what floribundas should be all about.

This is a superior summertime rose, but its blossoms may have difficulty opening properly when nights turn cool in the fall. Just as the first petals should be unfurling, the bud will swell up and begin to rot. Many roses with as many petals as 'Home & Garden' share this cool-weather problem, which is called "balling."

JARDINS DE BAGATELLE

CLASS: Hybrid tea   BLOOM SIZE: 4"
BLOOM COLOR: White   HARDINESS: Zones 5b–9
INTRODUCED: Meilland, France, 1986

An elegant hybrid tea, producing stem upon long stem of urn-shaped blooms. These are ivory, with splashes of peach or apricot deepening according to the weather. With high marks for fragrance, health, winter hardiness, and repeat bloom, 'Jardins de Bagatelle' is one of the most rewarding hybrid teas you can grow. It makes a great cut flower, and taking long stems will not deter its persistence to bloom again soon.

'KAREN BLIXEN'

KAREN BLIXEN

CLASS: Hybrid tea   BLOOM SIZE: 4½"

BLOOM COLOR: White   HARDINESS: Zones 5b–9

INTRODUCED: Poulsen, Denmark, 1992

A hybrid tea that blooms as much as a floribunda. We expect the bloom of a good floribunda to completely obscure its foliage. Though this rarely happens with hybrid teas, the foliage of 'Karen Blixen' regularly disappears beneath its massive, pure white blooms. This makes a stunning effect in the garden, especially when a group of these roses are massed together. The blooms make great cut flowers too, and will last a long time if taken as buds. Its healthy dark green foliage and bushy habit make 'Karen Blixen' a hybrid tea that's attractive at rest as well.

Nurseries do not overestimate the public's eagerness to purchase roses with literary names, and the demand for a rose named after the author of *Out of Africa* may be less than for one named after anyone who is appearing on television this year. Thus, 'Karen Blixen' has been sold under many alternative names, including 'Isis', 'Roy Black', and 'Silver Anniversary'.

L'AIMANT

CLASS: Floribunda   BLOOM SIZE: 3½"

BLOOM COLOR: Pink   HARDINESS: Zones 5–9

INTRODUCED: Harkness, England, 1994

Some roses are exciting as soon as they are introduced, because they offer something completely new or promise improvement when it is obviously needed. 'L'Aimant' was not one of these exciting novelties, but I have come to value it more each year. It is one of the few floribundas that I am now growing in multiple locations around the garden.

The sturdy plant displays big sprays of wonderfully fragrant, fluffy bright pink blooms. At the same time, solitary blooms are appearing elsewhere on the plant, so something is always happening. It's not one of those floribundas that blooms only in huge sprays, all at once, and then takes two months off. An ideal bedding rose, it also works very well as a junior member (in height) in a border of David Austin's roses.

The plant is healthy and quite winter hardy. It gets better each year and has supplanted 'Sexy Rexy', which has unfortunately declined with age (and was never fragrant in the first place). Also sold as 'Victorian Spice'.

LADY ROSE

CLASS: Hybrid tea   BLOOM SIZE: 4"

BLOOM COLOR: Orange-red   HARDINESS: Zones 5b–9

INTRODUCED: Kordes, Germany, 1979

An excellent hybrid tea for bedding, consistent and healthy in all weather. 'Lady Rose' has flowers of darkest orange-red, saved from dullness by the pleasing way in which they fade to coral orange. Foliage is dense and prickly, and blooms appear in so many places over the plant that cutting one with a long stem is often not possible.

The plant has a perfect round habit, which in Europe is often displayed to great advantage budded as a tree rose. I don't know of an American nursery that offers 'Lady Rose' as a standard yet, but I think it would bring them many satisfied customers.

LAMBERT CLOSSE

CLASS: Shrub

BLOOM SIZE: 5"

BLOOM COLOR: Pink

HEIGHT: 3'

REPEAT BLOOM: Good

HARDINESS: Zones 4b–9

INTRODUCED: Ogilvie, Canada, 1994

This is not my favorite Canadian Explorer rose, but it is popular with many garden visitors because its blooms resemble those of hybrid teas. These appear in shades of pink on a tough, compact 3' plant that works well for bedding. If forced to choose, I would rather have the profusion of less complicated blooms found on other Explorers instead of the fewer-but-larger blooms of 'Lambert Closse'. But anyone seeking to grow blooms like hybrid teas in a severe-winter climate should look to 'Lambert Closse'.

'LIEBESZAUBER'

LIEBESZAUBER

CLASS: Hybrid tea

BLOOM SIZE: 5½"

BLOOM COLOR: Red

HARDINESS: Zones 5–9

INTRODUCED: Kordes, Germany, 1990

A horse of a hybrid tea, growing with tremendous vigor to 5' and producing outsize dark red blooms. 'Liebeszauber' is marketed as a climber in South Africa, and it will reach 10' or more in mild climates. Across the northern states, it will be one of the tallest and most productive elements in a bed of mixed varieties of hybrid teas. It possesses outstanding winter hardiness.

We all perceive fragrance differently, and 'Liebeszauber' disappoints me because it does not have the strong, rich fragrance of famous old red hybrid teas such as 'Crimson Glory' and 'Chrysler Imperial'. It does have a fragrance, though, and if you approach it without preconceptions you may find it quite pleasing.

American nurseries keen to increase their sales of this excellent rose helpfully translate the name as 'Love's Magic'.

LIMELIGHT

LIMELIGHT

CLASS: Hybrid tea

BLOOM SIZE: 3½"

BLOOM COLOR: Yellow

HARDINESS: Zones 6–9

INTRODUCED: Kordes, Germany, 1985

The best bright yellow hybrid tea, and a great bedding rose. Its biggest liability is its relatively small bloom size. This is no problem in the garden, where the quantity of bloom produced more than compensates for individual blooms that are a little puny. But 'Limelight' can look out of scale if you want to include it in a mixed bouquet of hybrid teas. In cool weather you may detect a slight green shading at the edges of the bloom. Its growth is extraordinarily leafy, and you may want to thin some foliage to let light and air into the center of the plant. This can encourage new basal growth and reduce the threat from spider mites and disease.

'LOVE AND PEACE'

LOVE AND PEACE

CLASS: Hybrid tea
BLOOM SIZE: 5"
BLOOM COLOR: Yellow/pink
HARDINESS: Zones 6–9
INTRODUCED: Lim/Twomey, USA, 2002

The same yellow-with-pink color scheme as its parent 'Peace' on an incredibly attractive hybrid tea bush, clothed to the ground in glossy green leaves. A healthy, trouble-free, easy-to-grow rose that lacks only fragrance, or novelty.

MARGARET MERRIL

CLASS: Floribunda
BLOOM SIZE: 3½"
BLOOM COLOR: White
HARDINESS: Zones 6–9
INTRODUCED: Harkness, England, 1978

Even as floribundas have improved so much over the past 10 years — super health, larger sprays, more intense colors — many still lack one essential rose ingredient: fragrance. This one has fragrance to spare in its elegant satiny white blooms, which typically appear in small clusters. The 'Margaret Merril' plant has a perfect 3' floribunda habit, blends well with roses

'MARGARET MERRIL'

of any other color, and is ideally suited for adding perfume to any mass planting of floribundas.

MY INDIFFERENT 'ICEBERG'

For 50 years 'Iceberg' has been one of the most famous roses in the world, the white floribunda that always looks so beautiful in rose books and in the world's most notable rose gardens. But try as I might, I cannot grow 'Iceberg' well. It grows, it blooms, it gets a little black spot, it survives the winter, but it never matches my expectations — or anyone else's. No one ever notices 'Iceberg' in my garden, unless they are specifically looking for it, in which case they try to say something polite. I've tried different plants of 'Iceberg' in different parts of my garden, finally concluding that this rose is simply not suited to my conditions, no matter how well it does everywhere else. However, thanks to 'Grace Abounding', 'Hakuun', and **'Margaret Merril'** (all of which do so well for me), I haven't experienced any big empty gaps where a white floribunda should be.

'MARIJKE KOOPMAN'

MARIJKE KOOPMAN

CLASS: Hybrid tea
BLOOM SIZE: 4½"
BLOOM COLOR: Pink
HARDINESS: Zones 5–9
INTRODUCED: Fryer, England, 1978

With a name like 'Marijke Koopman', it has to be good. And it is. This is absolutely the most dependable hybrid tea in my northern Ohio garden, producing dozens of long-stemmed, rich pink blooms all summer long, and well into fall. There are very few hybrid teas that one can plant and forget, but 'Marijke Koopman' is one. The older 'Pink Favorite' also offers excellent disease resistance in about the same color of rose, but does not produce nearly so many blooms as 'Marijke Koopman'. 'Marijke Koopman' disappoints only in its insufficient fragrance.

MARQUISE SPINOLA

CLASS: Shrub	REPEAT BLOOM: Good
BLOOM COLOR: Pink	HEIGHT: 2½'
BLOOM SIZE: 3"	HARDINESS: Zones 5–9
INTRODUCED: Guillot-Massad, France, 1996	

Although sold as a shrub rose, 'Marquise Spinola' has an ideal floribunda habit and is perfect for bedding, where it stands up well to all weather. It makes big sprays of pure pink blooms. These have more than 100 short petals and open completely flat. It has much more fragrance than most floribundas and an extraordinarily long life as a cut flower. Blooms can still look good after a week, which is quite unusual for a rose with so many petals.

MARTINE GUILLOT

CLASS: Shrub	REPEAT BLOOM: Good
BLOOM COLOR: White	HEIGHT: 4½'
BLOOM SIZE: 4"	HARDINESS: Zones 5–9
INTRODUCED: Guillot-Massad, France, 1996	

A spectacular rose for bedding and cutting, 'Martine Guillot' grows to 4½' tall, well clothed in dark foliage

'MARTINE GUILLOT'

and completely covered with fantastic sprays of white blooms. As buds these have the elegant, slender, spiraled shape of a nineteenth-century tea rose, with none of the weak stems associated with members of that class. A spray will consist of a dozen or more blooms, and a plant may bear a dozen or more sprays at once. The full effect is magnified by having multiple plants. I grow five in a row as part of a border of Générosa and English Roses and would not like to have any fewer.

'Martine Guillot' is the best member of Guillot's family of Générosa roses. In my garden, 'Martine Guillot' has proved itself on a par with the Canadian Explorer roses for winter hardiness. The rosarian Gwendolyn Gallagher reports that 'Martine Guillot' also thrives in the harsh climate of Hokkaido, Japan.

MEMOIRE

CLASS: Hybrid tea	BLOOM SIZE: 5"
BLOOM COLOR: White	HARDINESS: Zones 5b–9
INTRODUCED: Kordes, Germany, 1992	

An easy-to-grow hybrid tea, with well-shaped white blooms on top of glossy foliage. These last well when cut and often appear in clusters, which makes this rose even more impressive as a bedding rose. Like many white hybrid teas, it has a lemony fragrance. Sometimes sold as 'Ice Cream'.

MISTER LINCOLN

CLASS: Hybrid tea	BLOOM SIZE: 5"
BLOOM COLOR: Red	HARDINESS: Zones 5–9
INTRODUCED: Swim & Weeks, USA, 1965	

A dark red hybrid tea with intense fragrance, 'Mister Lincoln' matches many people's idea of the perfect rose. Its stems are long, its blooms large, and its color and fragrance perfectly aligned with our expectations. But 'Mister Lincoln' isn't perfect: its blooms can blast open quickly in hot weather, and powdery mildew will attack when autumn nights grow cool. The plant can appear leggy when it is not in bloom.

This was not the first rose named for Abraham Lincoln. One hundred years previously, when news of the president's assassination reached France, the nurserymen Moreau and Robert introduced 'Souvenir du Président Lincoln', a rich pink, repeat-blooming Bourbon that also has an intense, pleasing fragrance. 'Souvenir du Président Lincoln' makes a fine, bushy shrub and is actually a better bedding rose than 'Mister Lincoln', although its blooms rarely last more than a day when cut.

MRS JOHN LAING

CLASS: Hybrid perpetual   REPEAT BLOOM: Reliable
BLOOM COLOR: Pink   HEIGHT: 4'
BLOOM SIZE: 6"   HARDINESS: Zones 5b–9
INTRODUCED: Bennett, England, 1887

Huge, silvery pink flowers on a compact plant and blooms all summer long make 'Mrs John Laing' one of the best hybrid perpetuals for today's gardens. The plant won't look out of place in a bed of hybrid teas, so long as you don't mind flowers that are larger and much more fragrant than most. The blooms of 'Mrs John Laing' make extremely effective cut flowers. To last well as cut flowers, they should be taken when they are only half open.

This is one of the most enduring roses hybridized by Henry Bennett, an English cattle breeder who was among the first to approach rose breeding in a scientific way.

Small world department: In the mid-1980s, when I was staffing the information booth at a rose show in Akron, Ohio, a lady who stopped by the booth mentioned that a rose had been named after her great-grandmother. She wondered if anyone had ever heard of it: 'Mrs John Laing'. Not only had I heard of it, I had entered it in the class for "Most Fragrant Rose" that day. It didn't win, but it found an ardent admirer.

MOONDANCE

CLASS: Floribunda   BLOOM SIZE: 3"
BLOOM COLOR: White   HARDINESS: Zones 5–9
INTRODUCED: Zary, USA, 2007

When I first planted 'Moondance', it was without any great expectations, even though it had won the All-America Rose Selection award. (It had also been named the Jackson & Perkins "Floribunda of the Year," but that means only that it is a floribunda being introduced by Jackson & Perkins.) For me, the seed of doubt came from the knowledge that 'Moondance' was bred from 'Iceberg' — a rose that never performed well in my garden.

'Moondance' started out with tremendous vigor, new canes breaking all over the place, and big, beautiful

'MOONDANCE'

sprays of full-petaled white blooms. This great performance has continued through two summers. It even has a nice fragrance. The plant reaches 5' in no time, which is tall for a floribunda. I hadn't counted on that, but I'm not going to mess with success and will not be moving this rose.

MOONSTONE

CLASS: Hybrid tea   BLOOM SIZE: 5½"
BLOOM COLOR: White/pink HARDINESS: Zones 6–9
INTRODUCED: Carruth, USA, 1998

A big, beautiful rose on a sturdy plant. There have been an almost mind-numbing number of hybrid teas introduced over the past 15 years with this same white-with-pink-edge color scheme. Many are shy bloomers that produce few flowers and are of interest only to rose exhibitors. Although it also can produce perfect exhibition blooms, 'Moonstone' is the best of the lot for reliable garden display.

MORDEN BLUSH

CLASS: Shrub HEIGHT: 3'
BLOOM COLOR: Pink HARDINESS: Zones 5–9
REPEAT BLOOM: Good
INTRODUCED: Collicutt & Marshall, Canada, 1988

The best of the Canadian Parkland roses, 'Morden Blush' has both the most pleasing color and the most eagerness to bloom of any in this group. Its soft pink, frilly-petaled blooms appear in small clusters on a healthy, compact plant that fits in perfectly with a bed of floribundas. This is a reliable rose, but don't plant it expecting the rugged growth of many shrub roses. In fact, the northern gardener may find little live wood to prune in spring, because 'Morden Blush' is no more (or less) hardy than most contemporary floribundas.

NARZISSE

CLASS: Hybrid tea BLOOM SIZE: 4"
BLOOM COLOR: Yellow HARDINESS: Zones 5b–9
INTRODUCED: Krause, Germany, 1942

A rose that arrived in the wrong place at the wrong time. This wonderful yellow hybrid tea was lost for many years in the hoopla surrounding the introduction of 'Peace'. 'Narzisse' remains a dependable choice for long-stemmed, maize-yellow blooms, usually with perfectly spiraled form. They make great, fragrant cut flowers, and the plant is more winter-hardy than many yellow hybrid teas introduced decades later.

NIGHTINGALE

CLASS: Hybrid tea BLOOM SIZE: 5"
BLOOM COLOR: Pink HARDINESS: Zones 5–9
INTRODUCED: Herholdt, South Africa, 1970

'Nightingale' is one of the few hybrid teas that survived the rigors of the location that Susan and I had first selected to grow hybrid teas in our new garden (see page 20). Not only did it survive, it thrived. It's a big hybrid tea, with large blooms, fat stems, and foliage eager to grow out of proportion when it is fed. The sturdy blooms are a blend of shades of deep pink extending almost into mauve, lasting very well when cut. Although its South African breeder would have had no experience with cold winters, the genetics of 'Nightingale' ensure its survival in Ohio.

NOSTALGIE

CLASS: Hybrid tea BLOOM SIZE: 4½"
BLOOM COLOR: White/red HARDINESS: Zones 5b–9
INTRODUCED: Tantau, Germany, 1996

Most roses that can be called "startling" have some serious defect that rosarians happily overlook. 'Nostalgie' is a great exception: its stunning blooms of cream and crimson, swirled together, provide one of the most dramatic contrasts in rosedom. The plant is a perfectly normal hybrid tea, growing to a stocky 4', resisting disease well, and not worrying about winter. Taking long stems will prompt the production of larger blooms. Simply snipping off spent blooms will produce more abundant repeat flowering, but with each bloom a smaller size.

OKLAHOMA

CLASS: Hybrid tea BLOOM SIZE: 5"
BLOOM COLOR: Blackish red HARDINESS: Zones 6–9
INTRODUCED: Swim & Weeks, USA, 1964

A lot of nearly black hybrid teas have been introduced in recent years, but none have as big a bloom or as big a fragrance as 'Oklahoma'. This is the fragrance that most people mean when they say "rose": full, sweet, and persistent, like a grandmother's perfume. 'Oklahoma' is a true hybrid tea, bearing its blooms singly on top of long stems. It will develop powdery mildew when autumn nights turn cool but is a star performer in hot, dry weather.

PALOMA BLANCA

CLASS: Shrub REPEAT BLOOM: Reliable
BLOOM COLOR: White HEIGHT: 3½'
BLOOM SIZE: 3" HARDINESS: Zones 5–9
INTRODUCED: Buck, USA, 1984

A completely trouble-free white rose, sold as a shrub but with a compact habit that makes it perfect for bedding. Well-formed blooms appear in large, perfectly symmetrical sprays all summer long. They last well as cut flowers and can be faulted only for a light (imperceptible to some) fragrance.

'PARADISE'

PARADISE

CLASS: Hybrid tea   BLOOM SIZE: 4"
BLOOM COLOR: Lavender   HARDINESS: Zones 6–9
INTRODUCED: Weeks, USA, 1978

A landmark among lavender hybrid teas, the bold magenta border around its blooms marks a division between the pale mauve hybrid teas that came before and the brighter lavenders that were to come later. 'Paradise' needs sun to develop the most striking color. It is an ideal hybrid tea for bedding and cutting. While no more tender than the average hybrid tea, it performs much better when it doesn't lose all of its live wood each winter. For this reason, Zone 5 gardeners may want to plant it next to the house or in some other sheltered location.

PAROLE

CLASS: Hybrid tea   BLOOM SIZE: 7"
BLOOM COLOR: Salmon   HARDINESS: Zones 6–9
INTRODUCED: Kordes, Germany, 2002

Humongous hybrid tea blooms (this variety is also sold as 'Buxom Beauty' and 'XXL') from that curious point on the color wheel where deep pink almost meets orange. The flowers are saved from being mere novelties, or even a joke, by a winning fragrance and a plant that is much healthier than the typical hybrid tea.

PASCALI

CLASS: Hybrid tea   BLOOM SIZE: 4"
BLOOM COLOR: White   HARDINESS: Zones 6–9
INTRODUCED: Lens, Belgium, 1963

White hybrid teas come and go, and breeders pay little attention to them because white roses sell the least. (Some nurseries counteract this by arranging their catalog in alphabetical order, instead of lumping everything of the same color together. In this case, the roses at the end of the alphabet will have the poorest sales.) The heavy-blooming 'Pascali' has stood the test of time, producing stem after stem of perfectly formed blooms that make great cut flower bouquets. Pascali's upright habit means that it can, and should, be planted closer together than other hybrid teas in rose beds.

'PASCALI'

PAUL SHIRVILLE

CLASS: Hybrid tea   BLOOM SIZE: 4"
BLOOM COLOR: Pink   HARDINESS: Zones 6–9
INTRODUCED: Harkness, England, 1981

Ideal for bedding, 'Paul Shirville' is a hybrid tea with a wide habit that fills a bed well. Its large coral pink blooms usually appear in clusters and make great cut bouquets. Their powerful fragrance will be surprising to people who have grown used to scentless hybrid teas. 'Paul Shirville' blooms abundantly all summer, and it is especially profuse each autumn.

'PEACE'

PEACE

CLASS: Hybrid tea BLOOM SIZE: 6"
BLOOM COLOR: Yellow HARDINESS: Zones 5b–9
INTRODUCED: Meilland, France, 1942

A rose that everyone knows, and some rosarians remember as being even better than it is today due to the massive scale of its propagation over the past 60 years. 'Peace' has huge lemon blooms, edged with pink, on a bush that would have been out of scale with other hybrid teas of the 1940s and 50s. But it fits right in today, remaining a great bedding and cut-flower rose. Even if it isn't quite as good as it used to be.

FADING WITH TIME

Asexual reproduction of roses — by bud-grafting or cuttings — should produce plants that are exact replicas of the original. In theory this is the case, but in practice nurseries are often careless about propagation (budding the tiny eyes found directly under a bloom, rooting a blind shoot). Over time these sloppy practices can degrade a variety. The rosarian Bob Martin has referred to this as "replicative fading," after a problem created by the transporter device in an episode of *Star Trek: The Next Generation*. Any rose propagated by many nurseries over many years is likely to have been subjected to this degradation. It is certainly responsible for the several different forms of 'The Fairy' on sale today. When the British floribunda 'Amber Queen' unexpectedly received an All-America Rose Selection award in 1988, it was propagated with such careless abandon that plants introduced in the United States were immediately inferior to ones I had imported directly from England only a few years before.

Just as thoughtless propagation can degrade a variety, so can thoughtful propagation improve it. You can see this for yourself with a rose such as **'Peace'** that has "faded" with time. Here's how: To start, pick the best bloom you can find on your 'Peace' rosebush on the longest stem, and root that cutting (or bud-graft the fifth and sixth bud-eyes down from the bloom). You will likely get a 'Peace' that is better, by a tiny increment, than the plant that the bud eyes or cuttings came from. Repeat the process enough times and eventually you may produce a plant that is demonstrably better.

For quicker results, obtain cuttings from a garden that has grown the same plants of 'Peace' since its American introduction in 1946. The rose is tough and long-lived, lasting longer now than most of the rosarians who would have planted it right after World War II. But original plantings of 'Peace' can often still be found at church gardens and in municipal plantings. If it has been properly pruned and cared for, you may be immediately impressed by how new an old plant of 'Peace' can look.

PEACEKEEPER

CLASS: Floribunda BLOOM SIZE: 3"
BLOOM COLOR: Yellow blend HARDINESS: Zones 5–9
INTRODUCED: Harkness, England, 1994

A cheerful and reliable floribunda, which throws small sprays of hybrid-tea-shaped blooms with great regularity. These are a bright apricot yellow, fading gently to buff tones. The plant grows upright and is less bushy than most floribundas. It is far more winter hardy than most roses of this color. Like so many of the Harkness floribundas, 'Peacekeeper' has a delightful scent.

PETER FRANKENFELD

CLASS: Hybrid tea BLOOM SIZE: 5"
BLOOM COLOR: Pink HARDINESS: Zones 5–9
INTRODUCED: Kordes, Germany, 1966

A hybrid tea that is above average in every respect ends up being a real garden asset. 'Peter Frankenfeld' is a tough rose, healthy and very winter hardy, that produces a huge number of well-formed, fragrant, cerise pink blooms all summer long. These make great cut flowers.

PLAYBOY

CLASS: Floribunda BLOOM SIZE: 3½"
BLOOM COLOR: Yellow/red HARDINESS: Zones 5b–9
INTRODUCED: Cocker, Scotland, 1976

Semi-double blooms are an intensely bright yellow, edged with orange-red. The petals are ruffled just enough to display this shocking contrast at its most

'PLAYBOY'

PRETTY LADY

CLASS: Floribunda BLOOM SIZE: 3½"

BLOOM COLOR: Apricot HARDINESS: Zones 5–9

INTRODUCED: Scrivens, England, 1996

The toughest of the apricot-shaded floribundas, this rose is also very beautiful. Its blooms are large for a floribunda, with the high-centered shape of a hybrid tea. They are a blend of cream and peach, usually appearing in cuttable sprays, but solitary blooms are also common. I have seen a few black spots on my plant, but only because I was looking. (Len Scrivens used a variety of the species rose *Rosa davidii* in the breeding of this rose, which is reported to be completely black-spot-free in England.) It's a remarkably healthy and free-blooming rose in a color that will blend well with any other garden hue.

PRISCILLA BURTON

CLASS: Floribunda BLOOM SIZE: 3"

BLOOM COLOR: Crimson/white HARDINESS: Zones 5b–9

INTRODUCED: McGredy, Northern Ireland, 1978

With crimson-purple markings on a silver-white background, 'Priscilla Burton' is my favorite hand-painted rose. It grows a little gangly for a floribunda, and it will get a little black spot. These faults are easily disguised when it is planted in a bed with other floribundas. The extraordinary color variations displayed on its semi-double blooms will make it a talking point in any mixed planting.

dramatic. Viewed from a distance, the overall effect is of bright orange. Blooms arrive singly as well as in well-spaced clusters. They make good cut flowers if taken just as the petals are beginning to unfurl.

'Playboy' is a superior bedding rose. With its good health and holly foliage, the 2½' plant is attractive even when not in bloom and so useful throughout the landscape as well as for bedding. It makes an excellent tree rose. Unlike some Scottish roses, it does not sulk in the heat of summer.

PORTRAIT

CLASS: Hybrid tea BLOOM SIZE: 5"

BLOOM COLOR: Pink HARDINESS: Zones 5–9

INTRODUCED: Meyer, USA, 1972

This pink hybrid tea was raised by an amateur, Carl Meyer, who was a plumber in Cincinnati, Ohio. It won the All-America Rose Selection award and went on to be sold throughout Europe as 'Stéphanie de Monaco'. It's a rose that works: it blooms a lot, it has a strong fragrance, it makes long stems, and it has no problem surviving an Ohio winter. The color is more than just medium pink. The reverse of the petals are a darker shade, which allows the rose to change in appearance almost hourly as it opens.

'PRISCILLA BURTON'

HAND-PAINTED ROSES

When Sam McGredy IV used 'Frühlingsmorgen' to bring *Rosa spinosissima* blood into modern roses, it produced a color-variation effect that he called "hand-painted." Hand-painted roses typically have a deeper color that appears etched onto a lighter one in random patterns. Like snowflakes, no two flowers are the same. The most dramatic color variations come in cool weather; in heat the hand-painted effect can be almost completely lost.

The success of the hand-painted floribundas in the late 1970s and 1980s prompted the introduction of a few hand-painted hybrid teas, of which the most notable was McGredy's 'Maestro'. Paul Jerabek bred a hand-painted shrub rose called 'Peggy M'. Although McGredy has retired, the influence of his hand-painted strain continues, most recently in Jackson & Perkins' 2008 Floribunda of the Year, 'Lovestruck'.

in the United States). Dozens of confused roses have been slotted into this class in the generations since for sometimes dubious reasons — because they were too tall to be floribundas, for example, or had flowers too informal to be hybrid teas, or because a nursery had decided to introduce another rose in the exact same color that year as a floribunda or a hybrid tea.

However, 'Queen Elizabeth' is a good starter rose. Success with it can give novice gardeners the confidence to move on to varieties that offer much greater rewards for just a bit more effort. And a plant of 'Queen Elizabeth' always makes a great gift for anyone who thinks they can't grow roses.

From the same breeder, the pink hybrid tea 'Bewitched' offers modified 'Queen Elizabeth'-like growth, with well-formed blooms and great fragrance.

'REMEMBER ME'

QUEEN ELIZABETH

CLASS: Grandiflora
BLOOM COLOR: Pink
REPEAT BLOOM: Good
INTRODUCED: Lammerts, USA, 1955

BLOOM SIZE: 4½"
HEIGHT: 6'
HARDINESS: Zones 5–9

I happily admit that I don't really like 'Queen Elizabeth'. It's a vigorous performer, growing tall and producing scads of blooms that don't have any discernible form and aren't a very interesting shade of pink. And it fails the smell test (it doesn't have any). Without 'Queen Elizabeth' we never would have been troubled with the artificially created grandiflora classification (found only

REMEMBER ME

CLASS: Hybrid tea
BLOOM COLOR: Copper
INTRODUCED: Cocker, Scotland, 1984

BLOOM SIZE: 4"
HARDINESS: Zones 6–8

An unmistakable hybrid tea blending sunset orange with rich coppery tones. The bud often appears brown, but blooms unfurl into a lively blend of many shades. The plant is a picture of glossy-leaved good health, and one can fault 'Remember Me' only for a relatively small bloom size, compared to other hybrid teas. The largest, most colorful blooms often appear in the fall, and the plant winters very well.

This is one of the few satisfying roses bred from 'Pink Favorite', a remarkably disease-resistant 1956 American hybrid tea. In its day, 'Pink Favorite' was viewed as the rose that would usher in a new era of healthy hybrid teas, but in most cases its pollen did not cooperate.

'QUEEN ELIZABETH'

ROB ROY

CLASS: Floribunda

BLOOM SIZE: 3½"

BLOOM COLOR: Red

HARDINESS: Zones 5–9

INTRODUCED: Cocker, Scotland, 1970

The British used to describe floribundas like this as "floribunda, hybrid tea type." As more and more floribundas began to feature blooms shaped like those of hybrid teas, the description became redundant. But it still works for 'Rob Roy', which produces neat sprays of blood red blooms that spiral open in the characteristic manner of a hybrid tea. The blooms open quickly, which may limit their value as cut flowers but only increases the value of 'Rob Roy' as a bedding plant, covered once each summer month in a canopy of red.

'ROBERT DUNCAN'

ROBERT DUNCAN

CLASS: Hybrid perpetual

REPEAT BLOOM: Monthly

BLOOM COLOR: Pink

HEIGHT: 4½'

BLOOM SIZE: 4½"

HARDINESS: Zones 5b–9

INTRODUCED: Dickson, Northern Ireland, 1897

Much hybrid tea influence is apparent in this later hybrid perpetual. The blooms are pointed rather than rounded, and the bush has a restrained habit that makes it suitable for bedding. Repeat bloom is excellent. Flowers are rich pink with a lighter reverse, with genuine old garden rose fragrance.

Winters in Zone 5 often give us no choice as to how we prune this rose. The cold kills the plant back to the ground, and we are left to cut off the dead canes and hope it will resprout. However, if your climate gives you a choice, pruning can turn 'Robert Duncan' into one of two very different plants. Prune it very lightly and it will produce an explosion of blooms, some not very large, a few not very well-formed, but all quite impressive for garden display. Severe pruning, back to about 6", will generate long stems with large, exquisitely formed blossoms, both singly and as sprays. These are ideal for cutting (and exhibition).

ROSE GAUJARD

CLASS: Hybrid tea

BLOOM SIZE: 7"

BLOOM COLOR: Pink/white

HARDINESS: Zones 6–9

INTRODUCED: Gaujard, France 1957

An outsize hybrid tea capable of producing singularly impressive blooms. These are bright raspberry pink, with a white reverse. The extremely high-centered buds unfurl slowly, and the blooms appear to grow bigger every day for the better part of a week. The large, dark green leaves are in proportion with the huge blooms, and stems are routinely several feet long. If you disbud a basal break of 'Rose Gaujard' to leave just one flower bud, it will possibly become the largest rose you've ever grown.

RUBY WEDDING

CLASS: Hybrid tea

BLOOM SIZE: 4½"

BLOOM COLOR: Red

HARDINESS: Zones 5–9

INTRODUCED: Gregory, England, 1979

This red hybrid tea blooms and blooms all summer long. It doesn't have much scent, and it won't win any prizes at rose shows. But it's a nearly constant source for long-stemmed red roses, and it requires no special attention to perform well. Health is good, and it's very winter hardy for a hybrid tea.

SCENT-SATION

CLASS: Hybrid tea

BLOOM SIZE: 4½"

BLOOM COLOR: Coral

HARDINESS: Zones 6–9

INTRODUCED: Fryer, England, 1998

Coral, with a paler reverse, this hybrid tea is more orange in hot weather and more pink when it is cool. The soft colors of the unfurling blooms are highlighted by a yellow base that gradually disappears as the rose opens. The bushy, healthy plant is perfect for bedding, and the stems are always long enough to cut.

As one would expect from the name, this rose is quite fragrant.

Although its blooms can be smaller than normal for a hybrid tea in the summer, 'Scent-Sation' shows to excellent advantage in autumn, when it is more likely to be smothered in blooms than most of its neighbors.

'SCENTIMENTAL'

SCENTIMENTAL

CLASS: Floribunda   HARDINESS: Zones 5–9

BLOOM COLOR: Red striped with white

INTRODUCED: Carruth, USA, 1997

With fully double burgundy red blossoms swirled with creamy white, 'Scentimental' is the best striped rose for dependable, long-lasting bloom. This is a color combination often found in the striped old garden roses. In this case it arrives on a healthy plant with good bedding habit. And it's fragrant.

SHEILA'S PERFUME

CLASS: Floribunda   BLOOM SIZE: 3½"

BLOOM COLOR: Yellow/red   HARDINESS: Zones 5b–9

INTRODUCED: Sheridan, England, 1985

Possessing the best qualities of both a floribunda and a hybrid tea, 'Sheila's Perfume' produces sprays of

STRIPED ROSES

Bold red streaks on a paper white reverse; bright yellow swirled into pure orange; raspberry drizzled on cream; purple on a background that varies from white to pink, like a pinwheel frozen in time. Such stunning contrasts represent the good news about striped roses. The bad news is that some have a gangly growth habit, many are prone to disease, and few have blooms that look their best for more than an hour or two. Fortunately, this is changing as rose hybridizers have discovered how to create roses that once appeared only as mutations. The newly hybridized striped roses such as **'Scentimental'** offer real improvements.

The mutant striped roses all carry forward the particular qualities of the rose from which they sported. Thus pink-and-white 'Candy Stripe' preserves the large, blowsy blooms and dusky fragrance of its parent 'Pink Peace'; salmon-and-white 'Festival Fanfare' has the same large sprays and heavy bloom of its parent, 'Fred Loads'.

Many new striped roses are discovered each year in rose gardens and backyards. Some of these mutations prove impossible to propagate. Others can be reproduced but do not remain stable — displaying some striped blooms, perhaps, along with some that are half one color and half another, and still more that look indistinguishable from their parent. An effective striped rose — one that makes you say "wow" — should not require close examination to determine whether or not it is really striped. While most of the world's rose breeders are enthusiastically working to improve striped roses through hybridization, Indian researchers pioneered the creation of striped roses by using atomic radiation. Apart from the obvious risks involved, the results from this program have not, so far, offered roses that are very different from the many mutations that have appeared with no advance warning.

A European who spent a summer driving across the United States told me that her favorite place was the vast expanses of Texas. There, she said, everyone gave you a big wave because they were so happy just to see another person. And so it was for many years with striped roses. When hybridizers stumbled across them, they gave them names befitting their scarcity. And that is why we have roses called 'Rare Edition' and 'Oddball'.

A collection of striped roses will only be effective if displayed in separate parts of the garden. One striped rose will animate any rose bed or dooryard garden. Two different striped roses planted next to each other will begin to look confusing. A bed of several different striped roses will hurt your eyes.

classically spiraled blooms in a surprising blend of yellow and red. The medium-sized blooms are intensely fragrant and attractive at every stage — bud, developing flower, and fully open bloom. Its habit is upright to 3' in my primary floribunda rose bed, where this is one of only a few roses I

'SHEILA'S PERFUME'

SILVER JUBILEE

CLASS: Hybrid tea   BLOOM SIZE: 4½"
BLOOM COLOR: Orange/pink   HARDINESS: Zones 5b–9
INTRODUCED: Cocker, Scotland, 1978

Does much of the future of the hybrid tea reside in the genes of 'Silver Jubilee', a coral orange-pink blend introduced in Scotland in 1978? This rose ushered the winter-hardy, disease-resistant *Rosa kordesii* into the lineage of the hybrid tea. 'Silver Jubilee' is notable for its perfect compact habit, mirror-glossy foliage, and profusion of beautifully shaped blooms. One could not imagine a better hybrid tea for bedding. 'Silver Jubilee' is so eager to bloom that it often does not make long stems.

While its most successful offspring to date are floribundas, 'Silver Jubilee' remains a benchmark for what a hybrid tea rose can offer in our gardens: habit as pleasing as an azalea's, vigor equal to phlox, foliage as glossy as holly, and the exquisite blooms of a rose.

grow in multiples. It would be hard to imagine a more attractive rose for bedding and cutting.

SHI-UN

CLASS: Hybrid tea   BLOOM SIZE: 4"
BLOOM COLOR: Purple   HARDINESS: Zones 6–9
INTRODUCED: Suzuki, Japan, 1984

Shi-un means "purple cloud" in Japanese, and this hybrid tea resembles one each month when it is covered in blooms. They are really a little less harsh than purple, a rich lilac color with a powerful fragrance. Individual bloom size is smaller than average for a hybrid tea, but the plant more than makes up for this by producing so many blooms.

Japan has a climate similar to the United States, and roses that do well in one country should also be successful in the other. Many American roses have proven this in Japanese gardens, but few Japanese roses have been introduced in America. If there are others as good as 'Shi-un', I want to grow them.

'SILVER JUBILEE'

SMOOTH VELVET

CLASS: Hybrid tea
BLOOM SIZE: 4½"

BLOOM COLOR: Red
HARDINESS: Zones 6–9

INTRODUCED: Davidson, USA, 1986

This red hybrid tea is the easiest to find of Harvey Davidson's thornless creations. 'Smooth Velvet' produces its blooms on long stems, and it repeats quickly. It would be an ordinary red hybrid tea if it didn't lack thorns, so is most useful in a dedicated cutting garden, or in a situation where a thornless rose would be beneficial.

THORNLESS ROSES

Thorns don't have to be part of the rose package, and California rose breeder Harvey Davidson has made a specialty of developing roses without them. These have novelty interest, of course, but are also valuable for planting where children may be playing, and for gardeners who must take special care not to cut their skin. Plus it's remarkably easy to work with thornless roses in flower arrangements.

Davidson has bred thornless hybrid teas and floribundas in a variety of colors. These are marketed as "Smooth Touch" roses, and all have names beginning with **"Smooth."**

SOUVENIR DE LA MALMAISON

CLASS: Bourbon
REPEAT BLOOM: Good

BLOOM COLOR: Pink/cream
HEIGHT: 5' in Zone 5

BLOOM SIZE: 5"
HARDINESS: Zones 6–9

INTRODUCED: Béluze, France, 1843

I grow this Bourbon rose in a long bed of hybrid teas. It fits in perfectly there and blooms more abundantly than some of today's introductions. The flowers are an exquisitely beautiful confection of pearl pink and cream, with short petals quartered in a perfectly symmetrical arrangement. The blooms are extraordinarily fragrant, and they last well when cut. Stems are long and strong. 'Souvenir de la Malmaison' flowers as profusely at the end of the rose season as it does at the beginning. The plant is just as hardy as a typical hybrid tea. It is grateful for a shovelful of winter protection, but it will usually survive without it.

'SOUVENIR DE LA MALMAISON'

Named in memory of the garden where the Empress Josephine attempted to collect all of the world's roses. There are numerous mutations. In 'Leweson Gower' the pink is intensified, while in 'Kronprincessin Viktoria' it is eliminated, resulting in a pure white rose. 'Climbing Souvenir de la Malmaison' is a more vigorous version that flowers a lot less. 'Souvenir de St Anne's' has only about 12 petals, and so just one day of perfect beauty. But that can be a day to remember.

STADT DEN HELDER

CLASS: Floribunda
BLOOM SIZE: 2½"

BLOOM COLOR: Red
HARDINESS: Zones 5–9

INTRODUCED: Ilsink, Netherlands, 1979

For a generation, red floribundas were predictably stumpy little plants with huge, overcrowded sprays of often-ugly florets. 'Stadt den Helder' is the red floribunda that broke that mold. It grows tall, usually over 4' in my garden, and its sprays are nicely spaced with semi-double, bright red blooms. You will also find some blooms appearing all by themselves on nice long stems. It's a superior bedding plant, but it is also useful in the mixed border and as an accent planted among conifers or anywhere its bright, cheerful color is needed.

A light red rose bred from 'Stadt de Helder' and sharing all of its best qualities has recently been named 'Anne Graber', in honor of the former president of the Canadian Rose Society.

STEPHANIE DIANE

CLASS: Hybrid tea
BLOOM SIZE: 5"
BLOOM COLOR: Red
HARDINESS: Zones 5–9
INTRODUCED: Bees, England, 1971

A tall, easy-to-grow hybrid tea that produces large, many-petaled blooms. These are cherry red with a slightly paler reverse, and they almost always appear singly atop very long stems. This rose enjoys good health and excellent winter hardiness. Its major fault is that its blooms have too many petals to open easily during cool or rainy weather.

SUMMER DREAM

CLASS: Floribunda
BLOOM SIZE: 2½"
BLOOM COLOR: Apricot
HARDINESS: Zones 5–9
INTRODUCED: Fryer, England, 1988

Imagine the old polyanthas still sold as "spray roses" at some florists and you will have an impression of the petal-packed form of 'Summer Dream'. It has been super-sized into a floribunda and given a pleasing new soft apricot color, but the arrangement of both the petals in the bloom and the blooms on the spray is the same.

A great producer of long-lasting sprays, 'Summer Dream' performs well in all weather. Despite having so many petals, its blooms still open well when nights grow cool. Plus, the blooms aren't spoiled by rain. 'Summer Dream' has a growth habit more narrow than most floribundas, and for good bedding effect should be planted no further than 18" apart.

From the same breeder, 'Sweet Dream' is essentially a scaled-down version of this rose. Marketed as a "patio rose," it is good for growing in pots.

SUN FLARE

CLASS: Floribunda
BLOOM SIZE: 2½"
BLOOM COLOR: Yellow
HARDINESS: Zones 6–9
INTRODUCED: Warriner, USA, 1983

When I gardened in the city, I lined my front walk with two dozen plants of 'Sun Flare'. This floribunda enjoyed excellent health and produced hundreds of

'SUN FLARE'

impressively large sprays of lemon yellow blooms each year. I don't have a front walk anymore, and my gravel driveway is lined with shrub roses. Sadly, 'Sun Flare' has not been too happy out here in the country, requiring extra protection to make it through the winter with enough live wood to allow a vigorous start in the spring. I consider hybrid teas to be Zone 6 plants and provide winter protection accordingly here in Zone 5. But I expect floribundas to be a little more hardy. Planted with the bud union 1" below soil level, I don't provide winter protection for most floribundas after their first year. 'Sun Flare' is one that does need yearly winter protection, and it's an excellent example of a Zone 6 star that is not really suitable for Zone 5.

SUTTER'S GOLD

CLASS: Hybrid tea
BLOOM SIZE: 4"
BLOOM COLOR: Yellow
HARDINESS: Zones 6–9
INTRODUCED: Swim, USA, 1950

Red buds open to flowers of a rich golden color. Look closely and you will find the bud's red tones hanging in there, on the backs of the outer petals. The flowers soon mellow to yellow, often mottled with patches of the original gold. The plant is a little wiry, but always sprouting new growth and buds. 'Sutter's Gold' is among the most fragrant of all hybrid teas, and it is unfortunate that the blooms do not last well when cut.

'SUTTER'S GOLD'

In the postwar years, rose breeders concentrated relentlessly on the hybrid tea. One looked much like the next, and the emphasis was on bloom production rather than charm. This is one of the most enduring roses from that period, precisely because it isn't a flower factory. It's a great garden plant.

SWARTHMORE

CLASS: Hybrid tea   BLOOM SIZE: 5"
BLOOM COLOR: Pink   HARDINESS: Zones 5–9
INTRODUCED: Meilland, France, 1963

A stalwart hybrid tea, with large blooms on a vigorous plant. The buds are a deep but bright pink, opening up to reveal a smoky charcoal edge that is most prominent in hot, sunny weather. (If you protect the buds from the sun while they open, the deeper edge hardly appears at all.) This is a superior cut flower, and one of the easiest of all hybrid teas to grow.

TIFFANY

CLASS: Hybrid tea   BLOOM SIZE: 5"
BLOOM COLOR: Pink   HARDINESS: Zones 6–9
INTRODUCED: Lindquist, USA, 1954

Not all old garden roses had a great fragrance, but almost all of them that we still grow today do. And so it is becoming with hybrid teas. Those that are still being enjoyed 50 years after their debut are almost all attractive to the nose as well as to the eye. 'Tiffany' is very fragrant, with slender buds of salmon pink. These open into large flowers with a soft yellow flush shot through the center of the bloom. 'Tiffany' makes a rewarding cut flower and has a typical hybrid tea habit. It can catch powdery mildew when that disease is prevalent.

TOUCH OF CLASS

CLASS: Hybrid tea   BLOOM SIZE: 5"
BLOOM COLOR: Orange-pink   HARDINESS: Zones 6–9
INTRODUCED: Kriloff, France, 1984

Another example of a rose that is perfectly suited for one place or purpose, 'Touch of Class' was originally introduced in France as 'Maréchal LeClerc' and achieved no particular success. However, this rose turned out to have precisely the high-centered form specified for award-winning hybrid teas in the American Rose Society's *Guidelines for Judging Roses,* and with a new name in a new country it has become a great hit. 'Touch of Class' is salmon pink and almost always appears one bloom to a stem. These make great cut flowers, and the plant is more productive than many exhibition roses. Its only real fault is a tendency to mildew when nights turn cool.

'TOUCH OF CLASS'

'TROPICAL SUNSET'

TROPICAL SUNSET

CLASS: Hybrid tea   BLOOM SIZE: 5"

BLOOM COLOR: Orange striped   HARDINESS: Zones 6–9
   with yellow

INTRODUCED: McGredy, New Zealand, 1996

'Tropical Sunset' is one of the first in a new wave of striped hybrid teas that have been created via hybridization. (Its great-grandfather is the striped miniature 'Stars 'n' Stripes'.) A hybridized rose is generally more stable and predictable than a mutation (the traditional source for striped roses), which often will throw a cane that reverts to the original variety, or demonstrate other inconsistent behavior.

'Tropical Sunset' displays bold yellow stripes on an orange background. It opens quickly through the traditional stages of a hybrid tea — urn-shaped bud, high-centered bloom — and is most impressive and long-lasting as an open bloom. The vigorous plant is taller than the average hybrid tea and especially floriferous in autumn.

TRULY YOURS

CLASS: Hybrid tea   BLOOM SIZE: 6"

BLOOM COLOR: Pink   HARDINESS: Zones 6–9

INTRODUCED: Carruth, USA, 2006

Perfectly formed, humongous, soft pink blooms on a compact hybrid tea full of healthy red-green foliage. Absolutely covered in bloom several times each summer, this is a bedding rose that can make its neighbors look like laggards. Despite its short stature 'Truly

Yours' has no problem producing plenty of cut flowers on medium-length stems. How it performs after a really severe winter will determine whether or not this rose represents an improvement on 'Savoy Hotel', a similar recommendable rose of the late 1980s.

TRUMPETER

CLASS: Floribunda   BLOOM SIZE: 3"

BLOOM COLOR: Orange-red   HARDINESS: Zones 5b–9

INTRODUCED: McGredy, Northern Ireland, 1977

One of the very best compact floribundas, with clusters of orange-red florets so profuse that its foliage often disappears completely beneath them. In flower throughout the summer, it appears equally at ease in heat and during rainy spells. Its sturdy petals are quite weather resistant. Well worth growing in quantity for a massed effect, and also splendid as a half-standard (tree rose) budded at 18" or 24".

No matter how popular they once were, many roses run out of steam by the time they are 30. Tastes change, plantings get old, vigor declines as a rose is continually propagated, and new introductions feature incremental improvements. 'Trumpeter', however, shows no sign of falling out of favor.

URDH

CLASS: Hybrid perpetual   REPEAT BLOOM: Reliable

BLOOM COLOR: Pink   HEIGHT: 3½'

BLOOM SIZE: 4"   HARDINESS: Zones 5–9

INTRODUCED: Tantau, Germany, 1933

Introduced long after the hybrid tea had secured its supremacy, this late-in-the-day hybrid perpetual

'URDH'

provides an interesting look at where the class might have headed if hybridizers had continued working with it. Here is a compact plant that produces lots of rich pink blooms. Packed with petals and intensely fragrant, they almost all appear individually on long stems. These make good cut flowers if cut young. 'Urdh' is ideal for bedding, and it will add a delightful fragrance to any grouping of hybrid teas.

A sister seedling called 'Stämmler' is an interesting example of how two roses grown from the same seedpod can be different. It is a lighter shade of pink and shares the same incredible fragrance found in 'Urdh'. In my garden it has not produced as many blooms, and its habit strays from the 'Urdh' ideal.

VALENTINE HEART

CLASS: Floribunda   BLOOM SIZE: 3½"
BLOOM COLOR: Pink   HARDINESS: Zones 5–9
INTRODUCED: Dickson, Northern Ireland, 1989

An ideal bedding rose, 'Valentine Heart' rarely makes the large sprays typical of floribundas, but it still produces so many blooms at once that the effect is essentially the same. Its blooms are pure pink, with a delicate mauve cast apparent in certain light. The blooms contrast beautifully with the glossy, deep green foliage. Often this compact plant displays buds, opening blooms, and fully expanded flowers all at the same time. This is a memorable sight. 'Valentine Heart' is particularly good in autumn, looking fresh and new when some floribundas appear eager to shut down.

VATER RHEIN

CLASS: Hybrid tea   BLOOM SIZE: 4"
BLOOM COLOR: Red   HARDINESS: Zones 5–9
INTRODUCED: Kiese, Germany, 1922

The original nineteenth-century hybrid teas were healthy, vigorous plants well-suited for bedding. For example, 'Mme Caroline Testout' (introduced in 1890) can still be seen in its beautiful shade of pink in big beds all around Portland, Oregon. By the 1910s, however, the class had been hijacked by florists, and hybrid teas began to be bred for the greenhouse environment. Many of these hothouse flowers appear weak and spindly when grown outdoors, and downright exhausted by the time autumn rolls around.

'Vater Rhein' has unusual vigor for a hybrid tea of its era (the 1920s) and makes a fine bushy plant. Its many-petaled blooms offer both old-fashioned fragrance and the old-fashioned kind of red that admits generous portions of pink and maroon.

VETERANS' HONOR

CLASS: Hybrid tea   BLOOM SIZE: 5"
BLOOM COLOR: Red   HARDINESS: Zones 6–9
INTRODUCED: Zary, USA, 1995

Each decade brings a new candidate for the red hybrid tea we have all been waiting for. In the 1970s it was the oddly named 'Precious Platinum', which remains a useful garden rose in the Midwest. 'Olympiad', introduced for the Los Angeles Olympics in 1984, turned out to be a sprinter rather than a marathon competitor. The very tough 'Taxi', bred in Denmark where the winters are cold and the taxicabs are red, contended for a few years as 'Olympiad' began to fade. 'Veterans' Honor' was the best American red hybrid tea of the 1990s, and it may still be today. Its red color is particularly bright and rich. While your eyes tell you that this flower is entirely red — both tops of petals and reverse — if you were to tear open a petal you would discover that there is white inside. Time, so far, has been kind to this heavy-blooming hybrid tea, but as it lacks fragrance the search for the perfect red hybrid tea will continue.

VICK'S CAPRICE

CLASS: Hybrid perpetual   REPEAT BLOOM: Reliable
BLOOM COLOR: Striped cream   HEIGHT: 4'
BLOOM SIZE: 5"   HARDINESS: Zones 5b–8
INTRODUCED: Vick, USA, 1891

For repeat bloom and a powerful fragrance, 'Vick's Caprice' is the most dependable of the heritage striped roses. It's a hybrid perpetual of modest height that still makes a quality bedding rose, and it will be more at home with other roses than in a mixed border. A mutation of the French rose 'Archiduchesse Elisabeth d'Autriche' discovered in New York State, 'Vick's Caprice' varies tremendously in color (pink to purplish stripes) and effect (clear or muddy background). But with three crops of blooms in a season, the chances of getting a memorable week of 'Vick's Caprice' is stronger than from the more widely available striped hybrid perpetual 'Ferdinand Pichard'.

'VICK'S CAPRICE'

VIOLETTE PARFUMÉE

CLASS: Grandiflora   HEIGHT: 4½'

BLOOM COLOR: Purple   HARDINESS: Zones 5b–9

REPEAT BLOOM: Good

INTRODUCED: Dorieux, France, 1995

With one of the most wonderful fragrances ever bred into a rose, this is a trouble-free grower that goes about its business of producing flowers for cutting with no special requirements or demands. Blooms are lavender purple, often heavily mottled with lighter tones. 'Violette Parfumée' is one of the very best roses for including in a bouquet of roses for your house, or for sharing with people at your place of work, your church, your bank, your post office, or any place where it can be appreciated by everyone with a nose for roses.

Officially classified as a grandiflora in the United States (where it is sometimes sold as 'Melodie Parfumée'), this rose is considered a hybrid tea in every other country of the world. It should be treated in your garden exactly as any other hybrid tea.

WARM WISHES

CLASS: Hybrid tea   BLOOM SIZE: 5½"

BLOOM COLOR: Apricot/pink   HARDINESS: Zones 5b–9

INTRODUCED: Fryer, England, 1994

The healthiest apricot-shaded hybrid tea I've ever grown, 'Warm Wishes' is also reliably winter hardy (something that could not be said for apricot hybrid teas just a generation ago). Its large blooms unfurl from perfectly spiraled buds, apricot blended with quantities of pink that vary with the weather. They have a pleasing fragrance and recur surprisingly quickly for such a large rose. 'Warm Wishes' is an ideal bedding rose that also makes a wonderful cut flower.

Often sold as 'Sunset Celebration' in the United States.

CHAPTER 6

MINIATURE ROSES

As recently as the 1980s it was typical to hear visitors at rose shows express surprise at the very existence of miniature roses (or "baby roses," as the spectators often called them). Since then, the explosion of miniature roses offered for sale as potted plants in supermarkets and other unlikely locations has made them much less of a novelty, but even more of a challenge. While miniature roses were once available only through specialized nurseries that bred them for outdoor use, many of the miniatures sold as potted plants today are not tough enough to survive outdoors. Some are simply not winter hardy. Others are selected for their ability to produce one massive bloom explosion, after which they may be too exhausted to attempt anything else. For reliable garden miniature roses, shop at a reputable garden center or specialized mail order nursery. Almost all miniature roses offered for sale in the United States are grown on their own roots. In Zone 5, I do not offer them any extra protection over winter.

OPPOSITE Planted en masse, the miniature 'Rainbow's End' provides a profusion of color all summer long.

USING MINIATURES IN THE HOME LANDSCAPE

Outdoors, miniatures are perfectly suited for growing in tubs and other containers (see chapter 9 for details on container growing). These must be considerably larger than the 4" or 6" pots in which the supermarket miniatures are usually sold. In containers, miniatures can provide bright spots of color not only on the patio and deck, but on tables and ledges as well.

All miniatures are repeat-blooming, and the best of them will be in bloom almost every day of the summer. For this reason, they can serve as outstanding accent plants. Use them in the garden for a patch of brilliant color at the front of a mixed bed, or sprinkled among dwarf conifers in a foundation planting. There are a few miniatures that make great edging plants, but most are too gangly to fill that niche well.

Most miniatures will be happiest and most productive in a dedicated miniature rose bed. As with larger roses, an arrangement of two staggered rows works best, but in most climates you will be able to fit three rows of miniatures into a bed without too much danger of trampling the outliers, or not being able to reach the ones in the middle. Full morning sun followed by filtered afternoon shade is ideal. I plant miniatures on 1-foot centers; rosarians in California and the South use much wider spacing.

A bed of miniature roses often looks best alongside a walkway. Because the blooms of miniature roses are so much smaller, a bed situated in the middle of a lawn will be much less dramatic than a bed of hybrid teas or floribundas. A bed of hybrid teas can extend for 100' or more and still look interesting. It is hard to imagine a 100' bed of miniature roses looking impressive to anyone who isn't a collector of miniature roses.

The truly miniature roses bred in the 1950s and 1960s make impressive additions to rock gardens. Many of the most recent miniatures have a stiff, upright habit that doesn't work well with other tiny plants. These miniatures are useful in small beds by themselves, and they can also work very well when planted in a circular pattern around floribunda tree roses.

Larger than miniatures, the mini-floras are bred specifically for success at rose shows. Mini-flora plants are often ungainly and can be hard to use well in a garden setting, although their large buds usually produce attractive cut flowers. Some mini-floras require winter protection in Zone 5.

Unless otherwise noted, all of the following recommended miniatures will shine in a dedicated bed of miniature roses, producing an abundance of flowers to cut for small-scale bouquets and floral arrangements. Also note that "Repeat Bloom" is not listed for these roses, as all miniature roses are repeat bloomers.

ABOVE One of the most rewarding bicolor miniatures, 'Hot Tamale' will rebloom faster if the gardener would cut off these deadheads.

'BLACK JADE'

BUTTER CREAM

CLASS: Mini-flora
BLOOM COLOR: Yellow
BLOOM SIZE: 2"
INTRODUCED: Martin, USA, 2003

HEIGHT: 2'
HARDINESS: Zones 6–9

Many mini-floras are creaky constructions of gangly stems and out-of-proportion, disease-prone leaves, doing their best to support a bloom that is magnificently formed. 'Butter Cream' is the delightful exception. It has superior form, and it's also a great garden rose. Its soft yellow blooms appear in profusion on a healthy plant that is eager to repeat bloom and maintains an attractive bushy habit. The blendable color makes this a useful accent plant throughout the garden, in mixed plantings and at the front of the border. Winter hardiness appears variable. My plant will not survive without a blanket of oak leaves; other rosarians in my area of the country report no problems wintering 'Butter Cream'.

There is a pure white sister seedling called 'Peter Cottontail'.

RIGHT PLACE *Landscape and garden accent; mixed border; front of border*

'BUTTER CREAM'

BLACK JADE

CLASS: Miniature
BLOOM COLOR: Red
BLOOM SIZE: 1½"
INTRODUCED: Benardella, USA, 1985

HEIGHT: 18"
HARDINESS: Zones 5b–9

The closest thing to a black rose of any size, this miniature produces elegant hybrid-tea-type buds that are nearly black and spiral open into blooms of very dark red. Before very long, its bright golden stamens become visible in the depths of the unfolding petals, like a light at the end of the tunnel.

This is a true miniature, with petite blooms in scale with small foliage. The plant grows to about 18" in my climate and will need protection from powdery mildew. The flowers will be more attractive and longer-lasting if grown in a little shade.

RIGHT PLACE *Grows in part shade*

'CIDER CUP'

CIDER CUP

CLASS: Miniature   HEIGHT: 2'

BLOOM COLOR: Apricot   HARDINESS: Zones 6–9

BLOOM SIZE: 1"

INTRODUCED: Dickson, Northern Ireland, 1987

This is the most refined of the Patio Roses introduced by Dickson in the 1980s. 'Cider Cup' is apricot, its blooms often veined in bronze and fading eventually to pink. Its bud has the exquisite perfection of a hybrid tea, but because it has only about 18 petals it will open very quickly. The fully open blooms last well and are in perfect proportion to the dark green foliage. The plants grow to 2'. The budded plant I imported from the United Kingdom 20 years ago has proven more vigorous than cuttings subsequently grown from it. (In the United Kingdom, miniature roses are propagated as budded plants and may not have been evaluated for suitability of own-root propagation. In the United States it's the other way around.) Like all Patio Roses, 'Cider Cup' does very well when grown in a container.

RIGHT PLACE *Container planting*

PATIO ROSES

Patio Roses never caught on in the United States despite their good health, compact size, bushy habit, and incredible floriferousness. Most Patios have blooms the same size as traditional miniatures, but on a larger bush. They do not fit easily into the mini-flora class, which features blooms twice as large, and growing larger. If you want to try a Patio Rose, **'Cider Cup'** is the one to grow.

DR JOHN DICKMAN   (photo, page 27)

CLASS: Mini-flora   HEIGHT: 2½'

BLOOM COLOR: Mauve   HARDINESS: Zones 5b–9

BLOOM SIZE: 2"

INTRODUCED: Bridges, USA, 2003

Superbly formed blooms of mauve with a deeper edge; this is one of the best mini-floras. It is equally useful as a smaller bedding rose and in the cutting garden. Surrounded by white, yellow, or pale pink, its color really stands out. Unlike most miniatures and mini-floras, 'Dr John Dickman' has a excellent, unmistakable fragrance.

Named for the distinguished rose judge and longtime Question & Answer columnist in the *American Rose* magazine.

RIGHT PLACE *Cutting and bedding*

GIGGLES

CLASS: Miniature   HEIGHT: 3'

BLOOM COLOR: Pink   HARDINESS: Zones 5–9

BLOOM SIZE: 1½"

INTRODUCED: King, USA, 1987

Perfect 1" blooms like hybrid teas appear in profusion all summer long, on stems that are ideal for cutting. The color is a pleasing coral pink that holds steady throughout the life of the bloom.

The bushy plant grows to floribunda proportions. While it is certainly not suitable for edging or incorporation into any miniaturized garden scheme, it makes a healthy spot of color that requires no special care. Plant it anywhere you'd like to have a ready supply of small-scale cut flowers.

RIGHT PLACE *Garden accent*

HOT TAMALE

CLASS: Miniature   HEIGHT: 2'

BLOOM COLOR: Orange/yellow   HARDINESS: Zones 5–9

BLOOM SIZE: 1½"

INTRODUCED: Zary, USA, 1993

One of the healthiest bicolor miniatures. The blooms of 'Hot Tamale' are an intense orange, with a bright yellow petal base and reverse. They begin as perfect replicas of hybrid teas and finally open into a many-pointed star shape. 'Hot Tamale' fades gracefully to pink and

'HOT TAMALE'

white, and the 2' bush is often a kaleidoscope of color with new and fading blooms all together.

Excellent as a cut flower, and blooms even have a little fragrance.

RIGHT PLACE *Miniature rose bed; cutting garden*

HURDY GURDY

CLASS: Miniature
BLOOM COLOR: Red striped
  with white
INTRODUCED: McGredy, New Zealand, 1986
BLOOM SIZE: 1½"
HEIGHT: 3'
HARDINESS: Zones 5b–9

It isn't hard to find striped miniature roses these days, or gardeners spending time trying to get them to grow, or to get them to stop. Some, such as 'Earthquake', are temperamental and often fail to make good growth. Others, such as 'Stars 'n' Stripes', often send out bizarre, feet-long, nonproductive shoots that really disqualify them as miniatures since this growth will screen out everything behind it.

'Hurdy Gurdy' has plenty of vigor, but it grows in good proportion to a 3' mini-shrub covered in wildly striped blooms of deep red and white. It is almost always in bloom and should be placed with care — you are unlikely to notice whatever is next to it. For this reason it can be a good choice for planting with foliage plants rather than flowering companions.

RIGHT PLACE *Among foliage plants for color*

IRRESISTIBLE

CLASS: Miniature
BLOOM COLOR: White
BLOOM SIZE: 1½"
INTRODUCED: Bennett, USA, 1990
HEIGHT: 2'
HARDINESS: Zones 5b–9

Masses of full-petaled, blush white blooms on a sturdy plant. 'Irresistible' is notable for producing a huge number of blooms at one time. This makes it a great choice if you want miniature bouquets of one variety, and indeed rose show classes for mass bouquets of one variety proliferated after the introduction of this rose. 'Irresistible' also makes a striking choice for growing in a tub or as a miniature tree rose.

RIGHT PLACE *Miniature tree rose; container planting*

'IRRESISTIBLE'

JEAN KENNEALLY

CLASS: Miniature
BLOOM COLOR: Apricot
BLOOM SIZE: 1¼"
INTRODUCED: Bennett, USA, 1984
HEIGHT: over 3'
HARDINESS: Zones 5–9

A modern classic, 'Jean Kenneally' produces apricot-colored miniature blooms of perfect hybrid tea shape. The plant is not miniature in size, growing past 3' in my garden. The blooms usually appear in huge sprays, with each bloom having its own cutting-length stem within the spray. In addition to its other attributes, 'Jean Kenneally' is more winter hardy than most miniatures of its color introduced before or since.

RIGHT PLACE *Cutting garden*

'MAGIC CARROUSEL'

MAGIC CARROUSEL

CLASS: Miniature   HEIGHT: 20"

BLOOM COLOR: White/pink   HARDINESS: Zones 5–9

BLOOM SIZE: 1½"

INTRODUCED: Moore, USA, 1972

Pink buds open into surprisingly beautiful open blooms, white edged in deep pink. A perfect garden miniature with leaves, blooms, and height of plant all in proportion. 'Magic Carrousel' also lasts well as a cut flower. One of the most trouble-free and rewarding miniatures you can grow.

RIGHT PLACE *Miniature garden; container planting*

MINNIE PEARL

CLASS: Miniature   HEIGHT: 2½'

BLOOM COLOR: Pink   HARDINESS: Zones 5–9

BLOOM SIZE: 1½"

INTRODUCED: Saville, USA, 1982

Long, elegant buds of cream blended with soft pink. 'Minnie Pearl' is great for cutting miniature bouquets.

'MINNIE PEARL'

It also makes an attractive specimen plant, and it's quite winter hardy. For many years, I grew this rose in the hollow of an old tree stump. It survived well, even though its roots weren't protected in the ground — a necessary condition for most roses during an Ohio winter.

RIGHT PLACE *Garden accent*

'RAINBOW'S END'

RAINBOW'S END

CLASS: Miniature   HEIGHT: 2½'

BLOOM COLOR: Yellow/red   HARDINESS: Zones 5–9

BLOOM SIZE: 1½"

INTRODUCED: Saville, USA, 1984

A cheerful sight in the miniature rose bed, 'Rainbow's End' has bright yellow blooms edged in red. This is a healthy, dependable miniature, with repeat bloom coming quickly. It is perfectly winter hardy in Zone 5; this is something that cannot be said for many other miniatures of this color.

There is also a climbing mutation, which sometimes grows more than it blooms.

RIGHT PLACE *Miniature rose bed; container*

REGINA LEE

CLASS: Mini-flora   HEIGHT: 3'

BLOOM COLOR: White/red   HARDINESS: Zones 6–9

BLOOM SIZE: 2"

INTRODUCED: Wells, USA, 2005

A vigorous mini-flora that produces perfectly formed 2" blooms of white rimmed in scarlet. Each bloom unfolds slowly to reveal layer after layer of picotee edging to delightful effect. The blooms have a great deal of substance, lasting very well when cut and standing up to summer's heat in the garden.

RIGHT PLACE *Cutting garden*

'RISE 'N' SHINE'

RISE 'N' SHINE

CLASS: Miniature   HEIGHT: 2'

BLOOM COLOR: Yellow   HARDINESS: Zones 5–9

BLOOM SIZE: 1¼"

INTRODUCED: Moore, USA, 1977

The benchmark by which all yellow miniature roses should be judged, 'Rise 'n' Shine' is a pure bright yellow on a plant that is constantly making new buds. Formed roughly like small-scale hybrid tea blossoms at first, the blooms soon open to the shape of an eight-pointed star. In my garden, 'Rise 'n' Shine' is rarely out of bloom from Memorial Day until Halloween.

The bushy plant grows to about 2' tall and half as wide. It doesn't send out the gangly shoots that afflict many yellow miniatures, and it has no trouble surviving an Ohio winter. This miniature works very well as an edging plant, and it has long been popular as a miniature tree rose.

RIGHT PLACE *Edging; miniature tree rose*

'SCARLET MOSS'

SCARLET MOSS

CLASS: Miniature   HEIGHT: 18"

BLOOM COLOR: Red   HARDINESS: Zones 6–9

BLOOM SIZE: 1¼"

INTRODUCED: Moore, USA, 1988

Buds dense with prickly moss open to bright red, single-petaled blooms. An easy-to-grow innovation among miniature roses, 'Scarlet Moss' is also a brighter red color than any of the full-size moss roses. The plant grows low and is slightly spreading. This rose winters well once it is established; it will benefit from winter protection for its first two years. Growing it in a container can emphasize its tiny, mossy buds, which won't be lost amidst the greenery of their neighbors.

RIGHT PLACE *Container planting*

SI

CLASS: Miniature   HEIGHT: 8"

BLOOM COLOR: White   HARDINESS: Zones 5b–9

BLOOM SIZE: ¼"

INTRODUCED: Dot, Spain, 1957

The smallest rose in the world, and worth growing for its novelty value. 'Si' has white buds, shaded pale pink in cool weather, no larger than a kernel of wheat. The buds are much more charming than the insubstantial white flowers that follow. The plant reaches about 8" for me and offers repeat bloom very quickly. You'd need to use manicure scissors to deadhead it, but I have never found this to be necessary as the plant is apparently sterile and puts no effort into setting seeds.

Best grown in a pot so that garden visitors will not need to get down on their hands and knees to find and appreciate this curious little rose. 'Si' is one of the earliest of a subgroup of "micro-minis" that have fallen from favor among American rose enthusiasts, as tastes in miniature roses have, perhaps counterintuitively, favored those with larger blooms.

RIGHT PLACE *Container planting*

SIMON ROBINSON

CLASS: Miniature HEIGHT: 2½'
BLOOM COLOR: Pink HARDINESS: Zones 5–9
BLOOM SIZE: 1½"
INTRODUCED: Robinson, Channel Islands, 1982

Five-petaled discs of clearest pink cover this impressive miniature throughout the summer. One of the heaviest blooming of all roses, 'Simon Robinson' is best thought of as a mini-shrub. It's great as an accent plant, and it will grow into a uniform low hedge. It would also be a fantastic 2' tree rose, if any nursery offered it that way. Spent blooms must be constantly removed to prevent hip formation and encourage repeat bloom.

This rose's stated parentage, a cross between the species *Rosa wichurana* and the miniature 'New Penny', is improbable. Repeat blooming is a recessive trait in roses; a cross between a once-blooming rose (such as *Rosa wichurana*) and a repeat-blooming rose (such as 'New Penny') should produce only once-blooming roses in the first generation. If those seedlings were used for breeding, they could then produce repeat-blooming offspring. It is possible that a step or two has been omitted from the officially recorded parentage. It is also possible that 'Simon Robinson' is an exception to the usual rules of genetics. It certainly has the shiny, healthy leaves of *R. wichurana*, and the compact habit of 'New Penny'. Whatever its family background, it's a rose I wouldn't want to be without.

RIGHT PLACE *Tree rose; garden accent; low hedge*

'SIMON ROBINSON'

'SOROPTIMIST INTERNATIONAL'

SOROPTIMIST INTERNATIONAL

CLASS: Miniature HEIGHT: 2½'
BLOOM COLOR: Yellow/pink HARDINESS: Zones 5b–9
BLOOM SIZE: 2"
INTRODUCED: Benardella, USA, 1990

Creamy yellow edged in vivid pink, this is the epitome of the high-centered exhibition bloom in miniature. The many-petaled blooms have a very high center, reflexing into a perfect star shape. These usually appear one to a stem or in small clusters. The attraction of this rose is the perfect form of its cuttable blooms; it is not particularly profuse.

The plant is healthy and has a naturally spreading habit. To encourage more upright growth, prune to inward-facing eyes. This will produce a more attractive plant that has blooms with longer, straighter stems.

RIGHT PLACE *Miniature rose bed; cutting garden*

STARINA

CLASS: Miniature HEIGHT: 18"
BLOOM COLOR: Orange-red HARDINESS: Zones 5–9
BLOOM SIZE: 1"
INTRODUCED: Meilland, France, 1965

Scarlet orange over a golden base, this was one of the first miniatures to perfectly mimic the classic spiraled bud of a hybrid tea. It is also an ideally proportioned miniature, with the bushy plant reaching 18" tall and wide. This makes it useful for edging a border. It is natural to think of miniature roses as edgers, but many are in fact too gangly to do this well. 'Starina' can sometimes catch powdery mildew when that disease is rife, but it is otherwise a healthy rose.

RIGHT PLACE *Edging for a border.*

'SWEET CHARIOT'

SWEET CHARIOT

CLASS: Miniature HEIGHT: 18"
BLOOM COLOR: Purple HARDINESS: Zones 5–9
BLOOM SIZE: 1½"
INTRODUCED: Moore, USA, 1984

Sold as a miniature, this charming rose defies classification. Its blooms have the informal, fluffy form often found in polyanthas. Its habit is relaxed and spreading, much like a modest ground-cover rose. It's as healthy as a shrub rose. And the fragrance of its violet blooms recalls that of some of our favorite heritage roses.

How do you use a rose that can't be neatly categorized? Any way you want. Growing 18" tall by 2½' wide, 'Sweet Chariot' is great as an edging plant, in front of a bed of old garden roses or a larger mixed border. It can be tucked into a rock garden or any small spot where an old-fashioned look is desired. It's very happy in a pot, and it can even be grown in a hanging basket (be sure to water at least once a day). And it makes a fantastic miniature standard (see chapter 8 for more information on standards).

RIGHT PLACE *Ground cover; miniature tree rose; edging plant; rock garden; container planting; hanging basket*

TOP MARKS

CLASS: Miniature HEIGHT: 2'
BLOOM COLOR: Orange-red HARDINESS: Zones 5–9
BLOOM SIZE: 1"
INTRODUCED: Fryer, England, 1992

This leafy 2' plant is covered in shiny orange-red blooms that last a long time. The appeal of this rose is not in the charm of its double blooms, which are really not that charming when cut from the plant, but in the sheer profusion of the bloom and the length of time it persists. Eventually the blooms do become worn-out looking; when you're clipping them off, be careful not to nip any new buds that are on the way.

Useful in pots and in masses of three or five plants in a border for a strong dash of color.

RIGHT PLACE *Container planting; massed in border as accent*

'TOY CLOWN'

TOY CLOWN

CLASS: Miniature HEIGHT: 1'
BLOOM COLOR: White/pink HARDINESS: Zones 5–9
BLOOM SIZE: 1"
INTRODUCED: Moore, USA, 1966

A classic rose from an era when miniature roses were really petite. The small blooms are paper white with a diffuse red-pink edge. They have just enough petals to approximate the form of a hybrid tea, appearing on a 1' plant that is perfectly proportioned for the size of its blooms. Ideal for growing in pots, rock gardens, or as a featured item in a garden of small-scale plants. As rose exhibitors have demanded larger and larger miniature blooms, and nurseries cater to this insistence, the charm of genuine miniatures such as 'Toy Clown' is being forgotten.

RIGHT PLACE *Container planting; rock garden; garden accent*

CHAPTER 7

CLIMBING
ROSES

In climbers, roses fulfill their greatest garden potential but also present their biggest risk. Few garden highlights can outshine a climbing rose covered in bloom. It's a garden-design no-brainer: Take an otherwise empty, uninteresting vertical space, and fill it with a huge quantity of colorful roses. If it were that easy, however, every garden would feature at least one climbing rose. But for northern gardeners, there's the significant challenge of finding climbers that will survive winter, and with enough live wood to produce an early-season bloom explosion. Pick the wrong rose, and you'll end up with one of the saddest garden sights of all — an empty pergola or an unclimbed trellis. Nevertheless, there are roses that will rise to this challenge.

OPPOSITE 'Super Dorothy' climbs with clematis in the garden of Rick Strebler in Edinburg, Ohio.

CONVINCING CLIMBERS TO BLOOM THEIR BEST

Roses are genetically programmed to bloom at the end of their growing tips. This is called apical dominance. When we see a rose bush covered in bloom from top to bottom, it is because it has many shoots of varying lengths. To produce the maximum number of flowering shoots, rose canes should be trained horizontally. This turns apical dominance on its side, literally, and promotes bloom growth from every node. This is why old rambling roses do so well when grown along a fence, and why modern climbers bloom profusely when carefully twined around a pillar but often bloom sparsely when forced straight up an arch or trellis.

Lacking tendrils or other natural means of attachment, roses must be trained to climb, by fastening them to the supporting structure. Permanent ties are impractical, though, because roses are always losing and gaining wood. For example, portions of canes will die back in winter and you'll have to prune those away. You also remove growth when you cut flowering stems for arrangements.

Instead, it is best to train canes along trellis laths or along a fence bit by bit as they grow. Roses with sturdy canes, such as 'William Baffin', may only need to be tied every 12 inches or so. Those with more flexible growth, such as 'Wichmoss', will need twice as much support. Most of the work of training climbing roses is done in the spring and early summer, when growth is most rapid. If you're sending a rose up an arch or tall trellis, be prepared to follow it. You may need a ladder or at least a stepping stool to attach ties as the rose grows. To attach the rose canes you can use twine, sturdy twist-ties, or plastic-covered wire. Caution: Many climbing roses have thorns that deserve caution and respect. Rosarians have traditionally depended on goatskin gloves because rose prickles cannot penetrate them. Today, rose gloves manufactured from modern Robocop-style protective materials are also effective.

A WARNING AGAINST WEAVING

New rose canes often are pliable enough to weave through trellis work, but I don't recommend doing it. Come next spring, the northern gardener will need to remove those same canes, which will have been killed over winter, and it will be incredibly difficult to weave them back out.

If you find yourself in this predicament, the wisest course of action is usually to cut the cane into short sections, and then push each part out of the trellis or fence one at a time. This takes up a lot of time and can involve considerable interaction with thorns.

SUPPORT STRUCTURES

Any rose that grows to 6 feet or more can benefit from a support structure, which will allow it to achieve greater height than it would as a free-standing shrub. Matching the appropriate support to your climbing rose will enable it to give the best display of roses possible.

Arches

In Zone 5, I get the most garden value out of arches. That's because, with careful selection, I can find roses that have enough vigor to cover an arch and still have plenty of energy left to bloom well.

Arches are the perfect device for separating, and yet joining, different parts of the garden. To the garden visitor, an arch is an invitation, and an arch covered with a climbing rose in bloom is a special invitation. A series of arches is called an arcade, and if you have enough room it offers an intriguing way to showcase climbing roses. You can use a single variety of climbing rose for each arch in the series. Another nice effect is to choose two different cultivars, one for each side of the arch, and repeat them along the arcade. Or, you can use several different varieties to produce a gradually changing color scheme as you progress from one end of the arcade to the other.

Arches do not have to lead anywhere, and they can also become a garden highlight when situated over a bench. When arches do lead to a destination, think carefully about how wide to make them. Don't let an arch become an obstacle for your garden cart, lawn mower, or tractor. If the arch is wide enough for two people to pass under side-by-side, the problem of worn grass will be less likely.

Arches can be constructed of wood, metal, or plastic. Wood and metal both look less antiseptic, but they require more care. Northern gardeners may have an advantage when it comes to painting wood or metal. If their climber dies back each winter, a logical painting window presents itself. Southerners may have no choice but to painstakingly pry the climber away from its support in order to make painting possible. Metal gets hot in the sunlight, and while a vigorous climber will soon provide its own shade, a marginal one might actually suffer from burn. Arches need to be anchored to the ground; check to see if anchor materials are sold with your arch. If not, metal fence staples work well.

Trellises

Some climbing roses, such as 'Compassion' and 'Summer Wine', naturally want to spread as they grow. Roses like these are better suited to a trellis than a narrower arch. Trellises are also the better choice for climbing roses with less vigor, or those that might be less hardy in your climate. A trellis half-covered with a climbing rose will still look promising, as your eyes are drawn to the part that is covered. An uncovered arch will invariably look wrong as eyes will inevitably focus on the part that is empty.

Trellises are most often affixed to the wall of a house, garage, barn, or other structure. Roses grown on the south or east side of a house will benefit from increased winter hardiness in that protected microclimate. This is the place to try climbers that might be a stretch for your climate. The west side of a building works well when gusty winds are not expected to be a frequent problem. Only varieties able to flower well with reduced light should be attempted on the north side of a building.

Keep in mind that all plants grown close to a building will require extra water. Don't plant the rose too close to the structure — site it at least 2 feet away from the wall. Choose a variety that will flower in shades that will not disappear into the color of the building. White and yellow roses are ineffective against white buildings; orange and red roses don't show up against brick. And no, you can't make a white climber effective against a white building by growing it on a brightly colored trellis. That looks tacky. It's about the rose, not the trellis — the trellis should be as close to invisible as possible.

OPPOSITE Northern gardeners seeking a repeat-blooming, winter-hardy climber need look no further than 'William Baffin'.

Another way to install trellises is as freestanding garden features. Roses grown against these open trellises will really be on display, so take care to avoid any climber that won't bloom strongly. Free-standing trellises will need support posts that are sunk into the ground. Plant the rose about 1 foot from the trellis.

Climbing roses grown out in the open are much less prone to powdery mildew than those up against a house, but winter hardiness is also a crucial consideration. Keep in mind that roses grown against the shelter of a building usually grow a few extra feet taller and gain a half zone of winter hardiness; roses trained to a trellis in an open area won't have this benefit. A rose that grows 10 feet against the east wall of your house may only reach 8 feet when planted in the middle of your garden. Planting two different climbers on each side of a free-standing trellis can produce charming results when growth habits are complementary and blooms of each variety peek over from the other side.

One of the metal stock fencing panels sold at farm stores in 16-foot sections makes a great trellis. Just use a metal-cutting saw to cut it to the desired height (some stores will do this for you), pound it into the ground, and watch your climbing roses grow.

Pillars and Pergolas

The simplest support for a climbing rose is a pillar or post. Twining a climber around a post satisfies its need for horizontal growth and encourages it to produce its maximum amount of bloom, while actually disguising deficiencies such as sparse foliage. A well-grown pillar rose will produce a lot of bloom in a very small space, and a strong, bright color is usually more effective on a pillar than a pastel one. Only modest climbers are effective on a post. If a vigorous climber reaches the top of a pillar and wants to keep growing, chaos ensues.

Since they consume so little space, rose pillars can be placed almost anywhere. They will be highlights in a mixed border and can serve to mark out different areas of the garden. If you want to stretch a clothesline between two rose pillars, that works too. A post can be as simple as a 4 × 4 from the lumberyard; expensive, ready-made rose pillars are also available from boutique garden stores. Pillars and posts will need to be sunk into the ground about 18 inches. A posthole digger will be handy for this. Practical organic gardeners may want to install a bluebird house on top.

The next step beyond a post is a teepee-like structure of three support stakes. A tripod can accommodate a more vigorous rose, but because it consumes more ground space is less suitable as an exclamation point in the landscape. If you have plenty of room, a climbing rose on a tripod can become a magnet when viewed across an expanse of lawn. On a smaller scale it can serve to disguise small eyesores, or even provide shade for rose cuttings.

A pergola is designed for roses to grow up and then over, so they are enjoyed as both climbing plants and then as cascaders, their clusters of blooms suspended above us. A pergola is likely to be a disappointment in Zone 5, and impossible in Zone 4. Zone 6 gardeners can achieve this effect with careful selection of varieties. In Zone 7 and warmer, the use of pergolas is limited only by the amount of space you have on which to construct them. A pergola typically displays several different climbing varieties at once, each trained to a separate post that leads it up to the mesh that covers the top of the structure. In a mild climate, roses trained on a pergola may provide so much shade that you will not be able to grow grass underneath. In this case, shade-loving perennials can be situated along a brick or stone path inside the pergola.

ROSE FIRST, INFRASTRUCTURE LATER

Few garden exercises can be more frustrating than designing and installing a new arch, pergola, or some other structure intended to display a climbing rose, only to discover that the rose you've chosen to plant at the base of it is unhappy there. After living through this experience several times, ripping out the uncooperative rose, and waiting several years for its replacement to become established, I now grow the climbing rose first without support. I observe how it wants to grow, and then fashion a support structure to meet its needs. This method works fine, because unless you actually stomp on it, a rose will not be disturbed by posthole digging or other carefully done construction projects.

CLIMBERS AS GROUND COVERS

ABOVE 'Jeanne Lajoie' is the most rewarding of all of the climbing miniatures.

Rosarians of Victorian times sometimes pegged their hybrid perpetuals to the soil, forcing them to grow along the ground or into an attractive mound rather than become the tall, leggy plants they would develop into on their own. This method will work with all climbers and any tall rose, and garden boutiques offer special rose pegs for this purpose. These look remarkably like croquet hoops, which cost much less and work just as well. Many of the roses introduced as ramblers 100 years ago make terrific ground covers today — they just require a little help from a gardener able to peg them into a mound. Plan on spacing old ramblers trained this way 10 to 12 feet apart; in many cases one plant will be enough to do the trick. Pegged ramblers should be pruned just as their upright counterparts. Remove up to one-third of old growth after the rose blooms each year. In the spring, remove only obviously dead wood.

CHOOSING CLIMBING ROSES

The farther south you garden, the greater selection of suitable climbers you will enjoy. Many of the climbers that grow as free-standing shrubs in my garden will require (and reward) sturdy support in Zones 7 and south. I've tried and failed with a lot of climbers in Zone 5. The roses I've listed in this chapter have survived at least five Zone 5 winters (except for 'Crimson Sky' and 'Golden Gate'). These are the ones I would start with, if I were starting over.

ALCHYMIST

CLASS: Shrub (technically, but used as a climber)
BLOOM COLOR: Yellow
BLOOM SIZE: 5"
INTRODUCED: Kordes, Germany, 1956

REPEAT BLOOM: None
HEIGHT: 8'
HARDINESS: Zones 6–9

Huge blooms, each one a spectacle of more than 100 petals, arranged into an old-fashioned quartered shape. The effect of one bloom is dramatic, but they usually appear in sprays on an upright climber that reaches 8' for me. The flowers have a strong, sweet fragrance.

The breeder almost certainly named this for its gold color, which emerges from buds that can be a blend of amber, yellow, and pink. But the name could also be a tribute to Kordes' skill in coaxing such a rose out of its parent, a *Rosa eglanteria* seedling. 'Alchymist' is only marginally hardy in Zone 5, and since it flowers only on old wood a tough winter means no blooms for one year. I have enjoyed my best success with this rose when growing it up against a south wall.

RIGHT PLACE *Against a south-facing wall*

'ALOHA'

ALOHA

CLASS: Climbing hybrid tea
BLOOM COLOR: Pink
BLOOM SIZE: 6"
INTRODUCED: Boerner, USA, 1949

REPEAT BLOOM: Good
HEIGHT: 8'
HARDINESS: Zones 5–9

Provides plenty of coral pink color as a slightly sprawling large shrub, but it is most effective when trained as a pillar rose. Twined around a post, its pliable canes offer a more concentrated and impressive display. 'Aloha' can also be effective on a trellis, but it may take several years to make enough growth to cover it. This is a climber that can be counted on for healthy foliage, unless there is a black spot epidemic.

The rough-hewn hybrid tea blooms have a strong fragrance. Despite its large number of petals this rose opens well, even in damp weather. 'Aloha' was an important parent of the David Austin English Roses, and it remains a valuable rose in its own right.

RIGHT PLACE *Trellis or post*

'AMERICAN PILLAR'

AMERICAN PILLAR

CLASS: Rambler
BLOOM COLOR: Pink
REPEAT BLOOM: None
INTRODUCED: Van Fleet, USA, 1902

HEIGHT: up to 12'
HARDINESS: Zones 5–9

A familiar sight in the American countryside, often surviving long after the farmhouses whose dooryards it once adorned have fallen down. This is a vigorous rambler, growing to 12' and prone to form a thicket if it isn't given sturdy support and annual pruning. Its blooms are crimson pink with a white center, enlivened by bright golden stamens. There is only one annual bloom, but it begins late and lasts a long time. At its peak there will be more blooms than you could possibly count. 'American Pillar' is winter hardy and happy throughout the country, from the sunburnt prairies to coastal New England. Once its flowering season ends it is likely to suffer from powdery mildew.

RIGHT PLACE *Requires sturdy support*

'ANTIKE 89'

ANTIKE 89

CLASS: Large-flowered climber REPEAT BLOOM: Monthly
BLOOM COLOR: Red/white HEIGHT: 8'
HARDINESS: Zones 5–9
INTRODUCED: Kordes, Germany, 1989

"Genuine antiques bred here," could have been Kordes' motto for the creation of this free-blooming climber. The form of the large blooms is indeed antique — a rosette shape with perfectly incurved petals, sometimes forming a quartered effect. But the color is entirely modern, bright strawberry red mixed with cream. And so this rose exhibits two familiar elements (the form of the old and the color of the new) in one unexpected combination.

'Antike 89' usually makes a lot of blooms all at once, and then rests for about a month. When in bloom it can attract attention from a great distance, and its neighbors might be ignored.

Stiff upright growth means it can grow as a free-standing shrub, but it will attain more height when given support. Typically 8' for me, but I have seen much taller plants in the South. It is quite prickly, and by spacing it less than 3' apart you can create a tall, completely impenetrable hedge.

RIGHT PLACE *Train to a trellis; free-standing shrub; hedge*

ASCHERMITTWOCH

CLASS: Large-flowered climber HEIGHT: up to 10'
BLOOM COLOR: Gray HARDINESS: Zones 5–9
REPEAT BLOOM: None
INTRODUCED: Kordes, Germany, 1955

Ghostly gray blooms are set perfectly on bright green foliage. The fully double flowers are sometimes delicately tinted lilac or pink, and when the climber is covered in bloom in June its impact will change from hour to hour, as the sun casts shadows in different directions and clouds pass overhead. This climber grows with vigor to 10' in Zone 5 and requires a sturdy support.

With large blooms that open wide, 'Aschwermittwoch' works very effectively when it shares a trellis with clematis. In my garden the purple-red clematis 'Rosemoor' usually blooms at the same time as 'Aschermittwoch' and then continues, sporadically, through the summer. Descended from *Rosa eglanteria,* 'Aschermittwoch' does not repeat bloom but is reliably winter hardy.

RIGHT PLACE *Requires sturdy support; partner on trellis with clematis*

A PERFECT PAIR

Clematis are often recommended as the perfect companion plants for climbing roses. Indeed, a clematis vine will happily share the same trellis or arch on which a climbing rose grows, and sometimes embarrass the rose with its vigor. (See 'Super Dorothy' with clematis on page 170.) The rose and the clematis will each be on their own timetables. Much like characters in one of those tales from the Depression in which two people share an apartment but never actually meet because they work different shifts, the clematis will often be blooming when the rose is not.

Clematis in general can be more unpredictable than roses both in their willingness to bloom and in the time that they bloom. This can vary from garden to garden, and even within a large garden. When I find that a clematis is happy in my garden, I leave it planted where it is and, if necessary, bring in a climbing rose whose behavior I have already figured out to pair with it.

'BLOSSOMTIME'

BLOSSOMTIME

CLASS: Large-flowered climber   HEIGHT: 8'

BLOOM COLOR: Pink   HARDINESS: Zones 5–9

REPEAT BLOOM: Reliable

INTRODUCED: O'Neal, USA, 1951

This child of 'New Dawn' is a halfway climber, perfectly happy to grow without support as a large (8') shrub for me. Its silvery pink blooms are halfway between the form of an early hybrid tea and a modern David Austin English Rose. As buds they reflex in the manner of a hybrid tea, and then at some point the sheer quantity of petals makes it impossible for them to move any more. A rose that does not disappoint, 'Blossomtime' is full of health, fragrant, winter hardy, and almost always in bloom.

RIGHT PLACE *Free-standing shrub or climber*

BLUSHING LUCY

CLASS: Rambler   REPEAT BLOOM: None

BLOOM COLOR: Pink   HEIGHT: 10'

BLOOM SIZE: 2½"   HARDINESS: Zones 5–9

INTRODUCED: Williams, England, 1938

I never know what rose will bloom first in my garden each spring. It could be any one of three or four dozen candidates. Whichever one it turns out to be, it enjoys one or two days of attention before everything else starts blooming.

There's no contest, though, for the prize of last rose to bloom. Year after year, it's 'Blushing Lucy'. And that's good. In July, when once-blooming heritage roses are shutting down and repeat-blooming modern roses are resting before putting out another burst of color, there often isn't a lot of rose color. But there's always 'Blushing Lucy', a rambler of modest proportions that covers itself in blooms that begin a soft, delicate pink and fade through several stages of pearl and blush before arriving at white. The effect is of roses of many different shades on one spray.

Before our neighbors sold us three of their acres, they had installed a lot of bluebird houses on top of 8' posts. A perfect pillar rose, 'Blushing Lucy' winds around one of those, looking as if it had always been there. The bluebirds seem to like it too. In warmer climates I suspect this rose would be much more aggressive and a great candidate for a pergola. Its shiny green leaves are more healthy than the typical rambler, and bloom continues for almost a month.

A. H. Williams also bred a climbing rose called 'Lucy', but 'Blushing Lucy' is not a mutation of it, nor even closely related.

RIGHT PLACE *Post; ground cover*

'BLUSHING LUCY'

CHEVY CHASE

CLASS: Rambler   REPEAT BLOOM: None

BLOOM COLOR: Red   HEIGHT: 10'

BLOOM SIZE: 1½"   HARDINESS: Zones 5b–9

INTRODUCED: Hansen, USA, 1939

A quality red rambler, different from its brethren for these reasons: 1) Its red is pure, not an over-saturated pink. 2) It has strong resistance to powdery mildew. 3) It lacks the "grow first, ask questions later" gene and

'CHEVY CHASE'

may take a long time to establish. 'Chevy Chase' builds to about 10' in my garden, and it will not grow upright without strong support. Its small but full-petaled blooms appear in clusters all up and down the plant.

Named for the Maryland suburb of Washington, D.C., where it was bred, and where it is completely winter hardy. Up here in Zone 5, a really severe winter will set 'Chevy Chase' back for a year or two.

RIGHT PLACE *Requires strong support; ground cover*

CITY GIRL

CLASS: Large-flowered climber REPEAT BLOOM: Rapid
BLOOM COLOR: Apricot-pink HEIGHT: 8'
BLOOM SIZE: 3½" HARDINESS: Zones 5–9
INTRODUCED: Harkness, England, 1993

A shorter climber, perfectly happy to grow as an attractive free-standing shrub in cold climates. It is valuable for the beauty of its bright pastel apricot-and-pink flowers, and the speed with which it repeats bloom. 'City Girl' produces spiraled hybrid tea-type buds, which open wide to display an attractive yellow base. They have a pleasing fragrance and appear every month of the summer.

Most climbing roses look fresh and full of life when they are at their peak of bloom at the beginning of summer. Those like 'City Girl' that maintain their freshness throughout the dog days of summer are especially valuable in the garden. The pastel coloration of this rose is particularly attractive against a brick wall.

RIGHT PLACE *Free-standing shrub; especially useful against a brick wall or other dark background*

COMPASSION

CLASS: Large-flowered climber REPEAT BLOOM: Reliable
BLOOM COLOR: Salmon HEIGHT: 9'
BLOOM SIZE: 4" HARDINESS: Zones 5–9
INTRODUCED: Harkness, England, 1973

A leafy climber that is always making healthy new growth from the base of the plant. 'Compassion' produces hybrid tea-type flowers of the shade of salmon that leaps between pink and orange. They have a big fragrance that carries well throughout the garden. Even though these blooms appear on long stems, they make unsatisfactory cut flowers, quickly losing substance when removed from the plant.

'Compassion' appreciates a sturdy support and will reach 9' on a simple trellis in my garden. Its thick canes are difficult to train over an arch or in any creative direction. 'Compassion' blooms well throughout the summer. It suffers from a lot of dieback over winter, but it comes back strongly each spring.

There is a yellow mutation called 'Highfield'. Although it retains the wonderful fragrance of 'Compassion', 'Highfield' has lost some petals along with the pink and the orange, and its blooms appear insubstantial.

RIGHT PLACE *Requires a sturdy support*

'COMPASSION'

'CRIMSON SKY'

CRIMSON SKY

CLASS: Large-flowered climber   REPEAT BLOOM: Good

BLOOM COLOR: Red   HEIGHT: 8'

BLOOM SIZE: 6"   HARDINESS: Zones 5b–9

INTRODUCED: Meilland, France, 2007

Whopping big flowers of bright red make a strong impact, even when there aren't very many of them at once. The plant grows quickly to 8', and blooms typically appear singly and in clusters of three at the top of each cane. Despite the huge size of the blooms, they have only about 20 petals, which allow them to open easily in all weather. A perfect climber for a trellis, 'Crimson Sky' can also be effective as a tall, free-standing shrub.

This climber is marketed as an improvement on the 100-petaled 'Red Eden', which is misleading since, apart from being red climbing roses from the same breeder, they are not in any way similar.

RIGHT PLACE   *Trellis; free-standing shrub*

DEMOKRACIE

CLASS: Large-flowered climber   REPEAT BLOOM: Good

BLOOM COLOR: Red   HEIGHT: 10'

BLOOM SIZE: 2½"   HARDINESS: Zones 5–9

INTRODUCED: Böhm, Czechoslovakia, 1935

A vigorous, hardy climber in a strong red color, blooming more in spurts throughout the summer than in one huge

'DEMOKRACIE'

flush. Given strong support, 'Demokracie' can climb a one-story building, but vertical canes will not produce nearly as many blooms as those trained sideways. The roses sold as 'Improved Blaze' or 'Blaze, Everblooming' are almost always 'Demokracie'. This rose is seen everywhere, often doing well despite apparent neglect. With just a little care it will do so much better.

RIGHT PLACE   *Strong trellis; against a building*

'DORTMUND'

DORTMUND

CLASS: Kordesii   REPEAT BLOOM: Good

BLOOM COLOR: Red   HEIGHT: 6'

BLOOM SIZE: 4½"   HARDINESS: Zones 5–9

INTRODUCED: Kordes, Germany, 1953

This sturdy, short kordesii climber is happy to be trained around a pillar and can also be grown as a free-standing shrub. It rarely gets past 6' in my garden. Blooms are fire-engine red, with a white eye. They are single-petaled, quite large, but have no fragrance. The plant is healthy and trouble-free. In Zone 5 this rose will typically die back to around 1' each winter and grow very quickly to retain its previous height each new summer.

RIGHT PLACE   *Post; free-standing shrub*

ELEGANCE

CLASS: Large-flowered climber REPEAT BLOOM: None
BLOOM COLOR: Yellow SPREAD: 12'
BLOOM SIZE: 4" HARDINESS: Zones 6–9
INTRODUCED: Brownell, USA, 1937

A powerful climbing rose with thick flexible canes bearing large lemon yellow blooms with the perfectly spiraled form of a hybrid tea. These make great cut flowers, if you can bear to cut into the outdoor display, which occurs only once each year.

'Elegance' needs to be trained horizontally to bloom the most. In Zone 5 it will benefit substantially from being near a house or other source of radiated heat. Since it blooms only on old wood, spring pruning will eliminate blooms for that year. For this reason I tolerate winter-damaged wood on 'Elegance' that I would prune off of any repeat-blooming rose, waiting until just after it has completed its bloom to remove it.

Dark, healthy foliage and light-colored blooms make 'Elegance' an ideal companion for conifers. Leaving the base of the plant exposed to sunlight will help to encourage new basal breaks, which 'Elegance' will need to produce with regularity in areas with difficult winters.

RIGHT PLACE *Train horizontally; companion for conifers*

THE BROWNELLS

The Brownells of Little Compton, Rhode Island, bred a lot of hybrid teas that are still promoted as "sub-zero" roses by some discount mail-order nurseries (the kind that advertise amid the cereal coupons and Sansabelt slacks in the glossy advertising supplements to the Sunday newspaper). Their hybrid teas are unremarkable and not terribly winter hardy. Several of the Brownell climbers are uniquely beautiful, though, and **'Elegance'** is their best.

FREISINGER MORGENRÖTE

CLASS: Large-flowered climber HEIGHT: 6'
BLOOM COLOR: Multicolored HARDINESS: Zones 5–9
REPEAT BLOOM: Reliable
INTRODUCED: Kordes, Germany, 1986

A blend of orange and pink, with a golden heart and a little red at the edge, all mixed together in a bloom that is a reasonable facsimile of a hybrid tea in bud and looks just as attractive when fully open. This climber grows straight up to 6' in my garden, and will then flop about if not provided the support of a trellis or fence. The blooms appear on sprays that make perfect multicolored bouquets, lasting quite well when cut. 'Freisinger Morgenröte' is a strong repeat bloomer, eager to produce new sprays throughout the summer.

Since it takes major nurseries 10 years or longer to develop a new rose, it's amazing how often they introduce similar roses just a few years apart. Meilland of France followed 'Freisinger Morgenröte'with their own 'Arielle Dombasle' a few years later. 'Arielle Dombasle' has the same color effect and more fragrance, but it is not quite as winter hardy.

RIGHT PLACE *Trellis or fence*

GLORIANA 97

CLASS: Climbing miniature REPEAT BLOOM: Reliable
BLOOM COLOR: Purple HEIGHT: 7'
BLOOM SIZE: 2" HARDINESS: Zones 5–9
INTRODUCED: Warner, England, 1997

Even though this is the tallest of Warner's climbing miniatures, reaching over 7' for me, everything remains in perfect proportion: buds, blooms, and dainty leaves. The buds begin as deep pink, with a perfect buttonhole form, and gradually turn to soft purple as they unfold. 'Gloriana 97' blooms all up and down the height of the plant throughout the summer. It makes a striking accent in a mixed bed, and it can also be a mobile focal point when grown in a large tub on casters. I use it most effectively alternating with the 'Maypole' crab apples in a border of mixed shrubs; it continues the effect that the crab apples produce in spring all summer long.

RIGHT PLACE *Garden accent in mixed border; container planting*

GOLDEN GATE

CLASS: Large-flowered climber REPEAT BLOOM: Good
BLOOM COLOR: Yellow HEIGHT: 7'
BLOOM SIZE: 3½" HARDINESS: Zones 5–9
INTRODUCED: Kordes, Germany, 2005

This is a real breakthrough rose, two-thirds of the way to the perfect yellow climbing rose for northern climates. Its large blooms are intensely golden, open well in all weather, and do not fade. Although I have grown it for only three years, the plant has proven itself genuinely winter hardy. Its only failing is that is does not climb quite high enough. 'Golden Gate' tops out at about 7' and will do a beautiful job of covering a modest trellis. But in Zone 5, don't expect it to climb over an arch or cascade down from a pergola.

When ordering this excellent rose be sure not to confuse it with either of two mediocre hybrid teas also called 'Golden Gate'.

RIGHT PLACE *Trellis or post; large free-standing shrub*

HIGH HOPES

CLASS: Large-flowered climber	REPEAT BLOOM: Good
BLOOM COLOR: Pink	HEIGHT: 8'
BLOOM SIZE: 3"	HARDINESS: Zones 5–9
INTRODUCED: Harkness, England, 1992	

Elegantly shaped, seashell-pink buds open quickly into blooms just a shade lighter. These flowers are not large, but they typically appear in substantial clusters.

Many climbers are forgiven their faults if they really climb and they really bloom. Some disease? Ugly or missing foliage? Rosarians often excuse these problems with a "Whatever," even when the problems are directly at eye level, with blooms only higher up. 'High Hopes' needs no excuses. Its foliage is full, healthy, and an asset in its own right. I grow two plants of 'High Hopes' against the side of a mini barn that has been painted beige. The blooms reach above the black shingles at 8', and the wholesome foliage starts right from the ground.

RIGHT PLACE *Against a building; trellis*

ILLUSION

CLASS: Kordesii	REPEAT BLOOM: Continuous
BLOOM COLOR: Red	HEIGHT: 8'
BLOOM SIZE: 4"	HARDINESS: Zones 5–9
INTRODUCED: Kordes, Germany, 1961	

Blessed with wide petals in an unusual color combination — cinnabar red with a reverse of deepest pink — this rose displays its tightly packed sprays of large blooms against shiny kordesii foliage. While content to grow as a large free-standing shrub, 'Illusion' will take great advantage of a V-shape trellis, sending canes to 8' when offered this support in my climate. These canes will die back nearly to the ground in a typical Zone 5 winter, but new ones arise with such gusto in the

spring that the full effect of a climbing rose is restored in time for the first bloom. Repeat bloom is continuous through the summer.

It is rare to see any black spot on this rose, unless it is planted next to a particularly unhealthy neighbor. As with many kordesii roses, it can be faulted only for its lack of fragrance.

RIGHT PLACE *Free-standing shrub; V-shape trellis*

JEANNE LAJOIE

CLASS: Climbing miniature	REPEAT BLOOM: Reliable
BLOOM COLOR: Pink	HEIGHT: 7'
BLOOM SIZE: 1"	HARDINESS: Zones 4b–9
INTRODUCED: Sima, USA, 1975	

Plant this rose wherever you want to see a billowing mass of light pink blooms. Its June bloom is unbelievably profuse, and flowering continues strongly for the rest of the summer. Blooms are small and pompomlike and usually appear in big sprays. Although it grows over 7' tall, 'Jeanne Lajoie' does perfectly well as a free-standing shrub with no support. One of the most brilliant uses of 'Jeanne Lajoie' I've ever seen had it trained around a lamppost of about 7'. The bush had completely obscured both the post and the lamp, and when the light came on at night the multitude of blooms were illuminated from within, creating an incredible effect.

'JEANNE LAJOIE'

This rose illustrates the different perceptions of "climbing miniature" held by American rose breeders such as Sima and by Britain's Chris Warner. Climbing miniatures bred in the United States are usually big, sprawling plants covered with dainty blooms, while Warner's climbing miniatures are almost all narrow, upright plants ideal for fitting into confined spaces. None of the other American climbing miniatures is as good as 'Jeanne Lajoie'.

RIGHT PLACE *Free-standing shrub; trained around a post or along a fence*

'LAURA FORD'

LAURA FORD

CLASS: Climbing miniature REPEAT BLOOM: Good
BLOOM COLOR: Yellow HEIGHT: 6'
BLOOM SIZE: 1½" HARDINESS: Zones 5–9
INTRODUCED: Warner, England, 1989

The first of Chris Warner's climbing miniatures to enjoy widespread distribution, 'Laura Ford' grows straight up to 6', covered in bloom from top to bottom. Golden buds open to butter-yellow blooms kissed with pink. These are fully double but loosely formed, and they appear as open blooms for a longer period than they do as buds.

'Laura Ford' is perfect in any narrow space, such as an entryway. When planted 2' apart it will make an effective, thorny hedge.

Perfectly hardy in Zone 5. Unfortunately, this winter hardiness has been diluted in some of Warner's more recent yellow climbers.

RIGHT PLACE *Climber in narrow space, such as an entryway; hedge; container planting*

LEAPING SALMON

CLASS: Large-flowered climber REPEAT BLOOM: Reliable
BLOOM COLOR: Salmon HEIGHT: 8'
BLOOM SIZE: 5" HARDINESS: Zones 5–9
INTRODUCED: Pearce, England, 1983

As much a tall hybrid tea as a climber, 'Leaping Salmon' produces large blooms of a startling salmon orange. These appear singly or in clusters of three on top of very long stems and make great cut flowers. They have a pleasing fragrance and last a long time. While never offering the profuse display of many climbers, the appearance of even a few blooms on 'Leaping Salmon' always makes an impact.

Unsupported, 'Leaping Salmon' reaches 8' in my garden and blooms continuously throughout the summer. In a warmer climate it will require a sturdy trellis. It is several degrees hardier than many climbers bred in England.

RIGHT PLACE *Free-standing shrub; trellis in warmer climates*

LOUIS' RAMBLER

CLASS: Rambler REPEAT BLOOM: None
BLOOM COLOR: White HEIGHT: 8'
BLOOM SIZE: 1½" HARDINESS: Zones 4b–9
INTRODUCED: Lens, Belgium, 1997

A refined version of a wild rose, 'Louis' Rambler' has one bloom explosion each year, producing hundreds of huge sprays of five-petaled white blooms. These are enhanced by huge golden stamens, producing something close to a fried-egg effect. The display is stunning from hundreds of feet away, and just as breathtaking close up. A few months later the blooms have been replaced with thousands of bright orange hips.

'LOUIS' RAMBLER'

'Louis' Rambler' is super hardy and disease resistant, needing no care beyond removing worn-out wood and deciding what kind of support you want to provide it. It is considerably more winter hardy than any of the famous white ramblers introduced in the early years of the twentieth century. Left alone, it will make a beautiful free-standing shrub about 8' × 8'. It will climb a trellis to at least 12' and should cover any garden arch. Although I haven't tried this, I would have little doubt of its ability to go up one side of an arch and down the other.

This is the most reliable tree-scrambling rose in my climate, being perfectly happy to inhabit a semi-dwarf apple tree and display huge panicles of bloom amid its limbs. When planting a rose to climb a tree, preparation with an extra-large planting hole helps a lot. This will get the rose off to a solid start before it has to compete with tree roots. Patience is important

too, as it usually takes the rose about three years to get the idea of what is wanted. It is best to only attempt this with roses that are completely hardy in your climate, as it is often impractical or unsafe to climb a tree to prune a rose.

RIGHT PLACE *Free-standing shrub; trellis or garden arch; allow to climb in a tree*

LOVE KNOT

CLASS: Climbing miniature	REPEAT BLOOM: Rapid
BLOOM COLOR: Red	HEIGHT: 6'
BLOOM SIZE: 1½"	HARDINESS: Zones 5–9
INTRODUCED: Warner, England, 1999	

This is my favorite climbing miniature, displaying scores of blood-red blooms, each having the perfect form of a miniaturized hybrid tea on an upright plant. 'Love Knot' tops out at just 6' in my garden and requires no support. Its health is good — unusually good for a red rose — and repeat bloom speedy. Blooms should be cut tight, just as petals are beginning to unfurl, for long life as cut flowers.

'Love Knot' blooms all up and down its height, and it makes a great accent in any narrow space. It is also very effective as a courtyard (or front door) rose when grown in a large pot. Garden designers often speak of roses serving as exclamation points in a mixed border. It's a figurative expression, except in the case of 'Love Knot': the plant looks exactly like an exclamation point.

RIGHT PLACE *Accent in narrow space; container planting in a courtyard or by a door*

MME ALFRED CARRIÈRE

CLASS: Noisette	REPEAT BLOOM: Scattered
BLOOM COLOR: White	HEIGHT: 7'
BLOOM SIZE: 3"	HARDINESS: Zones 5b–9
INTRODUCED: Schwartz, France, 1879	

The toughest of the Noisette climbing roses, 'Mme Alfred Carrière' winters with no special fuss in my Ohio garden. Its creamy white blooms appear early in the season and continue, in a scattered fashion, throughout the summer. They appear on long stems on a lanky plant with few thorns. This is an excellent rose for growing against a brick wall, and, like all climbers, it will reach a greater height with support. Grown as a free-standing specimen plant, my 'Mme Alfred Carrière' reaches just past 7'. Every other Noisette I have tried has died over

THE GRAHAM THOMAS I LIKE

I once wrote in a magazine article that I didn't really like David Austin's 'Graham Thomas', compared to many of his other creations. 'Graham Thomas' is not reliably winter hardy for me, and its repeat bloom does not keep up with the size of the plant. This prompted lots of letters from people who love 'Graham Thomas', consider it their favorite rose, use it as a climber, and met Graham Thomas during visits to rose gardens in England. My opinion of the rose was certainly no reflection on the esteemed rosarian: I value all of the books by Graham Stuart Thomas and keep the ones about roses close at hand. I admire Gina Lollobrigida too, and I found her rose even worse.

One reader wrote to say, "I have a version of 'Graham Thomas' I promise you will like" and asked if he could send it to me. I said yes, of course, and the next spring I received 'Graham Thomas' *honeysuckle*. It is yellow just like the rose, grows like a horse, is never bothered by winter, and makes a stunning companion to **'Louis' Rambler'.** They grow together in my garden, completely intertwined and blooming at the same time, the yellow of the elongated honeysuckle blooms a perfect continuation of the yellow stamens in the blooms of 'Louis Rambler' and the white of 'Louis' Rambler' making the whole display perfect. The overwhelming fragrance of the *Lonicera* means that visitors may never notice the light but pleasing scent of 'Louis' Rambler.' But it's there when you grow the rose on its own, multiplied by however many tens of thousands of blooms appear at once.

Honeysuckle comes in many different colors, and some of the brighter ones can provide really startling contrasts with companion roses of suitable vigor.

'MME ALFRED CARRIÈRE'

winter. Actually, I think several of them have died in early spring, putting all of their effort into new growth before it is safe to do so. When a severe frost hits a rose at this vulnerable state it may not have the strength to recover. Hardier roses wait and leaf out later.

RIGHT PLACE *Against a brick wall; free-standing accent*

CHARLESTON'S CHARMING ROSES

The Noisette class of roses can be traced to a rose raised by John Champneys (some spell his last name *Champney*), a rice farmer in Charleston, South Carolina, in the early years of the nineteenth century. Noisettes remain an integral part of Charleston today, filling gardens with soft colors and sweet fragrance, flowing over fences, and blooming almost every month of the year. They intrigue visiting rosarians, who want to match them all up with their proper names. There are two other classes of roses that are distinctly American, but I can't think of any city where one can wander around and discover enchanting gardens filled with grandifloras or mini-floras at every turn.

MARIA LIESA

CLASS: Rambler
BLOOM COLOR: Pink
BLOOM SIZE: ¾"
INTRODUCED: Liebau, Germany, 1936
REPEAT BLOOM: None
HEIGHT: 10'
HARDINESS: Zones 4b–9

A vivid and easy-to-grow rambler, 'Maria Liesa' is troubled by none of the idiosyncracies that often afflict ramblers (mildew, blind shoots, and shoots that disappear into trees or over rooftops). It is also much more winter hardy than many ramblers. It grows powerfully to 10' in my garden, smothered in single-petaled blooms of an intense deep pink with a white eye. Training it horizontally will produce many more flowers during its one long annual bloom explosion, so this rose is much more suited to a fence or a wide trellis than an arch. Although thick, its canes are almost thornless and quite easy to train. It will make a stunningly effective ground cover if pegged down.

Almost always sold as ' Maria Lisa', but 'Maria Liesa' is the correct spelling according to rose scholar Charles Quest-Ritson. He explains that the breeder was Brother Alfons Liebau, an Augustinian monk who named the rose after Maria and Liesa, two women who worked at his monastery.

RIGHT PLACE *Train horizontally; ground cover*

MORNING JEWEL

CLASS: Large-flowered climber
BLOOM COLOR: Pink
BLOOM SIZE: 3½"
INTRODUCED: Cocker, Scotland, 1968
REPEAT BLOOM: Scattered
HEIGHT: 8'
HARDINESS: Zones 5–9

Healthy leaves, and lots of them, are the hallmark of this easy-to-grow climber. When trained, it will quickly cover an 8' trellis; this will look most attractive against a light-colored section of wall. Its leaves glisten with good health and are an attraction even when the plant is not in bloom. Its large, deep pink flowers have an informal charm, appearing in profusion at the beginning of each rose season. Bloom can be scattered after that, but the plant is always a picture of health. 'Morning Jewel' has better-than-average winter hardiness for a repeat-blooming climber.

RIGHT PLACE *Trellis*

NEW DAWN

CLASS: Rambler
REPEAT BLOOM: Reliable
BLOOM COLOR: Pink
HEIGHT: 9'
BLOOM SIZE: 3"
HARDINESS: Zones 4b–9
INTRODUCED: Dreer, USA, 1930

When people visit my Open Garden each year in June, the question they ask most frequently is: what climbing rose can I grow that repeats, that really climbs, and that will survive over winter? The answer is an easy one: 'New Dawn'. This rose will smother a modest-sized trellis, have no problems climbing its half of an arch, and looks great trained around a front door. Its healthy dark-green foliage will reach 9' with support in Ohio, providing a winning contrast to the soft pink blooms that appear in abundance every month of the summer. Its canes are extremely pliable and not too thorny, making it easy to guide around any support.

The first plant to receive patent protection, 'New Dawn' is a repeat-blooming mutation of the large-flowered wichurana rambler 'Dr W Van Fleet', with the same flowers and a more modest growth habit. 'Dr W Van Fleet' remains available, and it is a good choice for anyone who wants an even more vigorous climber with one long annual bloom period. Rosarians in southern California may not be able to tell the difference, as 'New Dawn' does not repeat well in climates without a cold winter.

'New Dawn' produced a worthwhile mutation of its own. Discovered in Czechoslovakia, 'Awakening' doubles the petal count of 'New Dawn' and arranges these petals in the classic quartered form of an old garden rose. Although just as healthy and winter hardy, in my experience it is not as eager to climb as 'New Dawn'.

RIGHT PLACE *Modest-size trellis; around a doorway*

'PAUL JERABEK'

PAUL JERABEK

CLASS: Large-flowered climber
REPEAT BLOOM: Reliable
BLOOM COLOR: White/pink
HEIGHT: 10'
BLOOM SIZE: 3½"
HARDINESS: Zones 5–9
INTRODUCED: Jerabek, USA, 2008

Brightly colored flowers — white with a pink edge — appear with almost startling regularity on a powerfully vigorous climber. The healthy dark green foliage makes a perfect backdrop for the blooms, which can appear both singly and in impressive sprays. This rose is very much like a bushier, winter-hardy version of the popular 1960s climber 'Handel', and it will reach 10' with support in northern Ohio. Although it is just now being introduced commercially, I have grown this rose for 10 years, enjoying its vigor and winter hardiness.

RIGHT PLACE *Trellis or arch; free-standing shrub in cold climates*

PAUL JERABEK'S WINTER-HARDY CLIMBERS

Paul Jerabek's namesake rose is the latest in a series of hardy climbers he bred that are perfectly suited to northern winters. These climbers are successful in the North not because of an extreme hardiness — they are not tip hardy north of Zone 6 — but because of a vigor that allows them to make so much new growth early each year. These are the perfect climbers for covering a trellis, offering continuous bloom throughout the summer. Among the best are 'Jules', a deep red, many-petaled rose; 'Roseford', clear light pink with a distinctive fragrance; 'Bev Dobson', which has elegantly shaped buds of deepest pink blended with silver; and the colorful 'Aunt Ruth', pink splashed onto semi-double, creamy white petals.

Ohio breeder Paul Jerabek was a modest man who never wanted to name one of his roses after himself. Only after his friends insisted did he finally agree, in his 98th year.

'NEW DAWN'

PHYLLIS BIDE

CLASS: Climbing polyantha

BLOOM COLOR: Yellow

BLOOM SIZE: 1½"

INTRODUCED: Bide, England, 1924

REPEAT BLOOM: Good

HEIGHT: 7'

HARDINESS: Zones 5–9

Almost never out of bloom, 'Phyllis Bide' produces multitudes of tiny blooms of buff yellow edged in apricot-pink. The buds show a hybrid tea shape at first before popping open into a fluffy ball. Reaching 7' in northern Ohio, a relaxed growth habit makes this a perfect choice to twine amid stiffer components in a border of taller plants. It's also very easy to train as a pillar rose, around a lamppost or any similar structure. Left to grow as a free-standing shrub, its foliage may appear sparse. While not particularly thorny, despite what some references say, 'Phyllis Bide' is not thornless.

This rose is somewhat uncomfortably classified as a climbing polyantha. There is no bush version, and I'm not sure a 2' 'Phyllis Bide' would remind us of a polyantha anyway. This rose is truly one of a kind.

The buds of David Austin's 'Janet' look just like super-sized versions of 'Phyllis Bide'. 'Janet', unfortunately, has not proven to be a winter-hardy choice for northern gardeners. 'Phyllis Bide' has been surviving tough winters for 85 years.

RIGHT PLACE *Post; free-standing shrub; tolerates shade*

PIERRE DE RONSARD

CLASS: Large-flowered climber

BLOOM COLOR: White

BLOOM SIZE: 6"

INTRODUCED: Meilland, France, 1988

REPEAT BLOOM: Good

HEIGHT: 8'

HARDINESS: Zones 5–9

If your picture of a climbing rose is a lithe and vigorous plant spilling over garden structures, 'Pierre de Ronsard' may cause you to think again. It is a stocky plant that takes a long time to climb, and without a series of mild winters may never be an effective climber in northern climates. Not to worry; when it doesn't climb it still makes a beautiful free-standing shrub, covered in gigantic blooms of creamy white edged in pink. The color of the blooms varies a lot with the climate, and its guard petals (those that open first) are often green in cool weather. The blooms are usually too heavy for the stems, causing them to nod. The taller the plant gets, the more attractive this feature is.

'Pierre de Ronsard' enjoys excellent health in Ohio and most other places. In southern California it can fall prey to rust. Often sold as 'Eden' or 'Eden 88'.

RIGHT PLACE *Free-standing shrub*

POLKA

CLASS: Large-flowered climber

BLOOM COLOR: Apricot

BLOOM SIZE: 4"

INTRODUCED: Meilland, France, 1992

REPEAT BLOOM: Good

HEIGHT: 10'

HARDINESS: Zones 5–9

Big fluffy blooms in a bronzy apricot color that is unexpected in a climber in northern climates. The plant enjoys excellent health and more winter hardiness than many hybrid teas of the same color.

'PHYLLIS BIDE'

'POLKA'

Although it is well worth growing for its bloom color, 'Polka' has a tendency to produce a lot of unproductive green growth. This is remedied by training its flexible canes horizontally, ideally along a fence. New flowering growth should appear from every node. If you don't have room for this, persistent pruning throughout the summer can encourage new flowering growth. This rose has no problem climbing to 10' in Ohio; the challenge is getting a good proportion of roses to cover that growth. When this happens, 'Polka' can be spectacular.

RIGHT PLACE *Horizontally along a fence*

RED FOUNTAIN

CLASS: Large-flowered climber	REPEAT BLOOM: Reliable
BLOOM COLOR: Red	HEIGHT: 8'
BLOOM SIZE: 3"	HARDINESS: Zones 5–9
INTRODUCED: Williams, USA, 1973	

A modest climber, but one that does not disappoint. My plant reaches only 8' with support, and it is covered for

'RED FOUNTAIN'

most of the summer with crinkly, bright red blooms, usually packed into tight clusters. It is equally effective trained on a trellis or wrapped around a post.

J. Benjamin Williams bred a lot of roses, including one called 'Tupperware'. In my experience, 'Red Fountain' will prove his most enduring legacy.

RIGHT PLACE *Trellis or post*

SANTANA

CLASS: Large-flowered climber	REPEAT BLOOM: Good
BLOOM COLOR: Red	HEIGHT: 7'
BLOOM SIZE: 4"	HARDINESS: Zones 5–9
INTRODUCED: Tantau, Germany, 1985	

More refined than many of the kordesiis to which it is closely related. Blood red 'Santana' is most attractive when fully open. Its large weatherproof blooms appear in small sprays, and they last a long time. The plant is unusually attractive in itself, clothed to the ground in healthy, glossy leaves.

Happy wrapped around a pillar or as a sturdy free-standing 7' shrub, 'Santana' is at its best (and tallest) when trained on a trellis. It makes a spectacular show against a light-colored wall.

RIGHT PLACE *Trellis or post; free-standing shrub; effective against a light-color wall*

SILVER MOON

CLASS: Rambler	REPEAT BLOOM: None
BLOOM COLOR: Silvery white	HEIGHT: 25' or taller
BLOOM SIZE: 4"	HARDINESS: Zones 5b–9
INTRODUCED: Van Fleet, USA, 1910	

This is a rampageous grower that can reach 25' or more. Yellow-tinted buds open to wide silvery blooms that make an outstanding display against the dark background provided by conifers, or an old red barn. Its one annual bloom can last a long time.

Although reasonably winter hardy, 'Silver Moon' is not a predictable bloomer in cold climates. Some years it may not bloom at all, and while its glossy green leaves are quite healthy they do not earn the space they claim when not accompanied by blooms. 'Silver Moon' is happiest in hot weather, and when in full bloom it is a highlight of the summer rose garden. Ideal for gamblers with large gardens.

RIGHT PLACE *Cover a barn; excellent with conifers or other dark-colored background*

'SUMMER WINE'

SUMMER WINE

CLASS: Large-flowered climber	REPEAT BLOOM: Good
BLOOM COLOR: Pink	HEIGHT: 7'
BLOOM SIZE: 3½"	HARDINESS: Zones 5–9
INTRODUCED: Kordes, Germany, 1985	

Perfectly simple 10-petaled pink blooms, reminiscent of the classic hybrid tea 'Dainty Bess' but on a robust, leafy plant. The large, fragrant blooms usually appear in clusters of five to seven.

A modest climber, attaining just 7' in Zone 5. 'Summer Wine' is easily manipulated and will accept training espalier-style against a wall. Grown in this manner it can cover an area as much as 12' wide.

RIGHT PLACE   *Free-standing shrub; train as espalier*

SUNDAY BEST

CLASS: Large-flowered climber	REPEAT BLOOM: Moderate
BLOOM COLOR: Red	HEIGHT: 7'
BLOOM SIZE: 2½"	HARDINESS: Zones 5b–9
INTRODUCED: Clark, Australia, 1924	

As much of a large, arching shrub as a climber, 'Sunday Best' produces sprays of single-petaled blooms, red with a white eye, all up and down its canes. Within each spray appear individual blooms at all stages of development, including some that may have aged poorly. The display can be almost blinding in June, and more modest flowering continues throughout the summer. My plant tops out at 7', and it does best when old canes are regularly removed. It requires no support in Ohio but will in warmer climates.

RIGHT PLACE   *Free-standing shrub*

ALISTER CLARK

Alister Clark was an Australian gentleman of leisure. When he wasn't hunting foxes or betting on race horses, he was breeding roses that would thrive in Victoria's hot, dry summers. Since much of my garden receives no supplementary watering, I have been eagerly testing the Clark creations, which are gradually becoming easier to find in the United States thanks to specialist nurseries such as Vintage Gardens. Unfortunately, many of the Clark roses won't survive an Ohio winter, no matter how happy they might be in our summer heat. **'Sunday Best'** is a happy exception.

SUPER DOROTHY

CLASS: Rambler	REPEAT BLOOM: Good
BLOOM COLOR: Pink	HEIGHT: 14'
BLOOM SIZE: 2"	HARDINESS: Zones 5–9
INTRODUCED: Hetzel, Germany, 1986	

An improvement over the beloved but mildewy old rambler 'Dorothy Perkins' in three respects. 1) It is quite mildew proof, 2) it repeats bloom, and 3) its flower sprays last well when cut.

The small variable pink blooms appear in huge panicles against a background of light green foliage.

'SUPER DOROTHY'

This is about the lightest green foliage one will find on a healthy rose. 'Super Dorothy' looks particularly good against a white background, but its naturally pale foliage may disconcert. I've had garden visitors ask me if I shouldn't give it some MiracleGro. But no, 'Super Dorothy' is plenty vigorous without any additional fertilizer boosts.

'Super Dorothy' grows with more vigor than design, and it can degenerate into a floppy mound if not provided with strong support. It is not as winter hardy as 'New Dawn' or 'William Baffin', but it has enough vigor to cover an arch with one summer's growth. In milder climates, it would be an excellent candidate to climb an apple tree.

RIGHT PLACE *Excellent against a white background; requires strong support; train on an arch; in warm climates, can climb in a tree*

SUPER ROSES

'Super Dorothy' is the best in the intriguing series of "Super" roses bred by Karl Hetzel in Germany. All five seek to reform a classic old rose. 'Super Excelsa' is a healthy version of the old rambler 'Excelsa', and 'Super Elfin' is a supercharged version of an obscure old floribunda. While 'The Fairy' hardly needs reformation, 'Super Fairy' is useful when thought of as a climbing version of the polyantha.

VEILCHENBLAU

CLASS: Rambler   REPEAT BLOOM: None
BLOOM COLOR: Purple   HEIGHT: 9'
BLOOM SIZE: 1½"   HARDINESS: Zones 5–9
INTRODUCED: Kiese, Germany, 1909

One spray of this rambler can display a calliope of colors from deep purple through gray, with stops at all of the lavender and mauve points in between. The small blooms typically appear in clusters of as many as three dozen. There is no repeat bloom, but small orange hips are often an autumn ornament. 'Veilchenblau' grows to about 9'. Since it is thornless, it is easy to train its canes horizontally, for more bloom, or up onto an arch, for maximum garden impact. It is both beautiful and practical when pegged as a ground cover, because its smooth canes are painless to weed around.

'VEILCHENBLAU'

Like all ramblers, 'Veilchenblau' may take several years to establish itself and begin performing at its best. It is perfectly happy in afternoon shade; indeed, its blooms appear at their best when grown that way. 'Veilchenblau' was the mother of many purple or mauve ramblers introduced in the 1910s and '20s. Many are quite interesting, but none are as winter hardy as their parent.

RIGHT PLACE *Train horizonally or on an arch; ground cover; enjoys afternoon shade*

WARM WELCOME

CLASS: Climbing miniature   REPEAT BLOOM: Good
BLOOM COLOR: Orange   HEIGHT: 5'
BLOOM SIZE: 1½"   HARDINESS: Zones 5–9
INTRODUCED: Warner, England, 1991

It's hard to find a quality rose that is really orange. Most roses that we refer to as orange are really red mixed with orange, or pink mixed with orange. This climbing miniature is truly orange, and its small, bright, semidouble blooms appear as beacons of cheer from a long way off. Close up you will see a small yellow eye at the center of the orange bloom.

'Warm Welcome' grows narrowly to just over 5' tall in my garden. Because it absolutely will not spread, it is very useful for planting in confined spaces. It makes a perfect foundation plant against a light-colored background; its stunning color will disappear into red brick but still glows amid deep green conifers. Prompt removal of spent blooms will speed new ones on their way.

RIGHT PLACE *Useful in narrow spaces; foundation planting against light-colored background*

WICHMOSS

CLASS: Rambler
BLOOM COLOR: Pink
BLOOM SIZE: 1½"
INTRODUCED: Barbier, France, 1911

REPEAT BLOOM: None
SPREAD: 20'
HARDINESS: Zones 4b–9

From an era when rose hybridizers were making lots of unlikely crosses just because they could, 'Wichmoss' is the result of a cross between *Rosa wichurana* and the classic moss rose 'Salet'. It's a novelty rose but also very useful, one of the most winter hardy of all ramblers. Its buds appear in big sprays, clear light pink and surrounded on their sepals and calyx by thick green moss. Like the moss of its parent, this has the fragrance of pine resin when rubbed between one's fingers. Blooms eventually fade to silvery white, but they last a long time as part of one annual display that can extend almost a month.

Left on its own, 'Wichmoss' can grow into a tangled mess. It is reformed by strong support, and it can be one of the most effective of all ramblers. Grown against a wall it may attract powdery mildew. 'Wichmoss' is at its best in an open situation, trained along a split-rail fence, where it can extend for as much as 20'.

After 'Wichmoss', no more climbing moss roses appeared until the late 1980s. None of them blooms as profusely as 'Wichmoss'.

RIGHT PLACE *Requires strong support; train along a split-rail fence in an open situation*

WILLIAM BAFFIN

CLASS: Kordesii
BLOOM COLOR: Pink
BLOOM SIZE: 3"
INTRODUCED: Svejda, Canada, 1983

REPEAT BLOOM: Strong
HEIGHT: 8'+
HARDINESS ZONES: 4–9

The toughest repeat-blooming climber for cold winter climates, 'William Baffin' will reach past 8' in gardens where other climbers struggle to bloom at all. Its semi-double flowers are strawberry pink with a paler reverse. They almost always appear in formidable sprays, and the plant makes new sprays all of the time.

'William Baffin' is a powerful grower, strong enough to support itself as a huge, free-standing shrub. But it is easily trained up a trellis or onto an arch, and gardeners in Zone 4 and the colder parts of Zone 5 may find no other rose as suitable for this purpose.

This rose is extra healthy but lacks fragrance.

'WILLIAM BAFFIN'

Gardeners will need a good saw to cut out old wood every few years.

RIGHT PLACE *Free-standing shrub; train on trellis or arch*

ZÉPHIRINE DROUHIN

CLASS: Bourbon
BLOOM COLOR: Pink
BLOOM SIZE: 4"
INTRODUCED: Bizot, France, 1868

REPEAT BLOOM: Reliable
HEIGHT: 10' in mild climates
HARDINESS: Zones 6–9

The famous thornless climber, this Bourbon rose is only marginally winter hardy in Zone 5. While southern gardeners can enjoy 'Zéphirine Drouhin' on trellises and over short arches, it won't even reach around a 6' pillar for me. I must provide supplementary winter protection to coax this rose along as a modest 4' bush in one of my mixed borders. It's a worthwhile struggle, because what this rose offers in continuous bloom and marvelous fragrance cannot be diminished by its vaguely unappealing cerise pink color. The blooms are loose in their arrangement, and they fall apart too quickly to make satisfactory cut flowers.

'Kathleen Harrop' is a mutation in paler pink, with one less row of petals. It is even less winter hardy, and I leave it to the enjoyment of my Southern rosarian friends.

RIGHT PLACE *Free-standing shrub*

'ZÉPHIRINE DROUHIN'

CHAPTER 8

TREE
ROSES

Any rose can become a tree rose. Known in the nursery trade as "standards," tree roses are created by grafting two or more bud eyes from a chosen rose onto a stem that is 18 to 36 inches tall. Multiple grafts are used to create a more fully rounded head, and to ensure redundancy in case of graft failures. (If one bud eye fails, the tree rose continues growing with what remains.)

OPPOSITE The compact habit and quick repeat bloom of the reliable Austin introduction 'Mary Rose' makes it one of the best tree roses.

Costly to produce and ship, a weeping standard, such as 'Rosarium Uetersen', is the most expensive kind of rose you can buy. It may also pay the most dividends.

MOST TREE ROSES are actually constructed of three parts grafted one atop the other: the rootstock; the long, straight stem; and the top growth. Each of these components is a different rose selected especially to suit the role it fills, but you will only ever see flowers from the top growth, which is known as the "head." There is nothing to stop a nurseryman from grafting two (or more) varieties onto the top of a tree rose stem, thus creating a standard of complementary (or perhaps shockingly different) varieties. Unless the two varieties marooned together at the top of a stick are closely matched in vigor, one will eventually outperform the other and the initial effect will be lost.

A rose grafted as a standard can rise above a perennial bed and be a star all summer long. I have seen rose standards used very effectively in herb and knotted gardens. Tree roses almost always look less elegant when planted en masse, as to line a driveway. When deciding to plant tree roses, think specimen tree, not forest.

TYPES OF TREE ROSES

A miniature standard is one with a stem of about 18 inches (sometimes shorter); a half-standard has a 24-inch stem. One can also find standards with one variety grafted halfway up the stem, and then another one at the top. These are called poodle standards, and they are usually most effective when grown in a container on a patio or deck. (I am always worried that someone who knows how much I love roses will give me one of these poodle standards as a gift, and then I will have to take care of it.)

Some tree roses can be 4, 5, or even 6 feet tall. These are typically grafted with a climbing or ground-cover variety that will trail down from the top of the tree rose and are called weeping standards. Weeping standards exceed the dimensional guidelines of the U.S. Postal Service and United Parcel Service, and because they are incredibly expensive to ship are rarely offered by mail-order nurseries. Because they're so rare, I would jump at the chance to purchase any that appear. Today, a tree rose with a 4- to 6-foot stem is more likely to be budded with a Meidiland variety than with a climbing rose. Although a tree rose with a 6-foot stem seems extravagant today, it would be dwarfed by some of the standards grown by nineteenth-century gardeners. We can only wonder at what the 18-foot standards grown by the Empress Josephine at her Malmaison garden must have been like.

RECOMMENDED ROSES FOR STANDARDS

Here are some particularly good roses to grow as standards or half-standards:

'Ambridge Rose' (page 131)
'Charlotte' (page 79)
'Electron' (page 135)
'Elina' (page 135)
'Happy Chappy' (page 92)
'Irresistible' (page 165)
'Mary Rose' (page 100)
'Regensberg' (page 107)
'Silver Jubilee' (page 153)
'Simon Robinson' (page 168)
'Sweet Chariot' (page 169)
'The Fairy' (page 119)
'Truly Yours' (page 157)
'Trumpeter' (page 157)
'Veterans' Honor' (page 158)
'Wildeve' (page 122)

'WILDEVE'

'HAPPY CHAPPY'

'VETERAN'S HONOR'

'IRRESISTIBLE'

'AMBRIDGE ROSE'

'ELINA'

'SIMON ROBINSON'

CHOOSING THE RIGHT VARIETIES

Any rose *can* become a tree rose, but not every rose *should* become one. Roses that grow bolt upright (such as 'Mister Lincoln' and 'Queen Elizabeth') usually look silly as tree roses. Roses with lush, bushy growth and abundant bloom make the most effective tree roses. A low-growing rose can often be more fully appreciated as a standard, where its blooms and fragrance will appear at eye and nose level. Roses with ugly foliage and disease problems should be avoided, as these problems will become ever more apparent directly at eye level. Nurseries vary their selection of tree roses from year to year, and there is no predicting what varieties might be offered in this form.

Raising them up above their neighbors liberates some roses from diseases that are spread in cramped quarters. Thus, a black-spot-prone rose such as 'Iceberg' is usually healthier as a tree rose than when grown closer to the ground.

CARING FOR TREE ROSES

Tree roses need the same basic care as most other roses. In addition, there are some special considerations in terms of staking, pruning, and winter protection.

Staking

Because they are vulnerable to bending over or even snapping in a heavy wind, standards must be secured to a sturdy stake, which is rarely an attractive addition. To avoid disturbing your tree rose's roots, position the stake after you have dug the planting hole and before planting the tree rose. This is another recommendation for siting tree roses as highlight points in a low border, where at least some of the support mechanism can be disguised, rather than all on their own out in a lawn.

Pruning

Tree roses should be pruned in the spring along with your other roses. Tree roses should be only lightly pruned for two reasons: 1) they do not look very attractive when cut back severely, and 2) they are less able to produce new basal growth, so every bit of growth becomes more precious. Once you cut it away, you may not be able to get it back. Throughout the summer, preserve foliage on your tree rose by not cutting blooms with long stems.

Winter Protection

Growing tree roses in a garden bed is a genuine challenge for the northern gardener. With no protection from the soil, the top graft is not hardy, and even a tree rose grafted with a very winter-hardy rose will not survive a typical Zone 5 winter. In Zones 6 and 7, tree roses can be successfully protected by bundling straw around the top, securing it with burlap and twine. In Zone 5 and colder, a tree rose must be tipped over and buried for the winter. This is done by carefully spading out around one side of the rootball, gently tipping the tree rose into a trench dug for the purpose, and then covering it with topsoil. Straw or some other insulation should then be placed over the trench to prevent freeze-and-thaw cycles that could heave the standard out of the ground. The time to resurrect your buried tree rose in the spring is when you are pruning your other roses, and before it has started to make new growth.

Obviously this method of winter protection limits the places in your landscape where tree roses can be employed, since many garden settings do not lend

LEFT Here the tree rose 'Polar Joy' is well-staked against the wind.

themselves to annual trenching. On the other hard, a tree rose set amid a bed of gladiolus can be buried with no problem at all.

To avoid disturbing its neighbors each winter, the standard rose can be grown in a giant pot sunk into the ground. As winter approaches, gently tug the rootball from the pot (which remains in the ground) — grasp the stem just above the soil level when you do this — and then bury the entire tree rose in a trench in your vegetable garden or annual flower bed for the winter. A 10-gallon pot is the minimum size required for this purpose. You will need to give your potted tree rose extra water during the summer, as most pots act as wicks when buried, drawing water away from the plant that is in them.

Standards grown in pots on a patio or deck can also be buried in any tilled-up part of the garden for winter, or they can be moved, pot and all, into a dark, sheltered place. An attached, unheated garage works perfectly for this if you avoid any windows or light sources that will trigger winter growth. The time to move tree roses to a protected place is when they have begun to go dormant, but before temperatures fall into the single digits (Fahrenheit). In northeastern Ohio, Thanksgiving weekend is almost always the perfect time for this. Water lightly throughout the winter; once every two or three weeks is usually sufficient. In the spring, move your tree rose to its outdoor location before it has a chance to begin active growth. The time when you are pruning your other roses will be right for this.

POLAR JOY

This rose is an amazing breakthrough that makes standard roses much easier for northern gardeners to grow. 'Polar Joy' (Lim, USA, 2006) is a standard that is all one variety rather than a collection of grafted parts. It grows on its own roots and is trained in the nursery field to form one long stem. After the stem reaches from 2' to 5' tall, the removal of side growth stops and the plant is allowed to grow out and form a top.

'Polar Joy' blooms in great masses of single-petaled medium pink blooms. I grow the 5' version, which is very effective at the center of a triangular bed of David Austin roses. When deadheaded regularly it will remain in bloom throughout the summer and well into fall. Any suckers or growths that appear along the standard stem should be promptly rubbed out. 'Polar Joy' is hardy to at least −26°F and requires no special winter protection. Like other tree roses it should be staked well so that it doesn't bend or snap in a strong wind. Placing the stake to the windward side of the standard generally reduces the pressure on the plant.

'POLAR JOY'

CHAPTER 9

ROSES IN CONTAINERS

Any rose will grow well in a container, so long as the pot is big enough and the rose is watered much more often than if it were planted in the ground. Containers allow us to bring a part of the rose garden onto the patio or deck. Cold-winter gardeners can also enjoy roses that would otherwise be too tender for their climate by growing them in containers, and protecting them in a sheltered place over winter. Some rosarians choose to grow many of their roses in containers just because they want to give the plants more specialized care. Others grow them in containers before planting them into the garden, to more fully evaluate their color and other characteristics.

OPPOSITE The versatile miniature 'Rainbow's End' shares its pot with a tumbling lobelia.

THE PERFECT CONTAINER ROSE is compact and constantly in bloom. It should also be disease resistant. Miniatures thrive in containers, and climbing miniatures can bring a pillar of portable color to any sunny outdoor living area.

CONTAINER ROSES AS GARDEN ELEMENTS

Container roses have two great advantages. First, they can be enjoyed anywhere that gets at least several hours of sun each day. Containers allow roses to bloom where we spend a lot of summer time: on the deck, patio, or sunny part of the porch, or perhaps around a pool. Apartment dwellers can enjoy container roses on a balcony, or sometimes a roof. Second, they are completely portable. If you have a lot of container roses, those that are doing particularly well can be grouped together as a display when you host a party or garden event. Conversely, container roses that are languishing can be banished to a remote "hospital" area.

Fragrant roses are especially valuable on patios, decks, or other locations where people will be seated for a period of time. People usually move through gardens and so catch only fragments of rose fragrance. Rose perfume is persistent, and it can be best enjoyed when containers of fragrant roses are placed near seating areas.

Gardeners with reduced mobility may find it easier to work with containerized roses. All gardeners will appreciate the convenience of a wheeled dolly placed under very large containers.

Roses do best when they aren't sharing their containers. There is no advantage to putting several roses in one big container. While lovely groupings can be made with combinations of potted roses, perennials, and annuals, the other plants will invariably be happier in their own smaller pots. An exception to this is potted tree roses. The bare area at the bottom of the pot can easily be camouflaged with annuals. I keep coming back to petunias for this; there are undoubtedly more exotic solutions as well.

LEFT The surprising new white floribunda 'Moondance' grows happily in a large pot with *Euphorbia* 'Diamond Frost'.

RECOMMENDED CONTAINER ROSES

The miniature roses included in this list are those particularly well-suited for container culture.

'EVELYN'

'Ambridge Rose' (page 131)
'Baby Love' (page 70)
'Cider Cup' (page 164)
'Evelyn' (page 85)
'Hakuun' (page 91)
'Laura Ford' (page 183)
'Magic Carrousel' (page 166)
'Petite de Hollande' (page 104)
'Playboy' (page 148)
'Regensberg' (page 107)
'Scarlet Moss' (page 167)
'Si' (page 167)
'Silver Jubilee' (page 153)
'Sonia Rykiel' (page 116)
'Sophy's Rose' (page 117)
'Trumpeter' (page 157)

'PLAYBOY'

'BABY LOVE'

'HAKUUN'

'SONIA RYKIEL'

'SILVER JUBILEE'

'MAGIC CAROUSEL'

PLANTING AND CARING FOR CONTAINER ROSES

Container roses do require extra care, especially more frequent watering. Their roots can't search for nutrients beyond the container, so they are completely dependent on what you provide. Northern gardeners must have a plan for protecting their container roses over winter.

Containers

A 5-gallon pot is large enough for growing a rose in most northern regions. Gardeners in areas where the growing almost never stops (such as southern California) and those who wish to coax exhibition blooms from their potted plants will need a container as large as 15 gallons. When choosing containers, balance the aesthetic and the practical. Although often more attractive, terra-cotta pots will require much more frequent watering than plastic ones.

Soil Mixes

Planting your roses in a lightweight soilless mix will make the container easier to move. Northern gardeners should keep this in mind since they will have to carry, or drag, their containers into the garage or some other unheated building for the winter. Roses can also be removed from their containers and buried in the vegetable garden or some other suitable place for the winter months (as described on page 196). Roses can remain happy in a container for as long as three years before repotting is necessary.

Planting Procedure

Use of a special soil mix is not required for container roses. Most of the time I use a mixture of a commercial soilless medium and "ditch dirt" (soil that the township trenches out of its drainage ditches and kindly drops off in my driveway). The advantage of a special mix is a reduced need for extra fertilization throughout the growing season.

When planting bud-grafted roses in containers, northern gardeners should not bury the bud union as they would when planting in the ground. The entire rose will need to be protected for winter anyway, and leaving the bud union exposed will help to promote new basal growth.

1. Trim the rose bush's roots to fit in the pot with approximately 2 inches of clearance on each side of the pot. Trim canes back to 12 inches or shorter.
2. Soak the roots in water for several minutes. An addition of vitamin B-1 (available at garden centers) to the water is beneficial.
3. Fill the pot approximately one-third full with soil mix. Add any amendments such as Dennis Konsmo's recipe or other slow-release fertilizer and mix in well. Add two shovelsful of soil mix on top of the amended soil in the bottom of the pot to keep the amendments from coming in direct contact with the roots. This will avoid root burn. Place the rose in the pot.

A SPECIAL RECIPE

Pacific Northwest rosarian Dennis Konsmo uses a custom-blended potting mix to grow fantastic roses outdoors in 15-gallon plastic containers. If your interest is in growing the very best container roses possible, you'll find that his formula will give excellent results. The proportions of the amendments can be reduced by one-third or two-thirds for use in 10- or 5-gallon pots.

His basic soil mix consists of equal parts (by volume) of sand, black topsoil, and bark or sawdust. He then mixes 3 parts of this basic soil mix with 1 part mushroom compost. From there he mixes together 1 cup of each of the following blend of amendments to add as he fills each 15-gallon container. You may want to wear a dust mask and gloves when mixing this combination.

  Fish meal

  Bone meal

  Blood meal

  Kelp meal

  Cottonseed meal

  0-45-0 triple superphosphate

  Dolomite limestone (the product Doloprill is a finely ground
    dolomite lime)

  Gypsum

If you're using Dennis Konsmo's recipe, fill a 15-gallon black plastic pot approximately one-third full of well-stirred basic soil mix. Add the blended amendments and mix completely with the soil mix. Cover with a shallow layer of unamended soil mix, to keep the roots from direct contact with the amendments. Follow the planting procedure described at right.

4. Fill around roots with additional soil mix until full. Water thoroughly to settle all soil tightly around roots. Mound soil or mulch over the bud union to about 6 or 8 inches above soil level. Remove this mound after three or four weeks when the roots are established.

Watering and Feeding

Containerized roses require daily watering, or more than once daily during prolonged heat waves. A drip irrigation system can be rigged up to automate the watering. This works perfectly well and saves time, but it may reduce the landscaping appeal of your potted roses, as they may appear as if they are on some kind of life-support system (which of course they are). Any well-balanced, timed-released fertilizer, applied according to label instructions, will nourish container roses. Specialized rose fertilizers are not necessary.

GROWING POTTED ROSES INDOORS

If you have a conservatory, roses will be relatively easy to grow in it. The true teas are favorite subjects, and many of the older hybrid teas with greenhouse connections can also be rewarding. No conservatory? Given a large enough south- or west-facing window, roses can be grown as houseplants. The effort required is intense, and the results will not be anything like what can be experienced for so much less effort outdoors, or from genera that really are suitable as houseplants. Nevertheless, keeping very tender varieties alive in a cool room is an annual winter ritual for dedicated rosarians in very cold climates. This should be viewed as a strategy for winter protection rather than a way to enjoy roses indoors. The amount of bloom produced will likely be small, and the plant will demonstrate its unreserved happiness at being returned to the outdoors when conditions becomes warm enough in the spring.

Potted up, the miniatures 'Child's Play' and 'Pinstripe' provide ideal front porch accents.

PART 3

GROWING
ROSES

After more than 30 years of growing roses, I have changed my thinking about many things. I fertilize less
than I used to, I spray much less
often, and I don't stress over most
pests. But some things don't change.
In northern climates, planting a rose
properly is essential for success. In
all regions, rose gardens need plenty
of water, and some pest problems
require an immediate response. Also,
I find that everything I do to encourage my roses to grow prompts weed
growth too. In the following chapters,
I'll describe the techniques I use to
grow healthy, beautiful roses, from
choosing and buying them wisely, to
planting and pruning, through a full
season of bloom, up until it's time to
apply protection for another winter.

CHAPTER 10

GETTING STARTED: BUYING AND PLANTING ROSES

Just two generations ago, most American gardeners lived within a Sunday drive of a nursery that grew its own roses. The varieties they grew were usually those best suited to the local conditions. One could visit this nursery in the summer or fall to see and select roses growing in the production fields. Picky rosarians would even tag the particular rose plants that they wanted to buy. These roses would then be delivered as soon as they were dug in the fall. By planting those bare-root roses in autumn, gardeners would benefit from weeks of uninterrupted root development, which resulted in plants that took off with no growth setbacks the following spring.

These days, most gardeners buy container roses, or order roses by mail. Properly planted, a rose should thrive for a generation or longer. Even though it may arrive at your house packed in a cardboard box, it's a living thing that depends on you to give it the start it needs toward a long and beautiful life.

TWENTY-FIRST-CENTURY ROSE SHOPPING

Local rose nurseries are almost all gone, replaced by shopping centers or tracts of houses. And bare-root roses available for planting in the fall are almost all gone too. Ontario's Pickering Nurseries may be the last remaining mail-order nursery that offers northern gardeners a chance to buy bare-root roses in the fall. This is an American phenomenon; in England and Europe, autumn planting of roses remains a normal practice. In this country, as rose production has moved out of local areas and become concentrated in Texas and California, rose crops are now not ripe in time for shipping during the northern gardener's autumn planting window (those weeks after a few frosts but before a hard freeze).

Lightweight and easy-to-pack in insulating material, bare-root roses (left) are available from mail-order nurseries. Some mail-order sources also ship potted roses (right).

Garden centers have changed as well. When I first started growing roses in the late 1970s, customers could visit a garden center in the spring and select bare-root roses out of large bins. No plastic wrap, no plantable boxes, no wax coatings. Just roses straight out of the grower's refrigerator, kept fresh in a little sawdust. Today all bare-root roses are potted up by the garden center or wholesale grower before sale. Some do this better than others, preserving roots in larger pots. Others are true butchers. Talk to serious rose growers in your area for recommendations of reliable local sources. In general, garden centers that make a point of advertising their rose selection, and that offer roses from several different wholesalers, are more likely to be careful when potting up roses. When you're selecting a local source for potted roses, the larger the pots the better.

The good news is that gardeners have never enjoyed more choice when ordering roses through the mail. Thousands of different roses are available, and these can be ordered as budded or own-root plants.

(See page 208 for an explanation of the relative advantages of budded vs. own-root roses).

Budded plants are always grown in nursery fields and are almost always shipped bare root. Traditionally in the United States, these plants have been graded as #1, #1½, or #2 plants, but these distinctions have little practical application. Any reputable American rose nursery will send you #1 grade plants, which will have at least three healthy canes. A few specialist nurseries growing hard-to-find varieties may offer you the choice of receiving #1½ grade plants, which may have only two canes, if #1s are not available. Both #1 and #1½ grade roses will grow perfectly well, and it is only because of the long growing seasons in Texas and California that American nurseries can offer so many giant rose plants for sale. A high proportion of roses sold in England and Europe would be graded as #1½ by American standards. I actually prefer smaller bare-root plants, because they are easier to get started. Most roses ordered from Canadian nurseries will be smaller

than those obtained from sources in the United States.

Grade #2 bare-root rose plants are tiny; they will fit in your mailbox, and perhaps even through the mail slot in your front door if you have one. The nurseries that offer such plants are unlikely to be selling desirable varieties anyway, so don't order #2 bare-root roses.

Own-root plants can be grown in production fields and shipped as bare-root plants as well. More often, though, own-root roses have been started in a greenhouse or hoophouse and grown in containers. The containers in which you receive them can range from miniature rose pots (approximately 2 inches square and not much deeper) to tree pots (2¾ inches square and 5½ inches deep), to quart and gallon containers. (In the nursery business, a 1-gallon container is actually 3 quarts in size, or ¾ gallon.) A few nurseries keep roses in even larger pots, and they may be willing to ship them if you are willing to absorb the huge costs involved in doing this.

Budded or Own-root

Long before anyone thought of making a T-cut into the stem of a wild rose and inserting the bud eye of a variety he or she wanted to reproduce, people were propagating roses on their own roots. Your great-grandmother may have rooted a cutting from her favorite rose under a pickle jar. Nurseries stuck cuttings by the hundreds out into a field and hoped they would root. The development of bud-grafting revolutionized commercial rose growing, because roses could be reproduced much more quickly. Also, it allowed roses that would be too weak to survive on their own roots to grow to saleable size thanks to the powerful rootstock roots supporting them.

Rosarians have been debating the merits of budded vs. own-root roses for generations, and some of the arguments have been extreme. For many years budded roses enjoyed the perception of being modern and scientifically advanced. Lately some of the arguments for own-root roses have included magical powers of winter hardiness, disease resistance, and floriferousness. Of course, there can be advantages to own-root roses, but they don't involve magic.

Own-root roses have one clear advantage. They will never produce rootstock suckers. Budded roses have one definite disadvantage. In the north, they must be planted carefully to avoid winter loss. Beyond these indisputable points, the question of budded or own-root may be a matter of personal preference, or simply a question of availability: some rose varieties are offered commercially only as budded plants, others only on their own roots. (See Planting Basics, page 213).

With changes in the economics of rose production, the producers of heirloom and collector's roses are being joined by major growers of modern roses in offering own-root roses. Budding roses is a skill, and because of agricultural import regulations, it cannot be outsourced to overseas locations. Sticking stems into dirt is unskilled labor, and to some extent it can even be done with machines.

HARDINESS AND HEALTH ISSUES

Two of the major advantages of own-root roses, advertisements tell us today, are improved winter hardiness and freedom from mosaic virus. However, since mosaic virus is spread in the propagation process, if you take a cutting from an infected plant and root it, you will get an own-root rose with mosaic virus. Conversely, if you propagate a virus-free plant onto virus-free rootstock, you will get a budded rose that is free of virus. Educated and responsible

---

PROS AND CONS OF BUD-GRAFTING

The bud union of this bud-grafted rose must be planted *at ground level* in Zone 6 and *below the ground* in Zones 5 and colder.

Today, those who favor budded roses are much less doctrinaire (except, of course, for those exhibitors who want all of their show roses on 'Fortuniana' rootstock). The use of rose rootstocks provides benefits for both nurserymen and gardeners. By bud-grafting onto a rootstock, the nursery can quickly increase its stock of a desirable new rose (or a resurrected old one). The rose thus becomes available to gardeners more quickly than it would if reproduced only via rooted cuttings. (One cutting will have four or more bud eyes, each of which can become a rose plant if budded.) And the buyer has a rose that will get off to a quick start in his or her garden. The downside to bud-grafted plants comes with the care one must take to plant them at the proper level, the issues of winter hardiness they raise, and the problem of rootstock suckers.

Bud-grafted roses don't "go wild," but their rootstocks do sometimes rise up. This can happen when the budded hybrid dies and the rootstock, still alive, starts growing. Additionally, when rootstocks are produced from cuttings as opposed to seed-grown stock, they will have active eyes that are just waiting to grow. In almost every case the rootstock will be more vigorous than the cultivar that was budded on to it; suckers must be removed or they will overwhelm and kill the variety you originally planted.

nurserymen take care to work only with virus-free roses, and thus it does not matter what propagation method they use.

As production of budded roses has shifted away from specialist growers to general plant wholesalers, budded roses have been sold to consumers in the North with instructions to plant the bud union 1 inch above the soil level. When my wife and I were representing the American Rose Society at our local big box home improvement store several years ago, we actually took a nursery marker and blotted out this ridiculous advice on a poster that the store had provided for us. Planting budded roses with the bud union above the soil is a guaranteed way to lose them in a northern Ohio winter. I don't think the retailers are telling people to do this in order to sell more roses next year. They are simply unaware of the different practices necessary to grow roses successfully in different parts of the country. In my experience, a budded rose planted at 1 inch below the soil level is just as hardy as an own-root rose.

A rose is no hardier than its genetics allows it to be, and growing it on its own roots doesn't make it any hardier. Captain George C. Thomas, Jr., one of the great American rosarians of the early twentieth century, conducted side-by-side trials of 50 budded and own-root roses of the same varieties and concluded that "own-root roses, outside of ramblers and species, need for success a climate without extremes of any kind." (Thomas, *The Practical Book of Outdoor Rose Growing*, Lippincott, 1914). This from a man who lived for his roses, so much so that on the day after he died his widow had the bulldozers out, obliterating them all.

Both budded and own-root roses can suffer from production problems. Some budded roses are grown with shanks so long that proper planting in northern gardens becomes difficult (see page 212–213).

Like all of the Canadian Explorer roses, 'George Vancouver' thrives on its own roots.

Many of us have from time to time received an own-root rose in a little pot that really doesn't have a developed root system. I dislike getting these rooted cuttings, which old-timers called bantlings. With a lot of tender loving care, these bantlings will grow into worthwhile plants, but only after the gardener has done a lot of the nursery's work.

Now that Jackson & Perkins is producing some of its roses on their own roots, it is marketing them as having a "fuller, more attractive shape." I do not believe that own-root plants necessarily have a fuller, more attractive shape — unless, of course, cultivars that naturally have a bushy growth habit have been chosen for this method of propagation.

When gardeners buy a hybridized rose creation, they expect the same plant that its creator, the rose breeder, originally selected for introduction. Some varieties, such as 'Peace' and 'Amber Queen', have been seriously "budded down" due to the propagation of weak eyes, either through carelessness or pressure to produce a lot of plants in a short period of time (see page 148). It is impossible for propagation of roses on their own roots to result in this type of diminished vigor, because a cutting that has weak eyes would simply not grow into a saleable plant.

BOTTOM LINE

If you are an experienced gardener dealing with a reputable nursery, it should not matter whether the rose you buy is budded or on its own roots. Like most rosarians, I do have some personal biases. For example, I'd just as soon have a Canadian Explorer rose on its own roots, and a hybrid tea on a rootstock. But if I want to grow a particular variety, I'll buy that rose in whatever form I can get it. Today, for many hard-to-find and heirloom roses, this means grown on their own roots. For most new hybrid teas and floribundas, it still means grown as budded plants.

After planting, gardeners rarely think about roses' roots. When I moved my garden I had a chance to look at all of them. And what I found out reinforced my thinking that there are advantages both to budding and to own roots. I discovered that my best plants had been budded initially, but over time they had established themselves on their own roots. (This can happen because roots can emerge from the stem bases or any part of a rose that is underground, or even just touching the soil surface.) Nothing gets a rose growing as quickly as a powerful rootstock. And there is nothing as seamless and trouble-free as a rose's own roots.

ROSE ROOTSTOCKS BLOOMS

Different rootstocks, or understocks, are used for budded roses in different parts of the world. These are the ones that American gardeners are likely to encounter. In most cases, a nursery will propagate its roses using only one rootstock, and thus, customers can't specify a preference. Northern gardeners will want to avoid rootstocks that won't be hardy in their climate. The following descriptions may also help you identify rootstock suckers when they appear.

'Dr Huey'

A climbing rose introduced in 1920, 'Dr Huey' has enjoyed a long career as a rootstock. Since this rose is a cultivar and not a species rose, it can't be grown from seed — it is propagated as cuttings. Rootstocks such as 'Dr Huey' produced from cuttings are more prone to sucker than seed-grown rootstocks. Its foliage is similar to that of a modern rose, so its suckers can be difficult to identify and remove. They produce maroon blooms on year-old wood. 'Dr Huey' was originally prized as a garden rose, and some who encounter its accidental appearance in their garden decide to keep it.

Ragged Robin

This is the nickname American nurserymen gave to a China rose raised in France, 'Gloire des Rosomanes', that was a ubiquitous rose rootstock a century ago. It fell out of favor with specialist rose growers because of its propensity to sucker and lack of winter hardiness, but it is still used by some general plant wholesale nurseries that haven't gotten the memo. This is one rootstock whose suckers will bloom in the first year, with masses of informal cherry red blooms. It is not dependably hardy north of Zone 6.

Rosa canina

Popular for its cold hardiness, *R. canina* can also improve the color intensity of wishy-washy roses. Its small leaflets make it easy to spot if it suckers. *R. canina* displays small blooms of blush and white on year-old wood. It is a useful hedging rose and is often seen along country lanes in England.

'Fortuniana'

Because it resists nematode attacks, this rootstock is essential for roses grown in Florida. 'Fortuniana' is also popular with rose exhibitors for its ability to produce large, long-stemmed blooms on a young plant. Although it can survive with heavy protection in Zone 6, this rootstock is not reliably hardy north of Zone 7.

Rosa laxa (*R. canina froebelli*)

This is the most popular rootstock in England, but it is not often used in North America. A form of *R. canina*, *R. laxa* accepts varieties that may be difficult to propagate otherwise, but it takes a year or more to settle in after transplanting. Suckers will appear similar to *R. canina*.

Rosa manettii (also called 'Manettii')

Not as popular as it once was, but still used by some growers in the South. *R. manettii* is not reliably winter hardy north of Zone 6. It suckers freely, with climbing, nearly thornless stems that produce medium-sized, single-petaled pink blooms in their second year.

Rosa multiflora

Still the most widely used rootstock, *R. multiflora* is adapted over a wide region. The thornless form is popular with nursery workers, who would otherwise suffer a lot of scratches. The thornless quality also makes its suckers easier to identify, but some nurseries use the form that has thorns. Suckers will produce masses of tiny white blooms in the second year, but by that time this powerful rootstock may have already swamped and killed the host plant. If *R. multiflora* rootstocks do spring up in your garden, dig them out and destroy them. (See page 236 for more information on the threats posed by *R. multiflora*.)

PLANTING ROSES

Some rose problems are easy to diagnose over the phone. Others don't become apparent until I visit the garden in question, and that is how I discovered that a novice gardener in my community had planted all of his roses upside down. Proper planting is essential for success with roses, and beyond "tops up, roots down," gardeners must position the bud union of grafted roses at the proper level for their climate. Every spring I see whole gardens of roses that died because they'd been planted with their bud unions above ground, or tree roses that perished because they were left outside all winter exposed to the cold.

Preparing Rose Beds

Almost any well-drained soil has the potential to grow good roses. (See Growing Roses in Raised Beds on page 215 for sites lacking good drainage.) All you need to add is sunshine and the right amendments, and then follow up with frequent watering and at least one annual feeding. The first step in readying a site for roses is to take a soil sample so that you will be able to add soil amendments in the appropriate amounts and adjust soil pH to the preferred 6.0–7.0 range.

After taking the sample, rather than digging out sod, the easiest way to proceed is to layer newspapers over the site, eight to twelve sheets thick, using bricks or rocks to keep them from blowing away. Two months later all grass or weeds will be dead, and the soil underneath the newspapers will be perfectly mellow and ready for working. If you have a rotary tiller, simply till in the newsprint. Or remove the newspapers and dig an individual hole for each rose. Double-digging (see Glossary) is fine, if you like to dig, but it is not necessary.

If you're tilling the site, this is the perfect time to add lime and other soil amendments, as listed at right. Till everything in well, let settle for several days, and plant your roses.

SOIL AMENDMENTS FOR ROSES

For best long-term growth, roses respond well to enriched soil, especially soil with an extra boost of phosphorus and magnesium. Roses may need more phosphorus than any other garden plant, and magnesium sulfate has a peculiar ability to stimulate new basal growth in roses.

Here's a good list of amendments for a rose bed. This is the quantity to add per 100 square feet of garden space:

- **18 cubic feet organic matter** (half peat moss; the remainder mature compost, shredded leaves, ground bark, rotted sawdust, well-rotted manure, or any similar organic matter)
- **5 cubic feet perlite or builder's sand** (omit if your soil is already sandy)
- **20 pounds gypsum**
- **15 pounds 0-45-0 fertilizer, or the equivalent amount of another phosphorus source** (such as colloidal phosphate; bone meal can also be used, but so much would be needed that it is best reserved for use in individual planting holes)
- **2 pounds Epsom salts** (magnesium sulfate)
- **Dolomitic limestone** (Unless your soil is quite alkaline, with a pH of 8.0 or above, you'll need to add at least 10 pounds of limestone to balance the very acidic peat moss. Add additional amounts if indicated by soil test.)

If you decide to dig an individual hole for each rose, add soil amendments as you go. One part amendments to two parts soil works well. If your soil test has shown that you have acidic soil, the most important of these amendments will be limestone, which moves extremely slowly through the soil. Those with extremely alkaline soil may want to add a little sulfur, keeping in mind that, unlike lime, a little sulfur goes a long way. Phosphorus is also most beneficial at planting time, since it does so much to help the roots get off to a strong start.

Bonemeal is very expensive when distributed across an entire bed, but it can be a good investment when 1 cup is added to each individual planting hole. If using a synthetic phosphorus source such as triple superphosphate (0-45-0), take care to keep it away from direct contact with the roots. Dig the hole a little deeper than needed, put in the phosphate, cover with soil, and then plant the rose.

How Much Space?

To determine the size of a rose bed, you'll need to first figure out how many roses you want to plant and at what spacing. Always leave extra room, because after your roses bloom for the first time, you'll want to go to a garden center and bring home some more. Here in Zone 5, I plant hybrid teas 20 inches apart. In warm climates, where roses will grow much larger, 30 to 36 inches is more common, and with hybrid teas as much as 48 inches apart in gardens that remain frost free.

Floribundas can be planted much closer together, especially if you are growing them primarily for garden effect rather than individual cut stems. Many of my floribundas are planted just 12 inches apart. Miniatures can be planted from 8 inches apart in cold climates (Zone 5) to 18 inches apart in warm climates. Shrubs, climbers, and old garden roses are so variable in size that it's impossible to recommend a specific spacing. It all depends on

COMPARISON OF LONG-SHANK AND GOOD BARE-ROOT ROSES

Long shanks (the area between the bud union and the beginning of the roots) can complicate the winter hardiness of bud-grafted roses.

PRUNING BARE-ROOT ROSES

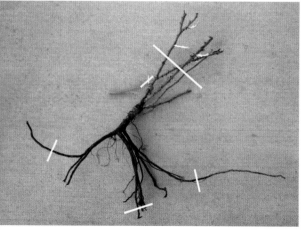 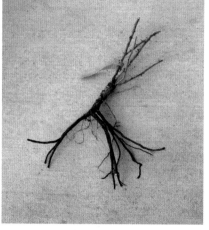

BEFORE PRUNING   **AFTER PRUNING**

Pruning removes watershoots (white growth that has appeared while the bare-root rose was in transit), straggly roots, and about one-third of the length of the canes.

your climate, the size of the variety you're planting, and the dimensions of what you've planted next to it. As a very general guideline, allow a planting distance of two-thirds of the expected height of the variety you are planting. Don't forget to leave ample room between the rose and the edge of the bed. For this, half the expected height of the rose is usually satisfactory.

Mail-Order Bare-Root Roses

Bare-root roses are plants that have been grown outdoors, usually in Ontario, Texas, or California. As they are harvested from the growing field, all soil is washed from their roots (hence bare root) and they are placed in cold storage for shipment at the appropriate time. Bare-root roses will be packed to endure shipping delays and will remain fresh for as long as several weeks. Obviously it is best to plant them right away, but if weather or some other factor prevents this the box can be kept in a cool place. Bare-root roses should be soaked in muddy water for 6 to 24 hours before planting. Some of the mud will adhere to the roots; this coating will help to keep them alive and fresh until new growth begins. If you have deep-enough buckets or larger containers, submerge the canes as well as the roots. Some rosarians also add a Vitamin B-1 solution (sold at garden centers) to this soak. There is anecdotal evidence that this will promote the kind of new root growth that gets a bare-root rose off to a good start, and the package will be labeled with the appropriate dilution rate for soaking bare root plants.

Mail-order nurseries have refined the timing of delivery of bare-root roses to a science, and if you order well in advance you should receive your roses at an ideal time for planting. Obviously, if you order late you may receive your roses late. For me, the perfect time for spring planting of bare-root roses is the first week in April.

I have planted bare-root roses as late as Memorial Day, and with a little extra care they have ended up performing very well by the end of that first summer.

PLANTING BASICS

Before planting bare-root roses, prune any damaged canes and trim away any damaged roots. New-fangled mechanical harvesters used by most rose producers leave bare-root roses with much shorter roots than they used to enjoy. But if any roots are longer than the hole you've dug, either deepen the hole or shorten the roots. Rose roots wrapped around the bottom of a planting hole will never spread properly, and the plant will suffer. If you receive bare-root roses in the spring with very long canes, the plant will get a quicker start if you shorten them to less than 10 inches before planting. Sometimes the rose will have sprouted new, white growth while in shipment. Break these white shoots off before planting, and strong green shoots will replace them.

If you live in Zone 6 or colder areas, it is essential to plant the bud union of a bud-grafted rose *below* the soil level. Gardeners in Zone 6 can usually plant the bud union just below soil level, expecting it to sink a little lower. In Zone 5, 1 to 2 inches deep works well. It's easy to position the bud union by placing a stick across the top of the planting hole once you think it has been dug deep enough. Many roses grown in California have extremely long shanks (the area between the bud union and the beginning of the roots). These are great in warm climates, where the bud union will be above ground, soaking up the sun. But it can be problematic in cold areas: planting the bud union 2 inches deep, followed by a 7-inch shank, puts the roots 9 inches or more below the surface of the soil. In areas with heavy soil and marginal drainage, roses will be unsuccessful in these circumstances. Even with perfect drainage, roots will remain colder for a longer period in the spring, retarding growth. Consider planting the rose at an angle, so that at least some of the roots are not so deep. As soon as growth begins, this sideways planting technique will not be noticeable.

The recommendation to plant bud unions even deeper, 4 or even 6 inches below the soil level, to achieve greater winter hardiness is not really practical. A budded rose will not be happy buried so far under the soil, especially in clay soil, and the end result will be either a dead rose or a plant that puts down roots and grows on its own roots. Over time, a rose planted with the bud union only 1 or 2 inches below ground will also create its own roots, with much less risk. Gardeners in Zones 3 and 4a may want to reconsider the use of budded roses, unless they are willing to dig up the plants and put them in storage each

PLANTING A BARE-ROOT ROSE

1. A stick is useful when positioning the bud union of a bud-grafted rose at the proper level for your zone.

2. Firm soil around the plant with your hands.

(Planting a Bare-Root Rose continued on page 214.)

3. Water slowly. Gurgling indicates air pockets that need to be filled in.

4. Tamp soil around plant after watering.

5. Distribute mulch after planting is complete.

6. Cover with a plastic bag to shade the plant until new growth begins. Beige-colored bags work best.

autumn, gladiolus style, or provide some extraordinary winter protection.

Gardeners in Zone 7 and warmer can position the bud union above the soil level. This is a big advantage, because sunlight stimulates basal breaks. Be careful if cultivating around your roses with exposed bud unions. Apart from the risk of snapping new breaks, wounds from garden implements to the bud union can introduce crown gall (see page 236).

Many rose books show a diagram of a bare-root rose being positioned over a cone of soil that has been constructed at the bottom of its planting hole. Very few roses actually come with roots that are shaped to fit over a cone, however. By gently packing your backfill and soil amendments around the roots (hands are much better for this purpose than feet) you will achieve the same result: a rose that does not shift around once it is planted. If you are planting a rose that has most of its canes concentrated on one side, place the empty side where it will catch the most sun. Sunlight stimulates new basal growth. Slowly tip a 5-gallon bucket of water over each newly planted rose. If you hear gurgling, firm the soil some more.

I feel lucky when I can plant bare-root roses in drizzly weather, and April in Ohio often obliges. Don't let your bare-root roses dry out. They should remain in their soaking buckets, in the shade, until their planting hole has been prepared. One of the easiest ways to stymie a new bare-root rose is to carry it around the garden with you while you are deciding where to plant it.

FOLLOW-UP CARE

After planting a bare-root rose, it must be protected from desiccation. If you are planting in the fall, simply hill it up with soil as described in the discussion on preparation for winter on page 248. You're then all set for the winter.

For spring planting, use soil or leaf mulch; alternatively, cover the canes with plastic grocery bags (beige ones work best). Some spring-planted roses may commence growth within two weeks after planting; others may take as long as six weeks to break out. As soon as you see new growth in the spring, remove the plastic bag, or begin to slowly wash away the soil or mulch mound with a gentle stream of water. Doing this on a cloudy day will make it easier for the plant to adjust.

If you unmound your new roses to find white shoots, it is essential to protect them from sunlight until they turn a normal green color. Unless you live in a windy location, sticking an old umbrella into the ground beside the rose will work very well for this purpose. Prune the canes of any rose that does not want to start growth. If a new rose appears completely recalcitrant, feeding with low doses of fish emulsion or seaweed extract usually helps.

Container Roses from Local Nurseries

The potted roses sold at garden centers and local nurseries are simply bare-root roses that have been recently containerized. In most cases, new roots will have knitted a rootball by the time the rose blooms, and this is a desirable time to plant them. It is best to plant on a cloudy day, and always make sure the plant is well watered and not under obvious stress before planting.

The bud union of bud-grafted roses always sits well above the soil level in potted roses. If you live in Zone 6 or colder, be certain that the bud union ends up below ground after you have finished planting. Once you have dug your planting hole, the potted rose can be placed in it to determine the relative position of the bud union. Dig deeper if need be.

The best way to remove a potted rose from its container is to gently grasp the shank of the rose (the area directly below

GROWING ROSES IN RAISED BEDS

Raised beds are useful in heavy soils where drainage needs to be improved. Groundcover roses also look charming as they tumble out of a raised bed. Floribundas can be showcased perfectly in a raised bed, and miniature roses can be cared for with less back-bending this way. Unless you have poor drainage, I see no advantage in planting very large shrub roses in raised beds. Roses growing in raised beds will lose some winter hardiness in northern gardens, so they're not the right spot for varieties of borderline hardiness in your zone.

Avoid using railroad ties to frame beds because they are treated with creosote, which can be poisonous to plants if it seeps out. Purpose-built landscape timbers are almost always better, even if they don't look quite so rustic. A raised bed will require soil to be imported from somewhere. The perfect solution would be to have some to spare elsewhere in your garden. (I built up a long raised bed for miniature roses as I hand-dug a small pond.) Store-bought topsoil will dry out very quickly, and it must be amended with peat moss or other organic matter.

Roses in raised beds will require more frequent watering. A drip irrigation system will work well, but soaker hoses can be placed in the bed with much less effort. Trimming the grass that grows up against the timbers or other material that form a raised bed will be an additional chore.

the bud union) and, while the pot is tipped sideways, tug it out. If the rose is in a fiber pot, you can also cut the pot away using sturdy shears. For potted own-root roses, such as Jackson & Perkins New Generation roses, there will not be a bud union and obvious shank. Simply grip as near to the base of the plant as you can, and pull gently. Own-root roses can be planted at the same level as they sat in their nursery pot. Simply use your hands to backfill garden soil to the proper level.

If you buy container roses early in the season, be prepared to plant them as bare-root roses, because all of the planting medium is likely to fall away as you remove the plant from its container. Conversely, if you unpot the rose and find the roots tangled up around the bottom of the rootball, then you'll need to cut these roots before planting. Otherwise, the roots may continue to circle after planting and never spread out into the surrounding soil. As garden centers economize by using smaller and smaller pots for their potted roses, this problem of poor growth due to root-bound rootballs is increasing. Start cutting into the root tangle and don't stop until you can pull the roots apart with

your hands. Then you can plant the rose.

After being planted, a potted rose will really appreciate a steady, slow drip of water from a hose. Sometimes a plant that had been growing vigorously in its pot may wilt after planting, despite all your best efforts. Providing some temporary shade along with the dripping hose will usually correct this problem within a few days.

Some garden centers force their potted roses to bloom earlier by growing them in greenhouses. These roses have usually been pushed hard with heavy applications of synthetic fertilizers, and they will be grateful to be treated gently by you. They will appreciate a few days to acclimate from the greenhouse to the outdoor environment. Keeping them well-watered in a mostly shady place is usually the perfect tonic.

Mail-Order Container Roses

Many of the hardest-to-find and most desirable garden roses may be available only from specialist mail-order nurseries, which offer own-root roses in small pots. If you buy some of these little plants, be aware that they'll need some pampering

before planting outdoors. Even roses known to be incredibly hardy and tough when mature are not strong enough to enter your garden directly from these tiny pots. The modest amounts of extra care that these roses require after you receive them will be amply repaid with years of garden pleasure.

Nurseries usually ship roses in small pots at the beginning of or during the growing season. They will almost always be in leaf and will sometimes have buds as well. Upon receiving roses in small pots, I place them in an old stock tank that gets only two or three hours of sun each day. The stock tank catches rain, so the new roses will be well watered and mostly shaded. A plastic storage tub would also work perfectly, or even a kids' wading pool (so long as the kids aren't expecting to use it). After a few days, transplant your little roses to larger pots. First, though, check for evidence of roots emerging from the bottom of the small pot. This is a sign that the rose really is an own-root rose and not just a rooted cutting that will require even more extensive care.

Many own-root roses are shipped in tree pots (2¾ inches square × 5½ inches deep). I repot roses in tree pots into 1-quart pots, and those already in 1-quarts go to 1-gallon. These larger pots then go back into the stock tank where they remain until new leaf growth is evident, fed with very dilute doses of fish emulsion and/or liquid seaweed extract.

Once new growth begins, I move the pots into a sunny nursery area, where they receive a tablespoon of slow-release fertilizer and daily watering. Those wishing to avoid synthetic fertilizers can continue to feed their potted roses with regular doses

An old stock tank used as a nursery area for potted roses that need extra care or are waiting to be transplanted.

of fish emulsion and seaweed extract. After six weeks or so, the 1-quart size gets promoted to 1-gallon size.

Once you have a healthy plant growing well in a 1-gallon pot, you can introduce it to the garden. Even the hardiest, toughest rose will be grateful for the extra time you gave it when young. I often plant these potted roses in September and make sure that they are well watered and have no weed intrusions for the remainder of the growing season. They all get a generous mound of soil for their first winter, heaped up as the growing season finishes, even though most will never need winter protection in future years. This protection should be provided in any garden where roses could be killed over winter by extreme temperatures. The soil mound will prevent the rootball, still mostly disconnected from the garden soil around it, from heaving out of the ground as the soil freezes and thaws. (See page 248 for directions for making a soil mound.)

CARE FOR MAIL-ORDER MINIATURES

Miniature roses grown and shipped in small pots can often be planted directly into a bed of miniature roses without any major problem. They will benefit from the steps outlined above, though, and repotting miniature roses is required when you plan to incorporate them into a perennial bed or other mixed planting. Getting miniatures well established in a quart-size pot before introducing them to a mixed garden will enable them to stand up to the perennial competition.

Transplanting

Occasionally you may need to transplant an established rose because its bed has become too shady or filled with tree roots. Sometimes a portion of a bed needs to be relocated because of a construction project. However, roses should not be thought of as chess pieces to be moved

1. Specialist nurseries often send hard-to-find roses in small tree pots. These own-root roses should first be promoted to a 1-gallon pot.

2. After establishing itself in this 1-gallon pot over a period of two or more months, the rose will be ready to move to a garden bed.

strategically from one part of the garden to another. When a rose is doing well I don't mess with success. No matter how beautiful I imagine a rose would look somewhere else in my garden, I never move any rose that is doing surprisingly well in a particular location. More often than not, after being transplanted the rose will return to its regularly scheduled attributes, and moving it back to its original location won't change it back into Super Rose. If I really think I would like to enjoy a strong-performing rose somewhere else in the garden, then I purchase or propagate another plant of the same variety. On the other hand, moving a poorly performing rose to a completely different area of

the garden often stimulates it toward better performance.

The easiest time to transplant a rose is in autumn. After the rose has stopped growing with summer's vigor, but before the ground has frozen, use a spade to make a sharp cut into the garden bed on all sides of the rose, about 10 to 12 inches from the base of the plant. This will sever some roots. Then dig down, and gently lift the rose out of the ground. Recent basal shoots may break off; this loss is inevitable. (In cold climates winter would have killed this soft growth anyway.) Take the rose immediately, with rootball attached, to its new location (where you will have already dug a spacious hole). If you are

1. With a sharp spade, slice into the soil on all four sides around the rose to be moved.

2. Remove the rose with as much soil as possible.

3. A wheelbarrow is not strictly necessary for moving the rose to its new location, but keeping the rootball intact is.

4. Dig a hole as you would to plant a new rose.

5. Plant the rose, keeping in mind the proper level for your zone if it is a bud-grafted rose.

6. Prune any damaged canes, and mulch to provide protection for the winter or until new growth begins.

Shade the plant until new growth begins with a plastic bag (see page 214), an overturned bucket, or a generous helping of mulch. Once new growth has begun, the covering can be removed. To avoid stress to the plant, do this on a cloudy or rainy day.

transplanting in autumn and the rootball falls apart, simply treat the rose as a bare-root plant. After transplanting, water the plant in well and watch to make sure it settles to an appropriate planting depth for your climate.

Even if the transplant is normally quite winter hardy, gardeners in Zones 6 and cooler should provide winter protection for the first winter after a rose is moved. See chapter 14 for more details. Gardeners in Zone 7 and warmer won't have to worry about winterkill but must take care that their transplanted rose is kept well-watered.

In cases of emergency, roses can be transplanted at any time that the ground is not frozen. A rose moved in summer will require almost constant care. Dig a larger rootball than recommended for autumn transplanting (and hope that it does not fall apart), provide shade with an umbrella or some other device, and leave a hose dripping into its root area. Treatment with a vitamin B-1 solution (sold at garden centers) might be beneficial. Do not feed anything stronger than quarter-strength fish emulsion or liquid seaweed until the plant shows definite signs of resuming normal growth.

As bud-grafted roses age, it becomes more difficult to identify an expanding bud union. Let's hope this elderly rose is in Zone 7 or warmer, because its bud union will be facing winter damage in colder climates.

CHAPTER 11

THE BASICS OF CARE:
FOOD, WATER, MULCH

There are all kinds of theories about what and how to feed roses. Fast-acting chemicals. Soil-enriching organics. Half as much, twice as often. Bulk feeding. The truth is, any feeding plan implemented in conjunction with a soil test will improve your roses. But water is nonnegotiable. Without sufficient water, roses cannot thrive.

WATERING ROSES

The old rule of 1 inch of rain per week is still applicable in many areas, but as long as your rose beds are well drained, your roses will be happy with two or three times as much. Drip irrigation is the perfect setup for watering roses generously while still conserving water. Soaker hoses are much less expensive than a drip irrigation system, initially, but they must be stored inside in cold winter areas. Both soaker hoses and drip irrigation systems supply water directly to the soil and thus to roots, minimizing water loss by not spraying it through the air.

Soaker hoses are plugged at one end and have hundreds of tiny holes that allow water to escape all along their length. In a large garden it is easy to move soaker hoses from one bed to another. Note that water output can vary depending on the quality and age of the hose, with water streaming out steadily at some points and hardly dripping through at others.

A drip irrigation system consists of a network of tiny pipes, usually placed underground, on which devices called emitters (which release water drop by drop) can be placed at any point. So, theoretically, each rose plant can have its own water source. A well-made drip irrigation system will deliver an exact amount of water. If delivery is controlled by a timer or even a computer, you can water your rose beds to your exact specifications, even when you are away from home.

Overhead watering with a sprinkler or hose makes leaves happy and will help prevent spider mites. It should be done in the morning to allow sufficient hours of sunlight for the leaves to dry off. (Leaves that remain wet overnight invite disease problems.) Of course, gardeners have no choice when rain might fall, and I always welcome it.

Knowing When to Water

I've mounted a rain gauge in my garden, and I record each day's rainfall. Whenever there hasn't been at least an inch of rain over the past five or six days, I prepare to water the hybrid teas, floribundas, and miniatures that grow near the house. During a hot, dry August, it may be necessary to water roses every day. But through it all, the old garden roses and shrubs that grow beyond the reach of my hoses receive no extra water at all.

It's also easy to monitor a rose bed's moisture level by sticking a finger into the soil underneath the mulch. Water whenever the soil feels dry more than 2 inches deep. Visual clues such as wilting leaves or drooping blooms indicate that the roses should have been watered days ago.

Roses planted in a mixed border will not require more water than their companions. Indeed, these densely planted beds — where all the roots are shaded and the "mulch" is other living plants — rarely need supplementary water.

By mid-September, when roses are beginning to prepare for winter, I water less so as not to encourage soft new growth. In my climate it is never necessary to water in winter.

FEEDING ROSES

The three major nutrients that all plants need are nitrogen, phosphorus, and potassium. All fertilizer packages are clearly labeled with the proportions of these three ingredients contained in the product. For example, a fertilizer labeled 10–24–15 contains 10 percent nitrogen; 24 percent phosphate (P_2O_5), a common form of phosphorus; and 15 percent potash (K_2O), a common form of potassium. Fertilizer blends may also include small amounts of minor and trace nutrients such as magnesium and boron; the rest is inert ingredients.

Synthetic fertilizers work quickly and cost less per pound of fertilizer value. They are the traditional favorites of rose exhibitors, greenhouse rose producers, and others who want to see quick results. In heavy soils, synthetics require a lot of water in order to reach the root system. In sandy soils, synthetic fertilizers can be quickly washed out of the root zone.

Organic fertilizers improve the soil as well as feeding the plant. Because they act more slowly than synthetics, organics are less likely to burn roots or prompt the lush, rapid growth that often attracts insects or disease. Commercially available organics usually cost more initially, but they represent a long-term investment in soil health.

Nitrogen

Nitrogen makes plants grow. Too little, and your plants will appear stunted. Too much, and you get the Jack and the Beanstalk effect of tall growth, often with elongated stems and leaves. Many rose varieties also react to surplus nitrogen by generating blind shoots, rose stems that produce no blooms. I always provide my roses with nitrogen at the beginning of

Soaker hoses are an ideal way to deliver water directly to rose roots.

THOUGHTS ON FEEDING ROSES

Soil Testing

It is a waste of time and money to embark on a complicated feeding program without first reviewing the results of a professional soil test. Local extension agencies rarely perform these tests themselves anymore but can refer you to a laboratory that does. The inexpensive Mr. Wizard-type soil test kits sold in garden centers should not be relied upon for consistently accurate results. (If you doubt this, simply test the same soil sample twice.)

Heavy Feeders

Roses require more food than most other garden flowers, and some roses require a lot more food than others. Hybrid perpetuals are the heaviest feeders I know, while hybrid rugosas seem to do just as well with a consistent water supply and no supplementary food.

Repeat Bloomers

In general, repeat-blooming roses need more frequent feeding than once-bloomers. I don't provide any food to my once-blooming roses once they are done blooming for the year.

Feeding Program

A simple but effective feeding program is one half cup of granular 12-12-12 fertilizer per rose per month, starting after pruning is completed and continuing until about six weeks before the first frost is expected.

Fish Fertilizers

A dose of fish fertilizer — whether whole fish, fish meal, or fish emulsion — can add a real boost to a rose feeding program throughout the growing season when applied as a supplement to a monthly feeding with a granular balanced fertilizer. Fish emulsion is sold "deodorized," but whole fish and fish meal will probably attract cats, dogs, raccoons, and other garden visitors.

Specialized Rose Foods

Roses can't read the labels of fertilizer products. A picture of a rose on a package is much less important than what the package actually contains, and whether those ingredients are proportioned in a way that will benefit your roses. Just like multivitamins, a specialized rose food will contain secondary and trace elements such as calcium and molybdenum, each of which is said to perform a specific function in overall rose performance. Most of these will already be present in your soil.

Alfalfa Meal

Alfalfa meal (sold as rabbit food) contains triacontanol, a growth stimulant valuable to roses. Applied liberally each spring, a cup or more around each plant, alfalfa meal does double duty as a soil conditioner. Alfalfa must be thoroughly mixed into the soil and is not an effective mulch. Some rosarians concoct an alfalfa tea for liquid feeding. Simply dissolve 1 cup of alfalfa meal in a 5-gallon bucket of water and pour around the base of rose plants as a tonic. Like anything else, organics can be overdone, and some rosarians who have gone overboard with alfalfa have developed near-toxic levels of boron in their soil. This has usually happened only following many years of applications, and a professional soil test will quickly reveal elevated boron levels.

Slow-Release Fertilizers

Slow-release fertilizers (also known as controlled-release fertilizers) are excellent for use with roses in containers. They eliminate the need to repeatedly scratch fertilizer into the area of delicate roots near the soil surface, or to embark on a more time-consuming program of liquid fertilizers. If using slow-release fertilizers, repot the rose at least once every three years, using entirely fresh potting mix. Gardeners in my area who have relied on slow-release fertilizers in their gardens have built up toxic (to plants) levels of potassium in their soil. This is not an argument against slow-release fertilizers so much as one in favor of soil tests.

Foliar Feeding

Foliar feeding can be an ideal summer tonic for roses, so long as they are well watered before application. Any commonly available soluble fertilizer gives the plants a real boost. Numerous studies have shown that, when applied at the same time as a systemic fungicide, a liquid fertilizer can help carry the fungicide into the foliage, making it more effective. Rich in trace elements, liquid seaweed makes a great foliar feed. Nothing works better than seaweed to improve rose foliage, but be aware that it could clog up your sprayer. I keep an inexpensive hose-end sprayer as my dedicated liquid seaweed applicator.

Fighting Acidity

Almost everything I do in my garden makes my soil more acidic. My peat moss is acidic, my mulches are acidic, my chemical fertilizers (and some of my organics) are acidic, and my rain is acidic. Even though I apply vast quantities of dolomitic limestone every spring and fall, my soil pH still hovers around 6.0. I till the limestone lightly in the soil, but it may take many years for the lime to migrate into the root zone. I am hopeful, though, that the lime I spread 10 years ago is already there and helping to buffer all that acidity. Still, so far as roses are concerned, a soil that is too acidic is better than one that is too alkaline.

Value of Gypsum

When I gardened in clay, I relied on gypsum to help loosen the soil. Now that I am in sandy loam, I still like gypsum, for its ability to flush salts out of rose beds. I try to apply gypsum every second year, at a rate of 3 pounds per 100 square feet. It can be applied at the same time as any fertilizer.

the growing season. After late summer, excessive nitrogen will encourage soft, new growth and reduce a plant's winter hardiness.

If I want to give my roses a kick-start right after pruning, a high-nitrogen fertilizer does just that. Ureaform is the old-time favorite chemical nitrogen fertilizer. It works quickly, but it can also burn plants if label recommendations are exceeded. Excellent organic sources for nitrogen include corn gluten meal and products made from leather waste. Always apply according to label directions. Note that many lawn fertilizers are high in nitrogen. If using a chemical lawn fertilizer on roses, be certain that it does not include any herbicides as added ingredients, as these will damage your roses.

Phosphorus

Phosphorus promotes healthy root systems, bloom production, and bloom size. With too little phosphorus, bloom production will drop; in severe cases the leaves at the bottom of the plant will turn purplish red. Roses really benefit from a phosphorus reservoir, such as bone meal, colloidal phosphate, or triple superphosphate installed at planting time (see page 211). I continue to add phosphorus to all of my rose beds at least once a year. If your roses develop a serious phosphorus deficiency, (and a soil test confirms that this is not a result of phosphorus being locked up due to high soil pH) you can inject a phosphorus source around the base of each plant using a bulb planter. The other alternative if many plants are affected is to dig up the suffering roses and rebuild the bed, following the directions from a soil-testing lab for amending the soil to increase phosphorus.

Potassium

Potassium works much like motor oil, smoothing the way for all of the other nutrients and micronutrients. A lack of potassium can be indicated by poor blossom color and leaves with yellow tips. Potassium is often lacking in sandy and red clay soils and in areas that are poorly drained. A modest application of potassium four to six weeks before frost can help roses prepare for winter, essentially helping them to increase the concentration of sugar in their sap, which will act as an antifreeze. Sulfate of potash (0–0–50) can be applied to existing rose beds at a rate of 1 pound per 100 square feet. Note that sulfate of potash contains a lot of magnesium, and if used in concert with dolomitic limestone (also high in magnesium) there is a danger of magnesium overload.

Other Nutrients

Deficiencies usually manifest themselves as discolored foliage, but if you test your soil, you will discover the deficiency long before your roses begin to suffer. A deficiency of magnesium can be corrected by adding Epsom salts; sprinkling a handful around each bush in spring and then again in early summer can promote the creation of new basal breaks. Whenever I have a rose plant that is failing to make new basal shoots, I give it a sprinkling of Epsom salts.

Iron, even when abundant in the soil, can be locked out by a low pH. Iron deficiency produces chlorosis, with leaves turning yellow while their veins remain green. Roses do very well with a slightly acidic pH of between 6.0 and 7.0 (7.0 being neutral on the pH scale of acidity and alkalinity). Bringing a more acidic pH into balance, by adding lime, will make the iron available once again as well as improving the availability of other nutrients.

Hybrid perpetuals, such as 'Baronne Prévost' (left), are the heaviest feeders I know, while hybrid rugosas, such as 'Cibles' (right), seem to do just as well with a consistent water supply and no supplementary food.

MULCH

A gardener who does nothing more than water roses and replenish their mulch will enjoy reasonable results. Mulch is important for keeping soil temperatures steady, conserving water, and preventing weeds. Some mulches also enrich the soil. Most of my garden is now mulched in bark, which needs to be replenished only once each year. Around most heritage roses and large shrubs, I use the large bark pieces, which last for several years.

I apply mulch around a new rose as soon as I have planted and watered it. I leave a ring of bare soil about 8 to 10 inches in diameter around each plant so that any new basal shoots will face no obstructions.

Whatever mulch you use, don't lay it on too thick. Soil needs to breathe, and if soil organisms are smothered, your roses will suffer. Three inches is a good thickness to aim for — deep enough to stifle weeds, not too deep to suffocate soil. A moderate amount of mulch, continuously replenished, will yield much better results than a mountain of mulch applied all at once.

Mulching Options

Organic mulches, such as leaf mold and manure, provide extra humus as they break down. Bacteria feed on this humus, liberating nitrogen in a form plants can use. Mulches should not, however, be confused with fertilizers and are not a substitute for them.

Horse manure. In my part of the country, horse farms are replacing dairy farms. We have gone through all three stages of the Horse Manure Glut. First, signs spring up offering "Free Manure," and gardeners bring buckets and baskets to the farm to carry some home. But there is still too much manure, so eventually the sign will say something like "We Load." And so gardeners take their pickups and have the horse farm personnel fill them with manure. At some extraordinarily tidy farms, the manure will be waiting, neatly bagged. After a few years we achieve manure nirvana with the sign, "Free Manure, Will Deliver."

Horse manure is a great tonic for tired soils, but it does have drawbacks as a mulch. First, it will contain weed seeds. Horses do not feed on oats alone, and a rose bed mulched with aged manure will begin to sprout various plants of the pasture. Second, manures (of any kind) provide an ideal environment for the spread of rose midge (see page 230).

Chicken manure is also available for free in many areas. I dislike it because it is sticky and difficult to work with, and it often remains too "hot" to use even after years of composting. The risk that chicken manure will burn my plants outweighs any benefits it may offer.

Leaf compost produced by regional, county, and municipal recycling agencies is ideal for use with roses. This can usually be delivered by the truckload (often you must be a resident of the appropriate jurisdiction). This is typically black and crumbly, and instantly attractive on top of the rose bed. I think there is no better background for displaying healthy rose foliage and blooms. This too will contain a variety of weed seeds, and some of these can be quite surprising. One shipment I received from Cleveland contained some syringes, but I would be even more concerned about reports of persistent herbicide residues. Roses are intolerant of herbicides, and a mulch that contained them could prove disastrous. Don't need a truckload? Smaller batches of leaf mulch are easy to produce on your own, either with a dedicated leaf shredder or by running a lawn mower over short stacks of fallen leaves. Aged over winter, this can be ready to use next year. Leaves stuffed into plastic bags will also compost themselves over time. Let your neighbors do the raking and bagging. All you need to do is drive through the neighborhood and collect. Store the bags in an out-of-the-way place, and use when needed next year.

Bark mulch is available everywhere, from fine nurseries to corner gas stations. It does a great job of smothering weeds but will consume a lot of nitrogen as it decomposes. Adding supplemental nitrogen is essential when using bark mulch or the hardwood mulch that is also available free from utility company trimming crews. I apply one handful of high nitrogen fertilizer (such as urea, 45–0–0) on top of the soil for each bushel of mulch that will cover it.

Mulching Prevents Weeds

The best way I know to squelch weeds is to spread a layer of newspaper, at least eight sheets thick, and cover it with shredded hardwood or bark mulch. This takes care of everything in the rose bed, and since it separates the mulch from the soil will even reduce the call for supplementary nitrogen usually needed when using these kinds of mulch.

Those who use tools to cultivate the soil around their roses will inevitably break off their share of new shoots and basal breaks. Take care to keep such damage to a minimum, because nicking the base of the plant with a garden implement can open a door for crown gall (see page 236). Deep tilling of rose beds with miniature tillers should be avoided, as it will inevitably sever valuable surface feeder roots.

MULCHING ROSE PLANTS

1. I worry about how I will control weeds once all newspapers migrate to the Internet. A layer of newsprint 6–8 sheets thick will smother most weeds and prevent new ones from sprouting.

2. Spreading bark mulch over the papers keeps them in place, and provides a much more attractive appearance.

3. I replenish the mulch each year. The newspapers last for about three years before the whole bed needs to be papered and mulched again.

The best way to control grass in a rose bed is to pull it out as soon as you spot it. Grass is most pernicious when it appears in the center of rose plants, where it is impossible to mulch and often very thorny to weed. If grass has invaded your rose beds in this way, you can use a selective herbicide to bring it under control. The one I have used for this purpose is called *clethodim*. While no foliar damage is apparent to rose plants even after clethodim is sprayed directly over them, they will grow sluggishly for the remainder of the season. So clethodim should be used only in extreme cases of grass invasion.

I do use glyphosate herbicide to edge my rose beds, applying it with a rolling applicator. This works very well, and it helps to keep invasive grasses such as quack grass out of the roses. I don't have to avoid windy days when applying herbicide in this way, but I have found that some weed-killer damage can spread to roses even when it is foggy or very humid. So I avoid using glyphosate under those conditions. If poison ivy or Canada thistles appear around your roses, it will take more than one application of glyphosate to kill them. For poison ivy, using more poisons seems fair. For thistles, I put on my rose gloves (thistle as well as thorn proof) and pull them out.

Roses suffering herbicide damage will show exaggerated, elongated growth, usually paler green than normal. Any buds produced will be tiny. Any flowers that attempt to open will be malformed. Roses are rarely killed by one misapplication of herbicide, and heavy rains or garden hose soakings will help carry them back toward normality.

STONE AND PEBBLES

Architectural mulch (such as decorative stones or pebbles) may or may not look attractive in your garden. I don't believe that artificially colored pebbles ever look good in a rose bed. These types of mulches will make it difficult to apply organic soil amendments, and the inconvenience of having to push mulch aside to do anything and then having to pull it back, may force you into depending on liquid and foliar fertilizers. Unless water is constantly run through it, architectural mulches make convenient hideouts for spider mites. One place I have seen architectural mulch used effectively is in a dooryard planting of tree roses, where it would have been too shady to grow much of anything at ground level.

CHAPTER 12

DEALING WITH PROBLEMS: INSECT AND ANIMAL PESTS, BLIND SHOOTS, AND DISEASES

Some rosarians actually enjoy the battleground aspects of protecting roses from pests and diseases. Their garages contain an arsenal of insecticides and fungicides; they regularly patrol their garden for any sign of infestation; and once a week they dress up in protective gear somewhat resembling a space suit to blast their roses with the latest that chemical science has to offer. But I find peace in the garden, and don't want to do battle with any part of it.

I stopped spraying most of my roses with chemicals about seven years ago. Instead of worrying about protecting myself against pesticides, I am now fascinated by the brigades of natural forces such as ladybugs and praying mantises that have occupied large portions of the garden. And I enjoy hosting more birds than ever before, adding a perpetual and ever-changing soundtrack to the garden.

I do still protect hybrid teas, miniatures, and some floribundas with fungicides. With some newer products this can be done monthly, so I spray these roses only five times a year (from mid-May through mid-September). If I had no interest in exhibiting my roses, I would choose to grow only roses that need no spraying at all, and I might even enjoy them more.

The best way to avoid rose diseases is to plant varieties that are disease-resistant. Good air circulation is also essential, and a rose plant that receives a steady supply of water — no drought and no wet feet — will be less susceptible. While there aren't yet varieties bred for insect resistance, the well-watered, well-fed rose is also less likely to be weakened by insect attacks.

None of the potential problems described on the following pages should discourage you from growing roses. It is unlikely that you will ever see more than a few of them at any one time, and the amount of effort that you devote to controlling them depends on how close to absolute perfection you want your roses to grow. Roses are still beautiful even when they aren't absolutely perfect.

INSECTS

Most of the pests described below can be found throughout the United States and southern Canada. Some of them appear regularly in my garden; apart from nematodes, I have dealt with all of them at least once. We rarely see earwigs anymore, and we ignore leaf-cutter bees. Though a pest, no action should be taken against leaf-cutter bees because they are important pollinators. Most garden insects are beneficial, or at least neutral. Although some such as Japanese beetles are instantly recognizable, my most serious insect enemy has been the nearly invisible rose midge.

Aphids

Aphids are tiny, soft-bodied, winged insects particularly attracted to the soft new rose growth of spring. These green (or sometimes red, pink, or white) insects suck life from succulent rose growth, which can become distorted in a severe infestation.

Aphids produce a sticky substance known as honeydew, which is a favorite of ants. Ants will actually farm aphids for their honeydew, and if you see ants marching up and down your rose plants, the plants almost certainly have aphids. Just as I enjoy maple sugar candy, people in the Middle East enjoy honeydew as a favorite confection.

Aphids are fragile, and insecticides are not needed to keep them under control. I used to chase off aphids with a strong jet of water from the garden hose. Simply aiming the stream at tender new growth where aphids congregate, and repeating every day for five days, would completely discourage any aphids that were not killed. Today, I have legions of ladybug beetles standing guard, ready to feast on any aphids that appear.

BEFORE

AFTER

A spot of glue will prevent invasion from some cane borers. Add some food coloring to the glue to make sure you don't waste time and glue by sealing the same cane twice.

Cane Borers

Two kinds of cane borers threaten roses. The raspberry cane borer likes to burrow into succulent new basal breaks, causing them to wilt and die. There is really no prevention against this borer, but by quickly removing and destroying the infected shoot you may also catch the borer's larvae and prevent a new generation of attacks. Borers travel downward after entering a shoot, so cut low.

The rose cane borer drills into mature canes where you have made your pruning cuts. As the borer establishes itself inside the cane, growth will gradually begin to slow and then wilt. Many gardeners never experience any problem from this kind of borer; others are confounded by it. The borers can be thwarted by using a drop of glue, or a commercial sealant, on your pruning cuts. If you have a lot of roses, this is a lot of work that really slows everything down during pruning time, when fair weather can be hard to find. I don't recommend sealing pruning cuts unless you have actually experienced a severe cane borer attack. If you do seal with glue, adding food coloring to the glue will let you see in an instant which canes you have already sealed.

Earwigs

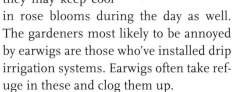

Earwigs are medium to large, soft-bodied insects that take refuge in rose blooms at night and chew their way out in the morning. During times of drought they may keep cool in rose blooms during the day as well. The gardeners most likely to be annoyed by earwigs are those who've installed drip irrigation systems. Earwigs often take refuge in these and clog them up.

Songbirds love earwigs, and if you see birds apparently attacking your roses, you are witnessing the best method of control.

Earwigs will rarely be a problem serious enough to warrant chemical remedies, which must be applied to the soil where earwigs lay their eggs.

Gall Wasps

A mossy green or brown gall, up to an inch in diameter, is created when this wasp stings a rose stem. *Rosa eglanteria* and its descendants are the roses most often affected, perhaps because the wasp is attracted to their fragrant foliage. If you find galls on your roses, chances are that the mossy rose gall wasp is the perpetrator. It is found throughout the United States and southern Canada. No real damage is done, and although not really beautiful, the galls are at least a curiosity. I always leave some on *R. eglanteria* to show garden visitors.

Inchworms

If your roses are growing in some shade, they may be subject to attack from inchworms. These tiny caterpillars descend from deciduous trees in the springtime and inch straight toward rose buds. Once an inchworm has burrowed into a rose bud it consumes the developing petals, preventing the flower from opening properly. If you find one inchworm you have a hundred, and there is no easy means of control. They can be hand-picked from roses, of course; spraying the giant oak and maple trees from which they typically descend is hardly practical.

Japanese Beetles

Since being introduced into New Jersey in 1916, Japanese beetles have now spread to 47 states. These metallic green-and-brown beetles are the most obvious insect pests in my Ohio garden. From the 4th of July to Labor Day, they feast and have sexual orgies on roses. If there are plenty of blooms, that is enough for them. If not, they will eat rose foliage too, reducing it to a lacelike appearance. Given a choice, Japanese beetles prefer light-colored, fragrant rose blooms to dark-colored ones without scent.

Japanese beetles appear after most once-blooming old garden roses have finished for the year, and for the most part are gone before repeat-blooming roses produce their finest blooms in the cool autumn weather. A few stray beetles can usually be found as late as October, but the first serious frost finishes them off.

Japanese beetles can be hand-picked anytime, but this method of control is particularly effective at dawn and dusk, when beetles are quiescent, or after a rainfall, when they are waterlogged. Beetles will reflexively tumble downward, so having a cup of soapy water with you will ensure their drowning.

Beetles can be killed by contact pesticides, including products as safe to humans as neem (used as a toothpaste in India). But however many you kill by contact today, just as many will be attracted to your roses tomorrow. Unless you are giving them out to your neighbors, beetle traps will be of no use. They attract Japanese beetles, and your roses are already doing that.

If you have a large garden and a lot of patience, milky spore disease is tremendously effective. Applied as a powder to the soil and turf surface, this bacterium kills beetle grubs in the soil and spreads into new areas each year. It may take four to six years to be fully effective, and it will not work if you have a small garden separated by pavement from neighbors who do not also apply milky spore.

During Japanese beetle season, particularly promising rose blooms can be protected with bonnets made of a lightweight fabric such as floating row cover, available from garden centers and mail-order outlets. Buds can be protected with waxed paper sandwich bags, twist-tied on to the rose stem. In most cases these sandwich bags will prove big enough until the bloom is one-third open and ready to cut.

Leaf-Cutter Bees

The leaf-cutter bee is an elegant pest. This bee cuts small, perfectly circular holes in rose foliage and uses this material to feather its nest. Because the bees never ingest the foliage, applying systemic insecticides is pointless. Nesting in wood, soil, or tubular lawn furniture, leaf-cutter bees are rarely more than a minor problem, and most gardeners find their precision work a thing of beauty. They are also important pollinators. Given a choice, leaf-cutter bees prefer the dull matte foliage found on most old garden roses to the glossy leaves of modern kinds.

Nematodes

Nematodes are tiny parasitic worms (very different from earthworms) that can attack rose roots. When infected, a rose plant will appear stunted. Its leaves will often display symptoms of mineral deficiencies, even if it has been provided with a rich diet. When dug up, nematode-infected roses will have tiny root systems.

Nematodes can't live through a severe winter and are therefore a problem only in mild climates such as in the Deep South. In Florida, roses are grown on *Rosa fortuniana* rootstock, which provides resistance to nematodes. Most independent garden centers in Florida offer roses on *Rosa fortuniana* rootstock.

Rose Chafer

This dull gray beetle is a little bigger than a Japanese beetle. Rose chafers enjoy rose foliage as much as blooms, and the foliage of many other plants as much as roses. In my garden they really prefer hollyhocks. They are sluggish, and if you do find them eating your roses or skeletonizing your rose foliage it is easy to catch and squish them. Although less satisfying, dropping these beetles into a jar of soapy water also works well for dispensing with them.

Rose Curcurlio

I imagine that some garden club members may have been frightened by slide shows featuring this weevil. But its long snout is much less impressive when we realize it arrives on an insect that is only a quarter-inch long in real life. The rose curculio uses its snout to eat deep holes into rose buds, which will then fail to open. It can be controlled by hand-picking. Serious infestations are rare, but they can be restrained by contact insecticides such as pyrethrum or insecticidal soap. Curiously, this is one rose pest that appears more troublesome in gardens where many different kinds of roses are grown together. Its larvae winter in rose hips, and if this pest has been a serious problem in your garden you should cut faded flowers to prevent rose hips from forming.

Rose Midge

You won't ever see a rose midge, and I hope you never see what they do to a garden. The microscopic rose midge is technically a maggot (the larva of a fly), and it destroys rose buds as they are forming. A severe infestation can rob the garden of all rose blooms, even as the plants grow healthily along. On close examination, it will appear as if the tender new shoots that should terminate in a bud have been blasted with a blowtorch. This burned appearance can also appear on side shoots and other new growth that might not have produced flower buds, as midge larvae feast on all succulent new growth. And worst of all, by the time you notice the damage they cause, the midge will have dropped to the ground to pupate and produce a new generation of midge flies. This is why the traditional means of control concentrate on getting rid of young midge flies by dousing the soil with a chemical drench before they emerge from the rose bed.

Rose midge was originally a greenhouse pest, with outbreaks first reported a century ago in Ontario and along the eastern seaboard. It has since spread outdoors and across the eastern United States. Its range is increasing, but outbreaks west of the Mississippi remain isolated.

I would love to learn that someone has discovered a rose midge predator or an environmentally sound method of bringing midges under control. Although sometimes recommended for this purpose, diatomaceous earth is completely ineffective: the microscopic larvae simply do not cut themselves climbing over the sharp particles. In the years after World War II, rosarians achieved total control of rose midge with dangerous chemicals that are outlawed today. None of the grub-killers on the market today work as well, and while I am open-minded about reports of infected gardens correcting themselves over time, I have not seen this myself. Reports from dedicated organic gardeners of controlling rose midge by covering rose beds in plastic are intriguing; in theory this should be an effective solution, but in practice it would be ugly and complicated as it would require placing the roses on an all-liquid diet.

Some hybrid perpetuals and other roses with particularly long sepals (such as Ralph Moore's 'Elegant Design') show resistance to rose midge because their botanical construction makes it difficult for midge larvae to get to the developing bud. William Radler, the creator of the Knock Out roses, has announced that he is actively working at breeding midge resistance in roses.

Be cautious of introducing midges into your garden via infected potted roses from garden centers. There are many reasons why a potted rose might have dead growing tips, including water or heat stress and even mineral deficiency. But if you see a sales lot filled with potted roses with no blooms or buds, run — don't walk — back to your car.

Midges reproduce especially well in manure mulches, so avoid them if you've had problems in the past. Keep in mind, though, that granular grub control agents won't work efficiently if you use a mulch made of giant bark pieces.

If you've ever doubted the wisdom of removing buds from newly planted or weak roses to get them to concentrate on their growth, just look at what the rose midge does. My rose bushes have never been as lush and green as when I've had midges. With no flowers to produce, they can spend all of their time and energy growing foliage. Really beautiful foliage.

Rose Slug

These larvae of sawflies skeletonize rose foliage. Left unchecked they can completely defoliate a plant. Rose slugs seem particularly fond of climbing roses; I have never seen them on miniatures. They typically feed at night, and the dedicated gardener armed with a flashlight could pick them off (from the undersides of the leaves) then.

The good news is that they usually appear in isolated parts of the garden and can be controlled by good garden sanitation. Rose slugs overwinter in debris, and they should never be a major problem in the well-kept garden.

Rose Stem Girdler

These beetle larvae bore into rose stems, causing them to  swell and sometimes break. It's easy to control them simply by removing and destroying infected stems. The rose stem girdler seeks out *Rosa hugonis,* but it can be found in other species and heritage roses as well. I have never seen it troubling modern roses.

Scale

Scale looks like a gray or light brown crust forming on rose stems. Up close, it will look like a lot of little clamshells on rose stems. These are the skeletons of the scale insect, which may or may not be residing inside the skeleton house. Although at least 20 different species of scale have been reported as rose pests, scale is rarely a widespread problem. Rose scale outbreaks are more likely on the West Coast than in other parts of North America.

This pest is easily controlled by simply cutting off the stem where the scale insect has chosen to nest. If you discover that scale is a persistent problem in your garden, a spray of lime sulfur when the roses are dormant can be effective. Dormant spray is applied before the rose begins growth in the spring, or after it has been stopped by freezes in the fall. Lime sulfur stains skin and clothing, so be sure to wear old clothes and cover all exposed skin when spraying. It discolors wood, brick, and stone too, so aim well. Never apply lime sulfur once your roses have begun any growth. Many climbing roses are particularly susceptible to injury from this type of spray.

Spittlebugs

This pest appears in the month after rose pruning, when vigorous new growth is underway. It settles into leaf axils where it surrounds itself with a white foamy material as it drains sap from the plant. Unchecked, spittlebugs can cause new shoots to

become deformed or even die. A strong jet of water will clear the foam. After that you can grab the $1/3$-inch-long spittlebug with your fingers (or, if you are squeamish, a pair of tweezers). Before squishing it you may want to examine the spittlebug under a magnifying glass, where it will look remarkably like a little frog. Fortunately, spittlebugs are not usually a problem later in the rose season.

Spider Mites

Arachnids rather than insects, spider mites were originally greenhouse pests but, like rose midges, they now thrive outdoors as well. They are found throughout North America, but they are most troublesome in hot, dry climates, or in any area experiencing a drought.

Spider mites live and nest on the undersides of rose leaves, sucking the life out of the leaf. Spider mites work from the ground up: you will first notice that lower leaves are dried out, and leaves higher on the plant may appear stippled. In the photo above, we see spider mite damage at an early stage, before the leaf has turned yellow or brown. Examination of the leaf underside will reveal grains like sand. If your eyesight is really keen you can discern these grains running around. It may be easier to see them if you hold a sheet of white paper under an infested leaf and tap the leaf. The mites will fall onto the paper, where they will appear similar to ground black pepper. Like other arachnids, mites do spin webs. But by the time any webs are noticeable, a spider mite infestation is really far advanced and rose plants may be completely compromised.

Mites are most active in hot, dry weather and rarely a problem when it is cool and damp. By recreating these conditions, such as with a frequent misting of cool water, you can bring mites under control. Proprietary miticides are also available. Keep in mind that mites lay new eggs daily, and most miticides don't kill eggs. To help prevent mites from gaining a foothold, it may help to keep weak, twiggy growth pruned away from the bottom and lower interior of your rose bushes. Many rosarians perform a "summer pruning" after the first flush of bloom to eliminate this weak growth near the center and bottom of the plant.

Mites are not insects and will not be killed by insecticides. The best way to ensure a mite infestation during hot, dry weather is to spray your roses with a broad-spectrum insecticide. You will kill the mites' insect predators and leave the door wide open for a mite attack on your roses.

Thrips

Thrips are tiny, sucking insects that are particularly insidious on light-colored roses. The singular of "thrips" is "thrips," proving that some arbiter of language also knew that the gardener never sees just one of this pest. They make buds turn brown, and blooms may be horribly discolored once they open. Sometimes damage can be so severe that buds will not open. Thrips are not rose-specific, and they often move straight from iris to roses in the spring. They can be controlled by misting buds with a systemic chemical insecticide. If you choose this plan of action, it is important to start early. Once thrips are deep inside rose petalage, no insecticide can reach them. Plan B is to wait until autumn, when thrips are often less active and don't do enough damage to merit retaliation. Among the organic remedies, I have not found water sprays or neem effective against thrips, but I plan to try spinosad (a nonsynthetic insecticide) the next time they pose a serious problem.

BLIND SHOOTS

One question I'm asked quite often is, "My roses appear to be growing well, but they aren't blooming. What's wrong?"

There are several possibilities, but first, let's rule out the idea that a lack of bees is to blame. Roses do not need bees to bloom, and as they are self-pollinating plants will even produce their fruit (rose hips) without any help. The presence or absence of bees has absolutely no effect on the number of blooms in your garden. Chances are, one of the five reasons below is the problem. I've listed them here in order of most likely to least likely culprit.

1. Lack of bloom could be due to rose midge (see page 230).
2. Too much nitrogen fertilizer has been applied. This problem will correct itself over time, more quickly if there are heavy rains or you deep-soak the beds.
3. The rootstock used by the nurseryman has suckered from the root level of a budded plant. This is usually an isolated incident, but if you garden in a cold climate and have just planted bud-grafted roses with the bud union above the ground, it is possible that

ELIMINATING SUCKERS

BEFORE

Here the gardener (me) did not pay attention to a plant, and understock suckers have gotten almost out of control.

DURING

It is important to remove suckers at the point at which they grow from the plant. Pruning them off at ground level only encourages them to grow faster. Don't use good pruners, as using pruners to dig into the soil is the surest way to ruin them.

AFTER

Watch for reemergence of suckers and act quickly to remove them.

you could discover a rose garden of rootstocks the next year. The likelihood that a budded rose will sucker is determined by several factors; rootstocks grown from cuttings are much more likely to sucker than those grown from seeds, and the care with which the nursery handles the plant while it is being grown can also make a difference. (See also page 210.)

Another possibility is that the budded part — the part you want — has died. When this happens, any budded rose is likely to send up growth from its surviving rootstock, and the rootstock should be dug out. Before you take action, though, make sure the shoots are indeed originating from the rootstock. There's an old wives' tale (which I usually hear from older men) that rootstock shoots can be identified as having leaves with seven to nine leaflets, compared to the five-leaflet leaves found on garden roses. Wherever this tale comes from, it is wrong. Many popular roses have leaves with seven to nine leaflets, especially when well fed, and some rootstocks (such as 'Dr Huey') typically have leaves with only five leaflets. Own-root roses cannot, of course, produce suckers. And no rose spontaneously "reverts" to a wild or primitive state.

When a rootstock suckers on a plant that is otherwise doing well, act quickly to remove it. Left alone, a vigorous rootstock will swamp most roses. Excavate gently around the base of the plant to discover the source of the rootstock, and remove it cleanly. Simply cutting off the rootstock where it appears at soil level will only serve to bring it back twice as fast.

4. In the spring, cold weather can retard bud development. This problem will correct itself when it gets warmer.

5. In the fall, numerous hybrid teas and floribundas (particularly those introduced in Europe since the 1980s) can throw long, nonproductive canes. This is a genetic rather than a cultural defect. The varieties that do this are usually those with the healthiest, glossiest foliage.

DISEASES

The key to preventing rose diseases is to choose varieties that are immune or resistant in the first place. Some rose varieties are particularly prone to black spot or powdery mildew, and no amount of prevention, chemical or organic, will alter this genetic reality. The use of any one chemical fungicide regularly and exclusively will result in disease organisms that develop resistance to that fungicide.

Disease prevention starts at pruning time. A well-pruned rose will resist disease much better than one that has been left with poor-pithed, winter-damaged wood or lots of twiggy growth in its center. These kinds of canes produce weak growth that is more vulnerable to infection, and disease symptoms will show up there first. Pruning time also presents an opportunity to clean up fallen leaves that can harbor disease.

Limit overhead watering to the morning hours, so that leaves have plenty of time to dry. This will help prevent disease. High-nitrogen chemical fertilizers can encourage the kind of fast growth that falls prey to powdery mildew, so use with caution.

Ohio isn't considered part of the Rust Belt because of its rose diseases. We rarely see rust, just as those in hot, dry climates are seldom troubled by black spot. But any of the rose diseases I describe below can appear anywhere in North America, when conditions are right, and they can infect any kind of rose.

Black Spot

Years ago, rose books told us that the black spot disease had caused economic upheaval and mass migrations of people, and had altered the historical course of several nations. That's because scientists of a century ago lacked the tools we have today, and some thought that rose black spot was the same fungus that caused the Irish Potato Famine. We now know differently.

Black spots appear on rose foliage, especially on lower leaves. Examined carefully, the spots will have a frilly border. Eventually the leaf will yellow and fall away.

A severe case will eventually defoliate a plant. While almost all roses have the vigor to send out a new batch of leaves, few will be able to withstand a second attack. Roses that enter winter without a good cloak of foliage are particularly prone to winterkill. And so black spot kills many more roses in the winter than it does in the summer.

Black spot is especially a problem under rainy conditions, because the disease spores germinate on wet leaf surfaces. Keep this in mind if you water your roses by overhead sprinkling. Your roses will love it, but avoid doing it at times when there isn't enough sun left in the day to dry the leaves. Of course, you have no control over when rain might fall, and it is inevitable that your rose leaves will get wet at night and may develop black spot. (Curiously, black spot does not develop on roses that are kept under a constant mist, 24/7. Greenhouse rose growers now use this technique to prevent black spot, but it is not a practical solution in most home-garden situations.)

A propensity for black spot came into roses via *Rosa foetida,* a species that introduced the yellow color into roses.

A FRAGRANT LINK

In the genetics of roses, fragrance and susceptibility to powdery mildew are linked. Many of the hybrid perpetuals with enough scent to perfume a room are at the greatest risk of disfiguration from this disease. As hybridizers have sought to give us roses that are more resistant to powdery mildew, some of the fragrance has been bred out as a consequence.

Grapes are subject to the same strain of powdery mildew that afflicts roses, and vineyard owners traditionally plant a climbing rose known to be mildew-susceptible at the end of each row of grapes as an early-warning system. ('Don Juan' is a favorite for this purpose at American vineyards.)

To this day, yellow roses are often more susceptible to black spot. The old once-blooming European roses — albas, damasks, centifolias and gallicas — are rarely troubled by it.

Once established, black spot is very difficult to control. Garden sanitation is important, as black spot spores persist in fallen leaves. A drastic pruning of repeat-blooming roses each spring can also go a long way toward controlling black spot if it was present in the previous year. Black spot will always appear first on weak canes that should have been pruned away in the first place. In the 1950s and '60s, blackspot was almost eliminated in big-city gardens, because all of the sulfur in the air acted as an omnipresent fungicide. At that time, since gardeners weren't complaining much about black spot, hybridizers weren't overly concerned about susceptibility. Now, in a time of less-polluted air, gardeners are discovering that many roses from that era are particularly prone to black spot.

As an alternative to chemical fungicides, the Cornell formula (based on potassium bicarbonate, and marketed as GreenCure) is an effective control when used according to label directions. In my experience, this product works well as a preventative, but it will not bring a serious black spot outbreak under control.

Powdery Mildew

Powdery mildew is a fungal disease that's often seen later in the rose season, when cool nights follow warm days. It will crinkle and discolor new growth, which appears a dusty white. In severe cases new buds will become distorted and fail to open properly. Powdery mildew can attack any rose, but it is particularly a problem on those that make strong new growth throughout the rose year. It is more often seen on tall roses than on short ones.

The most effective way to prevent powdery mildew is to provide good air circulation around your roses. Roses grown in an open area are much less prone to powdery mildew than those in a crowded garden setting. A climber growing along a split-rail or open-mesh fence will almost always be more healthy than one trained against a building. Overhead watering at midday can break the cycle of mildew infection, because the spores cannot germinate when the leaves are wet, but there is no remedy that will restore infected growth to its normal state. Since infections appear first at the top of the plant, it is easy to simply cut away the most severely infected areas with no harm at all done to the rest of the plant.

The Cornell formula (sold as GreenCure) provides control when applied before symptoms appear, as can some of the homemade baking-soda recipes. When applied to leaves already afflicted with powdery mildew, baking soda concoctions can eliminate the disease, creating a completely dead zone that after a few days will drop away, leaving a hole where the mildew once was. So this does not really represent an aesthetic improvement.

Downy Mildew

Not anything like powdery mildew, this serious fungal disease can defoliate and kill a rose very quickly. Downy mildew appears as pur-

plish splotches on rose foliage and stems; the downy part is visible only under a microscope. While black spot often first appears at the bottom of the plant, downy mildew is often first seen near the top. The quickest diagnosis is the touch test: when a rose is afflicted with downy mildew, affected leaves drop off the plant at the slightest touch. The wind will conduct this test for you, and plants with downy mildew can be very quickly defoliated.

Hybrid teas and miniatures appear to be most vulnerable. A few of David Austin's English Roses have also suffered from downy mildew in my garden. When I first began growing roses, downy mildew was most often found in California. It now turns up all over the country, and nurseries bear some responsibility for its distribution.

Nature provides control whenever temperatures stay above 81°F for at least 24 hours. That is usually enough to kill the disease. Downy mildew will be held dormant when temperatures are consistently in the 80s or above, but it will return with cooler weather if there is no 24-hour stretch of over 81°F. Some ingenious rosarians have battled downy mildew by connecting garden hoses to their hot-water heaters, but this can be dangerous so I recommend extreme caution if you decide to try this.

Rosarians seeking chemical conquest of this difficult disease have returned to the zinc-based fungicides popular in the 1960s.

Rust

Orange spots appear on the undersides of foliage and on rose stems. A plant with a serious case of rust fungus will defoliate, sometimes very quickly. Rust development is favored by the cool, humid summers and mild winters found in areas such as northern California. It is rarely a problem in areas with severe winters. Rust will often target old garden roses such as centifolias and mosses before modern roses.

I have been fortunate to see rust only a few times in my garden. In each case I have been able to control it by simply cutting away the diseased stem. Discard diseased prunings by burning or placing in the trash. Diseased growth should never be composted.

Rust winters over on fallen leaves, and thorough garden sanitation can do a lot to prevent it. If you end up with a rust outbreak, any black spot remedy (including the new bicarbonate products) should be effective.

Botrytis

This fungus appears during cool, rainy periods. It is first evident as a gray mold on rose buds; in advanced cases, the buds will be prevented from opening. Grapes infected with botrytis often produce interesting wines, but infected roses possess no redeeming features. Hybrid teas and roses with many petals are most susceptible. This disease can be found throughout North America, but it is rarely a problem in desert areas. It is most common in autumn, as the flowering season is coming to an end.

Most rosarians deal with botrytis simply by cutting off and discarding the infected buds, sealing them in a plastic bag to prevent the spores from spreading any more. Chemical science has recently offered effective, if expensive, remedies. I know of no organic solution beyond cutting the problem away.

Canker

This disease first appears as yellow or brown lesions on a rose stem. With time these become brown and sunken, and the stem can eventually die. The canker fungus is present in many soils, but it rarely finds enough points of entry to become a real problem. Canker is almost always introduced after a mechanical injury to a rose stem (caused by a careless gardener, or simply by thorns from a neighboring stem whipping in the wind). Canker is more common in nursery fields than in home gardens.

Affected stems should be pruned off. Most fungicides, chemical or organic, will prevent the canker from spreading from the stems to the foliage, where it causes

MOSAIC MYTHS

There are a lot of myths about rose mosaic (see page 236), and most of them cause gardeners to worry much more than they should. The facts: Mosaic can't be spread from one plant to another in your garden via aphids, by infected pruning tools, or by roots touching each other underground. The only way mosaic spreads is when roses are propagated. If you take a cutting or bud eye (the reddish swelling at a leaf axil from which new growth will emerge) from an infected plant, then the new plants you create will also have the virus. Or if you graft a bud eye from a healthy rose onto an infected rootstock, then the resulting plant will also be infected.

Some nurseries selling roses on their own roots advertise that own-root roses are inherently virus-free. This isn't true, and it all depends on the nursery starting with a clean mother plant. An own-root plant can be infected with mosaic just as easily as a budded one, if the propagating material used is infected.

Responsible nurseries do not propagate plants with mosaic virus; the virus is spread by irresponsible nursery practices. Today it is hard to find some classic roses of the 1950s or '60s without mosaic. Fortunately, infected propagating material can be cleaned up with heat treatment under laboratory conditions, and a few progressive nurseries such as Vintage Gardens now offer virus-indexed, healthy versions of old favorite hybrid teas. There is no need to dig up a plant infected with mosaic virus so long as it is still growing with vigor. Obviously infected plants should never be propagated.

small flecks and larger purplish spots that are sometimes confused with downy mildew.

Crown Gall

This tumorlike growth appears at the base of a rose plant. A bacterial rather than fungal disease, it can appear at the crown (or bud union, in a plant that has been bud-grafted) or at the base of an own-root rose. In either case, it appears where rose stems come into contact with soil. It can afflict any type of rose and is a common problem in rose nursery fields. It is especially troublesome in clay soils and where drainage is poor.

There is an expensive commercial product that will kill crown gall bacteria, but many rosarians have reported success dousing the infected area of the plant with a household disinfectant. Simply pour about 1 cup of the undiluted disinfectant over the gall-infected area. Avoid drenching leaves with the disinfectant.

The easiest remedy is to excise the gall with a sharp knife. You may find that once you cut into the gall it breaks into small pieces. If this happens it is important to gather up all of these pieces and remove them from the garden. In many cases the plant will survive. When it doesn't, it's a good idea to remove the soil where the plant failed, and to replace it with fresh dirt before planting a new rose. Be sure to disinfect any tools used to cut the gall.

Rose Mosaic

Rose mosaic is caused by a virus that is spread during the propagation process. The disease displays itself as variegated yellow patterns on rose foliage. Sometimes it will not become evident until the plant is stressed by heat or drought. With good cultural practices, it may lay dormant for years without ever disfiguring an otherwise-healthy plant.

Some people find mosaic attractive, and in many cases plants infected with it show no apparent loss of vigor or other qualities. Mosaic virus can infect any rose and has no geographical boundaries. The red blend hybrid tea 'Curiosity' from Scotland is an example of a virused rose with variegated foliage that has been introduced on purpose. (See Mosaic Myths on page 235.)

Rose Rosette

This is the wolf at every rosarian's door. Other diseases disfigure and weaken; rose rosette kills. Caused by a virus, rose rosette appears as a witch's broom, or crazy-looking new growth. Many roses normally produce new shoots that are red; here they will be intensely red, thorns will be exaggerated and soft, and buds will appear in unusually congested clusters. Rose rosette is spread by eriophyid mites as they feed on roses. Eventually the abnormal growth takes over the entire plant, which dies.

The eriophyid mites that spread rose rosette are particularly attracted to multiflora roses (*Rosa multiflora*). Thus a rose with multiflora in its genetics, such as most polyanthas and many old-fashioned ramblers, could be more vulnerable. The rose rosette problem is particularly acute in the Midwest, but it is spreading throughout the country.

THE MULTIFLORA CONNECTION

In the 1950s and '60s multiflora roses were planted for erosion control all along the interstate highway system. It quickly spread from the highway edges to farms, where it colonized pastureland. Multiflora is now registered as a noxious weed in many states. In the 1990s an Iowa scientist actually proposed introducing rose rosette to rid the countryside of multiflora.

If you live in a rural area, destroy all of the multiflora roses you can. If you live near a park where multiflora has sprung up and been confused for an ornamental plant, educate the park personnel and have it destroyed. The multiflora used as an rootstock on many of your roses is absolutely no threat so long as it remains underground. So long as rootstock suckers are not allowed to flourish, roses budded onto multiflora are not in any way more vulnerable to rose rosette.

In Ohio I have seen entire rose gardens destroyed in a year by rose rosette. Observant gardeners are usually able to control it by vigorous removal of all affected plants. If you see rose rosette symptoms in your garden, do not tell yourself that it will just go away. It won't. Do not tell yourself that you will deal with it later. You shouldn't wait.

The vector mite does not fly but is propelled by the breeze to new areas. There is some evidence that rose gardens surrounded by hedges or other similar barriers are at less risk, because the windborne mites have less access. Similarly, roses grown in harmony with other plants, rather than in beds all by themselves, should be less at risk.

Plants with rose rosette should be dug and burned, or discarded in a sealed plastic bag. There is anecdotal evidence that a large plant with just one affected cane can sometimes be saved by cutting out only that cane. Attempts to control the eriophyid mite with various chemical pesticides have been inconclusive.

ANIMAL PROBLEMS

Of all the animals I see in my garden — including the occasional coyote — only two cause serious damage to roses: deer and rabbits.

Deer

I never learned their real names, but we called them the Poachers and for as long as they were tenants on the old farmstead behind us, we never saw a squirrel or a turkey or many woodchucks. We marveled at the things we saw slung over their shoulders, on the way into their house. When we mentioned this once to the old farmer across the road, he smiled and said, "Mighty tough eatin', them raccoons."

Then the land behind us got sold to someone with dreams about development, and the Poachers were gone. We see lots of squirrels now, raccoons fish in our ponds, and when we call in the cat in the evening, sometimes there is a possum sitting there on the deck, wondering what's going on in the house.

And we have deer. These are not the scrawny, stressed-out deer one sees in the suburbs, stripping every leaf off of a magnolia or a rose. These are big healthy country deer, with a varied diet. They do not need to eat roses to survive, but they do find plump rose buds to be a treat. With a buffet stretching over several miles, our garden is dessert. A well-timed visit from deer could eliminate a week of summer's largest rose blooms, as they would walk through the gardens nibbling on the largest buds on top of the longest stems. They almost always ignored the small-sized rose blooms that were produced in large clusters.

By 1927 the white-tailed deer had been hunted to extinction in Ohio. Gradually they wandered back in from Pennsylvania, and I am old enough to remember when they were a novelty. At that time, my dad's route home from work was through a big park. Once in a while he would arrive with the announcement, "There's deer!" and we would all pile into the car to go and look at them.

We had to be very quiet, sitting in the car watching the deer. No bickering, even if it was our turn to sit by the window and someone else was there, because any commotion would frighten the deer away. The least bit of noise, and they'd show their white flag and disappear.

Things have changed. Today when I see deer up in the garden I can walk right up to them and get a quizzical, "What are you doing here?" look. And in this era of video games I don't think very many children would be impressed by the sight of a deer in a field or woods.

Deer are creatures of habit, and we've tried our best to get them to break the rose one. Here are things we've tried in our garden.

Deer love to graze in a rose garden. Healthy deer will simply munch rose buds, as we see here. When deer are stressed, they will strip foliage as well.

REPELLENTS

A taste or an odor that discourages deer from browsing on your roses is the simplest solution, when it works. I found that a Bitrex/latex-based repellent worked for a while. I would have continued to apply it but for two disadvantages: the solution clogged every sprayer I owned, and if I got any near my mouth it made me ill. Somehow, though, the deer got used to it. So then I switched to a garlic/egg-based repellent, which did not work at all. Its garlicky smell was not unpleasant; I almost liked it. While I have no reason to believe that the deer liked it too, it certainly did not discourage them from browsing the roses. Again, they were primarily interested in eating our plumpest rosebuds and rarely nibbled on foliage.

Bitrex/latex repellents leave a white coating on plants. The garlic repellent I used left behind a speckly but mostly clear residue. Neither disfigures the garden the way that sheets of clothes-dryer fabric softener do. But these worked for quite a while, attached with clothespins to roses in strategic locations. Eventually I was buying quite a lot of fabric softener sheets. Ringing up my purchase of many boxes of this product, the checkout lady told me, "You're a darling. I wish my husband thought fabric softeners were important."

Any unpleasant or unusual scent may deter deer for a while — thus, the success stories and Internet recommendations for elephant dung, coyote urine, and particular brands of deodorant soap. I have no faith in the long-term success of any of these deterrents.

DOGS

Our dog never chased deer. She would, however, bark at them, and when we heard her howling in the night we knew that the deer were here. Or that someone was driving far too slowly down the road. Or, possibly, someone was driving the same model truck as Susan's son had when he stopped by here with his rodeo gear and lassoed her, back when she was a puppy. In any case, the deer were not deterred in any way by a dog that merely barked.

A commercial orchard in the next township has installed an Invisible Fence system around their trees so they can keep Siberian husky dogs in the orchard to chase away deer. As our deer become more and more approachable, I am tempted to try to collar each of them and install an Invisible Fence to keep them out. This would save all of the trouble of taking care of Siberian husky dogs.

SCARE DEVICES

Motion-detector radios, motion-detector spotlights, and motion-detector sprinklers did not work for us. The deer did not appear to care one way or the other, even when we had the radio dial turned to talk radio or rap. We had the motion-detector sprinkler out long enough for some red-winged blackbirds to learn how to activate it — they seemed to enjoy playing in the spray. The resulting increase in our bird population may have indirectly led to a decline in insect pests.

BARRIERS

Sections of baling wire twined between branches of our fruit trees keeps the deer from nibbling in the orchard. But it is impractical for roses, which are both far more numerous and much less sturdy. Deer follow regular paths, and placing old tomato cages lengthwise across obvious deer pathways worked for about a week.

FENCES

Ultimately, a deer fence remained the only practical solution. I installed 10-foot

An 8-foot fence will keep deer out. The yellow flags are for snowmobilers and all-terrain vehicle operators.

metal poles at 10-foot intervals around the garden. Sunk 2 feet into the ground, they support wiring onto which I suspended an 8-foot fence. Deer can easily jump a 6-foot fence, so a fence must be at least 8 feet to stop them from coming over the top. Erecting a 7-foot fence at a 15-degree angle toward your garden may also achieve the effect of an 8-foot fence. Alternatively, two shorter fences about 4 feet apart will also keep deer out. Deer won't jump unless they can see a clear landing pad, so a shorter fence a few feet away from a row of well-grown roses will also work. Even though it was sold as deer fencing, the green mesh I installed at first was completely unsuitable. Deer could poke their antlers right through, and by the second summer entire patches had degraded in the sunlight. The black polypropylene fence I replaced it with is much more durable, and also nearly invisible from a distance. Bright yellow flags every few yards might not do much to warn color-blind deer, but they have cut down on all-terrain-vehicle and snowmobile incidents.

Depending on the elevation of their approach path, an opaque fence shorter than 8 feet may also work. Fencing should be stapled to the ground to prevent deer from crawling underneath.

Rabbits

Rabbits are also a serious rose pest. They make sharp horizontal cuts into rose stems, compared to the more ragged cuts made by deer. And while I have seen both rabbits and deer standing on their hind legs to nibble things in my garden, of course rabbits can't reach nearly as high. Rabbits do their most serious damage at the beginning of the growing season, when roses are producing lots of succulent new growth. Small, newly planted roses are especially vulnerable and can actually be killed by hungry rabbits.

Rabbits are easily deterred by rabbit fencing or motivated cats. Temporary fencing 30 inches high can be placed around individual roses or entire beds. By the time roses have set buds, the rabbits have moved on to more appetizing areas in my garden. If yours persist, you may need to consider permanent fencing.

Another way to deter rabbits in spring is to delay rose pruning. Last year's thorny canes will protect most of this year's tender new growth. Extra care will be needed when pruning finally occurs, and some new growth may be broken in the process. But in the meantime, rabbits will have found somewhere else to nibble.

Rabbit fencing protects the base of 'Polar Joy' tree rose during winter and spring. To improve aesthetics, the wire fencing can be removed during the summer flowering season, when the plastic wrap-around material will be sufficient to deter rabbits.

UNDERSTANDING PRUNING:
WHEN, HOW, AND WHY

Rose pruning is not a mysterious exercise once you understand the reasons why it's necessary. Pruning is vital because: 1) pruning removes dead and damaged wood, 2) pruning gets rid of weak or twiggy growth, and 3) pruning shapes the plant. In their natural state, roses are pruned by frost, fire, and rabbits and other animals. Because garden-grown roses are usually protected from these natural pruners, they will benefit from a gardener with a sharp pair of pruners. Pruning promotes strong new growth.

GENERAL PRUNING GUIDELINES

If you intend to garden without chemical fungicides you will discover that a thorough spring pruning is your most valuable line of defense. Apart from choosing disease-resistant roses in the first place, it is the most important thing you can do to enjoy healthy roses. Later in this chapter, I'll explain what's involved in deciding how and when to prune particular types of roses. First, though, here are some general guidelines about tools and timing.

Pruning Tools

Be sure to use a pair of good quality pruners, sharp enough to cut rose wood without tearing it. I rely on Felco's No. 2 pruners. Cutting through thick canes may require loppers. I've used the same pair of Corona loppers for more than 20 years. Gardeners in warm climates may be fortunate enough to need a pruning saw for some of their roses. Tough, thorn-proof gloves are essential, whichever tool you use.

Basic Pruning Cuts

Every pruning cut you make into live wood provides direction to the rose. A new shoot will always grow in the direction that the eye from which it sprouts is pointing, so sprawling plants can be made to grow more upright by pruning to an inward-facing eye. When you prune a stem back to a bud eye that is sprouting, that new growth will speed up. Prune to an eye with no apparent sign of activity, and new growth will take some time to appear. In this way spring bloom can be sped up or slowed down. The precision cuts practiced by exhibitors on hybrid teas to regulate the number of eyes that will sprout on each cane are not necessary on shrub and heritage roses — but be sure to always use sharp pruners, and cut just above an eye.

Some roses make a lot of twiggy growth at their center, surrounded by larger, healthier canes. This twiggy growth should be completely removed. Some roses make only twiggy growth — this should be shortened in the same way as larger canes are.

It's easy to allow large roses to become larger each year, but they will be much more productive if regularly thinned. To thin a rose, simply remove up to one-third of its canes, beginning with those at the center of the plant and any that appear very old or weak.

Spring Pruning

Spring is the best time to prune roses, but wait until after the threat of subfreezing temperatures has passed. Pruning too early can do more harm than good. Because pruning signals the rose to commence growth, early pruning may prompt a lot of new growth that will only be killed by subsequent freezes. Each rose bud eye has two auxiliary eyes that will try to sprout if the primary eye is killed. Once the auxiliary eyes are killed as well, the plant is in dire straits because it can't produce new green growth.

Nature almost always provides a reliable signal of when it is safe to prune. Where I live, the appearance of the first forsythia blooms is that signal. Because I have over 1,200 roses to prune, I must begin earlier than that. However, I confine all of my early pruning to the simple removal of dead wood. I try never to cut into live wood until the forsythia provides my go-ahead signal.

Damaged wood should also be removed during spring pruning. Rose canes that appear green from the outside are not necessarily healthy. Damaged wood can be identified only by its pith, which will be black, brown, gray, or beige instead of a healthy, creamy white. Pruning away wood with bad pith is the first line of defense against black spot and other fungal diseases, which always appear first on compromised wood.

Even bushes that suffer no dieback will maintain a better, more bushy appearance and will bloom more profusely if pruned regularly. In cases where there is no obvious problem wood to be removed, you can take away one-quarter or so of all top growth, or selectively remove entire aging canes, or both.

Pruning once-blooming roses in the spring before their annual bloom will eliminate some of the display. This may, however, be the only practical way to deal with congestion or dead wood at the heart of the plant. These problems will not be visible once the plant has started growing and is full of leaves. Canes that remain after the rose has been pruned will produce larger, more perfect blooms. Spring pruning of all canes on a once-blooming rose can eliminate all bloom for that year.

TOP LEFT Many rosarians won't enter their garden without their Felco #2 pruners.

TOP RIGHT Healthy white pith (left); damaged pith (right) indicates that the rose must still be pruned some more.

BOTTOM Approaching a rose after a northern winter, begin by removing all dead wood. Everything will make more sense once you've done that.

Summer Pruning

Pruning continues throughout the growing season. Each time you pick a rose, you prune the bush. Carefully cutting back a stem to the first outward-facing, five-leaflet leaf will give you the best chance for an ideal bloom or spray when the rose reblooms, and a plant that maintains a healthy open shape. However, simply removing the spent bloom (deadheading) is equally effective at stimulating new growth and bloom. Trials conducted by England's Royal National Rose Society have confirmed that beds of the same rose varieties have produced just as much bloom when pruned carefully by skilled gardeners as when simply attacked by untrained persons with hedge shears.

The point of summer pruning is to do something. Doing nothing will delay the next bloom cycle and may invite disease. However, many roses that don't offer repeat bloom do display attractive rose hips in autumn; these roses should not be deadheaded.

Cleaning out the clutter of weak and unproductive growth from the base of the plant in early summer will eliminate a possible foothold for black spot and spider mites. I have never used a cane sealant when pruning, but if borers were a big problem in my garden I would consider it.

ROSE PRUNING SPECIFICS

The two factors that determine how any particular rose is pruned are 1) What kind of rose is it? and 2) What kind of winter was it? Northern gardeners often have no choice about how to prune roses, because winter has made all of the decisions already. Simply cut into the dead wood, and cut back relentlessly until you reach clean, white pith. This may take plants down to just a few inches of live wood. In some cases, when there is no white pith at all, prune all above-ground canes away and hope that healthy new growth will be generated from below ground. If you have planted your roses correctly, this is possible in the case of both own-root and bud-grafted roses.

Hybrid Teas and Floribundas

First, remove all dead wood. Keep cutting back the canes until you reach healthy white pith. Next, remove all weak, twiggy, or unproductive growth. If you find canes rubbing against each other, remove the older one. Your goal is to open up the center of the plant, and you may need to remove some healthy wood to do this. If winter (or your winter protection methods) has left you enough live wood, leaving canes 12 to 18 inches long will provide the best overall display. However, if you want fewer but larger blooms or sprays, suitable for exhibition, cut the canes back to 4 to 6 inches.

A well-pruned hybrid tea or floribunda should form a vase or bowl shape, with the canes radiating outward from the center. When shaping strong, healthy canes, cut them at a 45-degree angle above an outward facing bud eye (the reddish bud from which new growth will emerge). An exception to this is hybrid teas that tend to sprawl, such as the old classic 'Crimson Glory'. These sprawlers can be somewhat reformed by pruning to an inward facing eye. This will encourage upright growth.

Miniatures

The principles of pruning miniatures are the same as for hybrid teas and floribundas, with everything on a smaller scale. Many miniatures are "smarter" than hybrid teas and won't try to put out vulnerable growth too early in the spring. Therefore, I often prune them before the hybrid teas.

Shrub Roses

With massive display of bloom being the strong point of many shrubs, and as many are quite winter hardy here in Zone 5, I often leave all the live wood in the spring, removing only twiggy growth and a few older canes. Every few years each shrub should get a more serious cutting back, in order to avoid becoming top-heavy. Pruning away one-third of the plant is an excellent idea for shrubs that have not had a serious cutting back in a year or two.

English Roses

These roses demonstrate a wide range of winter hardiness. Many of the apricot and yellow ones are as tender as hybrid teas, leaving the northern gardener with little discretion in how they are pruned. Others are quite winter hardy and can be treated as described above for shrub roses.

WHY I DON'T LIKE FALL PRUNING

Because pruning stimulates new growth, it is best done in the spring. The argument for autumn pruning is aesthetic rather than practical. While some rose bushes have an architectural beauty, in most cases, bare rose canes are ugly in the off-season. Pruning them away in the fall can improve the winter landscape. But autumn pruning will weaken roses in climates with severe winters; roses suffer winter dieback from the top, and if you shorten the top you shorten the path to real damage. Gardeners in cold climates should avoid fall pruning. Those in gusty locations should shorten any unsecured rose canes tall enough to rock back and forth in the wind. Roses whose roots are loosened in this manner are extremely vulnerable to winterkill.

1. BEFORE: This shrub rose ('Pearl Drift') has come through an Ohio winter with almost no winterkill.

2. DURING: With no dead wood to remove, the plant is shaped by pruning back to bud eyes where new growth as already begun.

3. AFTER: The plant has an attractive vase shape.

Many of the David Austin English Roses benefit from a serious cutting back after their first bloom of the season. Taking stems a foot or more in length when cutting flowers will actually encourage repeat bloom. This summer pruning will help to eliminate a tendency to produce vegetative summer growth at the expense of bloom. It will also help heavy-flowered varieties such as 'Abraham Darby' produce stronger stems.

Polyanthas

Most polyanthas are winter-hardy, wiry plants descended from *Rosa multiflora*. They suffer little winter dieback and can easily be prepared for a new season of bloom with a pair of hedge shears. Simply shear to desired height. Some polyanthas have higher doses of tender China blood and will benefit from more careful pruning. These varieties, including 'Mlle Cécille Brunner', can be identified by the dainty, hybrid tea-like blooms they produce and should be pruned as if they were shrub roses. Since polyanthas are often particularly susceptible to spider mite damage, some rosarians practice a summer pruning ritual of removing lower leaves from the plant after its first flush of bloom. This will rob the spider mites of their easiest footholds. It is not worth denuding the plant to get this benefit, so polyanthas that grow only 2 feet high should not be robbed of more than 6 inches of their foliage.

Species Roses

The roses that were here before we were require no pruning help from us at all, beyond the removal of obviously dead wood. I do prune *Rosa sericea pteracantha* severely each spring, in order to generate a more abundant supply of fresh, ultra-thorny canes.

Hybrid Rugosas

The purpose of pruning these super-hardy roses is primarily to shape the bush. Rugosas will not be happy if you try to use pruning techniques to squeeze them into a smaller place. Worn out canes will become apparent during the course of the growing season, and these can be removed as you notice them.

Hybrid Musks

These are graceful shrubs that look best when left alone. Winter takes its toll here in the north, so I often have a lot of dead wood to remove. Beyond that, I try to interfere as little as possible each spring. During the summer, hybrid musks respond happily to prompt removal of old blooms.

Albas

Among the most elegant of the old garden roses, and also the most winter hardy, albas should be left free to find their own shape. These are once-bloomers, so any pruning prior to bloom will reduce the number of flowers. Removing unproductive, twiggy growth in the interior of the plant will improve health. As the years go by, unproductive older canes should be removed to make room for new growth.

Bourbons

Here in Ohio, I have good luck pruning these repeat-bloomers exactly as I do hybrid teas. They are no more (or less) hardy, and while in a good summer many of them will make much more growth, the spring-pruning procedures remain the same. Those in warmer climates will enjoy Bourbons as much larger plants, which can be shortened by one-third each spring.

Centifolias and Once-blooming Mosses

Most are quite winter hardy and require only the removal of obviously dead wood. After their annual bloom, removal of a few older canes will help to rejuvenate the plant. Some mosses are too susceptible to black spot; their health can be improved by removing weak growth at the center of the plant. Occasionally centifolias and mosses will throw an unusually long new cane, which can be cut back to the height of the rest of the plant.

Chinas

Every rule has an exception, and the Chinas are the roses from which twiggy growth should not automatically be removed. In many cases, twiggy growth is all they have. In the unlikely event that winter has left me any green canes, I trim these gently and remove clutter-causing older canes from the center of the plant.

Damasks

These once-bloomers often form very attractive bushy plants with no intervention by the gardener. Still, they mind pruning less than other old garden roses and can be shaped as new growth begins after the spring bloom. This summer pruning will be effective if it addresses new growth, and a complete failure if it attempts to do

something extreme, such as shorten a plant by half. New canes that break out in awkward directions can be trimmed to an eye pointing in a more appropriate direction, and shoots that tower above their neighbors can be shortened. Old plants can be renewed by removing one-third of the canes each year for three successive years.

Gallicas

These once-bloomers often sucker into a thicket, which should be thinned to promote air circulation and stronger new growth. Old canes should be removed from the center of the bush; removing them at soil level will avoid unsightly stubs that may sprout into multiple smaller and less productive shoots. Gallicas respond well

---

USING YOUR PRUNERS IN SUMMER: TAKING CUTTINGS

Softwood rose cuttings can be made at anytime during the flowering season. I have best luck with cuttings started in June, because they will be well-rooted before facing their first winter. Cuttings can be rooted in pots (at least 5" deep) filled with a lightweight soilless mixture such as ProMix or inserted directly into a loamy patch of ground. Shade (80 percent) is essential for rooting cuttings. Unless you have a misting system, cuttings must be covered to maintain humidity levels. A mayonnaise or similar large jar works well to cover cuttings started in the ground; clear plastic bags are effective for those in pots.

Choose a particularly fine bloom or spray. When it shatters, check the stem to see if it is ready to root by breaking off a thorn. If it snaps easily, the stem is ready. If not, wait a few days. The bud eyes you will most want to include in your cutting are the fourth and fifth ones down from the base of the bloom.

Cut a section of stem 6" to 9" long and including these fourth and fifth eyes.

Make an angle cut just below the bud eye at the bottom of the stem you have cut. You can use an old pair of pruners for this; a ragged cut may encourage more rapid rooting. The bottom two eyes will go underground; remove all thorns around them. Remove all leaflets except for the top two. You may dip the bottom of the cutting in rooting hormone if you wish (it will be difficult to root some varieties without it). Insert into the ground or pot, cover, and keep moist and mostly shady. Failures will become obvious in 10 days or so. New growth could also be appearing by then. Many other cuttings may appear to enter a state of suspended animation, with no apparent growth. With luck, these ones are growing their roots first and new top growth will appear later.

If rooting in a pot, it will be easy to spot top growth and roots (appearing

from the drainage holes at the bottom of the pot). At this point, you can remove the cover, beginning for just a few hours at a time and misting frequently. When roses are rooted in the ground it is impossible to judge root growth. In most cases it will be wise to keep their jar covering in place for almost a year, and remove it when top growth begins to crowd the glass the following year.

Roses rooted in the ground and covered with a glass jar will need no other winter protection in Zone 5. Those started in pots can be wintered in a cold frame or in the basement under artificial lights.

Once they have grown up, roses rooted in pots can be treated just as those received from nurseries selling own-root roses (see page 216). Those rooted in the ground can be transplanted in the spring or fall as described on page 217.

to pruning, and because they rarely set attractive hips, pruning immediately after their bloom has faded has no ill effects. Indeed, hacking off the top third of the plant after blooming may be all you need to do in order to provoke another strong bloom the following year.

Hybrid Perpetuals

The hybrid perpetuals are a diverse and genetically complicated group. There is no one best way to prune all of them. In the 1951 *American Rose Annual* (published by the American Rose Society), Howard Tenner published an extensive article about how to prune specific varieties. Reading it made me much more successful with hybrid perpetuals, and I continue to refer to it today.

In general, those hybrid perpetuals prized for their profuse garden display should be pruned lightly (where winter permits), and those grown for the beauty of their individual blooms should be pruned more severely. These parameters continue throughout the growing season, with exhibition-type hybrid perpetuals cut back severely after each bloom. Even if you have no interest in rose exhibiting, this technique will generate more beautiful blooms in your garden.

Portlands and Repeat-blooming Mosses

These roses are often much less winter hardy than the damasks from which they descend, and my pruning strategy is often determined by what the winter has left me. Portlands make dense growth that may become prone to disease when not thinned out. Most of the repeat-blooming mosses have a growth habit that is much less dense than their Portland cousins, and these appear most productive when I leave them alone, removing only obviously dead wood.

BEFORE: Decide to prune gallicas early in the morning, when you feel most ambitious. Remove clutter from the middle of the plant, as well as all canes that are no longer productive.

AFTER: Shortening canes will eliminate this year's blooms, so my goal was to remove aging canes rather than to shorten young ones.

Teas

The true teas often kill themselves by starting to grow too soon in the spring. This growth is then repeatedly cut back by late freezes and frosts, and the plant is often weakened beyond its ability to recover. I grow only one tea ('Lady Hillingdon') successfully outdoors here in Zone 5. If I had more, I would definitely exercise patience and prune them last. Once frost-free nights are certain, teas benefit from careful shaping. They may resent losing too much live wood at one time, however.

Repeat-blooming Climbers

A winter-hardy climber will produce a framework of basal canes, from which many lateral canes will emerge. Training basal canes horizontally will greatly increase the number of lateral canes and thus the total amount of bloom. (See chapter 7 for more information on training climbing roses.) At pruning time, shorten lateral canes to three or four bud eyes. If a basal cane has become notably unproductive, it should be completely removed.

Once-blooming Climbers and Ramblers

These bloom only on old wood, just like the once-blooming old garden roses. However, many are not nearly as winter-hardy as the albas, gallicas, and damasks. With these climbers I often violate my rule about pruning until I strike white pith. If I were to insist on these roses having only white pith in their canes each spring, there would be many years in which I would not see them bloom at all. So rather than

1. BEFORE: We see substantial amounts of dead wood that must be removed.

2. DURING: Cut back to white pith (see page 241).

3. AFTER: The climber is ready to flower profusely in about six weeks.

sacrifice bloom, I remove only obviously dead wood, enjoy the display of bloom produced despite the compromised wood, and then remove all winter damage. Left alone, the poor-pithed canes usually wilt after blooming. A repeat-blooming rose would be seriously weakened by this. For once-blooming climbers, allowing bloom from bad wood is an effective (and beautiful) compromise.

Most ramblers produce a lot of basal breaks. By removing canes once they are three or four years old, these climbers will be constantly refreshed.

ROOT PRUNING

Roses that spread freely via suckering — this includes many gallicas, rugosas, and some other species roses, such as *R. arkansana* — can be contained by regular root pruning. Once a month during the growing season, take a sharp spade and use it to cut a perimeter beyond which you don't want the rose's roots to spread. Suckering roots won't be more than a foot deep, so there is no need to dig a trench — simply thrusting the spade into the soil will sever any spreading roots without disrupting the landscape at all.

CHAPTER 14

PREPARATION FOR WINTER:
TIMING AND TECHNIQUES

Winter protection begins in the summer. You don't want your roses racing into winter, so don't push them with high-nitrogen fertilizers late in the season. Nitrogen fertilizer will encourage soft, sappy growth that is easily killed in the winter. At the same time as you stop feeding nitrogen, four to six weeks before your first frost date, stop deadheading spent blooms. Allowing roses to set seeds and form hips sends a signal to the plant that summer's work is done and it's time to slow down. Scratching some high-potassium fertilizer into the soil in late summer can also help roses settle down for winter.

The harsher your winters, the more you'll need to worry about winter protection. Some roses, unfortunately, are doomed no matter what winter protection method is chosen. The three leading causes for loss over winter are:

- Selecting roses that are not winter hardy in your area. If you want to grow tender roses, you'll need to take extra-special measures to protect them during the winter, as described on page 250.
- Planting budded roses with the bud union above the soil level. For directions on setting the bud-graft at the proper level when planting, see page 213.

- Rocking loose by heavy winds. Tall, bud-grafted roses are most vulnerable to this, but even own-root roses can be lost when wind or frost heaving exposes the root area to winter's worst. The simplest solution in to shorten the canes as the rose enters winter. But for winter-hardy roses this may mean sacrificing perfectly good wood as well as blooms the following spring. In these cases, securing the rose to a sturdy stake and making sure the bud union is well covered with soil solves the problem.

PROTECTIVE MOUNDS

Most hybrid teas, some floribundas, and many English Roses are winter hardy without protection only to Zone 6. In Zone 5, the goal of winter protection is not to prevent the plants from freezing, but rather to maintain a steady temperature around the crown and eliminate the losses caused by sudden freezes and thaws. At the same time, a critical portion of the plant is being protected from desiccation. Snow is an outstanding insulator: areas with dependable snow cover can get along with less winter protection than those without it. In Zone 5, gardeners can protect their roses with a mound of mulch, sawdust, compost, or garden soil.

Step-by-Step

The time to protect roses is after several heavy frosts, but before the ground is frozen. In northern Ohio, this is traditionally Thanksgiving weekend. Winter protection should be in place before temperatures fall into the single digits (Fahrenheit).

1. If the rose has grown tall, shorten the canes enough to prevent the rose from rocking out of the ground in high winds.
2. If it is a budded plant and has been planted correctly, the bud union will already be underground. If the bud union is exposed, add dirt to elevate the soil level until it is buried 1 to 2 inches deep. This part of the procedure is not temporary; you will want to raise the level of the bed to keep the bud union underground for the rest of the plant's life.
3. Build a mound of sawdust, compost, or soil over the base of the plant, covering the canes to a height of about 1 foot. If you use soil, take it from another part of the garden, since digging near your roses may damage their roots. Since soil is heavy, this can be a lot of work. After hauling a few barrow loads of soil, ordering a load of sawdust almost always seems like a good idea.

Resist the temptation to remove the protective mound too early in the spring. Premature removal may erase all of the benefits, as new growth will be killed by spring frosts. But waiting to remove it too late will cause damage to new shoots that

---

MOUNDING SOIL OR MULCH

Winter can arrive quickly. Do not hesitate to provide protection, even if plants are still growing. All new growth will be lost in any case; your goal is to preserve live canes underneath your protection.

begin to sprout underneath the protective mound. Any implement is likely to damage this new growth. It is safest to use your hands, gently, or to gradually wash away the mound using a soft stream of water. The compost or sawdust that formed your winter protection can simply be spread around the bed. Some soil may need to be returned to its original location. Any leaves that can't be easily turned into the soil can be composted.

Late spring frosts are the bane of gardeners in the middle portion of the country, and removing winter protection too early is as dangerous as not applying it at all. The first forsythia bloom is a reliable signal that it is safe to uncover and prune your roses.

Don't give up too early on a plant that shows no sign of life in the spring. Some roses seriously damaged by a severe winter may not send out new growth until weeks after pruning time. I prune my roses in early April, but I wait until Memorial Day to dig out an apparently lifeless rose. A tug on the rose may give you a clue: if it resists your pull, it may still have life. If you feel the death rattle, go ahead and dig it out.

OTHER METHODS

Building protective mounds may be too much work for some gardeners. There are several other methods of winter protection worth trying.

Landscaping blankets. Nurserymen use these blankets made of polypropylene foam to protect groups of containerized plants. While landscaping blankets are quite effective at protecting plants from cold and work well to cover rectangular beds, their disadvantages include the likelihood of tearing due to contact with thorny rose canes and the creation of an environment conducive to rodents. They can also be quite ugly when used in the home landscape, and they present a storage problem during the other eight months of the year. Because they can cover a large area in little time, these blankets are a reasonable choice when winter arrives much earlier than expected, or when a gardener is unable to build protective mounds.

Styrofoam cones. Cold-climate rosarians often use these cones to protect hybrid teas. They are effective at preserving life at the base of the plant. Disadvantages start with the fact that most of the canes need to be cut away to fit under the cone. If it turns out to be a mild winter, your roses will end up in worse shape than they would have been if you'd done nothing. If you grow more than a few roses, storage of the rose cones can present a problem. Some highly motivated rosarians construct entire temporary cold frames out of Styrofoam, surrounding and covering their rose beds with these each fall. Once again, canes must be cut back severely for this to work, and the Styrofoam must be well-secured to the ground to keep gnawing animals out.

Burial. Zone 4 rose enthusiasts use a technique called the Minnesota Tip, partially digging up their hybrid teas, tipping them over, and burying them. This is a lot of work, but nearly completely effective.

Indoor storage. Those attempting to grow tender roses in colder parts of Zone 4 and Zone 3 may succeed only by digging them completely out of the ground and keeping them over winter in a root cellar or some other chilly but frost-free place.

CAGED PROTECTION

If you wish to use winter protection that you can blow away in spring (hardwood leaves, or the feather-light sawdust produced in modern mills), you'll need something to keep it in place. Place a cylinder of chicken wire around the mound and anchor the wire in place with two stakes. You may also construct cylinders out of old newspapers, or purchase preformed plastic rings designed for this purpose from garden centers. Oak and beech leaves work perfectly as winter protection. Maple leaves should be avoided because they will become gooey, which can lead to rot.

PROTECTING TENDER ROSES

The best way to help tender roses survive winter is to grow them in containers. (For information on planting and caring for roses in containers, see chapter 9.) For the winter, you'll need to move the containers to a sheltered place such as an unheated garage or a root cellar. At least one well-known rosarian sets all of his potted roses on wheels so that they can easily be wheeled in and out of the garage, depending on weather conditions. If using a garage, avoid windows, because sunlight can stimulate unwanted new growth. For this reason, unheated sunrooms are unsuitable for winter storage of potted roses. Unless your storage area has limited vertical space, there is no advantage in pruning potted roses prior to storage. Be sure to provide a light watering each month. In the spring, remove the potted roses from the storage area at pruning time and prune as normal.

Alternatively, you can remove the plants from their containers and bury them in an easily tillable place such as the vegetable or annual flower garden. Dig a trench about 18 inches deep. Prune the tops of your roses down to 12 inches, but leave all of the roots. Bundling roses together with twine will save space and make it easier to retrieve the roses in the spring. You will need to shake the potting mix away from the roots so that the plants will fit closely together in a bundle. Set the roses lengthwise into the trench, cover with soil, and mark the location well. Use caution when digging them out in the spring, as it doesn't take much effort with a spade to break a budded rose at the bud union.

APPENDIX

GLOSSARY

All-America Rose Selections (AARS). A commercial organization that selects one to five new roses to promote each year. AARS winners have been evaluated throughout the country, and they often prove to be dependable choices.

Balling. A condition whereby a many-petaled rose fails to open completely due to cold weather, excess humidity, or other factors. Its bud remains in a ball shape.

Bare root. A plant from which all the soil has been removed for shipment from the nursery. Both budded and own-root roses can be purchased bare root.

Basal break. Strong new growth appearing from the base of a plant. Ultimately, roses depend on the formation of basal breaks for long-term success.

Bedding rose. A rose suitable for growing in a bed with other roses. Most floribundas are ideal bedding roses.

Border. A long, often narrow, bed planted with ornamentals. Perennial borders are very popular, but borders can also consist of all shrubs or a mixed collection of deciduous shrubs such as roses, along with perennials and bulbs.

Boss. A group of stamens. These are often an attractive feature on single-petaled roses.

Budded rose. A rose that has been grafted onto a rootstock. *See also* own-root rose.

Bud-grafting. The process of grafting a rose onto a rootstock. Also called budding.

Bud eye. Also called an eye, a point along a stem where a leaf is attached and from which new growth can emerge.

Bud union. The crown on a budded plant where the grafted top meets the rootstock. In cold climates, the bud union of roses must be planted underground.

Cropper. Nickname for a rose that produces all of its roses in one great flush and then rests before blooming again.

Cultivar. Short for cultivated variety. Any named rose that is not a species rose is a cultivar.

Disbud. To selectively remove buds when they are tiny. Removing the side buds around a developing bud on a hybrid tea will encourage a larger bloom. Removing the central bud from a floribunda spray will encourage more of the florets to open at the same time. To minimize scarring, side buds are best removed when they are pea-sized.

Double-digging. A soil preparation procedure that is popular for building rose beds. Dig one spade's length down, remove all soil. Next, loosen the soil in the underlying layer. Repeat along the bed, turning each shovelful into the previously dug spot. Double digging is not necessary, but it can be worthwhile if you like to dig.

Effective. Landscaping term for a plant or design that creates a pleasing effect, as in "'Elina' is an effective tree rose."

Endcap. A plant or group of plants used effectively at the end of a bed or border.

Eye. *See* Bud eye

Floret. One of the rose blooms in a spray.

Grafting. *See* Bud-grafting

Guard petals. The outermost rose petals in a bloom. They are the first to open and are usually not fully developed.

Heritage roses. Another name for old garden roses.

Hip. The seedpod of a rose, which develops after the flower falls away. Many species and rugosa roses have particularly attractive hips. Rose hips are rich in vitamin C and edible if they haven't been sprayed with chemicals.

Hybrid. A plant created by crossing two species or cultivars. Hybrids will not grow true from seed and must be reproduced asexually (such as by cuttings or bud-grafting).

Modern Roses. Technically any rose belonging to a class that came into existence after 1867. Many of the early hybrid teas do not look very modern today, and all of the old-fashioned looking David Austin roses are also Modern Roses. Most, but not all, Modern Roses are repeat-blooming. *See also* old garden roses.

Old garden rose. Any rose belonging to a class of roses that was in existence at the time of the introduction of the putative first hybrid tea ('La France', in 1867). Most old garden roses are old, but a hybrid perpetual, for example, introduced today would still be an old garden rose. Old garden roses include both repeat- and once-blooming cultivars. Also called heritage roses. *See also* Modern Roses.

Own-root rose. Roses grown on their own roots without a rootstock. *See also* budded rose.

Panicle. A spray of flowers, specifically a large one with many small florets.

Petaloids. Small, imperfectly formed petals found at the center of an open rose bloom.

Pith. The interior of a rose cane. When pruning, rosarians search for white (living) pith.

Quartered. The attractive form into which some 100-petaled roses can organize themselves. A perfectly quartered rose will display four symmetrical sections, sometimes with a button-eye in the middle.

Reverse. The backside of rose petals. These are the first to reveal themselves when a bud is unfolding. When the bloom is fully open they will be less visible. The term is usually used when the reverse is a different color from the top of the petals. 'Candella' is a red rose with a white reverse.

Rootstock. The rooted base onto which a rose is budgrafted. Also called understock.

Secateurs. Hand-held pruners.

Shank. The woody section immediately under the bud union of a bud-grafted rose, before the roots begin. Long shanks are undesirable in cold climates.

Sport. An atypical form of a plant that arrives spontaneously as a mutation. Many climbing roses are sports of their bush counterparts. Color mutations are usually, but not always, lighter than their parents.

Spray. A group of blooms on one stem.

Stable selection. A mutation that has been successfully propagated without reverting to the appearance of the parent plant from which it sported.

Stamen. The pollen-bearing organ in a flower. Rose stamens are often brown; blooms with golden or purple stamens are often particularly attractive when fully open.

Standard. A tree or shrub trained to a single bare stem and a rounded top. A rose standard is also called a tree rose.

Tree rose. *See* standard.

Understock. *See* rootstock.

Weatherspotting. The splotches that appear on some rose blooms after rain, fog, or cool nights. Roses resistant to weatherspotting are especially valuable in coastal climates.

RESOURCES

RECOMMENDED MAIL-ORDER NURSERIES

Corn Hill Nursery, Ltd.
Corn Hill, New Brunswick
506-756-3635
www.cornhillnursery.com
  Specialist in winter-hardy roses. Bare-root roses, most grown on their own roots.

David Austin Roses Limited
Tyler, Texas
800-328-8893
www.davidaustinroses.com
  David Austin's English Roses, along with old garden roses and a selection of climbers, hybrid teas, and floribundas. Bare-root, budded plants.

Edmunds' Roses
Randolph, Wisconsin
888-481-7673
www.edmundsroses.com
  Specialist in exhibition hybrid teas. Budded plants are shipped bare root.

EuroDesert Roses
Morongo Valley, California
760-408-5151
www.eurodesertroses.com
  Rare, unusual, and hard-to-find varieties, including many Sangerhausen roses.

Forestfarm
Williams, Oregon
541-846-7269
www.forestfarm.com
  A source for species roses, grown on their own roots and shipped in pots.

Heirloom Roses
St. Paul, Oregon
503-538-1576
www.heirloomroses.com
  Old garden and shrub roses, as well as recent introductions from Europe and a wide selection of miniature roses, all grown in pots on their own roots.

Jackson & Perkins Co.
Hodges, South Carolina
800-872-7673
www.jacksonandperkins.com
  The latest in hybrid teas and floribundas. Bare-root, budded plants as well as an increasing number of own-root plants, shipped both bare root and in pots.

North Creek Farm
Phippsburg, Maine
207-389-1341
www.northcreekfarm.org
  Hardy roses, most on their own roots, in a small catalog full of common sense.

Palatine Roses
Niagara-on-the-Lake, Ontario
905-468-8627
www.palatineroses.com
  A mail-order source for some of the latest Kordes introductions. All roses are budded on seedling *Rosa multiflora* understock and shipped bare root.

Pickering Nurseries, Inc.
Port Hope, Ontario
866-269-9282
www.pickeringnurseries.com
  Wide-ranging selection of old garden, climbing, and modern roses budded on *Rosa multiflora* understock and shipped bare root in spring and fall.

RECOMMENDED MAIL-ORDER NURSERIES (CONTINUED)

Rosemary's Roses
Columbia, California
209-536-9415
A carefully chosen selection of heritage and modern roses, grown in containers on their own roots. Shipping bare-root in winter.

Roses Unlimited
Laurens, South Carolina
864-682-7673
www.rosesunlimiteddownroot.com
Heritage roses, the largest selection of older All-America Rose Selection winners available anywhere, and an increasing selection of new introductions from around the world. All grown in pots on their own roots.

Vintage Gardens
Sebastopol, California
707-829-2035
www.vintagegardens.com
An incredible selection of heritage roses, grown on their own roots and shipped in pots. Their huge catalog is an important reference tool.

Witherspoon Rose Culture
Durham, North Carolina
800-643-0315
www.witherspoonrose.com
A mail-order source for Weeks brand roses bred by Tom Carruth. Budded plants shipped bare-root.

THE COMBINED ROSE LIST

Edited by Beverly R. Dobson and Peter Schneider, the *Combined Rose List* is the annual directory of all roses known to be in commerce, matched to the mail-order nurseries that offer them. Recent editions have included details about more than 15,000 roses, including all of the roses mentioned in this book. Full details can be found at: *www.combinedroselist.com* or by writing to:

Peter Schneider
Box 677
Mantua, OH 44255

BOOKS

American Rose Society. *American Rose Annual,* 1916–1990 (Harrisburg, PA, Columbus, OH, and Shreveport, LA).
Originally founded as a professional organization for florists and later devoted to the often-esoteric requirements of rose exhibitors, the American Rose Society still managed to provide lots of valuable information in its *Annuals,* such as Howard Tenner's treatise on pruning hybrid perpetuals in the 1951 edition. Old ARS *Annuals* are readily available from dealers in used gardening books on and off the Internet.

Beales, Peter. *Classic Roses* (New York: Holt, Rinehart, and Winston, 1985).
A pictorial encyclopedia of the old garden roses. This book helped spark a renewed interest in heritage roses among mainstream gardeners.

Bunyard, Edward. *Old Garden Roses* (London: Country Life, 1936; reprinted New York: Coleman, 1978).
A graceful, almost poetic study of the once-blooming old garden roses.

Ellwanger, H. B. *The Rose* (New York: Dodd, Mead, & Company, 1882).
One of the first important rose books written from an American perspective. Opinions jump off every page of a valuable reference that is uncommonly fun to read.

Harkness, Jack. *Roses* (London: Dent, 1978).
The best book on roses I have ever read, combining botany, history, and horticulture in a seamless and beautifully written way.

Harkness, Jack. *The Makers of Heavenly Roses* (London: Souvenir Press, 1985).
The real-life stories of the individuals and families who created the roses we grow. I am disappointed that this book has never been made into a miniseries.

Horst, R. Kenneth, and Raymond Cloyd. *Compendium of Rose Diseases and Pests* (St. Paul, MN: American Phytopathological Society, 2008).
The go-to guide when things go wrong.

Joyaux, François. *La Rose de France* (Paris: Imperie Nationale, 1998).
A beautiful and comprehensive encyclopedia of the gallica roses. In French, but the illustrations speak for themselves.

Krüssman, Gerd. *The Complete Book of Roses* (Portland, OR: Timber Press, 1981).
The author died before this massive book was completed and so it is somewhat uneven. It remains a useful source for much rose and rose-related information (and trivia) that cannot be found anywhere else. Originally published in German as *Rosen, Rosen, Rosen.*

LeRougetel, Hazel. *A Heritage of Roses* (London: Unwin Hyman, 1988).
A fascinating and valuable book, rich in original research. It is the one most important source for information about the Pemberton and Bentall hybrid musks and polyanthas.

Lord, Tony. *Designing With Roses* (North Pomfret, VT: Trafalgar Square, 1999).
The best inspirational guide for using roses in the landscape, although cold-climate gardeners should note that many of the suggested companion plants are not winter-hardy in cold-winter regions.

Martin, Clair G. *100 English Roses for the American Garden* (New York: Workman, 1997).
An American perspective on the David Austin introductions.

Martin, Robert G. Jr. *Showing Good Roses* (Pasadena, CA: RoseShow.com, 2001).
The only contemporary how-to book for American rose exhibitors. Fortunately, it is very good.

Osborne, Robert. *Hardy Roses* (Pownal, VT: Garden Way, 1991).
A guide to the Canadian Explorer roses and winter hardy roses in general, with organic growing techniques and much practical information.

Paul, William. *The Rose Garden* (London: Sherwood, Gilbert, & Piper, 1848).
British nurseryman William Paul wrote this book when he was 26 and produced regular updates until his death in 1902. He was probably the last man living to know everything there is to know about roses.

Phillips, Roger and Martyn Rix. *The Random House Book of Roses* (New York: Random House, 1998).
The best picture book for identifying roses, with photos showing close-ups of stems, leaves, and flower characteristics.

Quest-Ritson, Charles and Brigid Quest-Ritson. *The American Rose Society Encyclopedia of Roses* (New York: DK Publishing, Inc., 2003).
A representative illustrated encyclopedia of rose varieties, including all types of roses from all parts of the world. Originally published in England by the Royal Horticultural Society as *The Royal Horticultural Society Encyclopedia of Roses,* it does not always conform to the ARS's classification system.

Quest-Ritson, Charles. *Climbing Roses of the World* (Portland, OR: Timber Press, 2003).
A scholarly and nearly comprehensive examination, with 200 beautiful color plates.

Thomas, Graham Stuart. *The Graham Stuart Thomas Rose Book* (Portland, OR: SagaPress/Timber Press, 1994).
His classic volumes *The Old Shrub Roses, Shrub Roses of Today,* and *Climbing Roses Old and New* all under one cover, with substantial revisions and updates.

Verrier, Suzanne. *Rosa Rugosa* (Deer Park, WI: Capability's Books, 1991).
A common-sense guide to the rugosa roses, including descriptions of nearly all available up to that time.

Young, Norman. *The Complete Rosarian* (London: Macmillan, 1971).
A fascinating book from an original thinker and occasional debunker.

USDA ZONE MAP

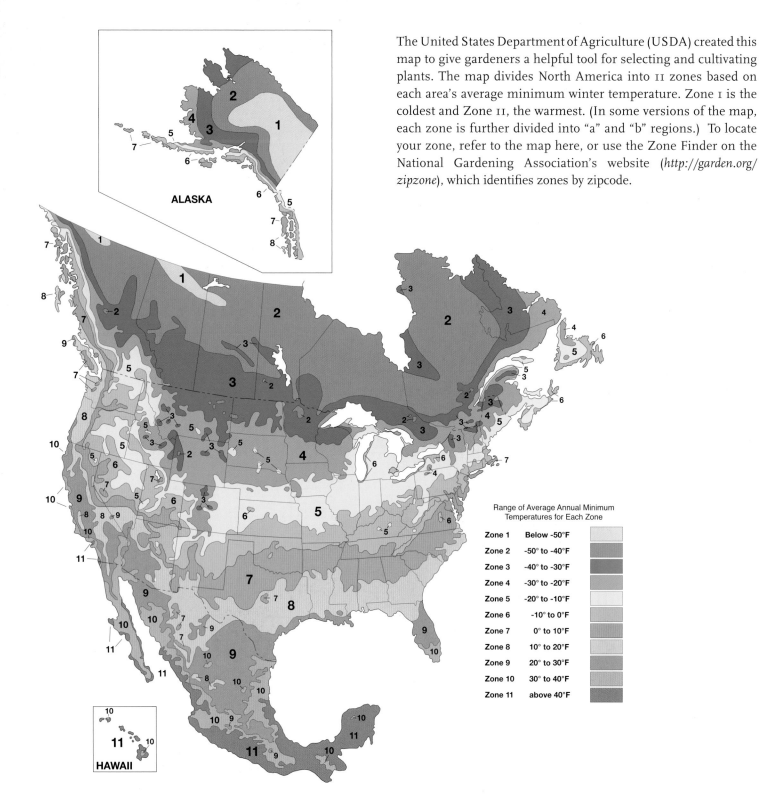

The United States Department of Agriculture (USDA) created this map to give gardeners a helpful tool for selecting and cultivating plants. The map divides North America into 11 zones based on each area's average minimum winter temperature. Zone 1 is the coldest and Zone 11, the warmest. (In some versions of the map, each zone is further divided into "a" and "b" regions.) To locate your zone, refer to the map here, or use the Zone Finder on the National Gardening Association's website (*http://garden.org/zipzone*), which identifies zones by zipcode.

ALASKA

HAWAII

Range of Average Annual Minimum
Temperatures for Each Zone

Zone 1	Below -50°F
Zone 2	-50° to -40°F
Zone 3	-40° to -30°F
Zone 4	-30° to -20°F
Zone 5	-20° to -10°F
Zone 6	-10° to 0°F
Zone 7	0° to 10°F
Zone 8	10° to 20°F
Zone 9	20° to 30°F
Zone 10	30° to 40°F
Zone 11	above 40°F

ROSES BY CLASSIFICATION

In my garage I have a plywood board onto which I tack the name tags of all of the roses that die in my garden. It's a reminder not to make the same mistake twice, and proof that northern Ohio can be challenging for roses. But this climate can also be incredibly rewarding, and this list of roses is the opposite of my Loss Board — it includes only those that have thrived here in Zone 5. While I have organized the book according to how these roses may be best used, here they appear according to their classifications.

'COLETTE'

ALBA/HYBRID ALBA
'Alba Semi-plena', p. 46
'Blush Hip', p. 75
'Félicité Parmentier', p. 86
'Lemon Blush', p. 54
'Mme Plantier'

BOURBON
'Mme Isaac Péreire', p. 98
'Souvenir de la Malmaison', p. 154
'Variegata di Bologna', p. 121
'Zéphirine Drouhin', p. 191

CENTIFOLIA
'Fantin-Latour', p. 49
'Petite de Hollande', p. 104

CHINA
'Eugène de Beauharnais', p. 85
'Hermosa', p. 94

CLIMBING HYBRID TEA
'Aloha', p. 176

CLIMBING MINIATURE
'Gloriana 97', p. 181
'Jeanne Lajoie', p. 181
'Laura Ford', p. 183
'Love Knot', p. 184
'Warm Welcome', p. 190

CLIMBING POLYANTHA
'Phyllis Bide', p. 187

DAMASK
'Bella Donna', p. 72
'Celsiana', p. 77
'Ispahan', p. 51
'Léda', p. 96
'La Ville de Bruxelles', p. 53
'Mme Hardy', p. 97

FLORIBUNDA
'Angel Face', p. 68
'Aspirin-Rose', p. 69
'Bella Rosa', p. 72
'Bernstein-Rose', p. 132
'Betty Prior', p. 74
'Centenaire de Lourdes', p. 78
'Chanelle', p. 133
'Charles Aznavour', p. 133
'Chorus', p. 134
'Day Breaker', p. 134
'Dicky', p. 134
'Domstadt Fulda', p. 134
'English Miss', p. 135
'Escapade', p. 137
'Fabergé' , p. 136
Gebrüder Grimm', p. 137
'Gelber Engel', p. 137
'Gene Boerner', p. 138
'Glad Tidings', p. 138
'Goldelse', p. 139
'Goldmarie', p. 139
'Grace Abounding', p. 143
'Hakuun', p. 143
'Hannah Gordon', p. 139
'H C Andersen', p. 139
'Heaven on Earth', p. 92
'Home & Garden', p. 139
'Hot Cocoa', p. 94
'International Herald Tribune', p. 95
'Kathleen Ferrier', p. 95
'L'Aimant', p. 141
'Margaret Merril', p. 143
'Moondance', p. 145
'Mountbatten', p. 101
'Nearly Wild', p. 102

'Old Port', p. 102
'Peacekeeper', p. 148
'Playboy', p. 148
'Pretty Lady', p. 149
'Princess Alice', p. 106
'Priscilla Burton', p. 149
'Regensberg', p. 107
'Rob Roy', p. 151
'Scentimental', p. 152
'Sheila's Perfume', p. 153
'Stadt den Helder', p. 154
'Summer Dream', p. 155
'Sun Flare', p. 155
'Trumpeter', p. 157
'Valentine Heart', p. 158

GALLICA
'Belle de Crécy', p. 72
'Belle Isis', p. 73
'Cardinal de Richelieu', 76
'Charles de Mills', p. 79
'Complicata', p. 80
'James Mason', p. 51
'La Belle Sultane', p. 53
'Perle von Weissenstein', p. 104
'Rosa Mundi', p. 109
'Scharlachglut', p. 61

GRANDIFLORA
'Queen Elizabeth', p. 150
'Violette Parfumée', p. 159

HYBRID MUSK
'Belinda', p. 71
'Focus', p. 88
'Marjorie Fair', p. 99
'Moonlight', p. 101
'Peter John', p. 56
'Pink Prosperity', p. 105

HYBRID MUSK (continued)
'Plaisanterie', p. 105
'Rosalita', p. 111
'Rush', p. 111
'Sally Holmes', p. 113

HYBRID PERPETUAL
'Baronne Prévost', p. 70
'Clio', p. 134
'Général Jacqueminot', p. 89
'Jubilee', p. 52
'Marchesa Boccella', p. 55
'Mrs John Laing', p. 145
'Robert Duncan', p. 151
'Souvenir du Docteur Jamain', p. 117
'Urdh', p. 157
'Vick's Caprice', p. 158

HYBRID RUGOSA
'Agnes', p. 68
'Cibles', p. 47
'Conrad Ferdinand Meyer', p. 80
'Hansa', p. 91
'Henry Hudson', p. 93
'Jens Munk', p. 51
'Linda Campbell', p. 54
'Rosalina', p. 110
'Scabrosa', p. 113
'Thérèse Bugnet', p. 121
'Turbo', p. 121
'White Roadrunner', p. 122

HYBRID SPINOSISSIMA
'Anna Zinkeisen', p. 68
'Stanwell Perpetual', p. 118

HYBRID TEA
'Alexander', p. 131
'Aotearoa New Zealand', p. 131
'Auguste Renoir', p. 131
'Belle Époque', p. 132
'Bride's Dream', p. 132
'Brigadoon', p. 132
'Candella', p. 133
'Dainty Bess', p. 83
'Double Delight', p. 135
'Electron', p. 128
'Elina', p. 135
'Folklore', p. 136

'Fountain', p. 137
'Garden Party', p. 137
'Gemini', p. 138
'Jardins de Bagatelle', p. 140
'Jema', p. 140
'John F Kennedy', p. 140
'Karen Blixen', p. 141
'Lady Rose', p. 141
'Liebeszauber', p. 142
'Limelight', p. 142
'Love and Peace', p. 143
'Marijke Koopman', p. 143
'Memoire', p. 144
'Mister Lincoln', p. 144
'Moonstone', p. 145
'Narzisse', p. 146
'Nightingale', p. 146
'Nostalgie', p. 146
'Oklahoma', p. 146
'Paradise', p. 147
'Parole', p. 147
'Pascali', p. 147
'Paul Shirville', p. 147
'Peace', p. 148
'Peter Frankenfeld', p. 148
'Portrait', p. 149
'Remember Me', p. 150
'Rose Gaujard', p. 151
'Ruby Wedding', p. 151
'Scent-Sation', p. 151
'Sebastian Kneipp', p. 114
'Shi-un', p. 153
'Silver Jubilee', p. 141
'Smooth Velvet', p. 154
'Stephanie Diane', p. 155
'Sutter's Gold', p. 155
'Swarthmore', p. 156
'The McCartney Rose', p. 120
'Tiffany', p. 156
'Touch Of Class', p. 156
'Tropical Sunset', p. 157
'Truly Yours', p. 157
'Vater Rhein', p. 158
'Veterans' Honor', p. 158
'Warm Wishes', p. 159

KORDESII
'Dortmund', p. 180
'Illusion', p. 182

'Leverkusen', p. 97
'William Baffin', p. 191

LARGE-FLOWERED CLIMBER
'Antike 89', p. 177
'Aschermittwoch', p. 177
'Blossomtime', p. 178
'City Girl', p. 179
'Compassion', p. 179
'Crimson Sky', p. 180
'Demokracie', p. 180
'Elegance', p. 181
'Freisinger Morgenröte', p. 181
'Golden Gate', p. 181
'High Hopes', p. 182
'Leaping Salmon', p. 183
'Morning Jewel', p. 185
'Paul Jerabek', p. 186
'Pierre De Ronsard', p. 187
'Polka', p. 187
'Red Fountain', p. 188
'Rosarium Uetersen', p. 60
'Santana', p. 188
'Summer Wine', p. 189
'Sunday Best', p. 189

MINIATURE
'Baby Love', p. 70
'Black Jade', p. 163
'Cider Cup', p. 164
'Giggles', p. 164
'Hot Tamale', p. 164
'Hurdy Gurdy', p. 165
'Irresistible', p. 165
'Jean Kenneally', p. 165
'Magic Carrousel', p. 166
'Minnie Pearl', p. 166
'Rainbow's End', p. 166
'Rise 'n' Shine', p. 167
'Scarlet Moss', p. 167
'Si', p. 167
'Simon Robinson', p. 168
'Soroptimist International', p. 168
'Starina', p. 168
'Sweet Chariot', p. 169
'Top Marks', p. 169
'Toy Clown', p. 169

MINI-FLORA
'Butter Cream', p. 163
'Dr John Dickman', p. 164
'Regina Lee', p. 166

MOSS
'Salet', p. 112
'Scarlet Moss', p. 167

MYSTERY
'Ralph's South African Rose', p. 57

NOISETTE
'Mme Alfred Carrière', p. 184

POLYANTHA
'Baby Faurax', p. 69
'Britannia', p. 76
'Maman Turbat', p. 99
'Marie-Jeanne', p. 99
'Mlle Cécile Brunner', p. 98
'Snowbelt', p. 115
'The Fairy', p. 119
'Yesterday', p. 123
'Zenaitta', p. 123

PORTLAND
'Comte de Chambord', p. 80
'Indigo', p. 94
'Rose de Rescht', p. 111
'Yolande D'Aragon', p. 123

RAMBLER
'American Pillar', p. 176
'Blushing Lucy', p. 178
'Chevy Chase', p. 178
'Louis' Rambler', p. 183
'Maria Liesa', p. 185
'New Dawn', p. 186
'Silver Moon', p. 188
'Super Dorothy', p. 189
'Veilchenblau', p. 190
'Wichmoss', p. 191

SHRUB
'A Shropshire Lad', p. 46
'Abraham Darby', p. 67
'Adelaide Hoodless', p. 67

'Alchymist', p. 176
'Ambridge Rose', p. 131
'Armada', p. 69
'Basye's Purple Rose', p. 71
'Belinda's Dream', p. 71
'Belle Story', p. 73
'Birdie Blye', p. 75
'Bonica', p. 75
'Captain Samuel Holland', p. 47
'Cardinal Hume', p. 77
'Carefree Delight', p. 77
'Champlain', p. 78
'Charlotte', p. 79
'Colette', p. 48
'Constance Spry', p. 48
'Coral Meidiland', p. 81
'Country Dancer', p. 82
'Country Living', p. 83
'Crown Princess Margareta', p. 83
'Daydream', p. 83
'Distant Drums', p. 84
'Dornröschenschloss Sababurg', p. 49
'Eglantyne', p. 84
'Evelyn', p. 85
'Fair Bianca', p. 136
'Felicitas', p. 86
'Festival Fanfare', p. 87
'Fisherman's Friend', p. 87
'Flower Carpet', p. 87
'Flower Girl', p. 88
'Frühlingsmorgen', p. 88
'Fuchsia Meidiland', p. 89
'George Vancouver', p. 89
'Geschwind's Nordlandrose', p. 50
'Great Wall', p. 90
'Greetings', p. 91
'Happy Chappy', p. 92
'Heritage', p. 93
'Home Run', p. 50
'Jacqueline du Pré', p. 95
'John Cabot', p. 52
'Lady Elsie May', p. 96
'Lambert Closse', p. 142
'Little Rambler', p. 97
'Marquise Spinola', p. 144
'Martine Guillot', p. 144
'Mary Rose', p. 100
'Morden Blush', p. 146

'Morgenrot', p. 101
'My Hero', p. 101
'Nashville', p. 102
'Open Arms', p. 103
'Oranges 'n' Lemons', p. 103
'Palmengarten Frankfurt', p. 103
'Paloma Blanca', p. 146
'Pearl Drift', p. 104
'Pleine de Grâce', p. 106
'Queen Mother', p. 106
'Rainbow Knock Out', p. 107
'Red Ribbons', p. 107
'Rhapsody in Blue', p. 107
'Romanze', p. 108
'Scepter'd Isle', p. 114
'Simplicity', p. 115
'Sommermorgen', p. 116
'Sonia Rykiel', p. 116
'Sophy's Rose', p. 117
'Spirit of Freedom', p. 117
'Teasing Georgia', p. 118
'The Countryman', p. 119
'The Ingenious Mr Fairchild', p. 120
'The Mayflower', p. 120
'Wildeve', p. 122
'Windrush', p. 122

SPECIES
Rosa arkansana, p. 108
Rosa eglanteria, p. 57
Rosa glauca, p. 109
Rosa pendulina, p. 110
Rosa pomifera, p. 58
Rosa roxburghii normalis, p. 59
Rosa sericea pteracantha, p. 110
Rosa virginiana, p. 60

SPECIES HYBRID
'Bourgogne', p. 46
'Corylus', p. 81
'Pink Surprise', p. 115
'Schoener's Nutkana', p. 114
'St John's Rose', p. 111

TEA
'Lady Hillingdon', p. 96

PHOTOGRAPHY CREDITS

© Ian Adams: 2, 4, 5, 15, 16 (top center, middle left and right, bottom right), 21 top, 22 left, 23 right, 25 left, 28, 29 top and middle, 30 right, 32, 33, 34, 36, 37 bottom, 42 right, 44, 45, 46, 47 right, 48, 49, 50, 52 bottom, 53 right, 54 left, 55 left, 56, 59, 65 top, 69, 72, 74, 76, 80, 81, 86 (middle and bottom), 89, 92 bottom, 94 bottom, 98, 99, 103, 105, 106 left, 108 bottom, 110, 111, 112, 116, 124, 126–127, 129, 137, 138 top, 140, 144, 148, 151, 157 right, 159, 170, 171, 172, 176 right, 177, 178 right, 179 top, 182, 183 right, 186 bottom, 189, 190, 191, 201 (middle right), 204–208, 212, 213, 214, 216–220, 224 right, 225, 227, 228 (top center and right), 232 (bottom three), 236 right, 238–241, 243, 245–249, 251

David Austin Roses, Ltd.: 3 bottom, 8, 16 top left, 29 bottom, 62, 77 bottom, 122 bottom, 155, 192

© David Cappaert, Michigan State University, Bugwood.org: 229 center

N. Cattlin/flpa-images.co.uk: 229 right, 231 top right, 232 top, 236 left

Whitney Cranshaw, Colorado State University, Bugwood.org: 231 bottom left

Division of Plant Industry Archive, Florida Department of Agriculture and Consumer Services, Bugwood.org: 234 bottom

GAP Photos Ltd.: (Visions) 37 middle, (Oliver Mathews) 57, 88, (Jerry Harpur) 106, (FhF Greenmedia) 109, (Friedrich Strauss) 233, (Brian North) 234 top, (Geoff Kidd) 235 right, 236 top

© Saxon Holt: 194, 198, 203

© Paul E. Jerabek, 9/7/1909–6/30/2008: 3 top, 10–11, 19 (top and bottom left), 35, 37 top, 51, 52 top, 53 left, 70 right, 91 left, 115 right, 118 top, 142 right, 143 (bottom left and right), 147 left, 149 bottom, 150 right, 156 right, 163 left, 165 168 bottom, 169 left, 178 left, 183 left, 186 top, 195 bottom right, 201 center, 224 left

© Bill Johnson: 228 (top left, bottom), 229 top left, 230 top, 231 (top left and center), 235 left

© Rosemary Kautzky: 6–7, 12, 13, 16 (top right, bottom left), 18, 19 right, 20, 21 (middle and bottom), 22 right, 23 left, 24, 25 right, 26, 27 top, 31, 38–39, 40, 42 left, 43, 47 left, 54 right, 55 right, 60, 61, 64, 65 (middle left and right, bottom), 66, 67, 68, 70 left, 71, 73, 75, 77 top, 78, 79, 82, 83, 84, 85, 86 top, 87, 90, 91 right, 92 top, 93, 94 top, 95, 96, 97, 100, 101, 102, 104, 107, 108 top, 113, 114, 115 left, 117, 118 bottom, 120, 121, 122 top, 123, 130–136, 138 bottom, 139, 141, 142 left, 143 top, 145, 147 right, 149 top, 150 left, 152, 153, 154, 156 left, 157 left, 160, 162, 163 right, 164, 166, 167, 168 top, 169 right, 175, 176 left, 179 right, 180, 185, 187, 188, 195 (all except bottom right), 196, 197, 200, 201 (all except middle center and right), 209, 221, 237

© Randy Lady: 25 bottom

© Kenneth Munzlinger/iStockphoto.com: 229 bottom left

© Jim Schutte: 30 left

Mars Vilaubi: 230 bottom

INDEX

Page references in *italics* indicate photos.

A

'A Shropshire Lad', 46
AARS. *See* All-America Rose Selection
'Abraham Darby', 67, *67*, 243
accent plants, roses as, 42
'Adelaide Hoodless', 67
'Agnes', 68
albas, *28*, 29, 257
    pruning of, 243
    See also specific cultivars
'Alba Semi-plena', 46
'Alchymist', 176
'Alexander', *16*, 131, *131*
All-America Rose Selection (AARS), 13, 14,
    21, 56, 75, 84, 145, 148, 149
'Aloha', 176, *176*
'Amber Queen', 148, 209
'Ambridge Rose', 131, *195*
'American Pillar', 75, 176, *176*
American Rose (magazine), 164
American Rose Society, 49–50, 94, 103, 209
    American Rose Annual, 245
    Guidelines for Judging Roses, 156
'America's Choice', 139
'Angel Face', 68, *68*
animal problems, 237–39
    barriers/fences, 238, *238*, *239*
    deer/repellents, 237, *237*–38
    dogs, 238
    rabbits, 239, *239*
    scare devices, 238
'Anisley Dickson', 134
'Anna Zinkeisen', 68
'Anne Graber', 155
'Anne Harkness', 106
'Antike 89', 177, *177*
'Aotearoa'/'Aotearoa New Zealand', 131
apical dominance, 172

Apothecary's Rose, the. *See Rosa gallica*
    officinalis
'Appleblossom Flower Carpet', 23, 70, 87,
    88
Apple Rose. *See Rosa pomifera*
arches, roses for
    'Louis' Rambler', *183*, 183–84
    'Paul Jerabek', 186, *186*
    'Super Dorothy', *170*, 171, 177, *189*,
        189–90
    'Veilchenblau', 32, 65, 190, *190*
    'William Baffin', 66, *66*, *172*, 172, 173,
        191, *191*
'Archiduchesse Elisabeth d'Autriche', 158
'Arielle Dombasle', 181
'Armada', 69, *69*
'Aschermittwoch', 177
'Aspirin-Rose', 69
'Auguste Renoir', 131–32
'Aunt Ruth', 186
Austin, David, 19, 77, 141, 197
    cut flowers, many-petaled, 129
    first rose introduction of, 48
    mail-order information, 253
author's garden, 14, 126, *126*–27
autumn blooms, 35
autumn damasks. *See* Portlands
autumn planting, 206, 217, 219
'Awakening', 186
awards, 13
    AARS, 56, 148, 149
    German ADR (Anerkannte Deutsche
        Rose), 108
    James Mason Award, 51
    "Rose of the Century," 111
    See also All-American Rose Selection

B

'Baby Blanket', 116
'Baby Faurax', 69, *69*
'Baby Love', 50, 70, *70*, *201*
'Baby Rambler', 97
"baby roses," 161
'Ballerina', 71, 99, 119
"balling," 140
banks and terraces. *See* groundcover roses
Baptisia australis (false indigo), 89
bare-root roses, 206, 207, *207*, 212
    by mail order, 212–13
    planting of, 206, 213, *213*–14, 215
    pruning of, 212, *212*
    soaking of, 212, 215
    watershoots on, 212
'Baronne Prévost', *19*, 70, *70*, 224, *224*
basic rose care, 220–26
'Basye's Purple Rose', 71
Beales, Peter, 51
bedding roses, 125–59
    selection of, 130
beds and borders, 64
    layout of bed, 128
    miniatures in, 162
    mixed borders, 64, 66, 221
    raised beds, 215
    site selection, bedding garden, 126
    spacing of rose plants, 128
'Belinda', *25*, *65*, 71, *71*
'Belinda's Dream', 71
'Bella Donna', *16*, 72, *72*
'Bella Rosa', 72
'Belle de Crécy', *29*, 72–73
'Belle Époque', 132
'Belle Isis', 73
'Belle Story', 73, *73*
beneficial insects, 66

'Benjamin Britten', *8, 9*
Bennett, Henry, 145
Bentall, Ann, 119
'Bernstein-Rose', 132
'Betty Prior', *21,* 74, *74*
'Bev Dobson', 186
'Bewitched', 150
'Birdie Blye', 75
'Bizarre Triomphant', 79
'Black Jade', *65,* 163, *163*
black roses, 53
'Blaze, Everblooming', 180
blooms
    cycles and, 128
    describing, 18–19
    size of, 35
    See also petal problems
'Blossomtime', *178, 178*
blue roses, 53
'Blush Hip', 75
'Blushing Lucy', *178, 178*
"Blush" series, the, 54
Boerner, Gene ("Papa Floribunda"), 20, 138
'Bonica', *75,* 75–76
books on roses, 254–55
borders and beds. *See* beds and borders
bouquet companion flowers, 130
Bourbons, 33, *33,* 257
    pruning of, 243–44
    See also specific cultivars
'Bourgogne', *46,* 46–47
boutonniere rose, 27, 98
'Bowled Over', 139
"Bowling Ball Rose, The," 139
breeding roses, 69
    breeders of roses, 20. *See also* specific
        cultivars
    crossing of species roses, 82
    "go and come" characteristics, 90
    "replicative fading," 148
    self-pollination, 232
    See also rose breeders; specific rose
        breeder
'Bride's Dream', 132

'Brigadoon', 133, *133*
'Bright Smile', 76
'Britannia', 76
Brownells, the, 181
brown roses, 94
Buck, Dr. Griffith, 58, 84
bud-grafted roses
    aging, bud unions and, *219, 219*
    bud eyes and, 193
    fading with time, 148
    hybrid roses and, 58
    planting, bud union and, 213, *213,* 215,
        250
    pros and cons of, 208
    rose mosaic and, 235
    See also rootstock
'Buff Beauty', 101
'Butter Cream', *163, 163*
'Buxom Beauty', 147
buying roses. *See* shopping for roses
'By Appointment', 106

C

Canadian Explorer roses, 47, 52, 70, 78, 84,
    86, 89–90, 97, 144, 209, *209*
Canadian Parkland roses, 97, 146
Canadian Rose Society, 155
'Cancer', 23
'Candella', 133, 253
'Candy Stripe', 152
'Canterbury', 118
'Captain Samuel Holland', 42, *43,* 47, *47*
'Cardinal de Richelieu', *76,* 76–77
'Cardinal Hume', 77
care for roses, basics, 220–26
'Carefree Beauty', 58
'Carefree Delight', *77, 77*
'Carmenetta', 109
Carruth, Tom, 20
cautions, rose selections and, 66
'Celsiana', *77,* 77–78
'Centenaire de Lourdes', 78
'Centenaire de Lourdes Rouge', 78
centifolia, 29, *29,* 257

'Champlain', *78, 78*
Champneys, John, 185
'Chanelle', 133
'Charles Aznavour', 133, *133*
'Charles de Mills', *79, 79*
Charleston, South Carolina, 185
'Charlotte', *79, 79*
chemicals, 5, 227
    beneficial insects and, 66
    chlethodim, 226
    Cornell formula (GreenCure), 234
    fungicides, 112, 223, 227, 234
    weedkillers, 44
Chestnut Rose. *See Rosa roxburghii normalis*
'Chevy Chase', 178–79, *179*
'Child's Play', *203, 203*
China roses, 31, 257
    as "monthly roses," 94
    pruning of, 244
    See also specific cultivars
'Chorus', 134
'Christopher Columbus', 102
'Chrysler Imperial', 142
'Cibles', 25, *47, 47,* 224, *224*
'Cider Cup', *164, 164*
'City Girl', 179
'City of London', 95
Clark, Alister, 189
Classic Roses (Beales), 51
classification of roses, 35
clematis, climbing roses and, 177
Clematis paniculata, 64, 64
Cleveland Rose Society, 56
climbing miniatures, 26, *27,* 257
    American/British differences in, 183
    See also specific cultivars
climbing roses, 26, *26,* 171–91
    basal breaks of, 246
    choosing right varieties, 175
    clematis paired with, 177
    as ground covers, 175
    hybrid tea, 257
    pruning of, 245–46, *246*
    polyantha, 257

training canes of, 172, 173
winter-hardy climbers, 186
See also ramblers; specific cultivars
'Climbing Souvenir de la Malmaison', 154
'Clio', 134
Cocker nursery, 20
'Colette', 42, *42*, 48, *48*
'Colonial White', 97
color contrasts, 128
Combined Rose List (Dobson and Schneider, eds.), 254
'Compassion', 173, 179, *179*
'Complicata', 80
'Comte de Chambord', 32, 80, *80*
conditioning cut roses, 130
'Conrad Ferdinand Meyer', 80–81
'Constance Spry', 48, *48*, 49, *73*, *91*, 131
container roses
from local nurseries, 215–16
by mail order, 216–17
protecting tender roses, 250
rootball and, 216, 217
See also growing roses in containers
'Coral Flower Carpet', 88
'Coral Meidiland', *24*, 81
'Corylus', 81–82, *82*
'Country Dancer', 82, *82*
'Country Living', 83
'Crested Moss', 30, *30*, 112
'Crimson Glory', 142, 242
'Crimson Sky', 175, 180, *180*
'Crocus Rose', 137
"croppers," 128
crossing roses. *See* breeding roses
'Crown Princess Margareta', *22*, 83
'Curiosity', *236*
cutting roses, 125–59
conditioning cut roses, 130
cut flowers, 128, *129*–30
cuttings of rose plants, 58, 235, 244

D

'Dainty Bess', 83, *83*, 189
damasks, 29, *29*, 257

pruning of, 244
See also specific cultivars
David Austin's English Roses. *See under* Austin, David
Davidson, Harvey, 154
'Day Breaker', 134, *134*
'Daydream', *83*, 83–84
dead wood, rose canes, 241, *241*
'Demokracie', 180, *180*
'Denise Grey', 76
'Dentelle de Bruges', 105, *105*
desiccation, protection from, 215
'Deuil de Paul Fontaine', 112
Dickson family/nursery, 20, 135
'Cider Cup', 164
'Dicky', 134
dieback, 241
disease-resistant varieties, 227
diseases
black spot, *233*, 233–34
botrytis, 235
canker, 235–36
crown gall, 236, *236*
downy mildew, 234–35
powdery mildew, 112, 174, 234, *234*
rose mosaic, 208, 235, 236, *236*
rose rosette, 236–37
rust, 235
'Distant Drums', 37, *37*, 84, *84*
Dobson, Beverly R., 254
'Domstadt Fulda', 128, 134–35
'Don Juan', 234
dooryard gardens, 130, *130*
'Dopey', 23
Dorieux, Francois, 20
'Dornröschenschloss Sababurg', 49
'Dorothy Perkins', 189
'Dortmund', 180, *180*
'Double Delight', 13, *13*, 14, 20, 31, 135, 137
double-digging, 211
double roses, 19, *19*
'Douceur Normande', 81
'Dr Huey', 14, 61
as rootstock, 210, 233

'Dr John Dickman', *27*, 164
'Dr W Van Fleet', 75, 186

E

Earth-Kind roses, 25
'Earthquake', 165
'Eden'/'Eden 88', 187
eglantine roses, 58, 85
'Eglantyne', *84*, 84–85
'Electron', 128, 129, *129*, 135
'Elegance', 181
'Elegant Design', 230
'Elina', 135, *195*, 252
Elizabeth Park, Hartford, Connecticut, 126
embankments. *See* groundcover roses
emblem/symbol, rose as, 7
English Alba hybrids, 22
'English Miss," 135–36
English Musk hybrids, 22
English Roses. *See* Austin, David
'Escapade', 85, *85*, 137
'Esmeralda', 85
'Eugène de Beauharnais', 85
Euphorbia 'Diamond Frost', 200, *200*
European rose classes, original, 28, 233
'European Touch', 136
'Evelyn', 67, 85–86, *86*, *201*
Everett, Clyde, *72*
'Excelsa', 190

F

'Fabergé', 136
Fagan, Gwen, 57
failures with rose plants, 13
'Fair Bianca', *12*, 13, 136, *136*
Fairchild, Thomas, 120
'Fairy Castle', 49
'Fairy Snow', 113
'Fantin-Latour', *29*, 49, 49–50
Fantin-Latour, Henri, 49–50
feeder roots, 66
feeding roses, 221–23
feeding program, 222
fertilizers, 222–23

feeding roses (continued)
  foliar feeding, 222
  gypsum, value of, 223
  manure, 224–25
  nitrogen, 221–22
  other nutrients, 223
  phosphorus, 221, 223
  potassium, 221, 223
  specialized foods, 222
  winter preparation and, 247
'Felicitas', 86, 86
'Félicité Parmentier', 86, 86
Fellows Riverside Gardens (Youngstown, Ohio), 128, 129
fence/horizontal training, roses for
  apical dominance and, 172
  'Elegance', 181
  'Freisinger Morgenröte', 181
  'Jeanne Lajoie', 27, 175, 175, 182, 182–83
  'Maria Liesa', 36, 185
  'Polka', 187–88, 188
  'Summer Wine', 173, 188, 188
  'Veilchenblau', 32, 65, 190, 190
  'Wichmoss', 191
'Ferdinand Pichard', 158
fertilizers. See under feeding roses
'Festival Fanfare', 87, 152
'Fisherman's Friend', 87
floral preservatives, cut flowers, 130
floribundas, 21, 21, 125, 257
  in beds and borders, 64
  pruning of, 242
  space requirements for, 211
  See also specific cultivars
'Flower Carpet', 23, 38–39, 41, 70, 87, 87
Flower Carpet roses, 22, 22–23, 87–88, 96
  "Next Generation" of, 88
  See also specific cultivars
'Flower Girl', 88
'Focus', 88
foliage
  discolored foliage, 223
  foliar feeding, 222–23
'Folklore', 136

'Fortuniana', 210
'Fountain', 137
foxglove, 62, 63
fragrance, 7, 69
  of moss roses, 30
  most fragrant roses, 33, 37
  of old garden roses, 28
  on patios, container roses and, 200
  perfume industry catalyst, 29
  powdery mildew and, 234
  "pure rose," 112
'Fred Loads', 87, 113, 152
'Freisinger Morgenröte', 181
"Frühlings-" hybrid spinosissimas, 89
'Frühlingsmorgen', 88, 88–89, 150
'Fuchsia Meidiland', 89
'Full Sail', 131
fungicides. See under chemicals

G

'Gala Charles Aznavour', 134
Gallagher, Gwendolyn, 144
gallicas, 29, 29, 257
  pruning of, 244–45, 245
  See also specific cultivars
garden centers. See under shopping for roses
Garden of Roses of Legend and Romance (Wooster, Ohio), 98
'Garden Party', 137
garden sanitation, 234
'Gebrüder Grimm', 137
'Gelber Engel', 137–38, 138
'Gemini', 138, 138
'Gene Boerner', 138
'Général Jacqueminot' ("General Jack"), 34, 89
Générosa roses, 23, 23, 116, 126, 144. See also specific cultivars
'George Vancouver', 89–90, 90, 209, 209
German ADR (Anerkannte Deutsche Rose) award, 108
'Gertrude Jekyll', 62, 63
'Geschwind's Nordlandrose', 50, 50
Geschwind, Rudolph, 50

'Giggles', 164
'Glad Tidings', 138
'Gloire des Mousseux', 112
'Gloire des Rosomanes' (Ragged Robin), 210
'Gloriana 97', 181
gloves, thorns and, 172
'Goethe', 112
'Goldelse', 139
'Golden Celebration', 120
'Golden Gate', 175, 181–82
'Goldmarie'/'Goldmarie 82', 139
'Grace Abounding', 90, 143
graded roses, 207
grafting. See bud-grafted roses
'Graham Thomas', 184
'Graham Thomas' honeysuckle, 184
grandifloras, 21, 21, 257. See also specific cultivars
'Great Wall', 90, 90–91
'Green Velvet' boxwood, 67
'Greetings', 91
'Grimm Brother's Fairy Tale', 137
groundcover roses, 32, 36, 64, 116
  climbers as, 175
growing roses in containers, 199–203, 200, 201, 203
  containers for, 202
  as garden elements, 200
  indoor growing of, 203
  planting and caring for, 202–3
  planting procedure for, 202–3
  potting mix recipe, 202
  recommended roses, 201, 201
  soil mixes for, 202
  watering and feeding of, 203
  See also container roses
Guillot nursery, 20, 23, 116
  Générosa roses, 126, 126–27

H

'Hakuun' ("white cloud"), 91, 91, 143, 201
'Handel', 186
hand-painted roses, 150
'Hannah Gordon', 139, 139

'Hansa', 91, 91–92

'Hansaland', 55

'Happy Chappy', 92, 92, 195

hardiness zones. *See* USDA Zones

Harkness, Jack, 20, 22, 77, 95, 106, 148

'Harkness Marigold', 106

Harkness nursery, 20

'Harlow Carr', 118

'H C Andersen', 139

'Heaven on Earth', 92, 92–93

hedges, roses as, 44–45, 45

height of roses, 35

'Heirloom', 115

heirloom roses, 209. *See also* old garden
    roses

'Henry Hudson', 93, 93

herbicides. *See* chemicals

'Heritage', 93, 93–94

Heritage of Roses, A (LeRougetel), 119

heritage roses, 10, 51. *See also* old garden
    roses

'Hermosa', 94

Hetzel, Karl, 190

'Highfield', 179

'High Hopes', 182

Hokkaido, 25

Holmes, Robert, 113

Holy Rose of Abyssinia. *See* 'St John's Rose'

'Home & Garden', 139–40, 140

'Home Run', 50

honeysuckle, 184

Hoodless, Adelaide, 67

horizontal training. *See* fences/horizontal
    training, roses for

'Hot Cocoa', 94, 94

'Hot Tamale', 162, 162, 164–65

House of Meilland, 48

'Hurdy Gurdy', 165

Hurst, C. C., 111–12

hybridizers. *See* rose breeders

hybrid musks, 25, 25, 115, 257–58

    pruning of, 243

    See also Pemberton/Bentall hybrid
        musks; specific cultivars

hybrid perpetuals, 34, 34, 222, 224, 224, 230,
    258

    pruning of, 245

hybrid polyantha, 74

hybrid roses, propagation of, 58

hybrid rugosas, 258

    Grootendorst series, 120

    new colors and, 25

    pruning of, 243

    watering, nutrients for, 224

    See also Rosa rugosa; specific cultivars

hybrid spinossimas, 89, 258

hybrid tea roses, 9, 31, 125, 258

    as "blooms on a stick," 64

    as genesis of modern rose, 20

    pruning of, 242

    putative first, 20, 28, 116

    See also specific cultivars

I

'Iceberg', 143, 145

'Ice Cream', 144

'Ice Meidiland', 81

'Illusion', 182

'Improved Blaze', 180

'Independence', 131

'Indigo', 94, 94–95

insecticides. *See* chemicals

insect pests, 228–32

    aphids, 228, 228

    cane borers, 228, 228

    earwigs, 228, 228–29

    gall wasps, 229, 229

    inchworms, 229, 229

    Japanese beetles, 229, 229

    leaf-cutter bees, 229, 229

    nematodes, 229–30

    rose chafer, 230, 230

    rose curcurlio, 230, 230

    rose midge, 230

    rose slug, 230–31

    rose stem girdler, 231, 231

    scale, 231

    spider mites, 231, 231

    spittlebugs, 231, 231

    thrips, 232

'International Herald Tribune', 95

'Irresistible', 165, 165, 195

'Isis'. *See* 'Karen Blixen'

'Ispahan', 51

J

Jackson & Perkins, 20, 24, 115, 138, 209

    mail-order information, 253

    New Generation roses, 216

'Jacqueline du Pré', 95, 95

'Jacques Cartier', 56

'James Mason', 10, 10–11, 51, 51

James Mason Award, 51

'Janet', 187

'Jardins de Bagatelle', 140

'Jean Kenneally', 165

'Jeanne Lajoie', 27, 175, 175, 182, 182–83

Jebb, Eglantyne, 85

'Jema', 140

'Jens Munk', 51–52, 52

Jerabek, Paul, 22

'John Cabot', 52

'John F Kennedy', 140

'J P Connell', 97

'Jubilee', 52, 52–53

'Jules', 186

'Just Joey', 74, 140

K

'Kaleidoscope', 84

'Karen Blixen', 141, 141

'Kathleen Ferrier', 95

'Kathleen Harrop', 191

"Katy Road Pink," 58

Knock Out roses, 23, 23, 230

    'Rainbow Knock Out', 107, 107

    See also specific cultivars

Konsmo, Dennis, 202

Kordes, Wilhelm, 78, 90, 176

kordesiis, 26, 97, 258

Kordes nursery, 20

    'Antike 89', 177

Kordes nursery *(continued)*
    'Goldmarie'/'Goldmarie 82', 139
'Kronprincessin Viktoria', 154

L
'La Belle Sultane', *19,* 53, *53*
labels, long-lasting, 49
'Lady Elsie May', 96, *96*
'Lady Hillingdon', 96, 245
'Lady Rose', 141
'La France', 20, 252
    as first hybrid tea, 28
'L'Aimant', 141
'Lambert Closse', 142
"Large-flowered climbers," 26, 258
'Laura Ford', *183, 183*
'La Ville de Bruxelles', 29, *53,* 53–54
lawn roses, 44
'Leander', 118
Leander group, 22
'Leaping Salmon', 183
'Léda' (Painted Damask), 96
'Lemon Blush', 54, *54*
Lens, Louis, 25, 57, 77, 105, 111
LeRougetel, Hazel, 82, 119
'Leverkusen', 97
'Leweson Gower', 154
Liebau, Brother Alfons, 185
'Liebeszauber', 142, *142*
lifespan, roses, 13
Lim, Ping, 91
'Limelight', 142, *142*
'Linda Campbell', 54–55
'Little Rambler', 97
Lloyd, Christopher, 133
lobelia, *198,* 199
long-shank roses, 212, *212*
long-stemmed roses, 20, 31
    conditioning of, 130
Lonicera, 184
lost roses, 58
'Louis' Rambler', *183,* 183–84
'Louis Riel', 109
'Love and Peace', 143, *143*

'Love Knot', 184
'Love's Magic', 142
'Lovestruck', 150
'Lübecker Rotspon', 138
'Lucy', 178
'Lunar Mist', 48

M
Mad Gallicas, 72
'Magic Carrousel', 166, *166, 201*
mail-order container roses, 216–17
mail-order nurseries, 253–54
'Mainaufeuer', 107
'Maman Turbat', *16,* 99, *99*
'Manetti', 31, 210
many-petaled roses, 129
'Marchesa Boccella', 55, *55*–56
'Maréchal LeClerc', 156
'Margaret Merril', 143, *143*
'Maria Liesa', *36,* 185
'Maria Lisa', 185
'Marie-Jeanne', 99, *99*
'Marijke Koopman', *143,* 143–44
'Maritime Guillot', 126, *126*–27
'Marjorie Fair', 99–100, *100*
markers for plant labels, 49
'Marquiese Bocella', 56
'Marquise Spinola', 144
Martin, Bob, 148
'Martine Guillot', 116, 144, *144*
'Mary Rose', 100, *100, 192, 193*
Mason, James and Clarissa, 51
'Matilda', 134
'Maypole' crab apples, 181
McGredy, Sam, IV, 20, 150
McGredy nursery, 20
Meidiland roses, 24, *24,* 81. *See also* specific
    cultivars
Meilland, Alain, 42, 53
Meilland nursery, 20, 48, 181
'Melodie Parfumée', 159
'Memoire', 144
'Métis', 82
Meyer, Carl, 149

"micro-minis," 168
miniature roses, 26, 27, 161–69, 258
    'Black Jade', *65,* 163, *163*
    'Cider Cup', 164, *164*
    'Giggles', 164
    in home landscape, 162
    'Hot Tamale', 162, *162,* 164–65
    'Hurdy Gurdy', 165
    'Irresistible', 165, *165, 195*
    'Jean Kenneally', 165
    'Magic Carrousel', 166, *166, 201*
    by mail order, care for, 217
    'Minnie Pearl', 166, *166*
    pruning of, 242
    'Rainbow's End', *160,* 161, 166, *166,*
        198, 199
    'Rise 'n' Shine', 167, *167*
    'Scarlet Moss', *30,* 167, *167*
    'Si', 167–68, *195*
    'Simon Robinson', 168, *168, 195*
    'Soroptimist International', 168, *168*
    space requirements for, 211
    'Starina', 168
    'Sweet Chariot', 169, *169*
    'Top Marks', 169
    'Toy Clown', 169, *169*
mini-floras, 27, *27,* 162, 259. *See also* specific
    cultivars
Minnesota Tip winter preparation, 249
'Minnie Pearl', 166, *166*
'Mister Lincoln', 144–46, *195*
mixed borders. *See under* beds and
    borders
'Mlle Cécile Brunner' (Sweetheart Rose),
    98–99, 243
'Mme Alfred Carrière', *31,* 184–85, *185*
'Mme Boll', *80*
'Mme Caroline Testout', 158
'Mme Ernst Calvat', 98
'Mme Hardy', 97, *97*–98
'Mme Isaac Péreire', *33,* 98, *98*
'Mme Plantier', *28,* 55, *55*
modern roses, 20–27
    climbing miniatures, 26, *27*

David Austin's English Roses. *See under* Austin, David
Earth-Kind roses, 25
floribundas, 21, *21*, 125, 150, 211, 242
Flower Carpet roses, 22, 22–23, 87–88, 96
Générosa roses, 23, *23*, 116, 126, 144
grandifloras, 21, *21*
hybrid musks, 25, *25*, 115, 243
hybrid teas, 9, 20, *20*, 28, 31, 116, 125, 242
Knock Out roses, 23, *23*, 107, *107*, 230
kordesiis, 26, 97
Meidiland roses, 24, *24*, 81
mini-floras, 27, *27*, 162
Oso Easy roses, 24
polyanthas, 21, *21*–22, 116, 120, 155, 243
Portlands and, 32, *32*, 119, 245
rugosas, 25, *25*, 110. *See also* hybrid rugosas
shrub roses, 22, *22*, 242, 243
Simplicity roses, 24, *24*
strengths/shortcomings of, 34
See also climbing roses; miniature roses; specific cultivars
monocropping, 66
"monthly roses," 94
'Moondance', 145, *145*, 200, *200*
'Moonlight', 101
'Moonstone', 145
Moore, Ralph, 26, 57
'Morden Blush', 52, 146
Morden roses, 52
'Morden Sunrise', 97
Moreau and Robert, 144
'Morgenrot', 101
'Morning Jewel', 185
moss roses, 30, *30*, 259
  'Deuil de Paul Fontaine', 112
  pruning of, 244
  See also specific cultivars
'Mountbatten', 101
'Mrs John Laing', 145

'Mrs Jones', 78
mulch, 128, *214*, 224–26
  newspaper layer as, 225, *225*
  options for, 224–25
  stone and pebbles as, 226
  weed prevention and, 225–26
'Mullard Jubilee', 135
multiflora roses, 236
Musk Rose of Shakespeare, 25
'Mutabilis', 105
mutations, 100
'My Hero', *101*, 101–2
Mystery, 259

N

naming roses, 23, 137, 140
'Narzisse', 146
'Nashville', 102
'Nearly Wild', 102, *102*
Nepeta 'Six Hills Giant', *62*, 63
'New Dawn', 69, 178, 186, *186*
'New Penny', 168
'New Zealand', 131
'Nicole', 139
'Nightingale', 146
Noack roses, 22
Noisettes, 31, *31*, 185, 259. *See also* specific cultivars
'Nostalgie', 146
'Nova Zembla', 81
nurseries. *See* mail-order nurseries; specific nursery
nursery area, stock tank as, 216, *216*
nutrients
  soil amendments, 211, 223
  See also feeding roses
'Nymphenburg', 56

O

'Oddball', 152
'Oderic Vital', 70
'Oklahoma', 146
old garden roses, 14, *28*, 28–34, 58, 211–212
  albas, *28*, 29, 243

centifolias, 29, *29*, 30, 244
China roses, 31, 94, 244
damasks, 29, *29*, 244
gallicas, 29, *29*, 244–45, *245*
hybrid perpetuals, 34, *34*, 222, 224, *224*, 230, 245
moss roses, 30, *30*, 112, 244
Noisettes, 31, *31*, 185
tea roses, 31, 245
See also heirloom roses; heritage roses; specific cultivars
'Old Port', 102–3
Old Rose hybrids, 22
'Olympiad', 158
once-blooming mosses, 30, 244
once-blooming roses, 28, 241
'Open Arms', 103
orange roses, 131
'Oranges 'n' Lemons', 103
Oso Easy roses, 24. *See also* specific cultivars
own-root roses, 207, 208
  from local nurseries, 216
  by mail order, 216

P

Painted Damask. *See* 'Léda'
'Palmengarten Frankfurt', 103
'Paloma Blanca', 146
"Papa Floribunda." *See* Boerner, Gene
'Paradise', 147, *147*
Park of Roses (Columbus, Ohio), 77
'Parole', 147
'Pascali', *19*, 57, 147, *147*
patented roses, 13, 100
Patio Roses, 155, 164
'Paul Jerabek', 186, *186*
'Paul Shirville', 147
'Peace', 14, 48, 143, 146, 148, *148*, 209
'Peacekeeper', 148
'Pearl Drift', 104
'Peaudouce', 135
'Peggy M', 150
Pelargonin (pigment), 131
Pemberton, Rev. Joseph, 25, 115, 119

Pemberton/Bentall hybrid musks, 71, 77, 101, 105
'Penelope', 101
Penzance, Lord and Lady, 58
'Peppermint', 109
perfume industry catalyst, 29
pergolas and pillars, 174
'Perle von Weissenstein', 104
Perry, Astor, 140
pesticides. *See* chemicals
pests. *See* animal problems; insect pests
petal problems
 "balling," 140
 lack of bloom, 232
 poor blossom color, 223
 weatherspotting, 132
'Peter Frankenfeld', 148
'Peter John', 56
'Petite de Hollande', 104, *104*
'Phyllis Bide', *65*, 187, *187*
Pickering Nurseries, 98, 206, 253
'Pierre de Ronsard', 187
pillars and pergolas, 174
'Pink Favorite', 144, 150
'Pink Meidiland', 81
'Pink Peace', 152
'Pink Prosperity', 105, *105*
'Pink Roadrunner', 122
'Pink Simplicity', 115
'Pink Surprise', *45*, *56*, 56–57
'Pinstripe', 203, *203*
pith, healthy and damaged, 241, *241*
'Plaisanterie', 105, *105*
planting location, choice of, 66
planting roses, 211–19
 autumn planting, 206, 217
 bare-root roses, 213, *213*–14, 215
 bed preparation, 211
 bud union and, 213, *213*, 215
 container roses, 215–17
 follow-up care, bare-root roses, 215
 in raised beds, 215
 repotting young roses, 217
 soil amendments, 211

space requirements, 211–12
 spring planting, 215
 transplanting, 217–19, *218*
 zones and, 213, 215
'Playboy', 148–49, *149*, 201
'Pleine de Grâce', *16*, 106, *106*
'Polar Joy', 196, *196*, 197, *197*, 239, *239*
'Polka', 187–88, *188*
polyanthas, *21*, 21–22, 259
 first development of, 116
 Koster series, 22, 120
 pruning of, 243
 as "spray roses," 155
 See also specific cultivars
poodle standards, 194
"Portage County Rose," 72
Portlands (autumn damasks), 32, *32*, 119, 245, 259. *See also* specific cultivars
'Portrait', *149*
posts, roses for
 'Aloha', 176, *176*
 'Blushing Lucy', 178, *178*
 'Dortmund', 180, *180*
 'Golden Gate', 181–82
 'Jeanne Lajoie', *27*, 175, *175*, 182, 182–83
 'Phyllis Bide', 187, *187*
 'Red Fountain', 188, *188*
 'Santana', 188
Poulsen nursery, 20
Practical Book of Outdoor Rose Growing, The (Thomas), 209
'Precious Platinum', 158
'Pretty Lady', 149
'Princess Alice', 106, *106*
'Priscilla Burton', 149, *149*
problem solving, 64
 blind shoots, *232*, 232–33
 See also animal problems; diseases; insect pests
propagation. *See* breeding roses; bud-grafted roses; cuttings of rose plants; rootstock
protection
 petals, weatherspotting and, 132
 of rose transplants, *219*

See also winter preparation
pruning, 240–46
 of bare-root roses, 212, *212*
 basic cuts, 240–41, *241*
 diseases and, 233
 fall pruning, 242
 general guidelines for, 240–42
 root pruning, 246
 specifics, by rose type, 242–46
 spring pruning, 241, 249
 summer pruning, 231, 242, 244
 tools for, 240
 trimming blind shoots, 232, *232*
 watershoots and, 212

Q

'Queen Elizabeth', *16*, *21*, 21, 124, 125, 130, *130*, 150, 195
'Queen Mother', 106–7
Quest-Ritson, Charles, 185

R

Radler, William, 23, 230
Ragged Robin (rootstock), 210
'Rainbow Knock Out', 23, 107, *107*
'Rainbow's End', *160*, 161, 166, *166*, 198, 199
raised beds, 215
'Ralph's South African Rose', 57
ramblers, 32, *32*, 259. *See also* climbing roses; specific cultivars
'Rare Edition', 152
"Razzleberry" roses, 23
'Red Ballerina', 99
'Red Eden', 180
'Red Flower Carpet', *22*, 88
'Red Fountain', 188, *188*
Redleaf Rose. See *Rosa glauca*
'Red Meidiland', 81
'Redoute', 100
'Red Ribbons', 107
'Regensberg', 107
'Regina Lee', 166–67
'Remember Me', 150, *150*

repeat-blooming roses, 28, 63, 222
    China roses, 31
    miniatures as, 162
    pruning of, 245
    shrub roses, 42
"replicative fading," 148
repotting young roses, 217
'Rhapsody in Blue', 107–8, *108*
right rose, choosing, 10, 13, 35
    for standards, 195
'Rise 'n' Shine', 167, *167*
'Robert Duncan', 151, *151*
'Rob Roy', 151
'Robusta', 55
'Rochester Cathedral', 77
Romantica roses, 42, *42*
'Romantic Roadrunner', 122
'Romanze', 108
roots, feeder, 66
rootstock, 31
    bud-grafting onto, 208
    Rosa canina, 61
    Rosa fortuniana, 230
    Rosa multiflora, 61
    suckers on, 233
    types of, 210
    See also bud-grafted roses
Rosa, 5
    arkansana, 67, 108–9
        'Peppermint', *108*, 109
        root pruning of, 246
    bracteata (The Macartney Rose), 57, 121
    californica, 68
    canina, 61
        froebelli, 210
    carolina alba, 60
    davidii, 70, 149
    eglanteria (Sweet Briar Rose), 57, 57–58,
        85, 176, 177, 229
    filipes, 57
    foetida, 233
        perisiana, 68
    fortuniana, 230

gallica, 111–12
    officinalis (Apothecary's Rose, the),
        109
    versicolor ('Rosa Mundi'), *109*,
        109–10
    glauca (Redleaf Rose), 18, *18*, 109
    helenae, 57, 111
    hugonis, 231
    kordesii, 52, *78*, 153
    laxa (*R. canina froebelli*), 210
    manettii ('Manettii'), 210
    multiflora (multiflora roses), 61, 210,
        236–37, 243
    mundi. See *Rosa gallica versicolor*
    nitida, 82
    palustris, 18
    pendulina, 46, 110
    pomifera (Apple Rose), 58–59
        'Duplex' or Wolley-Dod's Rose,
        59
    richardii ('St John's Rose'), 111
    roxburghii normalis (Chestnut Rose),
        44, 44, 59, 59
    rubiginosa (Sweet Briar Rose), 57
    rubrifolia, 109
    rugosa, 18, 68, 82
    sancta ('St John's Rose'), 111
    sericea, 18, 110
        pteracantha, 110, 243
    soulieana, 116
    spinosissima, 68, 150
    virginiana, 60
        alba, 60
        plena ('Rose d'Amour'), 60
    wichurana, 18, 168, 191
    See also specific cultivars
'Rosalina', 110
'Rosalita', 111
'Rosa Mundi.' See *Rosa gallica versicolor*
'Rosarium Uetersen', 42, *42*, 60, *60*, 194,
    194
rose blooms, describing, 18–19
rose breeders, 20
    rose naming rights, 137

    See also breeding roses; specific
        cultivars
rose classification, 35, 257–58
'Rose d'Amour', 60
'Rose de Rescht', 111, *111*
'Roseford', 186
'Rose Gaujard', 37, *37*, 151
rose hips, 36, 44, 232, 247
'Rosemoor', 177
"Rose of the Century" award, 111
Roses at the Cape of Good Hope (Fagan), 57
Rose Society, 140
Roses of Yesterday & Today (catalogue), 112
'Royal Bonica', 76
Royal Botanical Garden (Burlington,
    Ontario, Canada), 73
Royal National Rose Society (England), 242
'Roy Black', 141
'Ruby Wedding', 151
rugosas, 25, *25*, 110. *See also* hybrid rugosas;
    Rosa rugosa; specific cultivars
'Rush', 111
"russet" roses, 94

S

'Salet', 112, 191
'Sally Holmes', 111, *113*, *113*, 129
Sangerhausen Rosarium, Germany, 47
'Santana', 188
'Sappho', 46
'Save the Children', 85
'Savoy Hotel', 157
'Scabrosa', *36*, *113*, 113–14
'Scarlet Fire'/'Scarlet Glow', 61
'Scarlet Flower Carpet', 88
'Scarlet Moss', *30*, 167, *167*
'Scentimental', 152, *152*
'Scent-Sation', 151–52
'Scepter'd Isle', 114, *114*
'Scharlachglut', *18*, 61, *61*
'Schloss Balthazar', 139
Schneider, Peter, 254
Schoener, Georg, 114
'Schoener's Nutkana', 114

Scrivens, Len, 149
'Sebastian Kneipp', 114, 115
'Seduction', 133
selection of roses. *See* right rose,
    choosing
semi-double roses, 19, *19*
sentimental value of roses, 13
'Setina', 94
'Sexy Rexy', 141
shade, roses in, 36, 65–66
'Sheila's Perfume', 152, 153, *153*
'Shi-un', 153
shopping for roses, 206–10
    bare-root roses, 206, 207, *207*
    budded plants, 207, 208
    garden centers and, 13, 207, 216
    grades of plants, 207
    hardiness/health issues, 208–9
    own-root plants, 207, 208
shrub roses, *22*, 22, 259
    pruning of, 242, *243*
    See also climbing roses; specific
        cultivars
'Si', 167–68
'Silver Anniversary', 141
'Silver Jubilee', 69, 153, *153*, 201
'Silver Moon', 75, 188
Sima, 182–83
'Simon Robinson', 168, *168*, 195
'Simplicity', 24, 115, *115*
Simplicity roses, *24*, 24. *See also* specific
    cultivars
single-petaled roses, 18, *18*, 129
site selection, 44–45
    hedges, roses as, 44–45, *45*
    lawn roses and, 44
    wild settings, roses in, 44
'Skyrocket' junipers, 67
slow-death syndrome, avoiding, 13
"Smooth Touch" thornless roses, 154
'Smooth Velvet', 154
'Snowbelt', *115*, 115–16, 123
'Snowfire', 133
'Snow Hill' salvia, 120

softwood rose cuttings, 244
soil
    acidity, fighting, 223
    amendments for, 211, 223
    pH levels in, 211, 223
    soil mixes, 202
    testing of, 14, 222
'Sommermorgen', 116
'Sondermeldung' ("Special
    Announcement"), 131
'Songbird Rose, The', 106
'Sonia Rykiel', *23*, 116, *116*, 117, *201*
'Sophy's Rose', 117, *117*
'Soroptimist International', 168, *168*
'Souvenir de la Malmaison', 154, *154*
'Souvenir de St Anne's', 154
'Souvenir du Docteur Jamain', 117
'Souvenir du Président Lincoln', 144
'Special Child', 69
special purposes, roses for, 36–37
species roses, 18, 243, 259
    for edges of woodlands, 65
    See also Rosa
specimen roses, 41–42
spinosissima, 89, 118. See also *Rosa
    spinosissima*
'Spirit of Freedom', *117*, 117–18
'Spirit of Picardy', 118
"sports," searching for, 100
'Stadt den Helder', 137, 154–55
'Stämmler', 158
standalone roses, 41–61
"standards." *See* tree roses
'Stanwell Perpetual', 118, *118*
'Starina', 168
'Stars 'n' Stripes', 157, 165
'Stéphanie de Monaco', 149
'Stephanie Diane', 155
'St John's Rose' (Holy Rose of Abyssinia),
    111–12
Strebler, Rick, *72*, 171
'Striped Mary Rose', 100
striped roses, 152
"sub-zero" roses, 181

'Summer Dream' (American hybrid tea),
    64, *64*
'Summer Dream' (floribunda), 155
'Summer Wine', 173, 189, *189*
'Sunday Best', 189
'Sun Flare', 155, *155*
'Sunset Celebration', 159
sun/shade mix for roses, 65, 128
'Super Dorothy', *170*, 171, 177, *189*, 189–90
'Super Elfin', 190
'Super Excelsa', 190
'Super Fairy', 190
support structures, 173–74
    arches, 173
    pillars and pergolas, 174
    rose first, structure later, 174
    See also specific structure
'Surf Rider', 113
'Sutter's Gold', 155–56, *156*
Svejda, Felicitas, 86
'Swarthmore', 156
'Sweet Bouquet', 88
Sweet Briar Rose. See *Rosa eglanteria*
'Sweet Chariot', 169, *169*
Sweetheart Rose. *See* 'Mlle Cécile Brunner'
symbol/emblem, rose as, 7

T

'Tahitian Moon', 97
Tantau nursery, 20
'Taxi', 158
tea roses, 31, 259
    pruning of, 245
    See also hybrid tea roses; specific
        cultivars
'Teasing Georgia', *118*, 118–19
Tenner, Howard, 245
Texas A&M University, 25
'The Countryman', 100, 119
'The Crab', 23
'The Fairy', *21*, 21–22, *119*, 119, 148, 190
'The Ingenious Mr. Fairchild', 120
'The Mayflower', 70, 120
'The Macartney Rose', 121

'The McCartney Rose', 120–21
'Thérèse Bugnet', 16, 40, 41, 121, 121
Thomas, Capt. George C., Jr., 209
Thomas, Graham Stuart, 184
thornless roses, 36, 154
"throwaway" miniatures, 26
'Tiffany', 156
'Topaz Jewel', 68
'Top Marks', 169
'Touch of Class', 35, 156, 156
'Toy Clown', 169, 169
transplanting roses, 217, 218, 219, 219
tree roses, 193–97, 200
    caring for, 196–97
    choosing right varieties, 195
    poodle standards, 194
    pruning of, 196
    rabbit fencing for, 239, 239
    roses recommended for, 195, 195
    staking of, 196
    three parts of, 194
    types of, 194
    weeping standards, 194
    winter protection for, 196–97
trellises, 173–74
    V-shape trellis, 182
    weaving canes, warning against, 173
trellises, roses for
    'Aloha', 176, 176
    'Antike 89', 177, 177
    'Aschermittwoch', 177
    'Crimson Sky', 175, 180, 180
    'Demokracie', 180, 180
    'Freisinger Morgenröte', 181
    'Golden Gate', 175, 181–82
    'High Hopes', 182
    'Illusion', 182
    'Leaping Salmon', 183
    'Louis' Rambler', 183, 183–84
    'Morning Jewel', 185
    'New Dawn', 69, 178, 186, 186
    'Paul Jerabek', 186, 186
    'Red Fountain', 188, 188
    'Santana', 188

'William Baffin', 66, 66, 172, 172, 173, 191, 191
'Tropical Sunset', 157, 157
'Truly Yours', 157
'Trumpeter', 157
'Tupperware', 188
'Turbo', 121

U

understocks. See rootstock
unpatented roses, 13
'Urdh', 37, 37, 157, 157–58
USDA Zones, 14, 31, 64, 175, 248

V

'Valentine Heart', 158
Van Fleet, Dr. Walter, 75
'Variegata di Bolgna', 121–22
'Vater Rhein', 158
'Veilchenblau', 32, 65, 190, 190
very double roses, 19, 19
'Veterans' Honor', 158, 195
'Vick's Caprice', 158, 159
'Vick's Perpetual', 14, 15
Victorian age, 30
'Victorian Spice', 141
Vintage Gardens, 254
'Violette Parfumée', 159
virus-free roses, 208, 227
V-shape trellis, 182

W

'Warm Welcome', 190
'Warm Wishes', 159
Warner, Chris, 26, 103, 181, 183
watering roses, 220–21
    drip irrigation system, 220
    next to buildings, 173
    overhead watering, 220, 233
    soaker hoses, 220, 221, 221
    when to water, 221
weatherspotting, 132
weed prevention, 225–26
Weeks, O. L. (Ollie), 20

Weeks roses, 20
weeping standards, 194, 194
'White Roadrunner', 122
'Wichmoss', 191
'Wildeve', 122, 122, 195
wild settings, roses in, 44
'William Baffin', 66, 66, 172, 172, 173, 191, 191
Williams, A. H., 178
Williams, J. Benjamin, 188
'Winchester Cathedral', 100
'Windrush', 16, 122, 122–23
winterkill, 219, 242
winter landscape, 44, 242
winter preparation, 247–50
    burial of rose plants, 249
    caged protection, 249, 249
    indoor plant storage, 249
    landscaping blankets, 249
    losses, main causes for, 247
    protective mounds, 247–48, 248
    styrofoam cones, 249
    for tender roses, 250
    See also protection
Wolley-Dod, Charles, 59
Wolley-Dod's Rose. See Rosa pomifera

X

'XXL', 147

Y

'Yellow Flower Carpet', 88
'Yellow Romantica', 48
yellow winter-hardy shrub roses, 97
'Yesterday', 123, 123
'Yolande d' Aragon', 123

Z

"Zeke's Pink," 72
'Zenaitta', 123
'Zéphirine Drouhin', 191, 191
zones. See USDA zones

OTHER STOREY TITLES
YOU WILL ENJOY

Designer Plant Combinations, by Scott Calhoun.
   More than 100 creative combinations, planted by top garden designers across the country, to inspire home gardeners to put plants
   together in unexpected but stunning groupings.
   240 pages. Paper. ISBN 978-1-60342-077-8.

Fallscaping, by Nancy J. Ondra and Stephanie Cohen.
   A comprehensive guide to the best plants for brightening late-season
   landscapes.
   240 pages. Paper with flaps. ISBN 978-1-58017-680-4.

Foliage, by Nancy J. Ondra.
   An eye-opening garden guide to the brilliant colors and textures
   of dozens of plants, all chosen for the unique appeal of their leaves.
   304 pages. Paper with flaps. ISBN 978-1-58017-648-4.
   Hardcover with jacket. ISBN 978-1-58017-654-5.

*The Gardener's A–Z Guide to Growing Flowers from
Seed to Bloom,* by Eileen Powell.
   An encyclopedic reference on choosing, sowing, transplanting,
   and caring for 576 annuals, perennials, and bulbs.
   528 pages. Paper. ISBN 978-1-58017-517-3.

Grasses, by Nancy J. Ondra.
   Photographs and plans for 20 gardens that highlight the beauty
   of grasses in combination with perennials, annuals, and shrubs.
   144 pages. Paper with flaps. ISBN 978-1-58017-423-7.

The Perennial Gardener's Design Primer, by Stephanie
Cohen and Nancy J. Ondra.
   A lively, authoritative guide to creating perennial gardens using
   basic design principles for putting plants together in pleasing and
   practical ways.
   320 pages. Paper. ISBN 978-1-58017-543-2.
   Hardcover with jacket. ISBN 978-1-58017-545-6.

These and other books from Storey Publishing are available
wherever quality books are sold or by calling 1-800-441-5700.
Visit us at *www.storey.com.*